When God Says, "No"

When God Says, "No"

Reshaping Prayer and Learning to Listen

THOMAS R. HAUFF

RESOURCE *Publications* · Eugene, Oregon

WHEN GOD SAYS, "NO"
Reshaping Prayer and Learning to Listen

Copyright © 2011 Thomas R. Hauff. All rights reserved. Except for brief quotations in critical publications or reviews, no part of this book may be reproduced in any manner without prior written permission from the publisher. Write: Permissions, Wipf and Stock Publishers, 199 W. 8th Ave., Suite 3, Eugene, OR 97401.

Scripture taken from the NEW AMERICAN STANDARD BIBLE®, Copyright © 1960, 1962, 1963, 1968, 1971, 1972, 1973, 1975, 1977, 1995 by The Lockman Foundation. Used by permission. www.Lockman.org

Resource Publications
An Imprint of Wipf and Stock Publishers
199 W. 8th Ave., Suite 3
Eugene, OR 97401

www.wipfandstock.com

ISBN 13: 978-1-61097-063-1

Manufactured in the U.S.A.

To all those who desire authentic prayer

> "Do not be hasty in word or impulsive in thought
> to bring up a matter in the presence of God.
> For God is in heaven and you are on the earth;
> therefore let your words be few."
>
> — Ecclesiastes 5:2

Contents

Foreword / xi
Preface / xv
Acknowledgments / xvii

I. PEOPLE DON'T ENJOY PRAYER • 1
II. REASONS PEOPLE DON'T ENJOY PRAYER • 9
   A. PRAYER IS HAPHAZARD • 12
      1. *We Have No System to Follow* • 13
      2. *We Don't Know How to Pray* • 17
      3. *We Don't Know How God Will Answer* • 24
      4. *We Don't Interpret the Answer We Receive Honestly* • 29
      5. *We Don't Reshape Our Requests* • 39
   B. THE TRUE GOALS OF PRAYER ARE IGNORED • 40
      1. *The True Goal of Prayer #1: Effectiveness and Accomplishment* • 45
      2. *The True Goal of Prayer #2: Spiritual Maturity* • 50
      3. *The True Goal of Prayer #3: Endurance in the Present Life* • 60
   C. PRAYER IS BORING • 67
   D. OUR APPROACH IS FLAWED • 72
      1. *Nagging God* • 74
         a) Luke 11:5–13 • 77
         b) Luke 18:1–8 • 84
         c) Mark 7:24–30 • 86
         d) Repeated Prayer for the Lost • 89
      2. *Lobbying God With Numbers* • 131
      3. *Lottery Syndrome* • 137

III. WHAT ARE OUR REAL EXPECTATIONS? • 164
   A. "BLESS US" • 173
   B. "COMFORT" • 182
   C. "PROTECT US" • 186
   D. "HEAL US" • 189
   E. "BE WITH US" • 191
   F. "LIFT UP" • 192
IV. MITIGATING OUR PROBLEMS—AND CREATING MORE OF THEM • 194
V. MODELS OF PRAYER IN THE BIBLE • 212
   A. THE LORD'S PRAYER (MATTHEW 6:9–13) • 214
      1. Our Father Who Is in Heaven • 216
      2. Hallowed Be Your Name • 228
      3. Your Kingdom Come • 236
      4. Your Will Be Done on Earth as It Is in Heaven • 241
      5. Give Us This Day Our Daily Bread • 245
      6. Forgive Us Our Debts as We Have Forgiven Our Debtors • 251
      7. Lead Us Not into Temptation But Deliver Us from Evil • 256
      8. For Yours Is the Kingdom and Power and the Glory Forever • 260
      9. Guidance from the Lord's Prayer—Summary • 261
   B. PAUL'S PRAYER FOR THE EPHESIANS (EPHESIANS 1:15–19) • 262
      1. The Background Setting • 264
      2. The Over-Arching Theme • 265
      3. The Prayer's Foundation—Knowledge • 266
      4. Giving Thanks • 270
      5. Consistency in Prayer • 275
      6. Wisdom and Revelation • 277

       7. *Better Goals in Prayer* • *283*
          a) Knowing the Hope of Our Calling • 284
          b) Knowing God's Inheritance • 286
          c) Knowing God's Power • 287
    C. DAVID'S PRAYER OF THANKS
        (2 SAMUEL 7:18–29) • 289
       1. *The Background* • *289*
       2. *David's Prayer* • *300*

VI. SUGGESTIONS FOR PRAYER SUMMARY • 310

Bibliography • 313

Foreword

In this book, you have a simple stack of paper in your hands, neatly organized, bound with string and glue, but it bears an iron-like quality. "Iron sharpens iron," Proverbs 27:17 says, "so one man sharpens another." In this case, Tom Hauff is one iron Christian, as it were, and you are the other. This book is a chisel. It is a draw file. It is a sharpening tool crafted by a brother in Christ whose own troublesome experiences with prayer prompted him to forge a thoughtful path through the "Christianese" jargon, the unspoken assumptions, and the skin-deep habits that plague so many believers' prayers. Tom moves us toward a life of genuine communication with God. And so, if prayer has become pointless or dull to you, prepare for a sharpening. If motivation to speak with God is more like an obligation, it is time to get honed. And if you flat-out dislike praying for any reason, wondering if God actually listens to a single word you say, then be encouraged. You are not alone. Many Christians are straining and striving to understand prayer. The good news is that Jesus never asked us to press on toward maturity by ourselves; he invites us into his Church where he is always building up men like Tom—fellow Christians who keep us sharp.

Hold tight to that sharpening metaphor as you dive into this book because, while knife or ax sharpening can be a fine time indeed, personal heart-and-mind sharpening is not usually too pleasant; the rusty dullness of ignorance, pride, and greed needs to be chiseled away and filed down. So, unless you love wasting time, which hopefully you don't, you must start with an honest self-assessment about your prayers and the real state you are in—the way you approach God and the things you say to him.

What exactly do I say to him, and why do I say it? Does he listen? When do I ask him for things, and what are they? Does he give them to me? When it seems like he's not listening, do I say, "Whatever. Mystery!"? Do I even think about prayer at all? Is it useful? Productive? Ambiguous? Fruitless? Wherever you are, begin with an honest look inside yourself, and know that the sharpening process might sting, even hurt, but it is so good in the end.

Tom reveals the fundamental characteristic of communication—listening—and examines its presence or lack thereof in our prayer practices. Building upon clearly articulated biblical foundations, he constructs a concrete approach to prayer that will move you to speak with God confidently, knowing for certain that he listens and responds to all of your prayers. Tom will help you develop smart and functional approaches to prayer that move you deeper into a respectful, loving relationship with Jesus. Sounds almost exaggerated, doesn't it? After all, it is only a paper-and-ink book. I'll give you a brief anecdote to prove the point.

I am a Bible and theology student, a teacher, and a youth pastor in downtown Portland, Oregon. A few years back, I had been serving alongside my wife, Ali, both of us "praying" and teaching others to pray as we enjoyed life and ministry together. When she became pregnant the first time, we were overjoyed until the baby died in her womb. The miscarriage was a total blindside, and we suffered intense pain. When she became pregnant a second time, our joy blended with fear, and we offered up white-knuckle requests to God, pleading to him for the safe delivery of a healthy baby. Seems like a worthy request, right? We weren't asking for a Ferrari or superpowers; we just wanted the baby to survive. No doubt, God values life and fulfills our desires, doesn't he? As the stressful months passed and her second trimester drew near, we clenched our fists even tighter, begging God to carry out our will. And then that baby died, too.

Meanwhile, Tom was working on this book, and I had the privilege of hearing him process his thoughts as he crafted arguments and proved his points. Without directly challenging the prayers of my wife and I, his writings revealed the truth behind what we were doing . . . or, as the case turned out to be, what we were not doing. His meticulously honest engagement with the scriptures hit hard and even shocked me because he illuminated profound biblical truths about prayer that I had simply missed all along, opting instead to wallow in the familiar and wade in the lukewarm waters of nonsense. Ali and I had not been communicating with God; we had been hurling demands and expectations at him, unknowingly disguising them as requests, paying no attention to his responses or to our own theological beliefs. We simply hurled. And hurled. And hurled. But then Tom's words inspired us to pause.

What if God was saying, "No" to our request for a healthy baby? Or maybe, "Not yet." What if he was teaching and training us to understand him and trust his wisdom? What if he wanted me to know that prayer was never meant to reverse the consequences of the fall? What if God wanted me to learn how to pray during trials rather than trying to pray them away? Even while making a request that seemed pure and worthy of a "yes" answer, what if we had listened to God, who says he opens and closes the womb according to his will, and then actively rested in his plan, caring first about his will and our relationship with him? If God was trying to teach us any of these things, and now I am positive that he was, then the meager ritual of clenched-fist begging only blinded us. For three months of that second pregnancy we felt distant from God and terrified. We hurled our appeal over and over and over again, considering such petitions "righteous" and "faithful." But like a useful iron tool, this book cut to the quick, and my wife and I finally started learning to reshape our requests to God in light of his clear responses.

When she became pregnant a third time, our home was white-knuckle-free. Fear and anxiety during prayer vanished. We knew God was listening, and we ourselves were learning—for the first time—to seriously listen to him. In the end, he did see fit to give us a precious girl, Annabelle, who will now grow up with a Mom and Dad who teach her that mindless hurling is no way to talk to God. With the help of this book we will be teaching our little girl, each other, and the friends and family we have at church to pay attention to God's answers to their requests and reshape their prayers accordingly. Naturally, I am a thankful for so massive a blessing.

I'm thankful that you have stepped into this discussion, too, and I encourage you to wrestle with the text that follows. I wonder where you are in relationship to prayer. I wonder if you, too, are suffering the pains that accompany a feeling of spiritual drought in prayer. I wonder if, even right now, you have already started thinking about your own prayers and are considering those times that seem like clear evidence that God has become deaf to your voice. If that is the case, then press on. You will find excellent scholarship and thorough biblical research that Tom communicates with approachable, memorable writing. These are heady concepts delivered with ground-level language, and you will never talk to God the same way again.

A word to the wise: Be patient with Tom. He is going to rock your boat a little. He challenges habits that almost all of us learned to take for granted long ago, such as repetitive prayers for things like healing or the salvation of the lost. In cases like those, it is imperative that you patiently hold rebuttals until you have fairly listened to his whole argument. Yes, this is certainly a book about prayer, but it is simultaneously a course in thoughtful Bible study. Know this: Tom has not poured his love and energy and time into an op-ed puff piece about his emotional reactions or ambiguous impressions. If you want a comfortable devotional or a nuanced treatise on Christian feel-goodery, head back to the bookshelves. His work is careful and specific. His solutions are practical and realistic. His arguments are well-supported and precise. Though clearly made of paper and ink and glue and thread, this book crushes and cuts like iron at times—useful for chiseling, filing, and sharpening us into believers who effectively communicate with the God who gives life.

My prayer for you, the reader, is this: May the Holy Spirit reveal and illuminate God's truth about prayer to you, given through his Word, so that your discussions with him would become powerfully effective and fruitful. May the Holy Spirit protect you from Satan's deceptions while you read, as he urges you to comfortably close your mind, to remain immersed in suffocating assumptions and habits, and to say to yourself, as he did to Eve, "Did God really say that?" More than anything, may you be sharpened, and may you learn to love communicating with your Savior and Lord, Jesus Christ.

Ben Tertin
Imago Dei Community, Director of Youth

Preface

I NEVER INTENDED TO write this book. Frankly, I never thought much about writing any books. I have always, in the past, considered myself a teacher--not a writer. But in my teaching questions about prayer have come up over and over again. And the more these questions came up, the more I realized people desperately desire a wonderful prayer life, and yet so many fail to possess one. Moreover, I realized that I, the teacher, didn't have good answers to the questions students were asking about prayer. I, like my students, had never been taught to think honestly about prayer.

As I began to study, ponder, and teach about prayer seriously, one particular problem surfaced more frequently than the rest: God seems to say "no" a good deal of the time in our everyday lives. Moreover, to my chagrin, I realized that this thought was not just an academic observation. My personal prayers seemed to get a lot of "no" answers as well. I have never met someone who has always had their requests answered with "yes" from God. I have never met someone who would even declare they are *consistently* receiving "yes" answers from God. But I have met many who, when push comes to shove, and stark truth is being told, will admit that God does seem to say "no" a lot. That bothered me. And the more I spoke to others, the more we discussed it in classes, the more I realized it bothered a lot of people; for they were in the same boat as I. They were getting "no" answers as well. That ought not to be the case. And I think many would agree with me on that. All these "no" answers from God spawned this work.

This book explains why God is saying "no" to our prayers. I have done my best to avoid any sidestepping or ducking of issues. I hope it is useful to all that read it.

Acknowledgments

I could thank so many people for their influences in my life over the years: My family, my friends, my teachers, my bosses. Just about everything and everyone has taught me something good or bad about myself. But I will be brief here and note one person in particular as he pertains directly to this work: Mr. Ben Tertin. He was a student of mine who has turned into my close friend, confidant, and informal editor. I would never have written this work without his enthusiastic encouragement to take up the pen (so to speak). He is my student who is my teacher as well. Each week we talk, think, ponder, and sharpen one another. And without his goads, I would not have typed a word. Thanks for opening a door in my brain, Ben.

1

People Don't Enjoy Prayer

I HADN'T BEEN SLEEPING again. The cycles were constant in my life back then. I call it my routine. A few days of sound eight-hour nights—then a few weeks of sketchy, three- to four-hour nighttime wars. After that, my body finally exhausted and worn down, another few nights of hard, deep sleep. But never enough. Never Enough. And there were always the dreams. Usually violent dreams. Pent up anger that was never allowed to be vented during childhood found a way out at night. It always had, and it stayed with me for years. And then there was the talking. Waking my wife to tell her something nonsensical but vitally important, "Don't you see that?!" "Stop pushing me!" Occasionally I lashed out physically. Unconscious in mind, but body fully awake to terror. Sometimes I connected with her. Thank God never seriously. What kind of person beats their spouse in their sleep? But this is just background. I'm not really the topic of this story. I'm just the foil to another's performance.

I'd been doing my routine for years and was especially active that summer. It was hot in Coeur d'Alene, Idaho, and sticky-wet from rain as well during that one particular week. It was late at night and we were in bed: Kathy sound asleep; me in the throes of another sleeping war. The window was open in our second story apartment. It was the upper right in a fourplex of one-bedroom apartments. Our relatively new roommate, Shep the Wonder Cat, had been out all day and to her dismay, she was out tonight as well in the thunderous rain pouring from the sky. As I said, I'm not the topic of this story, Shep is our star performer.

Shep the Wonder Cat was not casually named. For a cat, Shep was smart. She knew her name and would come at the call, which I admit is not that impressive, but there was more. She would play fetch with a nerf ball, and she even learned to shake hands—paws—70 percent of the time. She apparently knew a good mark when she saw one as well. She'd been abandoned in the field next door and was a hobo until she wandered onto our porch one day and laid down. Now, we weren't really allowed to own a cat in our little fourplex, but we didn't technically own Shep either (though we did provide her with a cat house, food, and medical care for her many mishaps with other untoward felines in the neighborhood). I think maybe Shep thought she owned us. That would fit her worldview better.

As I said, Shep was smart. Sometimes she was too smart, like that night in the driving wind and rain. I had been up and talking the last few nights and was tossing again that night, but luckily woke before I started talking and kicking. I think Shep woke me. The wind was driving almost sideways into the window, and just under its howl I could hear a plaintive crying. I rolled out of bed and stepped to the window knowing instantly that poor Shep was in trouble. We had no screens so I could just lean out and survey the tiny patch of back yard, and as I scanned around—rain splashing against my face—there was nothing to hide under.

I finally looked straight down the back of the house thinking Shep might be cowering at the base of the back wall. She wasn't. Our eyes locked in the fuzzy glare of the freeway's high-intensity discharge lamps. Every now and then a bolt of lightning ripped through the sky some distance away and I could see her soaked, determined face clearly upturned to me as she hung on the back wall of the apartment building. Smart Shep could see our open window, she had the claws for the task, and she was assaulting the wall like a climber attacking K-2 in the sleet season, but she couldn't comprehend the obstruction that lay above her! Just above her was our downstairs neighbor's window directly below ours—our neighbor's *open* window! Shep was headed for a rude surprise if she had entered that window, for they *definitely* were not cat people.

Kathy called to me, breaking my dismayed fascination, "Are you ok?" I jerked around and whisper-yelled, "Shep's climbing the back wall!" I couldn't see Kathy in the dark, but I know she was thinking, "Great, he's at it again." A few nights ago it was "Ants in the headboard! Ants in the headboard! Don't you see them?!" Tonight it's "Shep is climbing the back wall!" She wasn't even going to get up. She was thinking that I needed to just work through whatever brain-wreck I was experiencing this night. But it wasn't a brain-wreck! I was awake! I turned back to Shep, who had stopped for a moment, silent, after seeing my face above her. Thinking of nothing else I hissed down at her, "Shep! No!"

She was just a cat. I know that. But I swear I saw something strangely human in her eyes at that moment. She looked directly into my eyes, held for a moment, and then just—let go. She didn't spin at first the way a cat should. She didn't even seem to be breathing. She just retracted her claws and fell backward, spread-eagle, belly up, eyes still locked on mine. It felt surreal. I'm sure a bolt of lightning lit both of us up for the split-second when she began to fall. The look on her face seemed to cry out to me with a question: "Why are you saying 'No!?'" And then the lightning was gone and dark grey, shadowy Shep was lost to my sight in the rain soaked night.

"No" is such an unexpected answer isn't it? Even for a cat.

We all know that generalizations are not very accurate at any detailed level. It doesn't matter what you generalize about, there are always facets of any subject that defy categorization in generalized terms. However, I have come to a belief about people and prayer I think might warrant a general statement: For the most part, people don't really enjoy prayer. People like the *idea* of prayer. People engage in activities they classify as prayer. But they do not really care for *authentic prayer*.[1] We are more than happy to dash off a few short *"Help me!"* prayers a day (or some such things), but when it comes to carrying on a deep and involved conversation with God on a personal level (as we do with friends for example), we are less than thrilled to partake.

That's one of those things we don't like to admit out loud, but I still suggest it is true. Look at the weekly prayer meeting in your church—if you have one. If people really loved praying, why are our prayer meetings always so small compared to our potlucks, Bible studies, and Sunday services? Why do people devour the latest popular *book on prayer* but spend a mere fraction of the time spent reading it on *actual* prayer?[2]

---

1. I say *authentic* prayer because surprisingly, statistics seem to reveal that Americans actually pray quite a bit. This is not really new. I've run across such assertions for years. For example, a Fox News poll a few years ago noted that "two thirds [of Americans] pray at least once a day." Online: http://www.foxnews.com/story/0,2933,141885,00.html. Interestingly enough, in a 2005 Barna Group research study pastors rated prayer as the lowest priority for their churches. Online: http://www.barna.org/barna-update/article/5-barna-update/185-church-priorities-for-2005-vary-considerably?q=counseling.

2. Here I must admit I see the irony in using a book on prayer to say people prefer to read books on prayer rather than actually spending time in prayer. I suppose my

Let me be even more honest and bring it home to a personal statement: I have not really enjoyed prayer. From what I've been told, from what I've often read about the how's and why's of actual prayer, and from evaluating much of my own prayer and that of others, it often seems like a bewildering waste of time (to be brutally honest).

I don't think I'm alone in that sentiment either. Having ministered among God's people since my conversion in high school (in Bible studies, music teams, Sunday schools, seminary and Bible college classes), I've become convinced that people find real prayer to be, at best, a difficult task to undertake and, at worst, an unwanted but required chore attached to their Christian faith. Additionally, when many of us do perform it, it leaves us with little joy, small comfort, and no excitement about the next time we have to do it. Prayer is often approached in the way we might approach cleaning the bathroom. We roll up our sleeves knowing a job needs doing, we take no pleasure in the work, and we wait until it's needed to go at it again. And once more, I must add, we never talk like this about it.

The fact is, like many, I've had my long bouts of just giving up on the whole thing. Maybe you're different. Maybe you haven't given up yet. But do you trudge to prayer time as though a hundred pound rock is sitting squarely on your shoulders—feeling the obligation to pray but having no desire or joy at the prospect? Be honest here. Don't answer that question with a shrug, or with the Christian platitudes you've heard all your life about how Jesus prayed all the time so we ought to also—and therefore you're totally psyched to get in there and pray. I'm asking directly, in the silence of your own head, telling the truth: Do you really *love to pray* and can't wait to do it again each day? I can answer a resounding yes when the question concerns studying my Bible or teaching on the Bible or meeting with believers. I have never been able to say *yes* when the topic is prayer. Can you?

I'm convinced many people feel this way about prayer inside where only they can see. And I'm equally convinced that it ought not to be this way. And if the Bible shows us anything, it shows us people who *don't* seem to have that problem. We simply do not find stories in the Bible

---

defense is that I'm trying to outline an approach to prayer that will help people develop their own prayer lives to such an extent that they will no longer need books on prayer—even this one.

that tell us how tedious and unfulfilling it is for the characters to go to prayer and how they struggle with having to do so.

This is not to say characters in the Bible are not pictured struggling *while in prayer* at times. Jacob is said to have "wrestled with God" for example in Genesis 32:24. Many take this to mean he struggled in prayer with God. Jesus himself is said to have sweated blood as he prayed over his upcoming crucifixion.[3] But such difficulty *in prayer* is different from difficulty in *coming to prayer*. The former is the difficulty of deep conversation with God, of wrestling with ideas and sorting out problems, of sharing intimacies, and learning to be honest with ourselves and our God. The latter, difficulty in coming *to* prayer, belies an inner dislike for the process.

Furthermore, on a practical level, when I look at what prayer is supposed to be— conversing with my God, who deeply loves me, and whom I deeply love—this disliking of prayer just makes no sense.[4] There's got to be something wrong with having to *force* ourselves to converse with our loving father. After all, when I look at my relationships with ordinary people I don't see this problem. Take, for example, my wife and friends. I love them. Certainly I love God just as much as I love them (most of us would say we love God even more). Consequently, I very rarely say to myself, "I really don't want to talk with my friends."

I've been married for over twenty seven years. There are those times where I *have* said that about my wife. It's normal to say such a thing *occasionally*, but it ought to be somewhat rare. If I were saying that I don't want to see or talk to my wife for days, months, even years, then most of us would say there is a problem there.[5] And even if it is not rare in your

---

3. Luke 22:44.

4. The reader might peruse Dallas Willard's book *Hearing God—Developing a Conversational Relationship with God*. By the title alone we see how importantly he thinks we should view interaction with God. In Willard's first chapter he asks a terrific question: "Can you make any sense at all of an intimate personal relationship where there are no specific communications?" (p. 29.) He's interested in the idea of us actually hearing from God personally, but I would point out that that idea is undergirded by an even more fundamental idea that we *actually talk* to those who are in an intimate personal relationship with us. Without interaction there is no "intimate personal relationship" in which to receive any communications. But we don't even want to talk to God oftentimes.

5. I'm speaking from some experience here as well. The fact is my own marriage has had some very deep troughs in the past. I think both my wife and I have, in the past, actually said we'd rather not see or talk to one another. And the truth is that really *is* a

marriage, I doubt we would think it's *normal* not to *want* to talk to our spouse, not to *look forward* to talking to him or her. The plain truth is we usually do look forward to talking to our spouses and friends. We even make time to do it if we're rushed during the day. We miss them when we don't do it. And we feel deprived and uncomfortable when we haven't talked to them for more than a day. That being said, when it comes to God, we often don't want to go to prayer with our loving father. And often when we do go to him, we describe prayer as a "difficult" part of our Christian walks. Oh sure, we don't mind a few requests tossed off now and again. We are OK with telling God how angry we are on occasion. But authentic, serious prayer time is not on the agenda for most of us.

It's not as though we're not excited about our general relationships with God, either. Some might suggest that a poor prayer life is just the tip of a poor Christian life all around. But I haven't really seen this as necessarily true. It seems to me that many devoted Christians love to study the word, love to hear his voice teaching them how to live and grow. We enjoy fellowship with other believers. We look forward to our weekly Bible study group, and again, if talking with believers around me is any indication, there is general enjoyment of most aspects of the Christian life. We truly do want to grow closer to our God, but for some reason, prayer is a sticking point for many of us. Think about that: *talking to God is hard for us*. It sounds odd even to say such a thing out loud. But still, if the truth be told, we just don't want more *real* prayer; if anything, we want less of it. How did prayer get to be this way for us?

Now maybe I've been too strong for some of you. Maybe you're in that category of people that don't *dislike* prayer. Perhaps you're one of those people who enjoy their prayer life immensely. What's interesting to me is that often even that type of person has described to me how *difficult* prayer is for them! And in all honesty, I've noted that many times they report the same types of problems in prayer that those who dislike prayer report: "I'm not really sure about the answer I've gotten," "I'm not sure what to pray for," "I'm not seeing any obvious outcomes of my prayers." Probably the biggest problem is the one Shep the Wonder Cat encountered as she stared up at me: "God says 'no' to me a lot!" Though

---

problem! Not desiring to talk to the ones you supposedly love is a sure indicator of a love that is on the rocks and needs to be reevaluated. And this is not some emotional feeling that can be manufactured. This takes work and a commitment to a love that is deeper than mere passing feelings.

I must say I've never heard someone come right out and say it like that. Usually we soften that truth for our own mental well being. I'd like to suggest that the person who enjoys their prayer life very often does, in fact, have the same problems that those who struggle with prayer have. However, the difference is that the one who does not struggle as much will oftentimes reinterpret what prayer should be like to accommodate what others find intolerable. That is, they remove the discomfort that others feel and in consequence they enjoy their prayer life more. But in many instances they've removed the difficulty at the expense of an authentic prayer life. I'll come back to this later when we discuss the problems of prayer.

In all honesty the rejection and dislike of prayer many of us harbor actually makes complete sense given what we are often told about prayer and our Christian walk in general. In fact, if we were we to actually practice our Bible studies, church meetings and fellowship groups the way we are told to practice prayer, we'd probably dislike them too. (And some of us do just that!)

I would also ask, frankly speaking, if prayer is so unsatisfying, why *would* we want more of it? It seems to me that people are smart and rational and especially *intentional*. Dedicated believers will often jump to partake even of hardship for their Lord. And they enjoy the process of doing so when they experience the presence of God in the midst of the toil. But prayer, as we are often taught to offer it, very often gives us no such sense of God's presence. It's just a struggle for us—even for those of us who diligently practice it daily. If such is the case, I ask again, why *would* we want more prayer? It's like asking for another crack of the switch during the spanking—no smart individual is going to pursue that.

This book is meant to address this problem of prayerlessness and the struggle of *feeling obligated* to pray. It will highlight the way we interpret God's answers to our prayers and the way our interpretations can actually harm our prayer lives at times. It is primarily dealing with the seasoned believer who cannot seem to get into the practice of prayer and the new believer who wants to start on the right foot. But there are also those believers who cannot seem to commit to any of the most basic spiritual disciplines that the church has embraced for its long history. They cannot consistently read their Bibles. They cannot consistently give liberally. Perhaps they cannot consistently even go to church. This latter group, and maybe you find yourself here, is not the main focus of this book, but I believe the problem they have is identical to the problem a prayer-less believer has. So such a person can learn from this book as well. Additionally, there is something here for the believer who diligently prays, but still wrestles with the questions that arise in all prayer, such as what to pray for and how to pray for it and especially what to do when God says no to you. Now, I know that sounds like I'm saying this book is for everyone. Maybe so, but if that is the case, it is only because God's truth can always find application in our lives; and I think I have hit on some of God's truth and I would like to share it.

I'm convinced that prayer, and all the spiritual disciplines, practiced rightly, ought not to be the struggle they often are. At least they ought not to be a struggle for participation. Like the athlete who *struggles* at times during practice, we ought to enjoy the process of the discipline of daily workouts. Prayer can actually resemble all the other spiritual disciplines we undertake with joy. And hopefully, in this book we will find a key that helps us learn to long for prayer as Jesus himself seems to have done during his earthly life.

Let me add one last point on prayer before we begin. There are many types of prayer. Sometimes we just want to vent to God. Sometimes we just want to meditate. Sometimes we just want to rehearse what we know about him. I'm looking most pointedly at the prayers of request we offer. It seems to me that these are the major sources of our problems in prayer. People seem all too happy and able to offer their praises and thanks to God. They seem completely comfortable with just expressing feelings. But when it comes to prayer as a conversation over a topic of request and guidance it becomes far more difficult. And it is precisely that sort of prayer that most interests me—the sort that asks something of God. This is because just like when we ask something of another person, we expect a response, and in that response we so often find no apparent help. And that is the crux of a big problem in prayer: God seems to look down from above and hiss "no" to many of us a lot. And like Shep the Wonder Cat, broken by a response she never expected, we retract our grip on prayer and begin an uncontrolled freefall into prayerlessness.

2

Reasons People Don't Enjoy Prayer

LET ME RELATE A story from the life of a friend I'll call Chris. For Chris, who was about ten, auto repair with his dad usually meant a rousing session of "holding the light." There were variations occasionally: sometimes it was a flashlight, sometimes a big caged shop light, sometimes a small penlight. Chris would stand on the hard concrete, holding his light, not knowing what was being fixed, how it functioned, or what the process of fixing it was. Every now and then he was sent to get a wrench or screwdriver. This was pretty much the pattern for all work projects around the house. Chris did what he was told with no explanations as to why anything was done, how to plan to do it, or what was the process for getting through it. The main goal was to get the job done, not to explain to young, inexperienced Chris how to do it.

It could be described, perhaps, as learning by osmosis—the subtle transfer of information from father to son. Chris, the young grasshopper; dad, the wise sage. "Watch grasshopper, and learn." Except it didn't work. Holding the light did not teach him how to approach changing a timing belt. Likewise the hauling of rock did not explain the planning of a sound retaining wall, nor did the steadying of a two-by-four clarify how to do carpentry. People need more information to undertake such things on their own. Chris wasn't given that information. He did what he was told, and he didn't learn.

All was going satisfactorily that particular Saturday morning as they worked on the truck. Chris held the light; dad worked. Unfortunately, the tranquility was shattered, when dad needed a wrench. Obviously it would be something out of Chris' light-holding expertise. Chris could stretch himself beyond his vast light-holding acumen and fetch tools on occasion. Not infrequently, however, he didn't actually know which tool to fetch, even when given a name for it. He had never been told the names of each type of wrench in any systematic way. Often he'd end up holding them up and having to ask if he had the right one. For a child it's hard to remember the names when you run the risk of being berated for picking the wrong one.

The point is, on that particular truck-fixing morning, his dad needed a wrench. It was truly a dilemma, and the wrench in the works was that he didn't say what particular wrench was needed. He didn't say, "Chris, go get me a so-and-so wrench." He said, "I need a wrench." Perhaps his dad believed that any moron could look over his shoulder and see the problem and the specific wrench needed to solve it. Moreover, his dad must have expected Chris to be attentive to the statement "I need a wrench" and to interpret it correctly as "Go get a three-eighths inch box end wrench" (or whatever the actual wrench was).

On two points their communication broke down. First, Chris did not know what type of wrench to fetch, and if he were being honest, he probably didn't care. Second, and more importantly, he was not attuned to that statement or its proper interpretation. After all, he was "holding the light." He was doing his job. His job rarely changed. Hold the light. As everyone knows, that's the critical requirement of the light-holding job. Light-holders hold the light. So, on that fateful Saturday morning, when he continued to hold the light and didn't go get the required wrench, his dad turned and shot at him, "What is wrong with you? Use your head! *Think!*"

Chris was shattered. Years later you could see it in his eyes. He had been holding the light so well. It was focused right on the offending bolt. In the past, he had received many tongue-lashings for *not* holding it correctly, and he had been berated with the same "What is wrong with you?!" and "Think!" for not holding the light attentively. But that day he was diligently doing what he was assigned, holding the light, focusing its beam on the work area.

Now, to be sure, Chris was not a stupid child. He lacked experience of the world and social interactions as all children do, but he could follow the line of thinking in those three clauses his father had used. "What is wrong with you" meant that there *was* something wrong with him and it needed fixing. "Use your head" meant he was not, at present, using his head and needed to get with the program. And "think" meant, obviously, he was not thinking. What else could these three clauses mean? Even thoughtless Chris could interpret those clauses accurately. And he had heard them enough times by the tender age of ten to have thought through these facts. Those were oft-quoted statements in his young life. They were roundabout ways of saying he was stupid, senseless, or unthinking.

"What's wrong with you!?"

His dad clearly thought there was *something* wrong with his son. Why else would a boy's father ask that question again and again? And Chris believed him. Chris thought there *was* something wrong with him for years and years. In his fifties it's still one of the first questions he hears in his head when he botches something or fails to understand something. "What's wrong with you?!" That Saturday morning Chris vowed to be different. He vowed to think from then on. He was determined to "use his head."

They didn't finish the job that day, and they were working at the truck again on the next. Chris was diligently holding the light when his dad muttered something and walked away to the tool box. Chris had been watching him fiddle with a bolt for some time—his dad's thick fingers were having a hard time grasping it in the cramped confines of the engine compartment. And, more importantly, this time Chris was *thinking*. He was thinking his little fingers could remove that bolt. So when his dad walked away, Chris reached in and unscrewed the bolt for him. He thought that was what they were doing—removing that bolt. Looking back on it however, there was really no valid reason for him to have thought that. He hadn't the slightest clue about what they were working on. He pulled the bolt out and turned to show his dad his success, but his dad bellowed at him, "What is wrong with you!?"

It struck Chris like a sledgehammer! He stammered back, "I *thought* . . . ," but he was cut off in midsentence by his dad's sharp, angry response, "*Don't Think!*"

Those two days seemed to epitomize a serious problem in Chris' young life. Looking back on it years later he learned to put a name on it—haphazardness.

One day: "Think!"

And the very next: "Don't think!"

It was an impossible rule for a child to comprehend. It was a rule that no one could live under. We humans cannot live arbitrarily. We can't live haphazardly.

I've put forward the generalization that, for the most part, people do not enjoy practicing prayer. Nor do they even want to enter into it on a regular basis. Underlying this generalization is the conviction that most prayer is not authentic. Therefore, we can have statistics that show people do actually pray, but I would counter it is not prayer such as that which we find in the Bible or, more specifically, see in Jesus' life. When we talk about the sort of prayer found in the pages of scripture, I'm convinced people are not nearly as interested. But naturally that raises the question: *Why don't people want to pray?* Or we might rephrase it as *Why don't they enjoy prayer enough to engage in it consistently and with verve?* Let me reiterate here that I don't believe people act irrationally. They dislike (or are disinterested in) prayer for some *good* reason. You often find believers who have no problems at all with church attendance, Bible study, even meditation on the word, but they still struggle with prayer. We often can't articulate what the problems are, but serious Christians don't just ignore what they know to be important just on a whim. In this section, I'm going to identify the biggest hindrances to prayer. I'm not going to try to solve them yet, but it's a good idea to state them clearly so that we have some idea of what we are trying to fix.

PRAYER IS HAPHAZARD

The first, and foremost, hurdle I see is that for many of us, prayer is just too *haphazard* in nature. What I mean by this is that, compared to the other spiritual disciplines people practice eagerly, prayer is extremely difficult to evaluate and often has no set rules of engagement. It often has no system, and we have no idea how to approach it or what the goal of the job is supposed to be. It is like Chris' childhood experience. It feels as though we get different answers to the same question. Or perhaps that we don't have any real idea of what the process should entail. Let me suggest five basic contributing factors in our prayers that make it haphazard in nature:

- We have no *system* of prayer as we do with other spiritual practices.
- We don't really *know how to pray*.
- Once our prayers ascend, we don't *know how God will answer*.
- Often we don't *interpret the answer* we receive *honestly*.
- And finally, we don't *re-shape our requests* in response to God's answers.

Each of these problems contributes to the overall sense that prayer is haphazard. And I want to stress that this sense of haphazardness is not a mundane problem. It can lead to serious problems that harm our Christian walks overall, as well as be a fundamental contributor to our lack of desire to pray. Usually people cannot live with this haphazardness indefinitely. I knew instinctively as a child that "Think!" one day and "Don't think!" the next was impossible to live by for all practical purposes. Consequently, people try to alleviate this haphazardness as much as possible. After we look at these five specific contributing factors, I will return to this idea of haphazardness in prayer and look at detrimental ways people sometimes try to fix the problem.

We Have No System To Follow

The first factor that makes our prayers haphazard is that our system of prayer (if we actually have one) is often woefully inadequate. More commonly, we don't actually have any system in the first place. This lack of system promotes haphazardness in prayer, which in turn leads to our lack of desire to pray. This is a bit like my own childhood experience of car projects. (I wonder if all boys have childhood stories of car projects.) I would watch my dad approach our family cars when they were running incorrectly, and he would work all sorts of magic on them. He was a whiz with fixing cars. They would always, every single time, end up running fine again. But I had no idea how that actually happened. He never told me there was a system to his fixing of engines. He tried certain things first and then went on to other things. It all looked haphazard to me and consequently, when I had grown up, I really had no idea even where to start when my own car began to run poorly.

Let's use a counter example that we may be more familiar with: Bible study. I very rarely hear committed, excited Christians say they don't look forward to their Bible study time. And when I ask them to describe it to me, I often find it very organized and methodical.[1]

There are many different approaches to Bible study, but in all of them people feel that attainable, measurable criteria can be achieved, and furthermore, they have a plan for achieving those criteria. Some people's Bible study consists of just reading, and the plan is to read through the

---

1. I should note that how organized and methodical a method is mostly in the eyes of the beholder. I may find their system unorganized, but the point is *they* find it organized and it provides them with a structured methodology to consistently follow.

Bible in a year. This is structure organized around simply reading texts. This approach seems to adopt the view that getting the big picture consistently will help clarify the small picture questions that come up in more focused study. Some spend more time in detailed studies. Perhaps they try to mark all the verbs and nouns, really keying in on the grammatical structure. This is system built on linguistic ideas. Still others try to look at texts in a more discourse oriented way and focus on the links between passages. This is structure built on discourse analysis. Most people partake of all these various approaches, trying to cover a certain amount of text, analyzing its grammar, syntax, and discourse structures, and then additionally making judgments on how it applies to our lives. I'm not all that interested in what approach people use, but it seems to me that they use *some system*. People don't usually just sit down, blankly, with a vague sense of wanting to cover *something*—whatever comes up.

But unfortunately, that's often how we approach our prayer lives. We sit down, close our eyes, and hope for the best. We might argue that this is the *spiritual* nature of prayer. But if the *spiritual* nature of prayer leads to such lack of system, are we admitting that Bible study has no *spiritual* component because it lends itself so easily to system? Or are we admitting that we are able to organize our Sunday school lessons because they are not really *spiritual* in any way? After all, lessons come from study, so study must apparently be non-spiritual because it has system built into it. In reality, we do think there is a spiritual component to Sunday school, Bible study, and church services, even though they partake very often of quite structured systems. We do not believe, practically speaking, that *spirituality* in and of itself infringes on the use of a concrete methodology. We expect God to speak to us through his word as we read and think and go through our *systems* of study. In point of fact, the spiritual facet is often relied on when our limited abilities to grasp the texts are exhausted. But unlike prayer, we don't start to study with the assumption that we should just begin even when we have no plan of attack. We've seen that person who just drops their Bible open each day and reads whatever passage comes up. But we've also realized that such an approach leads to a pretty disorganized and sub-par theology.[2]

---

2. A pastor I knew would describe this haphazard approach with the story of a man who dropped his Bible open one day and read "and Judas went out and hanged himself" and the next day dropped it open to "go and do likewise." Obviously such an approach would have some pretty big disadvantages.

The advantage to a *system* becomes apparent when you do things without one. Let me use a track and field example to illustrate. When I was in junior high school I was on the track team, and I was one of those who tried pole vaulting. I also ran a variety of sprints, but I especially liked to pole vault. Now the other events, the 200-, 100-, and fifty-yard sprints could be run with little direction. This is not to say world class sprinters don't follow systems, but when beginning, many runners can line up in the blocks and run with very little planning—the gun goes off and they run. Many of the fast kids did just that. (They even won a lot until they met someone who had been practicing with a system.)

But pole vaulting is nothing like that. There is a system you must learn to get the hang of flinging your legs up past your head and pushing yourself along a pole and over a bar. Many of my friends tried to pole vault, but they didn't want to master the system. They wanted to treat pole vaulting like sprinting— to just do it "naturally." They would grab a pole and have at it. And it simply did not work. This is not to say they didn't spend a good deal of time doing it. It just never went anywhere.

On the contrary, I set myself to learning the system in steps (as our coach directed). First I learned to carry the pole in the right position. Then I learned how to plant it in the right way. Then I learned how to pull the legs up at the hips. Then I learned to pull the legs up *and* push off with the arms. All of this was intended to get me used to being upside down with the ability to rotate my body in the air over the bar. Frankly, to attempt to learn to pole vault without a system is to attempt something impossible. My friends were too haphazard in their approach, and the end result was that I vaulted and they quit (or vaulted very poorly). We needed a plan to learn each movement. And during the practice sessions, I learned to use the goals of each step of the plan to evaluate how to proceed. If you can't plant the pole correctly, you can't push off correctly. If you've learned to plant the pole incorrectly, you must go back and re-learn the proper method to achieve your goal and move to the next step.[3]

In an even worse case which I saw on the field one day, a kid skipped the system and just vaulted from feel—unfortunately *with* a little success. He ended up flopping his body almost sideways in the air

---

3. Notice in the analogy I said "the" proper method. I'm not actually advocating one single proper method for prayer. But I would suggest that there are proper methods and improper methods.

over the bar. It was so awkward looking that everyone would stop and stare; they were amazed he could clear the bar. And it was truly unfortunate that he did often clear the bar because he was never going to go very far with his current efforts. Sure, he'd even won a couple meets, matched against raw ninth grade pole vaulters who often wouldn't even plant the pole correctly. But after a while he went up against people who really knew how to vault and the results were inevitable. He failed miserably and never even competed seriously again. He showed up every week, still giving his all, but there was no way it would ever pan out. And worse yet, with his obvious strength and flexibility he *could have been* a great vaulter. He settled for poor habits instead of methodical practice. This, by the way, is the difference between a *discipline* and just practice. A discipline is the application of proper means to achieve growth in some area. As the Apostle Paul said in his boxing analogy of how he "runs the race" of his Christian life: he does not "beat the air" aimlessly; he "disciplines" his body.[4]

We grasp this idea when it comes to much of our Christian lives, but for some reason we forsake it when we come to prayer.[5] Moreover, when I ask people what they do when they pray, it appears that they quite often don't even consider the possibility that prayer could or should have some sort of system. Almost never do I hear people explaining their prayer lives in the same terms they might use for their Bible study lives. Some have vague systems, such as praying around the world, or praying through their friends or family list. But that's often as far as it goes. And, like the young pole vaulter I previously mentioned who had no system but succeeded at times, some Christians have even had a little success in prayer and then just kept doggedly to their lack of system thinking it had worked. In reality though, it hasn't.

I propose that prayer needs a system on at least two levels. First, we ought to have a system for our prayers as a whole. We might call it a *macro-system*. Here we would have broad areas of concern. We might include things like missions, family, the church, our well-being, our friends, etc. Second, we ought to have some plan for our specific daily prayers.

---

4. 1 Cor 9:26–27.

5. It's interesting to me that at the school where I teach we have a course dedicated to Bible study methods, but we don't offer a course called *prayer methods*. Although I've been told that the associated Seminary does have a class on prayer. It seems as though we believe prayer *is* important, but not so important that we should have an actual *methodology* to undertake it.

We can call this a *micro-system*. Here we can think about things like what specifically we should pray for, how we pray for it, what sequence of prayer should we follow, what topics should be included and where ought they be placed in the sequence.

Without some sort of plan, we are like pole vaulters with no system. We fling ourselves around not knowing what should go where or what to make of it when we flop over the bar on any given lucky day. This lack of system creates a great deal of haphazardness in our prayer lives. The obvious solution is to find a system. We will try to develop one as we progress.

We Don't Know How to Pray

Prior to the question "How do I pray for things?" we might ask, "What should I pray for?" There is quite a big difference between those two questions. "What should I pray for?" is usually interested in what specific *topics* to bring up in prayer or what specific item I want from prayer. We'll look at that question in the following pages as well, but it seems to me the more important part of the question, "What should I pray for?" (and the part people really are in a quandary about) is: "How should I pray for things?" The first question has answers like:

- Pray for your health.
- Pray for your worries.
- Pray for wisdom.
- Pray for forgiveness.
- Pray your thanksgiving.
- Pray for friends.
- Pray for your country.[6]

It is my firm belief that most people really don't need to be convinced that they're allowed to bring *anything* to God in prayer. People

---

6. There is an older book by Herbert Lockyer called *All the Prayers of the Bible* that addresses all the prayers in the Bible with an emphasis on what problems or circumstances are being presented. Dr. Lockyer lists almost everything one can think of from "Prayers for Escape from Trials" to "Prayers as Praise." But as I note in the text, I don't believe most people need to be convinced of the truth that they can bring any *topic* to God in prayer.

seem to know that we can pray for almost any "topics" in that sense. It is much like conversations with close friends. We feel pretty secure bringing things up as discussion topics. As believers it is almost an instinct to talk to God. And when we talk to someone we love we tend to share whatever is on our minds. And if we even take a short moment to think about it, we realize that there is nothing we could hide from God anyway. So talking to him about some topic isn't revealing something he doesn't already know.[7] For the most part, I've found that people are more than willing to bring any topic up with God in prayer (at least privately).

The more pressing problem we often face is in knowing *how* to pray over what we bring to God. Here we might recall again my childhood experience of watching my dad fix cars, or undertaking most jobs. Except this time the problem is in knowing what to do. I understood oftentimes the goal of the job we were undertaking; for example, a common goal was to build something. But for me, I was never let in on how exactly one goes about it. How do you make the plan for it? What factors are important to remember in planning the work? Do you put rebar down first and then pour concrete or do you pour concrete and then push rebar into it? Could it be something different altogether? Does it matter? Figuring this out is especially difficult when the one you're emulating skips steps by doing them in his head outside of your sight.

In terms of prayer, how do we actually go about it? Should we repeat our prayers over and over? Should we pray specifically or generally? Should we pray for what others ask of us without alteration? These are all fundamental process questions. Later in the book we will look at how to pray more extensively, but at this point I want to highlight one foundational attitude that must accompany any prayer request we offer. It is, in my opinion, an absolute requirement in prayer, and it is found by examining a couple of exchanges between Moses and God. Our examples are not actually prayers, but rather are direct exchanges between man and God. I'm making the assumption that God's direct interaction with us is probably the same as his interaction with us in prayer—at least in the sense of how we talk about different topics.

As a first example, let's look at the third chapter of Exodus, in the Old Testament, where we find the record of Moses meeting God at the burning bush. Before I go any further let me point out that there is no

---

7. Here we might note some of the verses to this effect in scripture: 2 Chr 6:30; Job 28:23; 34:21; Pss 33:13; 94:11.

deep, developed relationship between God and Moses at this point. In fact, Moses probably didn't know God very well. After all, Moses had grown up in Egypt among Egyptians, trained by Egyptians and learning publicly about Egyptian gods and practices. He clearly had some relationship to his kinfolk, but it appears he did not have a close relationship with the God of his people. When he met God at the burning bush, he even had to ask what to call God. And he needed to be instructed on how to act in the presence of God. I mention this fact to point out that we are here going to compare ourselves not to someone who is a spiritual giant with God, but to a person who is probably a relative novice in respect to talking with God. And yet, there is a lot we can learn from the exchange. So let's proceed.

At the burning bush encounter, God gives Moses the mission of leading his chosen people of Israel up out of Egypt to the Promised Land.[8] When you read the rest of the passage, notice that Moses does not just take the mission and go. He has a lot of questions:

- "Who am I, that I should go to Pharaoh, and that I should bring the sons of Israel out of Egypt?"
- "What shall I say to them?" (I.e., to Israel when they ask who sent him.)
- "What if they will not believe me or listen to what I say?"
- What if my nature renders me incapable of the job? (This is in the form of a statement—Moses says "Please, Lord, I have never been eloquent . . . , I'm slow of speech and slow of tongue." Moses is wondering about his personal abilities to accomplish the mission.)

Now if anything should be taboo in a conversation with God, you would suspect it to be questioning God on his orders. It is the Lord God of the universe, after all. But up to this point in our text of Exodus (4:13), God patiently deals with every question Moses brings to him. There seems to be no topic that is taboo, even when Moses is questioning God about the orders he's just given him. And there is no hint that Moses is considered impertinent in God's eyes either. God just deals with each question as it arises. It is only at 4:14 that we are told: "Then the anger of the LORD burned against Moses." Why is that? Why after all those

8. Exod 3:10—4:10.

concerns and questions did God's anger flare up? Moses got his orders; why wasn't God angry with all the previous questions and fears?

The key is in Exodus 4:13. Moses' questions are not insolent up to that point. They are an example of a man trying to work out the details of a mission he is about to undertake. It makes perfect sense to wonder about things like what should be said to make it go smoothly and what should be done if certain contingencies occur. It also makes sense to evaluate the qualities we possess if we are expected to accomplish some feat. In fact, it makes sense for a *mature individual* to actually *have the questions*! All along God is not angry because Moses is just exploring the directive God has given. God gives him answers to the questions, sometimes by giving him signs to perform, sometimes by just reassuring him of the facts of the situation. In terms of our question, "How should I pray?" we might say it is acceptable to engage in some pretty pointed question and answer debates with God.

But in the end, after hearing all of God's answers and encouragements, Moses says in 4:13, Lord, I don't want to go! I'm paraphrasing of course. Moses is more discreet saying, "Lord, send the message by whoever you will." That sounds like he's on God's side, but in reality he's saying God should pick someone else—send the message by whoever you will—*except me*. In essence Moses is telling God he knows more about himself than God does and that God has made a mistake in picking him. God disagrees and is angry about Moses' lack of willingness, trust, and faith.

This interaction is oftentimes much like our prayers. We ask good questions and make good requests, or sometimes we ask bad questions and make bad requests. But in both cases God listens and answers us. Sometimes he says, "Yes," sometimes "No." Sometimes he says, "Don't worry about that." Sometimes he points out observations about reality that we've missed and that he wants us to think about. He sometimes, very rarely, tells us, "Don't ever pray over that particular topic."[9] But it

---

9. Of course there is that one statement in 1 John 5:16 that explicitly says, "If anyone sees his brother committing a sin not leading to death, he shall ask and God will for him give life to those who commit sin not leading to death. There is a sin leading to death; I do not say that he should make request for this." In this particular case, the sin leading to death is probably the denial of Jesus. And John wants us to know that it is out of bounds to pray that God save someone while they still deny Jesus. We might pray they hear the gospel preached, but we should not expect God to save those who deny the only way of salvation.

seems to me that God does not enjoy it when we talk to him, ask things of him, question his ideas, and then *ignore* his responses. And frankly, we wouldn't like that sort of conversation either. It's demeaning. Even the most challenging statements are acceptable in God's eyes, provided we *listen* to his responses, and reformulate our ideas in light of them, but when we just ignore the responses and tell God he's wrong (either overtly or covertly), I would imagine we offend him.

Just as a side note, another possible problem here could be Moses' interpretation of what God said in his answers. He could have, theoretically, heard what God said, interpreted it incorrectly, and consequently made some serious errors. But this didn't seem to be the case. In this instance Moses seems to have heard what God said, interpreted it correctly, and then just ignored it. Later we'll look specifically at the question of how we interpret God's answers and how misinterpretation can happen. Here, in our Moses story, there is no need for that investigation. The text gives no indication that Moses missed the point of God's answers. And God did not seem to think Moses misunderstood him either. Moses didn't pay any attention to them. He didn't *listen*. This, then, is a critical ingredient in how we pray: we must be ready to *listen*. Listening is going to come up in other discussions in this book, but I believe that it is so foundational that it needed to be highlighted early on. Without listening to God, our prayers are positively going to go astray. If I am not willing to really listen to the answers I get, even praying perfectly will avail me nothing. Unfortunately, as we all probably know, this foundational attitude of listening doesn't seem to be easily formed.

The second exchange between God and man is another story from Moses' life found in the Old Testament book of Numbers. Let me lay out the background of the exchange. In Numbers 20 we find Moses and the people of Israel at a place called the Wilderness of Zin. It was an arid wasteland, and the text tells us there was no water there. Consequently, the people were frustrated, and that led them into sin. They "contended" with Moses specifically about the lack of water and suggested that they would have been better off if they had died rather than come to such an arid, unforgiving rat-hole. Moreover, they accused Moses of leading them, and even their animals, into the desert only to die.[10]

---

10. I won't go into the myriad unspoken assertions that the people seem to have had in their grumbling: God is unfaithful to His word, God lied to them when He brought them out of Egypt, slavery in Egypt is preferable to serving the one, true, living God

Moses took these complaints to God and God gave Moses a solution. He told him to (1) take the rod he had given him earlier, (2) assemble the people, and (3) speak to a particular rock in order to bring forth water. This would show the people God was caring for their needs. Practically speaking, it would also solve the water shortage problem, but here is where a problem arises that is similar to the problem Moses had in his first meeting with God. He did not *listen* to the directions God had given him. The text goes on to say:

> [9] "So Moses took the rod from before the LORD, just as he had commanded him; [10] and Moses and Aaron gathered the assembly before the rock. And he said to them, 'Listen now, you rebels; shall we bring forth water for you out of this rock?' [11] Then Moses lifted up his hand and struck the rock twice with his rod; and water came forth abundantly, and the congregation and their beasts drank."[11]

Do you see the problem? God said to Moses, (1) take the rod, (2) assemble the people, and (3) speak to the rock. Moses' interpretation of God's statements was: (1) take the rod, (2) condemn the people harshly, and (3) strike the rock twice. Moses didn't really *listen* to God again, although he probably would have tried to defend himself by pointing out that in general he did what God wanted. After all, there was a rod, a gathering, and a rock involved. But in all truth, Moses did what he wanted and pretended it was what God had said to do.

Interestingly enough, God still supplied water to the people. Remember the pole-vaulter who actually got over the bar with dismal form? The people and Moses metaphorically got over the bar—they got what they were shooting for. Moreover, God was not going to punish others in this instance because Moses was unwilling to listen to his commands. Something good came from Moses' dismal effort, but Moses himself was going to have to learn a lesson. The text tells us: "But the LORD said to Moses and Aaron, 'Because you have not believed Me, to treat Me as holy in the sight of the sons of Israel, therefore you shall not bring this assembly into the land which I have given them.'"[12] Moses'

---

of the universe, etc. There were a lot of subtle, theologically sinful assumptions that accompanied the suggestion to Moses that they were led out Egypt just to die of thirst or hunger in the desert.

11. Num 20:9–11.

12. Num 20:12. Note that Aaron was apparently involved in this fiasco as well. But Moses, as the leader seems to take the brunt of the punishment in many ways.

punishment was that he would not lead the people into the Promised Land. And this punishment stuck in his craw! Amazingly enough, Moses responded by *not listening* to God again! We might point out as well that in God's indictment of Moses he says Moses didn't *believe* God. And this led to Moses treating God in an unholy fashion. Moses again understood God correctly. He just failed to believe what he was told, so he proceeded as he saw fit.

Let's see where this problem went for Moses later in life. If we turn to the book of Deuteronomy, chapter three, we find Moses and the people of Israel on the brink of coming into the Promised Land. Moses is recounting the long and difficult journey (both physical and spiritual) that Israel had completed and is preparing them for the final stage of entrance. In Moses' speech he notes that he had continuously been concerned about the punishment he received because of the striking of the rock. The text says:

> [23] "I also pleaded with the LORD at that time, saying, [24] 'O Lord GOD, You have begun to show Your servant Your greatness and Your strong hand; for what god is there in heaven or on earth who can do such works and mighty acts as Yours? [25] 'Let me, I pray, cross over and see the fair land that is beyond the Jordan, that good hill country and Lebanon.'"[13]

Moses was asking to be allowed to enter the land again, even though he had been told specifically that he was not going to have that blessing. Who knows how many times this prayer ascended to God? In light of the answer he records, I imagine it was more than once or twice. The key point is in God's response:

> [26] "But the LORD was angry with me on your account, and would not listen to me; and the LORD said to me, 'Enough! Speak to Me no more of this matter. [27] 'Go up to the top of Pisgah and lift up your eyes to the west and north and south and east, and see *it* with your eyes, for you shall not cross over this Jordan. [28] 'But charge Joshua and encourage him and strengthen him, for he shall go across at the head of this people, and he will give them as an inheritance the land which you will see.'"[14]

13. Deut 3:23–25.

14. Deut 3:26–28. Just as a side note, notice how Moses blames his predicament on the people of Israel! It is unfortunate that an old maxim is often true, "*No life is totally wasted—you can always be a bad example.*" Moses was one of the best examples we could ever follow in many things, but even the best people have their failings. In this case, Moses was struggling with his listening skills.

Notice God's anger again with Moses as he says, "Enough! Speak to Me no more of this matter." Moses again drew God's ire because he refused to take into account what God had already answered. In this instance it appears that over the whole of Moses' life he did not learn entirely the lesson of *listening* to God.

Our question—"How do I pray for something?"—can create a lot of haphazardness in our prayer lives. If we don't know how to pray we will probably flounder around, never settling on any approach. More likely we will not pray over things because we won't even know where to start. We have not fully answered the question of how to pray in this section (we'll look at that later), but I've suggested one foundational truth: we need to begin firmly with the belief that we will *listen* to what God says in response to us. Without this foundation, our prayers will take a terrible course and may end up stirring the anger of God.

We Don't Know How God Will Answer

Remember our opening story about Chris? One of the biggest frustrations Chris could remember having as a child was the fact that he couldn't figure out how his dad would respond to things. Obviously "Think!" on one day and "Don't think!" on the next is an extreme example, but he could remember many such contradictions on a regular basis. The basic problem was that he had no idea what to do or say because similar actions would produce contradictory responses. He could not read his father and anticipate what action would be correct in his eyes. Many times the only response he could come up with was to freeze up and do nothing. Of course that would create a whole new cluster of difficulties, but at least he could say he didn't actually *do anything* to deserve a tongue lashing. Ultimately, because he could not anticipate what his father would say, he would either act wrongly (proving his father right—that there was something wrong with him) or he would not act at all (again proving dad right—that he was not awake).

Of course the similarity between Chris' father and God breaks down when we look at God's responses; humans are contradictory at times. That's just part of our fallen nature. All dads contradict themselves on occasion, but God is never contradictory with us. If there is a lack of understanding, it is caused by our failure in some way, and if we cannot anticipate how God will answer us, it is because we have not paid attention to him, for he makes Himself clear when we listen. To say it again, God does not contradict himself when he responds.

This inability to read God is part of the problem Moses was having. He was not anticipating how God would respond, nor was he able to decipher what that response would be. Of course there is another facet that we must point out. Perhaps he was anticipating how God would respond but was sorely mistaken in his assumptions. I think this also explains many of the difficulties we encounter when trying to figure out how God will answer. We box him in by assuming we know exactly how he will answer and thereby leave him no option to answer at all (for all practical purposes that is).

My point here is that our prayers become haphazard because we do not know how God will respond to them. Some seem to view this as just the mystery of our eternal God. After all, scripture says: "Oh, the depth of the riches both of the wisdom and knowledge of God! How unsearchable are his judgments and unfathomable his ways! For who has known the mind of the Lord, or who became his counselor?"[15] Consequently, because God is unsearchable, we are often told (indirectly) to throw up our hands and declare *"Mystery!"* when considering the nature of God's actions, thoughts, and responses. Let me point out, however, that Paul uses this exact same text in 1 Corinthians 2:16 to indicate that we *can* know the mind of the Lord because we have the "mind of Christ." The great theologians through the ages have all agreed God is transcendent—that is, beyond us in a myriad of ways. But they also thoroughly agree that he is imminent as well—that we *can* know him on some level. Practically speaking, if we were unable to know him it would make no sense for him to speak with us, would it?

Let's think about this idea of not knowing how someone will respond in light of regular, daily conversation with people in general. Think back here for a moment about Chris and his dad working on the truck again. One day it was "Think!" and the next it was "Don't think!" In that case the mystery was coming from Chris' dad. But God surely is not so arbitrary, and still we often have the same response Chris had—complete confusion. There is a problem when we don't know how people (or God) will respond to us. Would his dad tell him to "Think!" today or would it be "Don't think!"? He never really could get clued into how his dad would respond to anything he did.

---

15. Rom 11:33–34.

Let me introduce some technical ideas here from a branch of linguistics that deals with something called frame theory. In this approach to the study of language the researcher looks at how we take people's statements and link them to situations we *expect* to occur. This helps us interpret what they are saying. In typical exchanges between people there is a great deal of focus on our expectations and inferences in conversation. The main idea behind frame theory is that we understand expressions from others partially by how we package them in our own minds.

If we are talking about dogs for example, I will undoubtedly do a number of things in my mind as I converse with someone to help me follow the conversation. I will perhaps formulate a picture of the ideal dog (or perhaps just one I know).[16] I will interpret words such as foot or eyes in terms of the limitations placed on such ideas by the over-arching concept of dog. I will even have expectations about the other person's content and comments based on the topic "dog." So, for example, when discussing a dog show I don't expect the other person to say something like, "She runs great and had a very nice four-barrel carburetor" after I ask a question about the show participants. Four-barrel carburetors don't usually enter into a conversation about dogs. But if someone did utter the shorter statement, "She runs great," I would think of that clause in terms of dogs running, not cars. I even reshape my ideas partially by the expectations I have of what the other person will say. So if someone does express the odd sentence, "She runs great and has a hearty engine," I will interpret the term "hearty engine" to fit into a discussion of dogs. I'll undoubtedly interpret the term to mean the animal's spirit or source of energy. That is, I make the effort to make the statement fit the context of "dog."

Think of the situation that would arise, however, if we could never anticipate what topics or ideas might come up in a conversation, if we never had a framework of possible context in which to put statements. We would quickly find ourselves at a complete loss. We would have to fish around for the right topic with no help from our expectations. We would likely be saying things that have no relevance to the conversation as well.

---

16. Some suggest that we actually store information in our brains in schematic or picture content. So when I hear the term "dog" I automatically bring up the diagram of "dog" that I store in long term memory.

Suppose I wanted to discuss finances with my wife and knew for a fact that she was one of those people who worry over the issue. Suppose further that we have limited savings which permit very little spending on toys. Wouldn't that shape my half of the conversation? I would probably not suggest to her, "Honey, I want to spend half our savings on a new guitar." I know what her answer would be. I know her and her internal make-up. And if I did say that to her, and she responded with, "I don't think we should do that" it would make little sense for me to follow up with, "Ok, honey, and after that how about we spend half of our savings on that new guitar I want."

In real life, I have some notion of how people respond and that notion shapes how I talk to them. And the better I know them, the better I am at predicting what they will understand, agree to, disagree with, or be angry about. Many students at our college know for a fact that to ask one particular professor for "grace" on an assignment will bring about a lecture on the nature of "grace" versus "a favor." It will not result in the extension of "grace" as they define it. After a few such interactions they don't even bring up the topic with him. The point is, the students have learned what makes sense to ask for and what does not, and they shape their interactions around their growing knowledge of that professor. Many more freshman will ask him that question than seniors. Seniors know how he will respond to it.

In like manner, we need to have some idea of how God will respond to us. If I pray diligently for a sports car every day to a God who does not give out sports cars, I'm effectively wasting my time (not to mention probably frustrating God to no end). If I pray for my cold to be healed over and over, and it turns out God uses colds to show me my frailty, I'm probably never going to learn my lesson because I'm focused solely on relieving the problem. It's critical that we know God and anticipate what he will respond with. Otherwise we will continue to suggest things to him that are, in blunt terms, ridiculous. So the question that naturally arises is: "How do I get to know God well enough to anticipate his desires?"

We might ask how you get to know anyone well enough to anticipate his or her desires. Doesn't it come down to spending time with that person, *listening* to what they say, watching how they act, and participating in their lives? In like manner we should do the same with God. We will get much better at knowing how God will respond by getting to know how he commonly acts and what he commonly expects. And the best place to begin finding that information is in scripture—the record of his actions. In fact the New Testament notes that the Old Testament was "written for our instruction" just so we can learn what God is like.[17]

I am suggesting, then, that we can to some extent anticipate how God will answer our prayers. But to become proficient at anticipating God's responses, we must take the time to get to know him. It's a chicken and egg circle in some senses. We know God better by learning to anticipate his responses better, and we learn to anticipate his responses better by getting to know him better. It's a growing cycle that builds on itself. In daily conversations we always anticipate what others will say to some extent, and this shapes our responses. When we think we cannot know what God will say to any situation, we surely cannot pray intelligently. Our prayers become haphazard because we don't have any idea what God is contributing to the conversation or even what general emphases he might typically focus on. We don't know what God likes and does not like in any practical way.

Of course there is another facet here that we will discuss more fully in the next section. Part of Chris' problem as a child was that his dad's interests and his own didn't mesh very well. Chris liked sports. His dad liked working on cars. Chris liked music and playing in his band. His dad liked to hole up in his shop alone. Chris liked to hang out with his friends. His dad didn't seem to have any he consistently interacted with. They were, and still are in many ways, different types of people constitutionally. Consequently, the things his dad did were often things Chris would not want to do and vice versa. There's no fault in this; it is just true sometimes. This is another problem we have with anticipating God's responses. We really don't want to anticipate them because we realize that they will not mesh with what we want. So we intentionally interpret God's answers wrongly. We are dishonest about what he is saying to us. As I said, we'll come back to this in a moment.

Let me finish discussing our present problem with a comment on why we may not like the idea of anticipating God's response. I think many of us might feel that to be able to anticipate how God typically will respond in a discussion is to imply that God is so small that he can be boxed into certain responses in some way. Let me be clear that I'm not saying any such thing. God is truly transcendent and unsearchable if

---

17. Rom 15:4. Cf. 1 Cor 10:11.

we are talking about the nature and make-up of his being. But in terms of relationship between God and man the truth is, we ourselves are the limiting factor. God *must* address us in ways we will understand for relationship to occur between us. We are so limited that we need concrete courses to follow in our interactions. Like a freeway that has boundaries on each side to keep traffic in some semblance of order and in the generally correct path. Our conversation cannot, and is not, open ended in that regard. We as humans need the ability to anticipate responses to make information coherent to us. In technical terms, we need to be able to *expect* certain contingencies in conversation in order to carry it out. Studies in the theory of expectation in conversation prove this time and again. I'm not advocating we can know God fully. I'm saying that his grace has been extended to us in our conversation with him in such a way as to let us talk to him as we normally do with other humans. And this is because it's the only way we humans can communicate. He is not expecting us to adopt some mystical method of communication. God doesn't mystically make it so we understand and talk with him in ways that are different from how we talk normally.

There is another question here that relates to this topic of understanding God. It is: "How does God actually guide us?" I'm going to address that question later in this chapter. There we will think on our expectations of what God will actually do on a daily basis for us rather than just how he will speak to us.

We Don't Interpret the Answer We Receive Honestly

As Chris grew up with his dad, one thing he said he learned was that dad didn't appreciate any questioning of his plans. His dad didn't want Chris to ever question *how* he approached a task, and Chris learned very quickly never to do that. The point being, that even though Chris had very little idea of how his dad would respond to things, he still was able to have some idea of what to expect from him. In any interaction, even those that are with people new to us, we always have some expectations in some way. Even if they are for something so small as an expectation of proper manners.

Although having no ability to anticipate God's responses is definitely a problem, I would contend that most committed Christians consciously or subconsciously actually *do* know that they must be able to anticipate how God will respond to them to some extent. Committed believers often are doing the very things that lead to a growing knowledge of what God is like and how he tends to respond to things. They read their Bibles, go to church, listen to sermons, attend Sunday school, read Christian literature, etc. They intentionally learn about God and get to know what he is like in all sorts of ways. Why do they do this? Because they know the truth of the matter. They need to know God better to better understand how he speaks and acts. They are subconsciously trying to learn how to anticipate him so they can communicate with him more effectively. And they do, in fact, learn to anticipate what types of answers he may give them to some extent. I think that the more serious problem that committed believers face is similar to Moses' more serious problem—they often can't or won't interpret the *clear* answers they receive correctly.

To be fair, this incorrect interpretation may be unintentional—they cannot interpret correctly for some real reason. With Chris' father there were real reasons he could not interpret what he was saying to him most of the time. As I've noted, the most problematic was the haphazard nature of his dad's responses. Similarly, sometimes we honestly don't know how God will respond to a new situation, and consequently we can't understand what he is saying to us. (However, I hasten to add once more, that it is not because God is inconsistent in his responses, but usually because we have not fully grasped the whole situation around us.)

But, in all honesty, it is more often the case that we don't understand what God is saying to us because we don't desire to understand it. We *will not* interpret what he says correctly. This is like Moses. He most assuredly understood what God had said about entering the Promised Land. He just didn't want to hear it. And in like fashion we don't want to hear what God says oftentimes either. Of course the reasons for this are many and varied, and we can't list them all. But let's look at some examples of this phenomenon in scripture and see some reasons others had for choosing to not understand God's clear speech.

First, we can list our example of Moses. No scripture tells us explicitly why Moses chose to reprimand the people and strike the rock when he was not commanded to do so. But looking at Moses' previous statements gives us some idea of his frame of mind and what may have shaped his actions.

We may begin by looking at Numbers 11. Israel had spent a year at Mount Horeb receiving the Law and building the tabernacle. We are told that in the second year from when they went out from Egypt, in the second month, God lifted his cloud and began the journey to the Promised Land.[18] It should have been a journey of just a couple of weeks. But soon after the march began, the people began to complain about things. In Numbers 11:5-6 they specifically griped about the lack of variety in their food, for they had been eating manna for awhile. More importantly they recalled with longing the food they used to "eat free" in Egypt. Of course they were forgetting that gathering manna each day as free people is preferable to eating "free" as slaves to the Egyptians.[19]

We are told Moses heard this griping and "was displeased." Literally it says it was "evil" in Moses' eyes.[20] This was a continual problem for Moses. Israel was constantly doing wrong and Moses constantly had to deal with it. In this case Moses went on a rant to God:

> [10] Now Moses heard the people weeping throughout their families, each man at the doorway of his tent; and the anger of the LORD was kindled greatly, and Moses was displeased. [11] So Moses said to the LORD, "Why have You been so hard on Your servant? And why have I not found favor in Your sight, that You have laid the burden of all this people on me? [12] Was it I who conceived all this people? Was it I who brought them forth, that You should say to me, 'Carry them in your bosom as a nurse carries a nursing infant, to the land which You swore to their fathers'? [13] Where am I to get meat to give to all this people? For they weep before me, saying, 'Give us meat that we may eat!' [14] I alone am not able to carry all this people, because it is too burdensome for me. [15] So if You are going to deal thus with me, please kill me at once, if I have found favor in Your sight, and do not let me see my wretchedness."[21]

Right from the start Moses was frustrated with the whole plan. The burden of leading was difficult to bear and especially so when Israel would resort to thankless whining over their situation and blaming Moses for their problems.

---

18. Num 10:11.

19. Remember also that Exodus 1:14 tells us the Egyptians "made their lives bitter with hard labor in mortar and bricks and at all kinds of labor in the field, all their labors which they rigorously imposed on them." Moreover, the king of Egypt came up with a plan to breed the Hebrews out of existence by slaughtering the male children and keeping only the females (probably to marry them to Egyptians; Exod 1:22).

20. Num 11:10.

21. Num 11:10-15.

Next, let's look at Numbers 13. Once the people had reached the Promised Land, God told Moses to send some spies out to reconnoiter. They looked over the whole land and found it very good, but they also noted that "the people who live in the land are strong, and the cities are fortified and very large; and moreover, we saw the descendants of Anak there."[22] In the end, Joshua and Caleb were the only two who wanted to go forward, according to plan, and take the land. The other spies lied to the people of Israel and told them, "The land through which we have gone, in spying it out, is a land that devours its inhabitants; and all the people whom we saw in it are men of great size."[23]

In response to this false report (and apparently paying no attention to Caleb and Joshua) Israel cried out in dismay and "grumbled against Moses and Aaron." Here is the text:

> [2] All the sons of Israel grumbled against Moses and Aaron; and the whole congregation said to them, "Would that we had died in the land of Egypt! Or would that we had died in this wilderness! [3] "Why is the LORD bringing us into this land, to fall by the sword? Our wives and our little ones will become plunder; would it not be better for us to return to Egypt?" [4] So they said to one another, "Let us appoint a leader and return to Egypt."[24]

Again, Moses was the brunt of their anger at the Lord. And in this case, they decided to throw him over for a new leader who would not just lead them with new policies, but would take them back to the slavery they had conveniently forgotten in Egypt!

In response to this gross sin God tells Moses he is fed up with Israel as well. He offers to "smite them with pestilence and dispossess them." Moreover, God offers to make a great nation out of Moses' line to replace them. In response to this Moses pleads for Israel on the basis of God's reputation. If Israel is destroyed, God will look like an impotent fool who could not bring his people out of slavery. In light of this argument God relents on his desire to destroy Israel, and instead he imposes the forty years of wandering in the desert. In other words, *Israel's* sin has condemned *Moses* to another forty years of hardship. You can imagine him sarcastically muttering, "Thanks guys!"

---

22. Num 13:28. The sons of Anak were men of extremely large stature and consequently the spies were intimidated by them. Cf. Num 13:33.

23. Num 13:32.

24. Num 14:2–4.

Reasons People Don't Enjoy Prayer

We could find more examples but need not belabor the point: Moses quite often had to clean up the mess Israel made and was often forced to suffer for their foolishness. I would suggest then that one reason Moses didn't listen to God in Numbers 20 was that he was harboring some deep-seated frustrations with the whole situation and wanted to vent his opinion. He did so, unfortunately, at the expense of God's holiness.[25] Even if Moses had legitimate reasons to be frustrated, he placed his own feelings over God's desires and holiness. Of course God never promised his servants a frustration-free life. I'm sure Jesus himself was often frustrated at the denseness of the people.[26] All of this is to say that, one reason we won't interpret what God tells us correctly is that we wish to express what *we want* over what *God wants*.

More examples of disregarding the clear instructions of God come from the life of King Saul. Samuel, the last judge of Israel, was tasked by God to anoint the first king of Israel—King Saul. In point of fact, Saul was not the best choice for the job for he was a king "like all the other nations" had.[27] This was the key problem with King Saul—he was not the King God would have chosen. He was selected on the basis of Israel's desires.[28] Even when Samuel explained what kings are really like, that they take the people's resources and make the people servants, Israel demanded a king saying, "No, but there shall be a king over us, that we also may be like all the nations, that our king may judge us and go out

---

25. Num 20:12.

26. We might note the story of the raising of Lazarus found in the Gospel of John, chapter 11. In John 11:38 we are told Jesus is "deeply moved within" when he heard some of the Jews wondering aloud if Jesus could have saved Lazarus from death since He had previously opened the eyes of the blind. The term translated "deeply moved within" often carries the connotation of being angry. It may have been the case that Jesus was angry and frustrated that the crowd seems to think the matter has concluded, as though death is some obstacle to the power of God. We might point out that Jesus clearly was not moved at sadness over the loss of Lazarus, for He had noted early on that his death was going to bring glory to God and that he would be "wakened from sleep" (John 11:11–44).

27. 1 Sam 8:5.

28. Just as a point of interest notice that God seems to sometimes give us what we desire as a way of teaching us how silly, and at times how evil, our desires can be. The most obvious example might come from Romans 1 where we are told that when the people chased after their sins (exchanging what they knew to be true of God), God "gave them over" to their desires and let them wallow in their sin. At times it may be the worst thing, on a practical level, that God gives us what we desire.

before us and fight our battles."[29] God met their demand with a king that matched all the qualities the other nations wanted in their king; Saul was tall, gallant, strong, handsome, and willful. The only problem was that this was nothing like the King God had in mind for his chosen people.[30]

Saul was anointed king of Israel by Samuel by the pouring of oil over his head. He was also given three signs that would validate the anointing as authentic.[31] After the signs came about, Saul was told to "go down before me [Samuel] to Gigal; and behold, I will come down to you to offer burnt offerings and sacrifice peace offerings. You shall wait seven days until I come to you and show you what you should do."[32] After this, Saul was again publically declared king at Mizpah.[33] It is very important to note here that Samuel wasn't just hogging the offertory limelight. Samuel's job was to offer the sacrifices. Saul's job was to be king. And Samuel was the one who knew what to do; Saul did not. So Samuel's directive to wait was important to follow.

Within that time period of seven days a war began, and Saul found himself in charge of the army of Israel. The Philistines were attacking and driving Israel into retreat. Saul waited out the seven days as Samuel had instructed but apparently during that seventh day Saul decided to go his own way. We are told:

> [8] Now he waited seven days, according to the appointed time set by Samuel, but Samuel did not come to Gilgal; and the people were scattering from him. [9] So Saul said, "Bring to me the burnt offering and the peace offerings." And he offered the burnt offering.[34]

It was not as though Saul didn't understand the directions Samuel, the prophet, judge and priest of God, had given him. We are told in the very next verses:

> [10] As soon as he finished offering the burnt offering, behold, Samuel came; and Saul went out to meet him *and* to greet him.

---

29. 1 Sam 8:19–20.

30. God even notes through Samuel that the people actually chose Saul in the strict sense that they set the requirements for who God would appoint (1 Sam 12:13).

31. 1 Sam 10:1–5.

32. 1 Sam 10:8.

33. 1 Sam 10:17, 24.

34. 1 Sam 13:8–9.

> [11] But Samuel said, "What have you done?" And Saul said, "Because I saw that the people were scattering from me, and that you did not come within the appointed days, and that the Philistines were assembling at Michmash, [12] therefore I said, 'Now the Philistines will come down against me at Gilgal, and I have not asked the favor of the LORD.' So I forced myself and offered the burnt offering."[35]

Here we are told two important things: (1) Saul didn't have to offer the sacrifices—Samuel did, in fact, keep his promise and arrive on time to offer them for the new king; (2) when questioned as to his motives, Saul didn't say he did not understand the directions. Instead he tried to excuse his actions in light of the circumstances around him—the people were scattering, Samuel hadn't arrived in a timely manner. He even says he "forced" himself to offer the sacrifice as though it was against his better judgment, but he had no choice! It is important to again note that by Mosaic Law only priests from the tribe of Levi could offer such sacrifices. Saul was not a priest, being from the tribe of Benjamin.

Saul felt Samuel was tardy in carrying out the promises. But the fact is, even if Samuel had waited until the last moment of day seven, Saul should have waited. At the very least, if Samuel was actually late, Saul could then have argued that the promise made to him about Samuel coming in seven days was broken. And therefore Saul was in a quandary as to how to proceed. But in this case, he didn't even wait the entire period, for on the seventh day, just after he went ahead, Samuel arrived just as he has said he would.

Here then is another reason we choose to ignore or misinterpret God's answers to us: we think his *timing* is incorrect. We prefer our own timeline of events. Let's go back to the pole-vaulting story for a moment. This is one of the reasons I believe my friends skipped the learning stages required to become good pole vaulters. They wanted to pole vault *right now*. They didn't want to wait and be instructed on the proper methods. The same thing would happen even more commonly with sprinters. They could all run and they wanted to run *now*. So they would ignore training and just get to the running.

I've seen a similar problem with college students over the years. They come to a Bible school to prepare for being a leader in the Christian community. If the Apostle Paul is to be trusted, there actually is some

---

35. 1 Sam 13:10–12.

requisite doctrinal, theological, historical and Biblical training needed to be an effective leader. But some students bail out of the process because the timing does not fit their desires. They want to be leaders in the church *now*—not after four years of Bible college or three years of seminary studies. God may have brought them to school with a plan, but that plan is abandoned because they want (with good intentions) to get to the forefront of the work. Not a few times have I heard something like "I'm not returning to school because I'm going out on the mission field" from students. They apparently come to the conclusion that getting out there is more important than finishing what God previously had "led" them to. Like Samuel, they want to get to God's work even if it means short-circuiting God's timing.

One more picture of why we choose to misunderstand what God tells us comes from Saul's later life. Later in his reign, Saul was told he was to be the instrument God uses to punish the people of Amalek. They had tried to hinder Israel as they came up to the Promised Land (Exod. 17:8–16). Because of this God promised to punish Amalek. Under Saul's leading Israel was to "strike Amalek and utterly destroy all that he has, and do not spare him; but put to death both man and woman, child and infant, ox and sheep, camel and donkey."[36] The text tells us Saul's response:

> [7] So Saul defeated the Amalekites, from Havilah as you go to Shur, which is east of Egypt. [8] He captured Agag the king of the Amalekites alive, and utterly destroyed all the people with the edge of the sword. [9] But Saul and the people spared Agag and the best of the sheep, the oxen, the fatlings, the lambs, and all that was good, and were not willing to destroy them utterly; but everything despised and worthless, that they utterly destroyed.[37]

Saul didn't destroy *all*. Instead, he spared Agag and all the best of everything. He only destroyed what was "despised and worthless."[38] When Samuel was sent to deal with the situation, Saul was oblivious to his misstep. He greeted Samuel, saying, "Blessed are you of the Lord! I have carried out the command of the Lord."[39] This is a picture of how completely we can deceive ourselves about our own motives and actions. Saul actu-

---

36. 1 Sam 15:3.
37. 1 Sam 15:7–9.
38. 1 Sam 15:9.
39. 1 Sam 15:13.

ally seems to believe he's followed God's instructions precisely. He goes so far as to defend his actions as actually fulfilling God's commands, saying, "I did obey the voice of the Lord, and went on the mission on which the Lord sent me, and have brought back Agag the king of Amalek, and have utterly destroyed the Amalekites."[40]

And when Samuel rather pointedly asks, "What then is this bleating of sheep in my ears, and the lowing of the oxen which I hear?" Saul does not respond in such a way as to suggest he didn't see the problem. Instead he does two things: (1) he blames the people for bringing the animals to him (15:15, 21), and (2) he says they are there only for use in sacrifice to God (15:15). In other words, when pushed, Saul knows deep down he has not followed what he was told to do. He offers what he thinks are mitigating circumstances. The people are sinners; he wants to offer sacrifices of good animals to God. Of course this doesn't explain the fact that Agag himself is still alive when he should have been slain already. Samuel rightly condemns Saul as "disobedient" and acting out of his own desire for spoil (15:19). It has nothing to do with misunderstanding or not knowing what God has said. It's a matter of Saul's will over God's will. In the end, when God's punishment has been handed down (the removal of his kingship), Saul finally confesses he did sin and that he placed his own fear of "the people" ahead of God's command (15:24).[41]

In this case we can say that another reason we won't interpret what God tells us honestly is that we prefer to let the circumstances of life determine whether we will heed God's word to us or not.

We can find many more examples in scripture of why we ignore or won't properly interpret what God says to us. But let me finish with one final example from the New Testament. In the Gospel of Matthew there is a story relating what happened when Jesus first told his disciples he was going to be killed. We are told that "From that time Jesus began to show his disciples that he must go to Jerusalem, and suffer many things from the elders and chief priests and scribes, and be killed, and be raised up on the third day."[42] In response to this troubling news, the text tells us that "Peter took him aside and began to rebuke him, saying, 'God forbid

---

40. 1 Sam 15:20.

41. I would note that even in his confession Saul tries to point to the people as the real problem. It sounds like he is asserting that had he not listened to them he would never had been in this predicament.

42. Matt 16:21.

it, Lord! This shall never happen to You.' But he [Jesus] turned and said to Peter, 'Get behind Me, Satan! You are a stumbling block to Me; for you are not setting your mind on God's interests, but man's.'"[43]

There is absolutely no reason to think Peter didn't understand what Jesus was saying. The text makes clear that Peter *did* fully understand what he was being told. His answer back to Jesus on the subject was "No way! That will never happen!" In other words, he didn't care for Jesus' clear thoughts on the subject; he preferred his own. What's interesting about this particular case is that Peter did not seem to be acting out of overt sin. In fact, we could make the case that he was acting out of his deep love for Jesus. But here we find a very important point: When we choose to ignore what God is telling us we can still act wrongly with all the right motives. Jesus goes so far as to insinuate that Peter is acting as a minion of Satan himself when he suggested Jesus should not die. The bottom line here is that when we choose to misinterpret or ignore God's directives, we can often align ourselves with evil. And here is the last reason I'll mention as to why we choose to misinterpret what God tells us: Because we think we know better than God does what is truly good.

Having listed a few examples of reasons why we don't interpret what God tells us honestly, we must come back to the main point of this section. It is my contention that because we are not honest in interpreting what God says to us, prayer appears to be haphazard. In this case we contribute to this state of affairs by choosing to not understand. And what could make conversation more haphazard than to intentionally misinterpret someone's statements to us? Even worse is the fact that, like Saul, we convince ourselves that we really *have* interpreted the discussion correctly.

The situation is something like this. Suppose my boss says directly to me, "I want to meet with you at 10 a.m." I agree to this plan but choose to insert the idea that "10 a.m." really means "11:12 a.m." because I like to listen to my radio show until 11 a.m. each morning. I might even justify myself by saying both times are in the morning, both come before lunch, and I'm still meeting with him. But the fact is, the meeting will most likely not occur at all because I'll be an hour late for it. And if I'm trying to understand what my boss says by looking at what actually happened, I'm sure to end up constantly misunderstanding my boss at every turn. The truth is, he told me exactly what he wanted, I understood it, and I

---

43. Matt 16:22–23.

chose to interpret it incorrectly for my own personal reasons. In the end though, when viewed solely from the perspective of what actually happened, our conversation appears very haphazard and unfruitful because we never got on the same page in any practical way. The next time he speaks to me, I will probably feel like our communication is hit or miss.

When all is said and done, prayer will always look and feel haphazard if we refuse to be honest about what God says to us, neither adding to nor subtracting from it.[44]

We Don't Reshape Our Requests

Did you ever want something so badly that it seemed to get stuck in a loop in your brain? I recall getting that first tuning-in to girls. Up to that point I had noticed girls, but like most kids, I put them out of my head with other pressing things like playing sports and hanging out with friends and what not. When I hit junior high, I suddenly noticed the fairer sex in a big way. And like all boys, girls kept getting more and more important to me as I aged. By the time I hit ninth grade I noticed girls a lot! And I recall one girl, whose name I cannot now even remember, in particular. For convenience let me call her Linda. I had become a Christian that year and thought that God wanted to help me out in every part of my life—dating included. So I prayed for Linda to approach me, shy as I was, for a couple of years. Perhaps I was not the brightest of kids. God never brought her to me. Still, I kept asking, over and over and over again. Sometimes my requests were downright silly: "Lord, may Linda show up at my window tonight." I'm not kidding. I was a dork. And I was a *consistent* dork. I prayed that same prayer for months at a time. Even though there were a number of pretty, smart, Christian girls right in front of me that I could have dated. But I continued my prayer for Linda for quite some time. The problem was that I was not re-shaping my requests in light of the answers I was getting from God. Linda was not being moved to show up at my window. God was not prodding her.

This is the final reason that I think prayer can become haphazard. It has to do with how we respond to God when we fully understand his

---

44. The reader may be saying at this point that this is exposing one of the basic problems in prayer again: It's hard to know what God actually says to us in any given situation. I think part of that idea stems from a flawed view of what God wants for us in the first place. We will address this in the section titled *"Our Approach is Flawed"* later in this chapter.

speech to us, and it is helpful to once again compare prayer to a conversation with a friend.

When we talk to others, one of the requirements to authentic communication is give and take. We have all met that person who seems to always bring conversations back to themselves, their ideas, their interests, their requests. It is clear that they are not really listening to your input. Rather, they are constantly formulating what they are about to say next to achieve their ends. If there is any listening going on, it is merely to link your words to their own desired subject. That sort of conversation grows old very quickly, and we tend not to want to speak to such a person.

In an authentic conversation we expect give and take. You speak; I listen. Then I make a point and you listen. Hopefully, as this progresses we build together a series of ideas. I hear your input and shape what I say in response to it in some way. In terms of requests, I take your answer and reform what I asked for into something that incorporates what you said—whether it be yes, no or something else.

How does lack of this encourage haphazardness in prayer? If we don't reshape our requests, we don't provide ourselves with information on what exactly God tends to say "yes" or "no" to. Suppose we pray a prayer for something and God says, "No." If I don't reshape my prayer in response to that and keep doggedly praying for the same thing, how have I learned what God *will* say "yes" to? I got stuck in a loop, praying that God bring Linda to me for a couple years. He was telling me "no," but I was persistently sticking with my prayer. He was even providing other girls right in front of me that wanted to date me as well. I didn't learn during that time what God will say "yes" to when it comes to girls. When God says "No" and I ignore it, I'm still ignorant of God's real desires, and therefore I'm still at a loss as to what to intelligently pray for. So again, I randomly pick and choose things haphazardly without any real surety that he is willing to grant what I request. This point is extremely important, so we will focus on this issue as we proceed.

THE TRUE GOALS OF PRAYER ARE IGNORED

Before we begin exploring some of the true goals of prayer, let me re-emphasize that I'm taking for granted that we ought to pray.[45] The Bible

---

45. If the reader wishes to verify this point she or he can peruse a number of key verses in the scriptures: Acts 1:14 says that the practice of the early church was to "devote themselves to prayer." Paul calls the believer to be "devoted to prayer" in Romans

speaks of prayer often—over 300 times if we count only the verses that mention some form of the word *pray*. There are instructions about prayer, records of actual prayers, directives to pray, recorded answers to prayer and other such prayer-related issues. I would venture to say that one cannot honestly read the Bible without coming to the conclusion that, at least in the Bible's view, prayer is both useful and important in the Christian life. I have assumed this point but reiterate it here to hammer home the necessity we have to fix anything that makes us dislike or disengage from prayer. And now I want to suggest another problem we face that renders our prayers haphazard and our practice of prayer distasteful: Ignorance of what the goals of prayer should be. I believe this is one of the most daunting problems we face.

Here I would draw the reader back to the situation I faced at times working with my father. He was not big on clueing me in to the goals of a job at any detailed level. I knew, for example, the end goal of what we did most of the time; we were fixing an engine, or repairing brakes, or laying concrete. But often I'd be given a job with no idea of its particular goal or purpose. I never knew what I was aiming at and why I needed that objective. It all felt very random to me.

Now let's get back to prayer. I want to restate clearly that I'm not talking about systems or methodologies here. In fact, that misunderstanding is probably part of this issue. Some people believe that mastering a *system* of prayer is the goal of prayer. Though again, we don't usually say this to ourselves openly. It is ironic that on the one hand, one of the problems I've noted is the fact that often we have no system at all to our prayers. This leads to haphazard prayer that is almost completely indefinable at times. And yet I would also suggest, on the other hand, that some have aimed at accomplishing a system or method of prayer as the end-goal itself. Neither approach is acceptable or functional.

This second approach to spirituality (attempting to merely master a *system*) is not limited to the spiritual discipline of prayer either. This problem exists in our practice of all the spiritual disciplines and is part of

---

12:12. In Ephesians 6:18 he says, "with all prayer and petition pray at all times in the Spirit." In Philippians 4:6 Paul says, "Be anxious for nothing, but in everything by prayer and supplication . . . let your requests be made known to God." In Colossians 4:2 he exhorts the believer to "devote yourselves to prayer, keeping alert in it." That Jesus, our master, took the time to engage in prayer consistently, and that we call ourselves his disciples should convince us that we ought to be praying. (After all, a disciple is one who learns and follows another.)

an overarching attitude addressed by Jesus in the Sermon on the Mount, which is found in the Gospel of Matthew, chapters 5–7. He teaches that it is not enough to keep the *letter* of the law, but one must achieve the *spirit* of the law. As an example, let me point out that usually we can easily master *not* physically killing others. But Jesus adds the deeper truth behind this—you should not even harbor anger against others. That is less easy to master. But we often think we have attained perfection when we have not physically killed anyone lately, though we harbor resentments and anger sometimes for years, paying no mind to them and believing it is the practice of not *actually killing* that is the end-goal.

But this is the very problem. To be honest, for the vast majority of us, it is easy not to kill people. I don't have to get out of bed each morning and remind myself on a daily basis "Now, Tom, no killing people today!" On the other hand, it is much more difficult to remove all hatred and anger from our minds. I would suggest that many of us might benefit from getting up each day and reminding ourselves, "Now, now, no hating people today!" We sometimes shrug this off with the idea that it's human to harbor a little hatred; it's just one of those things. This is especially true if it only flares up now and again or if we only hate a few people in our lives. More realistically we would not even classify our "hate" as hate at all. We use words like *distaste, anger, impatience,* etc. We very rarely just say to ourselves or others, "I hate so and so!" But what if we held that same standard of occasional occurrence for killing? What if we held the standard of allowance for special cases? My killing only flares up occasionally or I only kill a few people I especially dislike? Such standards wouldn't fly, would they? The point is, we sometimes chase artificial goals in our prayer lives, and when we meet them, we declare it a success even if it leaves whole areas of our lives untouched.

Let me wander off into the bushes for a moment to investigate some of the fallout of this particular belief that it is enough to achieve outward control of sin, but not inward. One effect I have seen time and again is that we can become self righteous. I have gotten the idea, when listening to believers talk at times, that they put great stock in their *not physically committing* some sin as opposed to those lesser believers (or downright pagans) who have. The sin is irrelevant. Sometimes people grow smug over not having actually committed adultery. Sometimes they are haughty about the fact that *they* never killed someone. More often it is more tame sins (if there are such animals) such as never telling *big lies* or stealing *large* amounts of money (e.g., millions in embezzlement or some such thing).

The point is that it is easy for Christians to keep themselves from committing many sins in our society, such as physically killing another person or embezzling a company's funds. This is born out by looking at crime in America. When talking about serious crimes (killing, raping, grand theft, etc.) most people do not commit them. And this applies to non-Christians as well as Christians. Our whole penal system is dealing with the malfeasance of something like five percent of the population. But the truth is, if we hold that as the standard (that we are not committing gross crimes or sins in this case), we can indulge in all sorts of equally heinous sin without ever thinking we have a problem in our lives.

Now obviously, when it comes to crime, the nature of the case is slightly different than when we talk about sin. We all accept lesser crimes almost with no thought because the effects seem so minimal that they demand no outrage. For example, the crime of people eating a grape or two at the store (stealing) is acceptable to most people. (Some even argue it is their right to taste the produce before they buy!) But most will not accept people embezzling a million dollars from a retirement fund. That kind of crime has, in most people's opinion, far more serious consequences than the loss of $100 dollars worth of grapes a month. In contrast, when we speak of sin we have no such dilution of import. God tolerates stealing of grapes in the same way he tolerates stealing a million dollars: neither is acceptable, and both are sins deserving death. Stealing is stealing. I'm suggesting that sometimes people use the *crimes* system rather than the *sins* system when they pray.

Now, we must make our way back to the main point. This has not been merely a detour into the bushes to point out that we can grow very arrogant toward other people's struggles when we hold such a limited idea of what sin entails. This view of sin and the arrogance it spawns can actually affect our prayer lives. If we have the idea that we are perfect (or close to it) because we don't *physically* manifest some sin, we tend to pray in ways that are dishonest. We pray with no thought to our own sanctification, and we pray disdainfully for those around us (or don't pray at all about them—losers that they are). We pray sometimes the blatantly dishonest way that we see the Pharisee pray in Jesus' parable in Luke 18:

> [11] "The Pharisee stood and was praying this to himself: 'God, I thank You that I am not like other people: swindlers, unjust, adulterers, or even like this tax collector. [12] 'I fast twice a week; I pay tithes of all that I get.'"[46]

Here is a person who has completely convinced himself that the lack of *outward expression* of sin is proof positive that not only has he mastered sin, but he is also innately better than others. This certainly is not a prayer God will listen to. In Luke, the author prefaces this parable by saying about Jesus: "And he also told this parable to some people *who trusted in themselves* that they were righteous, and *viewed others with contempt* [emphasis added]."[47] Those who hold this attitude are said to "trust in themselves"—not God. And they are those that "view others with contempt" setting up a hierarchy of who is most deserving of God's grace. One can hardly say this is an attitude God wants us to cultivate. And at the end of the vignette Jesus comments that the Pharisee was not *justified* when he left his prayers. I.e., his prayers were ignored, and he remained unforgiven for his sins.

Clearly there is a big problem when we fail to understand rightly the deeper goal of prayer and have as our goal the mere outward trappings of prayer. In terms of prayer we might attempt to master a system, such as having a half-hour prayer time each morning or praying the Lord's Prayer twice a day. Then, when we've accomplished that system, regardless of whether it is achieving the real goals of prayer or not, we think we've learned to pray. But we begin to dislike prayer because in truth; merely doing the system does not accomplish the true goals of prayer. Or if we don't go so far as to dislike prayer, we at least begin to assume it has no practical value.[48] Systems serve as an avenue on which to tread toward the true goals, but they are not the goals themselves. So we must ask: "What are the goals of prayer?" Let me present three fundamental goals we ought to shoot for in our prayer lives.

---

46. Luke 18:11–12.

47. Luke 18:9.

48. Though as I've said, even when we see no practical value in prayer, good Christians keep doggedly at it because they think they are being *faithful* in some way by persevering in an exercise that never bears any fruit.

True Goal of Prayer #1: Effectiveness and Accomplishment

The Lord's brother James gives us an important statement about prayer in James 5:16: "The effective prayer of a righteous man can accomplish much." There are two key components of prayer in this short statement that should be goals for our prayer lives.

The first important component is the type of prayer described by James. Take note of that word he uses: *effective*. He says the *effective* prayer accomplishes much, not just any ol' prayer. So we are forced to ask the question: What is an *effective* prayer like? Or, the more important question to us is: "How can I pray effective prayers?" Let's examine this for a moment by stepping back and asking a broader question: "What makes anything effective?"

We might answer that question with things like:

- It accomplishes what was intended.
- It is well crafted to fit the exact need.
- Perhaps it is what mathematicians would call elegant—that is, it accomplishes its purpose and at the same time is exquisitely clear, clean, and simple.
- It has understandable principles of operation.

Think of these sorts of things applied to some specific item now. We might ask, what makes an oven effective? We could apply our general answers more specifically:

- It actually cooks food (as it was intended to do).
- It has a chamber for cooking things without superfluous additions. (E.g., we don't want our ovens to have headlights, or internal radios. We want them to have heating elements, self cleaners, and other accoutrements that ease the actual practice of cooking food.)
- It is pretty and fits the décor of our kitchen—it is elegant in some way. And it has controls that are easy to use and not bulky or incomprehensible.[49]

---

49. I laugh when I think of a particular DVD player I bought a few years back. It was controlled on screen with symbols rather than text and they were almost incomprehensible. (One looked like fire with 2 crossed hammers over it! I thought that meant *set me on fire* perhaps.) The DVD had myriad abilities, but one could hardly decipher what the symbols meant to put them to use. This was the antithesis of elegance.

- Of paramount importance is the fact that I understand how to use it and what it should and should not accomplish. (I would hardly put my oven out in the driveway and try to find the "wash the car" switch. It was never designed for such a use, and whether I desire that or not, it will never achieve that end.)

One of the goals of anything we do should be effectiveness. This is one thing that my dad consistently showed me as I was growing up. He did things to be effective. I, like Chris, may not have understood how my dad would react to things at times, but one thing I really learned well from him was to stick with it. He worked on the car so that the car would run. He was tenacious about it. It would serve little purpose to spend hours or days working on a car without the goal of having it running at the end of the labor. Often that was how *I* would work. I think all boys had the chore of holding the light while their dads worked on cars. When I did that job, I just wanted to focus on my job—holding the light. Sometimes I didn't even care if it was pointed in the right direction—I was holding it. But I was not *effectively* holding it. For whatever reason, good or bad, the goal for me often degenerated into just having the flashlight in my hand. It didn't matter that it was shining on the fender. I was holding it, period. Luckily, as I grew older, I learned the lesson my dad intended for me. Do things to be *effective*.

This idea of effectiveness should permeate our idea of prayer. In truth, there should be some similarity between what we do in prayer and what we do in all our other pursuits. Prayer should not be some mystical entity whose goals and means are entirely divorced from everything else we undertake. I would liken this to the way we read and interpret the Bible. We don't desire some special, mystical way of reading the Bible that differs from how we read other texts. We use the same methodology to read a cook book as we do the New Testament. We are consistent in our approach to reading. We define words, we relate sentence parts, we parse verbs, conjugate nouns, recognize paragraph marks, identify genre, etc. This is not to say we don't change some things depending on the type of text we read. It is also consistent practice to read poetry differently from the way we read prose. But within each genre we still read consistently. We don't read one Psalm using the rules for poetry and the next with the rules for a technical manual.

On the broadest level, this should also be our rule when approaching our Christian life in general. When we are thinking about effectiveness, we should bring the same expectations to prayer that we bring to Bible study. We may use different practices with prayer, but in terms of being effective, I think we give away too much to the lord of haphazardness. And unfortunately, we do it in the name of spirituality.

So, like anything we do, to be *effective* prayer should:

- Accomplish what we intend it to.
- Actually fit the situation in which it arises.
- Be in some measure elegant (that is, clear, concise, and to the point).
- Be something with working principles that we understand.
- Be something we know how to use well.

James also says the effective prayer of a righteous man *accomplishes much*.[50] This is a second important component of prayer: It should *accomplish much*. After all, who wants to engage in prayer that accomplishes little, or worse yet, accomplishes nothing? Of course that begs the question (actually it begs a lot of questions, but here is just one): How do I measure accomplishment in my prayers? To answer, let's follow the same line we traced in discussing effectiveness, and ask, "How do I measure accomplishment in anything?"

At the school where I teach we have just undergone the process for accreditation under another agency. One thing they were very concerned about was the ability to concretely measure whether we were hitting our goals in all the areas in which we were working. It seemed like a lot of work at times to develop all the evaluation systems. But the truth is, if you can't measure how something is working, you can't know if it really *is* working. This is true both of business processes and of prayer, as well. The Bible certainly seems to portray the idea of accomplished prayer as important. And it often gives the measure of that accomplishment. Let's look at some examples to verify this.

One thing we should notice in scripture is that oftentimes the prayers and answers are not discussed in drawn out fashion. We find many descriptions that merely give the prayer and God's answer with

---

50. James 5:16.

little elaboration. I would point out that those are measurable, accomplished prayers. Here are some examples:

- In Genesis 20:17–18 Abraham prayed for Abimelech and his household, that the wives could conceive. In answer God opened the women's wombs. In this case there is an explanatory note that God had closed their wombs in the first place as a punishment of Abimelech.
- In Genesis 25:21 Isaac prayed for his wife Rebekah that she might have a baby, because she was barren. The text says, "The Lord answered him and Rebekah his wife conceived."
- In Numbers 11:1–2 God had sent a fire among sinning Israel. The people cried to Moses for help. The text says, "Moses prayed to the Lord and the fire died out."
- In 1 Samuel 1:10 Hannah prayed to God for a child (for she was barren). 1 Samuel 1:19–20 tells us that that "Elkanah had relations with Hannah his wife, and the LORD remembered her. It came about in due time, after Hannah had conceived, that she gave birth to a son."
- In Isaiah 37:1–29 the prophet Isaiah tells King Hezekiah that God has spoken against Sennacherib, king of Assyria "because you [Hezekiah] have prayed to me about him."
- In Jonah 2:1–10 Jonah prays to God for salvation from the belly of the fish and God makes the animal spit him up onto dry land.
- In Acts 9:40 we are told Peter prayed and then called a little girl back from death.
- In Acts 28:8 it says Paul prayed and then healed Publius of fever and dysentery.
- James 5:17 records the fact that when Elijah prayed earnestly for no rain it didn't rain for three years and six months. Then he prayed again and the sky poured rain.

These are just a few examples of texts with brief prayers that also mention measurable, accomplished effects. Now let's go on and list a few more and discuss them a bit more fully.

Although we might start almost anywhere, I think there are a number of interesting prayers found in the Old Testament book of Nehemiah that show the idea of accomplishment and measurability quite well. The first is in Nehemiah, chapter 2. Nehemiah was a Jew who was exiled in Persia for Israel's sins. He was the cupbearer to King Artaxerxes of Persia (who ruled from 464–424 BC). Nehemiah had an opportunity one day to ask the king if he might go home from Persia to Jerusalem to rebuild his home town. The text says:

> [4] Then the king said to me, "What would you request?" *So I prayed to the God of heaven.* [emphasis added] [5] I said to the king, "If it please the king, and if your servant has found favor before you, send me to Judah, to the city of my fathers' tombs, that I may rebuild it."[51]

Sandwiched between the king's query and Nehemiah's request is a short, one-line note that Nehemiah prayed to God. It doesn't say what for, but context seems to indicate that it was for success in his request to the king and his designs to go back home and rebuild Jerusalem.

What is interesting is how Nehemiah evaluates this prayer later. When the king grants his request, Nehemiah says it was "because the good hand of my God was on me."[52] Later, when he was in Jerusalem and had inspected the broken down walls of the city, he went to the Jewish leaders and urged them to help rebuild the city so it would not be a reproach. In this discussion with them he notes again that "I told them how the hand of my God had been favorable to me, and also about the king's words which he had spoken to me."[53] In both these instances he measures his prayer by what actually happened. He wanted to accomplish an end—going to Jerusalem and rebuilding the walls—and he prayed precisely for that. And he evaluated his prayer by what actually happened.

Later in the book we find another enlightening prayer. While the workers were rebuilding the walls of Jerusalem they were under attack from various detractors. Nehemiah 4:7 lists the key figures: "Sanballat, Tobiah, the Arabs, the Ammonites, and the Ashdodites." We are told that they conspired together to frustrate the work by causing a disturbance.

---

51. Neh 2:4–5.
52. Neh 2:8.
53. Neh 2:18.

In response to this it says about the builders: "But we prayed to our God, and because of them we set up a guard against them day and night."[54] The protective measures that Nehemiah put into place, along with the intelligence passed along by Jews living near the troublemakers, resulted in the thwarting of the disturbance. Nehemiah interprets this by saying, "God had frustrated their plan."[55] In other words, when Nehemiah looked at the situation and saw that the plan to disrupt the work of rebuilding had failed, he concluded that his prayer to God over the situation had been accomplished. And it was measurable by the lack of their opposition's success.

In no way am I saying that the majority of prayers in scripture are accompanied by a description of their accomplishment. But I am suggesting that when a prayer is discussed fully, it is usually accompanied by how it was accomplished and how that accomplishment was measured. Moreover, I'm suggesting that we ought to be able to measure whether our prayers are accomplished or not. Otherwise, James' statement that the effective prayer "accomplishes much" means nothing. If I cannot measure accomplishment, James isn't really giving me any useful information. James gives a precise example of what he means by presenting the effects of Elijah's prayers for drought and rain. James is saying that effective prayer accomplishes things that should be clear and measurable. That makes perfect sense. If we don't know if our prayers are accomplished, why pray them?

So, I've noted that James gives us one initial and important goal for our prayers with two components. Our prayers should be *effective* and they should actually *accomplish* something.

The True Goal of Prayer #2: Spiritual Maturity

Everyone has heard the dictum: "Give a man a fish and you've fed him for a day. Teach a man to fish and you've fed him for a lifetime." One thing we might note from this little proverb is that there are fish involved in both instances—both the giving and the teaching. But the goal of giving a man a fish is just to let him have a fish. The goal of teaching him to fish is that he might be a self provider of fish any time he wants one. Both approaches have goals, but most of us would agree that the second is a

---

54. Neh 4:9. Here we see that prayer was accompanied by action on the part of the petitioners. We will come back to this important notion later.

55. Neh 4:15.

loftier and more profitable goal for the man in regard to his whole life. In one instance he is, at best, a man with a fish. In the other he is a man who can get not just one fish, but any amount of fish he so desires. One action makes him dependent, the other makes him independent.

The fish proverb is much like shoe tying if you think about it. When we are little, we cannot tie our shoes. We run to our parents (or anyone we can find) to tie them for us. But sooner or later, if our parents are responsible, we are taught to tie our own shoes. Can you just imagine a forty-five-year-old asking someone to tie their shoes for them? Not a very attractive picture is it? No, we want to get to the independent shoe-tying stage much earlier in life. And once we know how to tie a shoe, the sky's the limit. I can tie any shoe with a string on it! The true goal of teaching a child to tie his or her shoe is not just having that particular shoe tied. The true goal is teaching the child to be a better, more functional person. Kids can take their shoe-tying skills out into the world and tie all sorts of footwear now. They are mature shoe wearers with their ability to tie laces.

In shoe-tying we find an example of another goal of prayer: Overall Christian maturity. We should not pray just to get something in particular. We should not pray just to have something in particular removed. We should not pray just to have gone through the motions of prayer. We ought to pray with a bigger goal in mind. We ought to see prayer as an avenue to maturity as Christians.

Now, before we get into this discussion, let me confess up front that I'm not hawking myself as Mr. Christian Maturity who knows it all and practices everything perfectly. So don't think because I'm talking about maturity as a goal for prayer that I've reached total maturity. I can assure you that I have not in any area. (And I know some detractors who would gladly verify that, I'm sure.) I've come to the belief that we are never going to be perfectly mature in this lifetime—perhaps not in the next in many ways as well.

Let me take a moment to address this problem of not being totally mature yet offering some ideas on maturity. I do so because I've heard this sort of objection used in all sorts of settings. It's the "you aren't there so you can't have a valid opinion on it" argument. For example one who has not had children might be disqualified from talking about child rearing. Or one is not a professional school teacher, so he can't offer any opinion on how to teach a class effectively. This is a weak argument. Obviously functional experience imparts good knowledge of how a thing works, but if a person is conscientious about acquiring information from all sorts of sources, such as those who have partaken of some activity, there is no reason they can't think intelligently about it and offer valid opinions. I've never been a medical doctor, but that does not mean I can't learn anatomy and comment on it.

Now, it is very often the case that we know a lot more about a topic than we can actually do in regards to it. I will use wood working as an example of what I mean here. I enjoy building things with wood. To that end, I watch wood working shows from time to time. I read magazines on how to use wood effectively. I own tools that allow me to make the best use of the wood I'm cutting and fitting. But when I look at my actual application of the knowledge I have, I realize I know more than I can effectively do. I've acquired a lot of information about wood working by reading, watching, and just talking to others. But my skill level is not equal to my knowledge level. That does not disqualify me from talking about wood working. In fact, I think it is a good thing in some ways. It lets me see where my skills can go from here. This seems to be the way of a lot of things in our lives. We learn a lot about them, and then try to implement them as best we can. And it's the same with Christian maturity. We learn a lot by reading our Bibles, going to church, talking with friends, etc. But we can't implement all we know (even though some of us think we can). A key here is that we implement consistently as much as we can of what we know. The more we implement, the more mature we are in regards to that thing. So maturity is definitely not just knowing about a thing—it is also practice in doing that thing. As the author of the book of Hebrews says, "But solid food is for the mature, who *because of practice* have their senses trained to discern good and evil."[56] Practice is the thing that really trains us and makes us mature, and practice is ongoing in all the spiritual disciplines. We may not be totally mature yet, but practice is moving us toward complete maturity, and for that reason we can comment freely on what maturity should be like—even when we've not reached it completely.

All that being said, it's extremely difficult to be mature in this day and age. Maturity does not seem to be well respected in our day-to-day society, which makes it difficult to acquire. (To be frank, I don't remember a time in my life when maturity was well respected.) I peruse the TV

---

56. Heb 5:14.

channels, note magazine covers, and scan newspapers, cringing at the thought that what I see is considered even semi-normal, grown-up, or mature (let alone even notable in any way).

I find people are often praised in our day to day society for being ignorant, poorly-educated, short-sighted, short-tempered, ill-mannered, aggressive, crude, and base. On television I see pre-teen children portrayed as capable of advising their adult parents on everything from retirement investing to medical needs. I see parents who behave like oafs and can barely figure out the world around them (and thus need their five-year-olds to help them handle life). I see everything from food to family-raising transformed into a competition. Usually when I look at my own failings, I find them to be attributes that are praised in our modern culture. If I'm rude to a person, society praises me for standing up for myself. If I desire to cheat on my taxes, I'm "puttin' it to the man," as a good American should. If I lust and commit infidelity, it's actually just the natural state of men and really is an exhibition of my manliness. The solid, mature, sensible person is nowhere to be found in the gangsta rap, bad girls, and reality show world of crude excess and emotional self incrimination poured into our heads at every turn of channel, station, or page. The person who wants to be less vulgar and more educated, well read, and informed is viewed as a prude and a snob. This is especially so if we desire to be a more godly person.

I hate to say this, but it appears that this disdain for sober maturity is often common in the Christian world as well. In many ways we have glorified the idea of "childlike" faith to the exclusion of mature belief. We use Jesus' admonition to be "childlike" as an excuse to be immature.[57] And oafish, silly behavior is often defined as lovable and relaxed, open and honest, admirable and transparent rather than what it is: childish and silly. We cry randomly to God, like children throwing a tantrum, and excuse it as "honest, open, childlike" emotion. We cling to the ability to *not* understand as though it's some kind of positive in our lives that we can trust naively in a God who apparently won't actually talk to us in an intelligent, understandable, or mature way. We glory in a God who wants us to talk to him, trustingly, openly, but who we firmly believe is never going to give us a straight answer (if he answers at all). We revel in the ability to throw up our hands and cry, "Mystery of God!" the moment we might have to think hard about something and decide what we believe.

---

57. Matt 18:13.

I don't think this is a positive thing in our lives. I think it's a cop-out in many ways, perpetuated by leaders that often are more interested in their parishioners' feelings than they are in their growth into mature Christians. I seriously doubt Jesus was considering Peter's feelings when he yelled at him, "Get behind me Satan!"[58] I think it is more likely that he was interested in Peter's true growth into the mature Apostle he was destined to become.

Maturity is definitely hard to find and hard to cultivate. And those who really seek it are often ridiculed as being too up-tight, too serious, too emotionally stunted, too out of touch with "real" life—too separated from "childlike" faith. But sober maturity is the lynch pin to an honest and enjoyable prayer life that both *feels* and, more importantly, truly *is* productive and rewarding. And there is no rule against maturity and joy being present at the same time. We seem to be presented with the choice of joy, fun, laughter, and pleasure on one hand and maturity on the other. But I don't know where that was ever made the rule. I suggest that the God of one is equally the God of the other. So we can be fun, joyful, excited, playful, *and* mature at the same time. I say again though, child-like does not *necessitate* child-ish.

Now, let's get back to the main point of this section, that a second goal of prayer should be *Christian maturity*. Let's think about this once again in the context of James's comments on prayer. "The effective prayer of a righteous man accomplishes much."[59] We have highlighted the ideas of *effectiveness* and *accomplishment* in the previous discussion. Notice now the other thought James has: it is the effective prayer of a *righteous* man. It is reasonable to equate *righteous* and *mature* in this passage.

Now, we might be tempted to say that James means righteous in the sense of *justified*. The prayer of a person who is saved by putting on the righteousness of Jesus accomplishes much compared to the prayer of one who is without such righteousness. But this really can't be the case. James is talking to Christians here. They all have righteousness if "righteousness" is defined as merely that which comes from *belief in Jesus* as Savior. James must certainly be talking about righteousness that is of a different quality than that found by our presence in Christ (or his presence in us if you prefer). It is something developed beyond the mere basics of trust in God for salvation. James is indicating that there are those Christians

---

58. Matt 16:23.
59. James 5:16.

who are *more* righteous than others and that such Christians' prayers accomplish more than other Christians' prayers. Again, he is not arguing that we should strive for only salvation-righteousness found in Jesus and that the person with such salvation-righteousness will accomplish much in prayer (as opposed to the pagan's prayer). He is saying that among all those who already have that form of righteousness, there is a subset of those who are somehow more righteous and that prayers offered by them will accomplish much.

The Greek word in James 5:16 which is translated as "righteous" carries the idea of being in accord with some standard. James is referring to the believer who is walking closely with God—one who is living a righteous life in the sense of meeting the standards that God expects of his children.[60] The fuller context gives us a key to this better righteousness:

> [13] Is anyone among you suffering? *Then* he must pray. Is anyone cheerful? He is to sing praises. [14] Is anyone among you sick? *Then* he must call for the elders of the church and they are to pray over him, anointing him with oil in the name of the Lord; [15] and the prayer offered in faith will restore the one who is sick, and the Lord will raise him up, and if he has committed sins, they will be forgiven him. [16] Therefore, confess your sins to one another, and pray for one another so that you may be healed. The effective prayer of a righteous man can accomplish much. [17] Elijah was a man with a nature like ours, and he prayed earnestly that it would not rain, and it did not rain on the earth for three years and six months. [18] Then he prayed again, and the sky poured rain and the earth produced its fruit.[61]

James makes a key point when he says a prayer "offered in faith" will accomplish its goal. I would direct the reader back to the beginning of the book of James at this point. In James 1:5–8 he says a similar thing about requesting wisdom from God. He counsels us to ask *in faith* with no wavering in our approach to God. Moreover, James concludes that a "double-minded" person should not expect to receive anything from

---

60. Again, I'm not arguing that perfection is the key here. But progressive growth and alignment with Jesus' expectations for a disciple seem to be important to being this kind of righteous. On the other hand, it would seem to imply that some believers are less aligned with God's desires for his children. Much like in human families you sometimes find one child who follows the rules and integrates well into the routines of the family and another child who refuses to integrate and follow the rules. Both are still children, but one is really better at family life and its responsibilities.

61. James 5:13–18.

God. Again, the prayer offered *in faith* is required—not just any prayer we might offer up. Being righteous is having strong, mature *faith*. James is making clear that we ought to be able to accomplish more in our prayers as we become more righteous, more mature as believers—more *faithful*. Being faithful is the engine behind accomplished prayer. But what is "being faithful" and how do you get faithfulness (and consequently accomplish what we ask for in prayer)?

The first thing I would answer is the central point of this section: We must have maturity as a *goal* of our prayer lives to be able to acquire strong faith. As in archery, prayer without aim is not likely to hit the target. If maturity is not our aim, we are unlikely to achieve it. Prayer is a testing and training ground for your skills in faith, and when we engage in prayer, we ought to be getting more faithful, more righteous, and more mature. It is somewhat disconcerting to me that whether I talk to seventy-year-olds or seventeen-year-olds I often hear the same things about prayer, especially when I start to ask specific questions about their prayer lives in terms of effectiveness and accomplishment. But shouldn't I be getting different comments? Suppose I asked a seventeen-year-old who had just begun baking about making a cake. Then I asked a seventy-year-old who had been baking all his life. Wouldn't it be reasonable to expect the seventy-year-old to have a lot better advice and practical information on baking than the seventeen-year-old? Shouldn't it be the same with prayer? After years and years of doing it, shouldn't we be more mature and have better answers and ideas when discussing prayer? Shouldn't we get to the point of being able to anticipate what is acceptable in prayer and what is not—what will probably be answered with a "yes" and what will not? In fact, shouldn't we be getting a *lot* of "yes" answers because we have become so effective at prayer?

This will only happen when we view our prayers not as a daily chore, but as a practice session intended to train us to be mature, faithful, and better at prayer. And here we must ask what makes our faith stronger? What makes us more faithful? Doesn't our faith become stronger when we see and experience God's faithfulness to us in tangible ways? I'm not suggesting our faith only grows stronger when we see signs expressed through answered prayer. Hebrews 11:1 makes clear that faith is "the assurance of things *hoped for*, the conviction of things *not seen* [emphasis added]." But, I am suggesting that our faith grows stronger when we get to know God better and, consequently, are able to pray without consistently demanding silly signs which he will say "no" to 90 percent of the time anyway. Faith grows when we experience God honestly and effectively in prayer. Faith doesn't grow because the answers to prayer are miraculous and we see them, but because we are in agreement with what should happen and the prayers themselves are in accord with God's wishes.

And on the other side of this, faith will actually shrink when we continue to hurl prayers at God which do not mesh with his will for us. When we repeatedly receive "no" answers from God to our prayers, faith is destroyed because prayer merely sets before us a seemingly unbreachable wall between God's desires and ours. And God will constantly say "no" to our prayers when they are not in agreement with his desires for us. He is a good father and he is not going to hand us anything that will harm us just because we ask for it—even when we ask repeatedly for many years.

A woman said to me the other day that she was confused about prayer. She didn't know when to pray for things, what to pray for, or what to expect from God in answer. I asked her why that was the case; what were her thoughts about the situation? She described to me briefly a prayer life that could do nothing but produce these very problems. She was committing just about every error I've mentioned in this book, and her Christian maturity was not being helped in any area of her life to boot. She was not reading her scriptures. She was not reevaluating her prayers in light of what God was saying. She was not entering into the life of the church in a committed way. The only outcome we should expect, when we have been praying to God immature prayers which he must ignore, is a constant stream of "no" answers. That's what any good father who is cultivating maturity would give to us. And that is precisely what God was doing with her. And she was worn down.

So here is an interesting truth about prayer: You are better at it when you are spiritually mature as well. So it turns out to be a circular process of praying, which produces more maturity (when done rightly), which then leads to more effective prayer, which in turn matures you even more, which leads to even more effective prayer, etc. etc. It is a cycle of prayer-maturing-prayer-maturing that should take place. On the flip side, immaturity in prayer leads to less meaningful prayer (with lots of "no" answers from God), which leads to more immaturity (because we wear down and give up), etc., etc. The cycle can go both ways. And again, it appears that many have taken the backwards route and ended up with a dislike for prayer in general because, if the truth be told, it's acting as a maturity and faith destroyer rather than an aid to growth.

The key point in this discussion lies in our taking seriously the idea that prayer is a spiritual *discipline* and not primarily an emotional outlet or spiritual candy machine. And as a spiritual discipline or training method, its primary goal is to strengthen and mature us.[62] It should make us more faithful as we partake of it. Unfortunately, our practice of prayer often does just the opposite. It leaves us feeling confused and bewildered. As I've been arguing in this book, we end up frustrated in prayer due to our practice of it. If we don't view prayer as a training method, it degenerates into small talk with God and loses one of its most important purposes.

Now, let's get back to James. How do we become this *faithful*, mature believer whose prayers are often answered with "yes" from God? How do we become this *faithful*, mature believer who is in accord with God's desires in the first place and, consequently, prays prayers that God, by his very nature, would agree to honor and grant?

One thing that seems clear is that you don't have to be some unique spiritual giant to acquire such prayer-accomplishing faith. James makes a point of telling us that Elijah the prophet was just "a man with a nature like ours."[63] But when he prayed for drought or rain, he saw results. How many of us could say that? Clearly Elijah's faith was something for us to examine. If he, being a "man with a nature like ours," could get to that place where even his weather prayers were answered, certainly we, with the same nature, have at least a small shot at attaining the same level in prayer. (I'm almost sure that every single reader has at one time or another prayed the, "Let it be sunny today" prayer. Wouldn't it be cool to be confident that even that prayer would actually be answered with a "yes"? More likely, we would wisely never pray such a fruitless prayer again.)

Why have we abandoned the idea of prayer as primarily a spiritual discipline? Let's first think about this phrase, "spiritual discipline." When

---

62. We find prayer listed among the spiritual disciplines in all sorts of books on Christian growth. Some that might be of interest to the reader are: *Celebration of Discipline* by Richard J. Foster; *Disciplines of a Godly Man* by R. Kent Hughes; *Spiritual Disciplines for the Christian Life* by Donald S. Whitney; *The Spirit of the Disciplines* by Dallas Willard. These are all modern books, but the church has had proponents of prayer as a spiritual discipline for its entire history.

63. Jas 5:17.

we use this description, I find that we sometimes get hung up on the term "discipline." Perhaps it was the way I was raised, but when I hear the term discipline I immediately think of getting yelled at or spanked. The idea of "punishment" is one of the definitions of the term discipline. But another definition is: "training to act in accordance with rules."[64] This is referring to the *practice* of something in order to train us to function correctly. This is the intended idea behind the description "spiritual discipline." All the spiritual disciplines are intended to train us to function correctly—to train our spirituality. If we can get past any notion of discipline in terms of punishment, I think it is easier to look at how prayer can be a training ground. Now, as I noted earlier, we must remember that spiritual disciplines are not an end in and of themselves. They are merely types of exercises that train us (i.e., mature us). Of course we must ask, "Train us to *do* what?" Or, "Train us to *be* whom?"

In this case, the spiritual disciplines are meant to train us in spirituality that we might become mature, faithful Christians. And remember that *faithful* means something more than just believing in Jesus for salvation. All Christians are faithful in that sense.

Although the topic under discussion is not prayer, the Apostle Paul tells us about the goal we are pursuing in our Christian walks in his discussion on spiritual gifting, found in Ephesians 4:11–13. In that passage he says spiritual gifts have been given to the body of Christ that we might do service and build one another up. And the outcome of this is that "we all attain to the unity of the faith, and of the knowledge of the Son of God, to a *mature* man [emphasis added], to the measure of the stature which belongs to the fullness of Christ."[65] In talking about the Christian life, the author of the book of Hebrews comments: "Therefore leaving the elementary teaching about the Christ, let us press on to *maturity* [emphasis added], not laying again a foundation of repentance from dead works and of faith toward God, of instruction about washings and laying on of hands, and the resurrection of the dead and eternal judgment."[66] Prayer, as a spiritual discipline, is to help us reach that maturity of which the Apostles wrote. It is intended to help bring us into the fullness of Christ. That last sentence can sound like a bit of vague *Christianese*, but

---

64. Dictionary.com, s.v. "Discipline."
65. Eph 4:13.
66. Heb 6:1–2.

I believe Paul is saying that we ought, in the end, to reflect Christ as he would act on a daily basis were he living the lives we live.

Although this section has led us down a number of rabbit trails, such as the nature of faith in general and the respect paid or denied to the concept of maturity, in the end the point is this: One of the main goals of prayer ought to be our maturity into the exact image of Jesus. And until we view prayer as a training method to achieve that goal, we will never be fulfilled in our prayer lives because we will have cut out a foundational purpose of prayer.

The True Goal of Prayer #3: Endurance In The Present Life

Bob was a student I once had in a Bible class. He was an "A" student. When a paper was assigned, he'd get an "A." If a test was given, he'd ace it. In fact, when you went through his college transcripts, he had mostly "A" grades in all his classes. If you asked Bob where some factoid was located in the Bible, he could tell you. He had definite opinions about the Holy Spirit and the committed Christian life as well. And if you were to ask him, Bob would say he was deeply devoted to God and had given himself over to the study of his word and to prayer to become more like him.

But Bob was, "A" grades notwithstanding and practically speaking, strange. As I watched him in class I noticed he rarely spoke to others, and when he did he seemed to put them off. My impression was that his expectations for how they should be living as Christians were rarely met, and it seemed to irritate him. On a consistent basis he would stand up and leave classes with no apparent reason.. He would clasp his hands and go into what looked like devout prayer by himself when sitting in a crowded classroom, drawing quizzical side glances from his fellow students. Often he would leave his Bible unopened throughout class, while staring blank-eyed out the window. His countenance looked miserable and somber most of the time, and he would sometimes just flop his head down on the classroom table, arms flung wide, as though he were overwhelmed by unhappiness. I felt sorry for Bob. My only personal contact with Bob, outside of class, occurred when he told me what a poor example of a Christian I was.

Have you ever known that sort of person? The one who knows their Bible well, prays consistently, and talks about Jesus with deep reverence, but doesn't seem to be able to apply any of it in a practical way? They seem unhappy with their own lives and generally irritated with everyone else's life as well. You wonder what they are trying to accomplish with all that "Christian" behavior. They apparently learn a great deal of scripture, they pray a lot, and they seem to desire a close relationship with God. Yet in the end, it doesn't work. They are just as miserable and incapable of functionally interacting with the Body of Christ as they were when they began.

Bob's problem is that he didn't seem to understand what all his Bible reading, prayer, and study should actually accomplish. He seemed to believe that by learning all that spiritual "stuff" life would be "cake." He seemed to think that by knowing the factoids his frustration with circumstances would cease. But in reality all that learning and effort does not necessarily ease situational frustrations. I'd say that it's not even reasonable to expect such an outcome. Jesus certainly was as spiritually in-tune as you could be, but that didn't remove any of the aggravation that accompanies his life in community with other believers.

By thinking this way, Bob had a problem similar to our third ignored goal of prayer. He had a misunderstanding of what he could or even should try to accomplish in prayer. And we believers often share the same problem. Our prayers are often centered on health issues, or solving problems, or receiving something from God. But especially with health-related prayers, I believe that we are often praying for things that are incompatible with the entire system God has set in motion in this world. Like Bob, we expect certain things from our prayers and, for all intents and purposes, there is no way those things can ever come about. And that is why we struggle.

Let's start with the big picture. In terms of the natural world's reality, we are living within the consequences of the fall of creation into sin. The book of Genesis tells us that nothing has been spared from this fallenness, and the book of Revelation tells us that the only cure is going to be God restoring (redeeming) his creation to the perfection it once had. In the meantime, part of the eternal plan of God is the use of this fallen situation to further his glory. And it appears that in the vast majority of cases God's glory is achieved by highlighting his grace and mercy to broken individuals in broken situations. His glory is also achieved by allowing suffering to be conquered through endurance and faith, bringing to our attention the sustaining, everlasting lovingkindness of our God—even during hardship.

Many of our prayers are attempts to short-circuit this process. We ask not for God's presence, but for the immediate removal of the consequences of the fall. For example, physical weakness is now a reality for mankind. So when infirmity comes upon us, it is not as though it is something out of the ordinary. In fact, it is something that should be expected! It is the ordained consequence of evil in the world that mankind suffer the breakdown of the physical body and physical death. Sometimes this happens slowly over a long lifetime; sometimes it happens quickly over the duration of a severe illness. Rather than recognizing and accepting this fact, we automatically pray for (and keep praying for) the removal of the infirmity as though God will withdraw the curse for us alone. But think of the ramifications of such prayer. Should we expect God to do this for our entire lives? Doesn't this expose the underlying belief that we ought not to ever grow old and die at all? That fact is, we are all going to suffer infirmity and die. Infirmity is in our life-blood because we walk in the fallen world and we are fallen along with it. Asking for God to take away our sicknesses is really asking God to ignore the fallenness that we possess. But God tends not to do that. When we think of biblical characters who didn't suffer death, most likely we think of Enoch.[67] And in that story, there is no indication that he asked for blessing. There is no indication that he prayed and God removed the infirmities that plague human existence. It just says God took him; and it appears God did so for his own reasons. Freedom from infirmity or death is not presented as an interest of Enoch's at all.

The Bible predominantly presents a picture of life accompanied by many types of suffering. When we pray for the "fixing" of our problems—physical, mental, situational—we often are asking for God to ignore the consequences of the fall and to treat us as though we do not have to suffer as the rest of mankind does.

Now, I'm not arguing that prayer over the sick or for the resolution of problems is always wrong. Even our passage in James declares that the prayer of the righteous, faithful person can accomplish healing. But I'm suggesting that oftentimes we make correction of the situation the *only* possible outcome that is acceptable in our eyes. And that shapes all our prayers into requests for things that, many times, are *not* possible because they consistently expect God to ignore the very fallenness that he ordains. In truth, every positively answered health prayer *is a miracle*

---

67. Gen 5:21–24.

in some way in that it is an example of God stepping in and reversing the fallen nature of the world. For example, when God says "yes" to the prayer to heal cancer, he is cancelling an effect of the brokenness inherent in our unredeemed bodies. But should we expect such miracles on a daily basis? If we should, why not just heal all cancer every time it's prayed for? Isn't that the logical question the unbeliever brings to the table? If removal of the consequences of the fall is the goal of prayer, why would God not just answer "yes" all the time? The answer is clear: prayer is not primarily intended to reverse the consequences of the fall. The prayers of the Bible almost never depict it acting that way. And when they do, it is considered a miracle for good reason. It is not *natural* to have it occur that way—it truly is *miraculous*.

Let's examine Jesus' prayer in the garden of Gethsemane when he asked that God remove the cup of tribulation he was about to suffer (i.e., his crucifixion).[68] Now let's be clear, Jesus didn't *want* to be crucified. Who would want that? But he also knew that the course of this world demanded that very thing. The suffering he underwent was for a purpose and to remove that suffering was to counter that purpose. So Jesus admitted that it was not *his* will that was paramount in the situation; it was God the Father's.[69] Like Jesus, we too often pray for the removal of hardship. But the difference between Jesus and us is that we don't really want *God's* will in the situation; we want the removal of hardship. We want *our* will. We ignore the fact that the hardship is often necessary to serve the purposes of God. I would point the reader to the opening verses of James again:

> [2] Consider it all joy, my brethren, when you encounter various trials,[3] knowing that the testing of your faith produces endurance. [4] And let endurance have *its* perfect result, so that you may be perfect and complete, lacking in nothing.[70]

Notice that James is not addressing the existence of trials. He assumes that trials will occur by saying *when* you encounter various trials and not *if* you encounter trials. His emphasis is on your attitude within the situation—not the removal of the situation. And notice also his advice is

---

68. Matt 26:39–44.

69. Cf. Isa 53:10, where God explains that it is his will for Christ to be "bruised" and "put to grief."

70. James 1:2–4.

given as a command and not a suggestion. He is saying we as believers must view our trials as opportunities for growth in order for them to achieve their necessary ends. Trials produce endurance, which leads to Christian maturity and is itself a sign of Christian maturity. Although he does not say as much, I would add that there is no promise here that just getting through a trial will accomplish this goal. We all have known people who have had many trials, and yet those trials don't change them for the better. Such people belly-ache, whine, and complain through their trials, never giving a thought to what might be learned from their difficulties. Such people may well *get through* the trial, but they will not have gained an enduring attitude which develops and exemplifies Christian maturity.

When we try to pray our trials away, rather than praying our way through them, we are really attempting to derail the process of growth that is so critical to our ultimate maturity. So, practically speaking, how do we approach prayer when under trial and distress? Is it wrong to ask for relief? Even Jesus asked for relief in the garden. Yet that request was framed in light of the ultimate goals of God first and the willingness to *stop* asking for relief when an answer is given. In Jesus' case, he seems to have known already what God's answer was, for he goes on and says, "Yet not as I will, but as You will."[71] We should reclassify this prayer from a request to a confession of desire on Jesus' part. He frames his prayer as a request to remove the cup of crucifixion, but he seems to acknowledge that that is not possible at the same time. This should be our pattern. We pray for the healing of cancer. But when cancer lingers, when God says, "No, I won't remove it," our prayers should follow a new path. God's will is the priority. As another example, Paul likewise prayed for the removal of his "thorn in the flesh," but when God said, "No," Paul moved on.[72]

There is one other point to make from James' directive to count it all joy when we encounter various trials. Notice it is not for God's benefit that the trials come to us. God is not pictured as taking enjoyment out of the trouble's we face. He does not delight in seeing us struggle and fail. These trials are for our benefit and we grow because of them. They are necessary for us and God wants to help us navigate them. James even goes on in the next few verses to explain that if we lack wisdom (in reference to dealing with our trials) we have the freedom and opportunity to

---

71. Matt 26:39.
72. 2 Cor 12:8–9.

ask for some from God, and he gives it "to all generously and without reproach."[73] So, far from being uncaring, God is completely with us in the trials we face and will give us the wisdom we need to handle them. But again, James doesn't say God will remove the trials. He will help us deal with them, and in doing so, we gain endurance which forms us into mature believers.

Here we might look at another great saint from the Old Testament for an example: Job. The beginning of the book of Job tells us Job was "blameless, upright, fearing God and turning away from evil."[74] Job was not some back-slidden, godless problem child who needed a good spiritual spanking. But Job was not perfect either. Sometimes we make the mistake of equating the two ideas of perfection and righteousness, but we must remember the fact that we can be righteous without being perfectly sinless. Job apparently lived the good, spiritual life in fear of the Lord. He sacrificed for his family, he prayed, he lived as God would desire and as well as a sinful human can live under our holy and perfect God.

But because he was not perfect, it was still necessary for God to allow him to undergo trials. So, we are told that God allowed Satan to inflict some very difficult situations on Job. Many members of his family were killed; his wealth was severely curtailed; and his body became sick and painfully diseased. But after all these difficulties we are told that Job did not "sin with his lips."[75] When his wife urged Job to "curse God and die" Job asked, "Shall we indeed accept good from God, and shall we not accept adversity?"[76] Job had a grasp of the fact that difficulties are allowed and used by God for his purposes in our lives.

Unfortunately, Job did not fully appreciate how important this truth was. He began to waver in this belief as the difficulties increased. His friends accused him of sinning heinously, and they concluded that his sins were the cause of the evils in Job's life. But Job had not sinned in the way they meant. His sins did not precipitate God's anger; he was not receiving heavenly punishment in the form of difficult trials. But as the pressure mounted, a part of his belief system was exposed that *did* need correction. Job had harbored the idea that God sometimes was unjust,

---

73. James 1:5.
74. Job 1:1.
75. Job 2:10.
76. Job 2:9–10.

uncaring, and at times even more helpful to the evil than the righteous! Such views are not compatible with a mature person of faith, and Job's trials were integral to the exposure of these false ideas. In the end Job was forced to deal directly with the difference in what he *thought* God was like, and what God *really* was like.[77]

All this is to say that Job's trials were the avenue by which he grew into maturity. He was already a *righteous* person at the start, and at the end God again says Job was his servant. [78] But Job had also needed to learn about God more fully and about his own misunderstandings of how things work and how he related to God. And it was through his troubles that this came about. I can't think of any other way this growth could have occurred. In walking in righteousness up to that point, Job had missed these things. How would continuing his life in the same way have altered his views? Without the trials, he would never have even considered his underlying beliefs, and merely removing the problems would not have helped him do so. The brokenness of the world and his own personal affliction served as perfect vehicles to bring about Job's change of viewpoint.

There is one last thing I would like to point out about Job: It is not as though the death of family members, loss of wealth, and personal illness were never going to happen to him. Such things usually affect every single person in the world sooner or later. We just accept them better when they occur in the manner *we think they should*. People should die in the right order and at the proper age; loss of wealth should happen when we are prepared for it; sickness should come when we are old and frail. Unfortunately, even when they do occur at the "proper" times, we still often try to pray them away. In truth, we often just want things our way. But God makes clear in Ecclesiastes chapter 3 that there is a God-ordained, correct time for everything under the sun and our opinion about the right timing isn't part of the equation.

We have mentioned three foundational goals of prayer in this section which are often ignored. First, prayer should be effective and should accomplish something. That seems logical for anything we do. Second,

---

77. In this case, Job had the misfortune of having God directly instruct him. That may sound good to us, but the exchange is twice prefaced by God telling Job to "gird up your loins like a man" (Job 38:3; 40:7). The idea here is that Job is supposed to get ready as though he is going to go to battle. That is probably the last thing you want the Lord God of the Universe to say to you.

78. Job 1:1; 42:7.

prayer should lead us to Christian maturity. It should be a spiritual *discipline* that trains us to be mature believers. And third, prayer should build endurance in our lives. It should not be a vehicle by which we constantly try to elude either (1) the trials needed to grow us into adult, faithful, enduring children of God or (2) the reality of the fallen world around us.

PRAYER IS BORING

At our school we give our students an opportunity to evaluate our classes at the end of every semester. This evaluation is conducted so that we have some sense of what students like and dislike in the course and so that we can alter the course if it doesn't seem to be connecting with them. It is not just a way of catering our classes to the whims of students, but it is a way to find out if we have missed anything that might have been useful to them. There are two types of evaluation methods. First, they fill out a sheet of questions about the class. That is pretty standard and frankly, as far as I am concerned, it is not all that helpful. Second, they have an opportunity to make free observations about the course. Here is where a professor might get some useful suggestions (provided the students take it seriously). Unfortunately, you also get a lot of useless information. Now, I'm not just talking about the vague, negative statements such as: "This class is awful!" or "I didn't learn a thing." Just as useless are the positive ones that say: "This teacher is the best!" or "I really liked the class." Don't get me wrong, like all professors, I would much rather receive the latter than the former, but in either case there is really nothing to work with. Neither gives me concrete items to look at and re-evaluate. At best I can take from such positive comments that the class works even if I leave it alone.

In one set of evaluations I once received a short comment on the class from one unnamed student: "I'm bored." Yes, this qualifies as one of the useless statements in terms of real evaluation. It told me more about that student, whoever he or she was, than it did about my class. But it also struck me as an especially important sentiment because boredom can be such a killer of motivation. When we are bored, we give up. And although I don't know for a fact who wrote that stellar observation, I could make a pretty good guess just by observing his or her behavior in class. Boredom kills participation. And this is a problem we have with prayer.

I would guess that most all of us have heard a child utter, "I'm bored," a few times in our lives. Sometimes it occurs at the most inopportune times—like during the quiet pause in Sunday's prayer time or sermon. I would bet that many of us have silently added our own, "Amen," to that sentiment. Children have the most lamentable property of feeling free to express exactly what they think. Of course this quality cannot go unchecked forever. In daily life we cannot say what we think anytime we wish with no qualifications. So, instead of uttering, "I'm bored," we act on that boredom in advance of the situation. The trouble children have is that early on they have no reference with which to evaluate what actually is boring. When they are young, they are hauled off to events whether they want to attend them or not, and then they must assess whether they are bored or not on the spot. But as we grow older, we gain more experience and can begin to make educated guesses about the *boringness* of whatever we are expected to attend or partake in.

Sometimes we are pleasantly surprised and enjoy whatever it is we did even though we thought it would be boring prior to doing it. But in general, I think we all have a pretty good sense about what we will find boring and what we will not. So we can often predict what is going to be boring for us. And here I must say it outright: Prayer is often boring. Synonyms for boring include *dull, tiresome,* and *tedious.* When something is boring, it wears you out, tires you, even can annoy you. Most of us would never say this out loud, but prayer is often just plain boring, wearying, even annoying. So the question is: Why is prayer so boring?

Earlier we thought of how prayer should be effective by thinking about how other things are effective. Let's do that here as well. Let's ask the question, "What makes *anything* boring?" I'm going to choose something that ought to be exciting as my example—a football game. My pastor loves to watch the University of Georgia Bulldogs. He grew up in Georgia and since he now lives in the Pacific Northwest, he misses it a great deal. As he was planning a trip back home, I once asked him what he misses most about Georgia. I expected him to say he missed his family being close by or something like that, but he said he most missed the fun and excitement of fall Georgia football. He and his friends and family would immerse themselves in SEC football for five months and it was just plain exhilarating for them.

But even he has watched a few of those games that he would describe as *boring.* So what could take something he so ardently loves to watch and looks forward to enthusiastically, and make it boring? In football, there are all sorts of things we might list. I want to take these reasons and expand them to prayer, because I think there are themes that run all through boring activities.

The game is played in a sloppy manner. People expect a certain amount of quality when they watch football. I recall a number of years back when the NFL was on strike and replacement players were brought in. The fans were not impressed. Even though the replacements played hard and gave their all, there was clearly less quality on the field. And I recall people noting how boring it was to watch such messy games. This too can be a quality of prayer at times. It can be sloppy.

Sloppy means that something is "careless," "untidy," or "slovenly."[79] Have you ever listened to other people's prayers and found yourself wondering, "When are you going to get to the point?" Perhaps you've been there yourself. Your prayers wander around imprecisely and carelessly. Sometimes it's as though we don't know what to say, so we just talk. One of my students described her own speech in this way: "It's an unconsciousness stream of thought just flowing out of my mouth."[80] Yet Jesus chastises the use of many words just for the sake of words.[81] Granted, in that passage Jesus seems to be more concerned with the use of words repetitively. But I would bet that when we find people carelessly throwing words at God in prayer, we also find them repeating things over and over. We will return to this idea of repetition later in the section on nagging God because I think it is a severe problem that has actually been adopted by many. Right now I just want to make the point that when we pray in a sloppy, imprecise, careless way, we often can grow bored of the process. Like watching a sloppily played game of football, we know that things can be done in a more careful, thorough and useful way and we get tired of mistakes and imprecision. Our minds begin to wander and soon we are either sitting there frustrated, or we are thinking about other things and not praying at all.

---

79. Dictionary.com, s.v. "Sloppy."

80. At the time she was lamenting the fact that it was so hard for her to put her ideas into ordered rational sentences for her English class. I had mentioned that it sounded as though she was writing the way she talked—working through ideas haphazardly. She agreed, but added the belief that she had no idea what she thought most of the time. It was just thought flowing out of her during talk.

81. Matt 6:7.

Sometimes we grow bored when *the game is not competitive.* Usually we mean by this that the outcome is obvious from the very beginning. There is nothing that is going to surprise or interest us in the contest.

When I was a kid, my folks would take my brothers and I fishing. One of the things I truly enjoyed about fishing in the Strait of Juan de Fuca was the surprise of what would come up on the line. Sometimes it was something you were aiming to catch—like a rock fish or a flounder. Sometimes it was something you would never in the world have wanted to catch—like a ratfish. I once pulled up a giant pacific octopus, and I remember freaking out as I excitedly looked over the side of the boat, eager for the first sight of my huge halibut or cod. Instead I stared wide eyed and horrified at a very red, seemingly very angry, tentacled monstrosity! I practically dropped the fishing pole in my dad's lap and high-tailed it for the other end of the boat. That was not the outcome I envisioned when I put the line in the water.

In the same way, prayer can become boring because we know the outcome before we begin. We sit; we close our eyes; we run through a list of items; we sit some more; we open our eyes; we quit. When there is nothing to spark our interest in the process, when our prayers become predictable, and we can guess with regularity the outcome of our requests, we can grow bored very quickly. This also ties into the problem of praying for things to which God must consistently say "no." We get into the pattern of expecting a "no" answer, knowing that the outcome of our prayers is, for all intents and purposes, obvious—there will be no change in the situation whatsoever. And when we get into the habit of expecting a "no" from God, we sooner or later stop playing the game of asking. We grow tired of the result, especially when we know the result before we even bow our heads—that nothing is going to change.

Of course one might argue that always receiving a "yes" from God also creates a situation where we know the result. But in that instance we also know there will be a change in the circumstances around us, so the boredom factor doesn't arise. Additionally, we just flat out enjoy getting "yes" answers, so again, boredom is not a problem. Much like a gambler who would always win, you get the same result, but somehow it just never gets old like losing does.

Another cause of boredom can be that *we don't care for the teams.* I'm going back to my football analogy here. I love to watch football, but I won't watch every game. I want to see my teams play. Living in the northwest, I want to see the Seattle Seahawks. When I was a kid and there were no Seattle Seahawks I chose the Minnesota Vikings as my favorite team. So I want especially to watch those two teams. Sometimes I will watch other games that are of interest for other reasons—they are especially competitive, they have players I want to see—but for the most part, I don't watch other games. I get bored because I just don't care about them one way or the other.

When we think of this phenomenon in terms of prayer, it seems to be a very large problem. There are a *lot* of things we might not care about in relation to prayer. We may not, for example, care much about the people around us, but prayer is almost impossible to undertake for others when we really don't care about them in the first place. We may not honestly care about what God has to say to us, but that is a big obstruction when we are trying to hold an authentic discussion with God. The thing is, God actually *will* answer us and expect things of us; he will make demands of us. Many times his ideas conflict with our own, and although we would never say it out loud, we really don't want to be confronted with his views. For that matter, we sometimes don't want to be confronted with our beliefs and ideas either. In truth, we may not care for the whole process of prayer at all. And when we don't care about prayer (usually for good reasons) we don't participate in it. Or when we do force ourselves to participate in it, we grow bored with the process.

I've seen this last exemplified by students in classes. Some students just don't like the process of education with its tests and homework and reading, but they know they want the degree that follows from participating in the schooling process. So they come to class and are bored out of their skulls. There is good information around them coming from their professors, their peers, the books, and the assignments, but they don't like the process, so they turn off—even while they are still coming to class and doing homework. They are bored by their own hand. Often we try to put this sort of boredom off on others. For the student, I've heard them say such and such a teacher is boring. They seem to be saying a number of different things to me when I hear this sort of comment. They may not like the personality or presentation of the professor. They may not like the details of the subject (they are only interested in one particular facet of something, for example). They don't like the class dynamic (people are too quiet, or too talkative about things that don't interest the student). But it seems to me, the real problem is the students themselves. The fact is they just don't care enough about the class to pursue it through the obstacles.

This is similar to my football watching habits. There are a lot of good games to watch, and if I really watched them I'd find all sorts of exciting and interesting play. But the bottom line is: I don't care. And unfortunately, I think many people feel the same about prayer: They just don't care about the whole thing, so they get bored when they have to participate.

I'm sure there are a lot more reasons we find things boring, but I think my point is clear. Prayer can sometimes be as boring as anything else we undertake. But I would point out, especially in light of the third reason we mentioned for boredom, that often things are boring to us because we bring a bored attitude to them. We mix a bored attitude with boring methods and ta-da: we end up being bored and unmotivated. What a surprise, huh?

OUR APPROACH IS FLAWED

I like to work out, and ever since I took my first weight lifting class in high school I have always "cranked iron." At one point in my life I decided I wanted to see how much muscle I could put on. When I was in college I was a whopping 145 lbs on my 5' 8" frame—in other words, I was skinny. I lifted and lifted, but I didn't get the results I wanted. I kept this lifting up for almost ten years until I had bulked up to a wild 165 lbs. Not too impressive, huh? One day I was lifting at a gym and I saw a guy I really envied. He worked at the gym and he was huge. I was impressed, and I wanted to know his secret, so I just walked up to him and asked if he'd help me.

He said he was more than happy to help and promptly asked to see my workout log. If you don't know, a workout log is a record of information related to your workouts. It can merely contain the actual workouts themselves, but it can also contain a lot more. Some have the food you eat each day, the time in a yearly cycle of workouts you are undertaking, how you feel emotionally, how much sleep you got that day, etc. I showed mine to him and after he glanced through it, he said dryly, "You don't lift enough weight to get big." I wasn't sure what to make of that statement. I was thinking that I lifted as much as I could lift. I lifted as hard as I could. But when I pointed that out to him, he just nodded and eyed me some more. Then, after a fairly long pause, he said he'd work with me but there was one requirement: I had to write down every single thing I ate for two weeks—*Every* single thing, with calorie counts. No skipping even a cup of coffee. My workout log had not contained that nutritional information and he apparently thought it would be important. He told me later this was actually a ploy to get me to quit. Apparently most people won't keep that detailed a log. They'll write down what they ate for a few days, but usually they give up. Well, he had never worked with a person like me. I tend to be tenacious about things when I want to accomplish them. So I went home and I did as he said; I wrote down every last item of food that crossed my lips. When next we met, two weeks later, he was stunned. He couldn't believe I'd done it so precisely. I wrote down every last thing I ate with calorie, fat, protein and carbohydrate numbers as well. And it was exactly what he needed to see. There was no way I was going to get bigger on the amount of food I was eating. I barely ate enough to maintain what muscle I had, let alone add any muscle. My approach was flawed from a nutritional standpoint, and that flawed approach would never allow me to add muscle weight. It didn't matter how much study I did on lifting weights and workout routines. It didn't matter how much effort I put out in daily workouts. The approach was flawed and would never work even though parts of it were exactly right.

Let's do a quick recap. We're looking at reasons why people don't enjoy prayer. So far we have said: (1) Prayer is haphazard; (2) We ignore some of the fundamental goals of prayer; and (3) prayer can be just plain boring. The fourth reason I believe people don't enjoy prayer undergirds these others to some extent. What I mean is that in many instances the first three occur because of this last reason: People are quite often taught a flawed approach to prayer. Like my flawed approach to getting bigger, they are doing things that can never work.

Sometimes it's overt—people are actively *given* faulty methods of prayer. Sometimes it's merely by example—we hear people praying in a faulty way and we emulate it. It's not that each of us is necessarily exposed to the same flawed approach, but many of us receive some kind of guidance in prayer which contains serious flaws. Now, anything people undertake is going to possess some flaws; I'm not arguing for perfection. Being flawed is human. And especially when we're talking about a process like prayer that takes a lot of practice, we expect mistakes and flaws. But here I'm talking about major flaws that ultimately inhibit authentic prayer and lead us to dislike or discontinue it. It is like my nutrition program. You can have some flaws in the system and still progress a bit. But if your way off all the time, you've got no chance of progressing.

Now you can see how the previous few suggestions build on this more fundamental problem. Whether the difficulty is that prayer is haphazard, or we have lost track of its goals, or it has become boring, we can generally say that all these particular troubles stem from some sort of general flaw. But even though haphazardness, loss of goals, and boredom relate to a larger problem of a flawed system, I'm not going to merely rehash in this section the same information I've just discussed in the previous ones. Here I'm going to talk about some obvious *major* flaws that recur over and over and produce their own specific problems. These are flaws that are even defended from scripture by their adherents as proper and obvious modes of prayer. They are not as easily handled as haphazardness, loss of goals, and boredom.

Nagging God

The first type of prayer which is defended by some, but is quite harmful to authentic prayer is *nagging*. Of course, we would never call it that. We use words like *persistent* or *enduring*. But in the end, when we analyze what we are really doing, it is nagging. We pray for something over and over again, regardless of God's answer. Think again about a friend or family member. Suppose you were asked for something and answered, "No." Then you were asked a hundred more times for it, (Some parents are nodding here in recognition of their little children, I'm sure.) You would probably say you were being nagged. Many times we don't get the answer we want in our prayers, but we keep praying our prayer regardless—we keep *nagging God*.

As a good example, let's think about illnesses. Many of us pray that people will be healed, but when they are not, we still keep praying that prayer. It is sometimes years and years of praying for healing. Perhaps the person goes through year after year of treatments, and yet we steadfastly are praying for "healing." Or maybe there is no treatment being given, and we just keep praying for healing anyway expecting that miracle healing. This can occur, for example, when a person has been incapacitated by an accident. We take any answer God gives and turn it into a "yes" with statements such as: "God heals in his own time." Of course, we must translate these proclamations to mean: "God allowed the ailment to remain, but that's ok because ultimately God will heal some time." Or we could mean to say: "God didn't heal, but I couldn't know that when I was praying the same prayer over and over again." To be blunt, we rationalize the truth. God said, "No," and we didn't care, so we kept on repeatedly asking for the same healing.

Some might think this is a cruel attack on a person who is praying for the healing of another. "How could that possibly be wrong?" we might ask. But let me remind the reader of another question. What were we *not* praying for while we spent time asking for healing repeatedly—with no results? Think again of an earthly father. If a child persists in asking for something they should not, a good earthly father is not going to give in just because they ask repeatedly or persistently. Imagine a five-year-old asking to jump off a 100 foot bridge into a lake. There is no way in a million years of asking that a conscientious father would allow any child to do that. And I would point out that not only would it be ludicrous to allow a five-year-old to do such a thing, but the child, by spending time on the request to leap off a bridge, is also missing out on all the requests they could have had answered with a "yes."

So in our case, when the sick person is not being healed, the question that should be asked is, "What might we learn from that?" Let's list what we might learn to pray for that they *could* receive:

- God's strength to endure pain.
- Insight into how to grow in their trust of God while suffering.
- How to be an example to others when life is painful.
- How to hope in our eternal promises rather than focus on the temporal, physical things before us.
- How we ourselves might grow in our trust of God's grace and working as we watch their suffering and ache for them.

The list of things we might profitably pray immense, for I've only noted a few items. But often we miss them all to repeat incessantly our prayer for healing. I would guess that many of us, having done this very thing, have grown weary and sick of our prayers as well, and in the dark of night, when we are being completely honest with ourselves, we have asked God what's wrong with him that he doesn't fix our friend. In other words, like Job, we go from poor theology that can be fixed, to crazy theology that paints God as wicked at worst and uncaring or impotent at best.

Let's go back to the picture of God as father to set the tone on this again. Imagine yourself as a child sitting at the table for dinner with your family and asking your dad, "Dad, will you pass me the salt?" Let's assume your father knows that you've not tried the food yet and that it is salted pretty well already. Or assume that he's concerned about your health and had instituted a lesser-salt regimen for the family. He answers *"no"* to your request. Assuming we love and trust our dad, what should be our next move? Do we spend the remaining forty-five minutes at dinner repeating the question—i.e., nagging him for the salt? Or do we perhaps ask more profitably, "Is there some reason why?" This would be much like Moses in the example we previously looked at. We are *exploring* the answer we get, not *ignoring* it. Realistically, we would then try to adjust our request. We would try to understand the situation in light of what our more knowledgeable father has said. We would not just fall into badgering him at every opportunity to get the salt we wanted. In fact, our dad would undoubtedly see that sort of behavior as extremely childish and he would chastise us for it.

It is unfortunate, but some actually believe scripture supports the idea of incessantly praying the same prayer over and over again. When I have spoken with people about the idea of how often we pray for something, I invariably hear some mention of three passages of scripture: Luke 11:5–13, Luke 18:1–8, and occasionally Mark 7:24–30. In addition I'm quite often asked the question, "Shouldn't I keep praying for the lost over and over?" This last is usually asked with a hint of distaste because they believe that I might be suggesting that their repetitive prayers for the lost are a waste of time.

All the listed passages have been wrestled with by many good scholars, so there is little need to rehash in great detail what has been said. But, let's look at each for a moment for two reasons: (1) just to put them to bed as bases for repetitive prayer; but also (2) to show how they might actually hinder real growth in prayer.[82]

---

82. Here I would especially direct the reader to David Crump's book *Knocking on Heaven's Door*. He has a good discussion of the Luke passages, arguing persuasively that they are not merely models of repetitive prayer. I prefer to go beyond his assertions however. He says, "My point is not to dissuade anyone from praying persistently or passionately, nor is it to discount the useful pastoral observations that many have made about the power of long-term petition to challenge personal priorities, to inculcate greater patience, or to deepen superficial faith" (p. 75). I would disagree with him on one point, going a bit further than he, and say we *ought* to dissuade people from praying

Luke 11:5–13

The first thing we have to do with each of these texts is look at the context that spawns them. Luke chapter 11 begins with a short story about the disciples asking Jesus to teach them to pray (Luke 11:1–4). The text tells us that Jesus had been praying, and when he finished they said, "Lord, teach us to pray just as John also taught his disciples."[83] Notice it's not really a question. They basically demand that Jesus do for them what John the Baptist had done for his disciples. Jesus acquiesces with no recorded hint of complaint, which leads me to believe that he thought it was a good idea to give them some specific instruction on prayer. And in this case Jesus is quite clear, and he gives them the short Lucan version of the Lord's Prayer. Here in Luke the prayer focuses on two things: (1) Praise to God (11:2); and (2) Requests of God (11:3–4).

Luke's main interest is in the idea of *request* in our prayers. He focuses on three specific requests in 11:3–4: Give us our daily needs (bread); forgive us our sins; and don't lead us astray (or let us wander into temptations).

The text we're interested in follows this, and reads:

> [5] Then he said to them, "Suppose one of you has a friend, and goes to him at midnight and says to him, 'Friend, lend me three loaves; [6] for a friend of mine has come to me from a journey, and I have nothing to set before him'; [7] and from inside he answers and says, 'Do not bother me; the door has already been shut and my children and I are in bed; I cannot get up and give you *anything*.' [8] "I tell you, even though he will not get up and give him *anything* because he is his friend, yet because of his persistence he will get up and give him as much as he needs. [9] "So I say to you, ask, and it will be given to you; seek, and you will find; knock, and it will be opened to you. [10] "For everyone who asks, receives; and he who seeks, finds; and to him who knocks, it will be opened. [11] "Now suppose one of you fathers is asked by his son for a fish; he will not give him a snake instead of a fish, will he? [12] "Or *if* he is asked for an egg, he will not give him a scorpion, will he? [13] "If you then, being evil, know how to give good gifts to your children,

---

persistently if we are going to define persistence as repeating a prayer over and over again regardless of what answer we receive. Such a view of persistence seems childish (not childlike) at best and dreadfully stunting and wasteful at worst.

83. Luke 11:1.

how much more will *your* heavenly Father give the Holy Spirit to those who ask him?"[84]

One thing we must admit is that Luke felt that this short scene expounds in some way the prayer Jesus has just given. And just so the reader doesn't have to wait, I believe the points he is focused on are (1) the *willingness* of God the father to give and (2) the *quality* of what he gives us. So Luke has recorded a prayer from Jesus that emphasizes asking things from God, and in light of that, a record of some of Jesus' thoughts on requesting things from God.

Before we get to those comments however, we might ask the question, why would we need to be instructed specifically on asking things of God? Jesus seems to assume that the disciples don't have a correct understanding of their relationship to God or of God's personal qualities as their father. Therefore, they need some instruction on the topic of asking things from God. (This book is testimony to my belief that we still need this instruction on that point.) In the text, it looks as though a few more questions have been asked but not recorded after Jesus' example prayer was given. Luke probably assumed any interested reader would ask the same questions, so he did not record them. These questions appear to include (1) "How is it we can ask so much of God?" (2) "How can we be sure God will give us what we ask for?" and (3) "Why would God give us things in the first place?" We might paraphrase this last questions as: "What is God like?" We want to know because it affects what he'll give to us. Is he a god who gives good things or bad?

I believe it is in answer to such questions that Jesus launches into the story about the friends and borrowing bread. I will divide this section into four parts:

- *Jesus' hypothetical situation* (Luke 11:5–7) —Here Jesus sets the stage with a story about a man who needs to ask something of his close friend.
- *Jesus' comment #1* (Luke 11:8)—After the story is given, Jesus then comments on two ideas. This first comment has to do with the motivation that drives the giving of the bread.
- *Jesus' comment #2* (Luke 11:9–10)—In this second comment, Jesus addresses the assurance the petitioner has of an answer.

---

84. Luke 11:5–13.

- *Jesus' explanation of God's motivation* (Luke 11:11-13)—In this last portion, Jesus compares God to people and asks us to think about the differences.

Let's look at each of these sections individually.

Jesus' hypothetical situation (Luke 11:5-7)

> [5] Then he said to them, "Suppose one of you has a friend, and goes to him at midnight and says to him, 'Friend, lend me three loaves; [6] for a friend of mine has come to me from a journey, and I have nothing to set before him'; [7] and from inside he answers and says, 'Do not bother me; the door has already been shut and my children and I are in bed; I cannot get up and give you *anything*.'[85]

Jesus has everyone imagine their own friendships as the setting of the story. He asks us to suppose we go to our friend late at night and ask to borrow three loaves of bread because we've had unexpected company and need some food. Just with this set-up the next line appears to be somewhat out of place in my view. When I think of my friends, I cannot imagine any of them not even opening the door, let alone shouting through it that I should go away because they've already gone to bed for the night. Yet that is what happens in this hypothetical story. My friend says he's in bed and that I should go away!

I'm reminded of a short conversation I had the other day with a neighbor of ours. She works at the local Costco we shop at, and we crossed paths while I was looking to buy an office chair. Somehow we got into a discussion about gardening, and she told us about an exchange she had with her husband a few days previously. She had asked him to move something around in the yard, and he had shaken his head and said, "No, I'm not going to do that." She said she had actually burst out laughing! Her husband never said "no" to her requests—he was always a helpful and caring husband. But we also knew he was sometimes a prankster, and I could envision him just saying "no" that way. It made me laugh too because it is so improbable. This is like our story from Luke. It sounds silly from the beginning when a "friend" turns you away without even opening the door. But that's what apparently happens in Jesus' hypothetical vignette.

---

85. Luke 11:5-7.

It is even more irritating that my friend tells me he is already in bed and can't get up to help, because clearly he is "up" enough to be yelling through the door at me to go away! And if it's his kids that are so in need of sleep, how helpful is that shouting through the door going to be anyway? Now perhaps I have misunderstood my friend's intent. Perhaps what my friend is trying to say is that even if he arises, he is not able to help. Perhaps he just doesn't have any bread lying around the house. Yet this is proven false by the outcome of the story where he hands over the loaves—as many as I need. In this case, it looks as though my friend simply does not want to help me out! (I'm imagining my involvement as Jesus suggested I do.)

That's the end of the hypothetical situation. I'm standing on the porch asking for just three loaves of bread and my friend is shouting through the door at me telling me to go away.

The natural question is, what do I do in light of my friend's hesitant attitude? Well, if this were me in real life, I would probably shake my head and go to another friend's house. But in the story, Jesus says I should imagine I'm so desperate that I begin to badger him through the door. Next comes Jesus' first comment on the situation.

Jesus' Comment #1

> ⁸"I tell you, even though he will not get up and give him *anything* because he is his friend, yet because of his persistence he will get up and give him as much as he needs."[86]

Jesus' first comment has to do with the motivation a person has for giving. He suggests a scenario that is different from what I imagine takes place. In Jesus' story, I stay and badger my friend through the door. Of course, this produces quite different results as well. My friend is not going to get back to sleep, and neither are his sleep-needy children. I'm apparently going to hammer away at the door until he finally *has* to give in to my demands. Jesus is interested in what actually drove my friend to open the door and hand over the bread. He notes that it is not our friendship that motivates him. It is my irritating persistence that finally drives him to open the bolt, and Jesus makes very clear that my friend really is in bed and has to get up to do it. (For my part, I am imagining he has to tip-toe across freezing cold linoleum on the floor too.)

---

86. Luke 11:8.

The point is, Jesus is telling us that there are different motivations that will drive humans to respond to our requests. Sometimes we can get what we want with people simply by being as irritating as possible. The squeaky wheel gets the grease and all that. The question I would ask about the whole situation is, what is this friendship going to be like from now on? Suppose I decide now that since I got the bread, I should use the same tactics I used that night for every request I have of my friend? I wonder how long my "friend" would be my "friend" if every time I asked something of him I ignored his reticence and just badgered and cajoled him until he gave in. Probably not long. But, in the short term, I could probably get a few things out of him with those tactics. Jesus is noting that such an approach *can work*. But his point is not that it is a good situation on either side. This is the exact opposite of the idea that "persistence" is a great attribute. From this story we can deduce that "persistence" works, but is it the best approach?

I would ask another question as well, what sort of "friend" is this anyway? As I said, I cannot imagine any of my real friends acting in that manner. If I had to brow-beat them into helping me when I'm in such dire straits, what would asking something simple of them be like? The fact is, this person is acting like he doesn't really want to be my friend at all. And chances are, he would not help me much when I needed it. So Jesus is really noting a pathetic truth here: We can, at times, use crude, persistent tactics and get what we want from people. But, Jesus goes on to tell us something that stands in *contrast* to this fact in his second comment.

Jesus' Comment #2

> ⁹ "So I say to you, ask, and it will be given to you; seek, and you will find; knock, and it will be opened to you. ¹⁰ For everyone who asks, receives; and he who seeks, finds; and to him who knocks, it will be opened."[87]

Jesus is emphasizing that he is telling us a truth here. He says in 11:8, "*I tell you . . .*," and here in 11:9 he says, "*and* I tell you . . . ." I.e., here is *another* truth you need to know about giving in addition to the truth that you can sometimes *badger* your human friends into handing things over. He is returning to the unspoken questions that spawned the discussion

---

87. Luke 11:9–10.

in the first place. He had taught the disciples to pray with examples of asking things of God. They probably had wondered how it is that we can ask so much from God in the first place. And now he shares a difference between God and humans (even our so-called friends). When we ask of God, he responds directly. If God were standing behind that door, I would not be standing on the porch yelling through it for a crummy three loaves of bread. When I ask of God, I receive. When I seek God, I find him. When I knock on his door, he opens it to me. God is not like humans—even my *friends*. How cool is that!?

Notice that Jesus has not yet addressed the motivation behind God's actions—he will do that with the following example. He is merely saying that in terms of receiving, finding, and being opened to, God is every bit the equal to any friend of ours—even if we can actually get them to give in to us by "persistent" badgering.

But the fact that God may be generous with us may not be any comfort to us. We might say, "So what if God will give me what I want? I still may have to badger him for it. So he is really no better than any friend I already have!" This is where we move to the final component of the discussion: Jesus' example of the motivation behind God's open giving.

Jesus' Explanation of God's Motivation

Here are Jesus' comments about God's motivation:

> [11] "Now suppose one of you fathers is asked by his son for a fish; he will not give him a snake instead of a fish, will he? [12] "Or *if* he is asked for an egg, he will not give him a scorpion, will he? [13] "If you then, being evil, know how to give good gifts to your children, how much more will *your* heavenly Father give the Holy Spirit to those who ask him?"[88]

The first thing we should note is that Jesus brings the relationship closer than just friend to friend. Recall he began his example prayer with our addressing God as *father*. We are going to look at that relationship closely later in chapter 5 because it sets the foundation for the entire prayer. But at present Jesus is defining the proper relationship between us and God. He is telling us that from that foundation we have a way of evaluating why and how we can ask things of God.

---

88. Luke 11:11–13.

Jesus' explanation begins with a question: "Now suppose one of you fathers is asked by his son for a fish; he will not give him a snake instead of a fish, will he?" Let me insert here that so often we read the questions in scripture as though they are just filler. Whenever you read a question in scripture, you should try to answer it before you go on. I imagine Jesus posing this question, and then just standing there while everyone mused over it: "Hmm, if I were asked for an egg by my son, would I give him a scorpion?"

Why would Jesus even raise this question? He's drawing our thought to the idea of *why* we give things to our children. A father gives, not out of badgering, but out of love. And even an earthly father knows what the right response is when asked for something by his child. When someone is badgered into giving, they are not interested in helping; they are helping for some reason other than love. In our story it is because the friend is irritated enough by the persistent badgering that he finally breaks down and gives the requested bread. In this second case of a father and child the motivation is the relationship between the two. And more importantly to Jesus, even faulty humans make the right choices in that relationship—they give what is requested from love.

Jesus drives this home by asking a question that points us to the distinction between God and men: "If you then, being evil, know how to give good gifts to your children, *how much more* [emphasis added] will your heavenly Father give the Holy Spirit to those who ask him?" [89] God, our heavenly father, certainly has *at least* the same amount of insight and love that we earthy fathers possess, and he certainly will give us what we ask for without delay based on that love for his children.

Jesus' point is not that we should emulate the badgering to get a friend to give in to our needs. His point is that we don't need to badger God for our needs because he knows what we need as only our loving father can. Moreover, he will meet those needs correctly when we ask.

Now, I want to stress that critical word: *need*. In Jesus' story, the request is not just a whim or desire; it is a real need. You may say to yourself the request for bread is not a need in the sense that the person who is visiting *has to have* some food. After all, the visitor will not starve

---

89. As a side note, notice the substitution of food in the examples with the Holy Spirit in Jesus' question. I would point out that here we see a metaphor for what the Holy Spirit is like in our lives. He is our sustenance in many ways, supplying us with what we need to function and live.

if he is deprived of a bit of bread late at night when he arrives. But in the sense of what was required of hosts in that setting by societal norms, it certainly *was* a need, and I would add that God understands the social *needs* (even the less important ones) as much as he understands the personal, critical ones of eating enough to survive.

So, in Luke 11:5–13 we are not being taught to pray over and over—nagging God—to move him to finally give us what we want. We are being taught that God gives to us because of the good motivation of being our heavenly father.

I would also point out again that a human father will never hand over something that a child wants just because he or she wants it badly enough. A good father will weigh the request and either say "yes" or "no" depending on his judgment as to whether the child should have the item. In like manner, God will not simply hand things out because we pray for them incessantly. He loves us too much to be that irresponsible.

Luke 18:1–8

The second passage that is often mistakenly understood to be teaching persistent, repeated prayer is Luke 18:1–8. This passage follows on the heels of a section that records Jesus' teaching about the coming kingdom of God. Luke 18:1–8 is not precisely about prayer; rather it is a discussion of justice. We often think the subject is prayer because Luke comments in 18:1 that Jesus was encouraging people to pray and not lose heart. But prayer in this parable is secondary to the exhortation to not lose heart in our expectations of God's right action. The parable reads:

> [1] Now he was telling them a parable to show that at all times they ought to pray and not to lose heart, [2] saying, "In a certain city there was a judge who did not fear God and did not respect man. [3] There was a widow in that city, and she kept coming to him, saying, 'Give me legal protection from my opponent.' [4] For a while he was unwilling; but afterward he said to himself, 'Even though I do not fear God nor respect man, [5] yet because this widow bothers me, I will give her legal protection, otherwise by continually coming she will wear me out.'" [6] And the Lord said, "Hear what the unrighteous judge said; [7] now, will not God bring about justice for his elect who cry to him day and night, and will he delay long over them? [8] I tell you that he will bring about justice for them

quickly. However, when the Son of Man comes, will he find faith on the earth?"[90]

This parable even has the title "Jesus Tells the Parable of the Persistent Widow" in one study Bible I own.[91] In this story a wicked judge is badgered by a widow for legal protection and even though he is evil, he relents and provides it because she won't go away otherwise. This story does, on the surface, seem to imply that just being persistent wins out in the end, but we need to put this idea to rest for good.

As noted above, Luke gives an explanation of the parable prior to listing it: "Now he [Jesus] was telling them a parable to show that at all times they ought to pray and not to lose heart."[92] We might ask, lose heart over what? In the context of the saying, Jesus was just talking about the coming Kingdom of God. It would make good sense to assume that we should not lose heart over that future joyous event. In fact, the other uses of the term translated "lose heart" in the New Testament seem to point to the same idea. This Greek term translated "not lose heart" is not all that common in the New Testament, occurring in only our passage in Luke 18, and also in 2 Corinthians 4:1,16; Galatians 6:9, Ephesians 3:13 and 2 Thessalonians 3:13.

In 2 Corinthians and Ephesians the term is used to encourage believers to not lose heart about their future and the truths of the Gospel. In 2 Corinthians 4 it is specifically about Paul's ministry and the hardships he faces. But his thought is that even with all the hardships he would not lose heart since his salvation and ministry are God given. In Ephesians 3:13, Paul asks the Ephesians not to lose heart at his sufferings and tribulations because, as amazing as it sounds, those sufferings were "for their glory." In both of these latter cases, losing heart would be to lose faith, because of the circumstances of suffering we see around us, in what we know is true.

If this is the intended meaning of the term in Luke 18, then Jesus is talking about not losing heart in the pursuit of our beliefs—probably the specific belief that a just God is going to act justly for us. The parable speaks to the truth that our righteous God *will definitely* act justly, especially in light of the fact that even evil judges know how to bring

---

90. Luke 18:1–8.

91. Luke 18:1–8 in *The Life Application Study Bible,* Grand Rapids: Zondervan, 2000.

92. Luke 18:1.

justice at times (though the parable points out that in this case, it is after being badgered into it).

The Galatians 6 and 2 Thessalonians 3 passages speak to the idea of not growing weary in doing good. If this is the idea Luke is presenting then Jesus is exhorting people to continue in their practice of prayer without growing weary; it is a general call to perseverance in prayer and right actions.

But Jesus' main point in the parable in Luke 18:1–8 concerns the faithfulness of God to deliver justice. He explains how even an evil judge will act responsibly toward those he despises when pestered long enough. In contrast, certainly our loving God and father will act responsibly toward his elect. After all, unlike the evil judge, God truly loves us and wants what is righteous for us. So Jesus' conclusion is that we should expect God to answer us, care for us, and listen to our prayers. Jesus exhorts the listeners to "hear what the unrighteous judge said." He means, the listener (reader) should pay attention to, and clearly understand, that even evil people will answer a call for justice at times. In this case, the pestering of the widow made even an evil judge act. Jesus then asks a question, "Will not God bring about justice for his elect who cry to him day and night, and will he delay long over them?"[93] The answer he expects is: "Of course God will bring justice, acting fairly and quickly!" Jesus is trying to make the people see that on the subject of justice God is no evil judge who has to be pestered over and over. God is far better and loving than such a judge. This is reminiscent of the comparison between God and an earthly father, isn't it? God is not like earthly beings in any way when it comes to caring for us.

Far from being an example of repeated, nagging prayer for something, Luke 18:1–8 is actually a statement about how we *need not* pester God for things. That may work with unrighteous judges on occasion, but God is far more responsive than some uncaring human judge; God will respond to us without nagging.

Mark 7:24–30

Mark chapter 7 is the final passage that often comes up when people think about repetitive prayer. In this passage a Syrophoenician woman keeps asking Jesus to heal her daughter, and Jesus finally does. In my experience it is usually less referenced when discussing repetitive prayer,

---

93. Luke 18:7.

but I it seems to me to be just as useful for defending repeated prayer as the other passages. In this case, Jesus himself is the one who is nagged into submission. The text reads:

> ²⁴ Jesus got up and went away from there to the region of Tyre. And when he had entered a house, he wanted no one to know *of it*; yet he could not escape notice. ²⁵ But after hearing of him, a woman whose little daughter had an unclean spirit immediately came and fell at his feet. ²⁶ Now the woman was a Gentile, of the Syrophoenician race. And she kept asking him to cast the demon out of her daughter. ²⁷ And he was saying to her, "Let the children be satisfied first, for it is not good to take the children's bread and throw it to the dogs." ²⁸ But she answered and said to him, "Yes, Lord, *but* even the dogs under the table feed on the children's crumbs." ²⁹ And he said to her, "Because of this answer go; the demon has gone out of your daughter." ³⁰ And going back to her home, she found the child lying on the bed, the demon having left.⁹⁴

The term translated "kept asking" in 7:26 is in what is called the *imperfect* tense, which often denotes ongoing or repeated action. Our English translations express this idea commonly by saying a person *kept on* doing such and such. So the woman is described as asking Jesus in an ongoing way, over and over again—she *kept asking* him to cast out the demon. Although sometimes the imperfect tense in the Greek language can imply a person doing something, then stopping, and then doing it again at another time, in this instance, she does not go away and come back to the request. She just keeps at it during this one meeting with Jesus.

Jesus' answer appears to be "no" at this particular moment, though possibly she interpreted it as a "wait" since Jesus said Israel must feed *first*—perhaps implying that she might receive her request later, *after* Israel is fed.⁹⁵ She, as a Gentile, must wait until Israel has "fed" on what Jesus is offering them.

---

94. Mark 7:24–30.

95. Apparently at this point in Jesus' ministry miraculous signs like the casting out of demons were focused on the children of Israel first and foremost. We might note Matthew 10:5–14 where Jesus gives instructions to his twelve Apostles prior to sending them out to preach the gospel. He says in 10:5–6, "Do not go in the way of the Gentiles, and do not enter any city of the Samaritans; but rather go to *the lost sheep of the house of Israel* [emphasis added]." For a portion of Jesus' ministry, he was solely focused on Israel and their acceptance of his messianic mission. When they rejected their Messiah, the gospel then fully opened to all.

The woman takes this answer and reiterates her request incorporating what Jesus has said. She agrees with his statement that the "children" should eat first, but she asserts that there is enough spillage, with enough power, to satisfy her needs without taking anything from those who are first. Jesus responds saying, "Because of this answer go; the demon has gone out of your daughter." In other words, that was a pretty convincing way to look at it, and so he granted her wish.

Now, did she persuade Jesus to heal by nagging him? I propose that she definitely did not; she actually revealed true maturity. She listened to what Jesus told her, recognized the truth of it, and reiterated her request *after* reshaping her desires to his own. She didn't ignore what he said or argue that he was wrong about who should eat first. Instead, she noted how her prayer was not intended to diminish his desires in any way. In fact, she obliquely praised him by noting that even the "crumbs" from his hand would satisfy her measly prayer. As we have noted, Jesus says that it is "because of this answer" that her request is granted. Her mature admission of *his* priorities over hers is what impresses Jesus. One wonders if he would have granted her request if she had responded to him with something like, "I don't care about those who come first; I want my child healed regardless!" I think not.

This story is also a good picture of how God responds to our responses. We pray to him; he responds. We then, in turn, have an opportunity to respond to him, and he listens to how we respond and acts accordingly. I would think that he responds differently depending on our response to him. When we ignore his answers and brutishly hurl the same prayer at him without reflection on what he has said, a good father will rightly ignore us and wait for us to rethink our position. So, as in Luke 11:5-13 and 18:1-8, here in Mark 7:24-30 we find no support for the idea of repeated prayer. Instead we find an example of a person who rightly listens to God and alters their prayer to align it with his desires.

I would also point out that it is very often the case that repetitive, nagging prayers do not satisfy us either. Even when we get what seems to be an answer, we very often are left with some real problems in regard to our personal growth. Questions like the following plague us:

- Why did God wait so long and let so much suffering occur?
- Did I do something to slow the pace of God's answer?
- Did God actually fix this problem, or did time and luck finally kick in?

As I've said before, sometimes we just cry, "Mystery of God!" and throw our hands up. But if, after all our time repeating the same prayer, we end up still not knowing how to pray any better than when we started, what have we gained? Praying prayers over and over—nagging God—is actually a sure fire way of hindering any real growth in our true understanding of God or prayer.

Repeated Prayer for the Lost

I was teaching on the repetitiveness of prayer one week in a Sunday school class and I used the example of praying for my dream car—a 1972 Chevelle. I noted that the Sonata I drove to church that day was the latest proof that God had not said "yes" to my years of asking. I also made clear my belief that I had wasted my prayer time on that Chevelle and that I should have taken the "no" answer and gone in another direction.

A woman in the class looked at me with perturbed countenance and said to me that that was fine for a silly car prayer, but she was praying for the salvation of her son—and that was far more important than a stupid car. At that moment it seemed to me that a wave of deep emotion swept through her as she thought about her boy. And why not? Who hasn't ached over the lost-ness of a loved one? Still, I felt I must ask her directly about the whole thing. So I asked her how she dealt with the fact that God had not saved her son for all these years—did that mean anything to her? I asked her if she thought God might be trying to tell her something by all those "no" answers? Could there be something else he might want her to pray for in her boy's life? I don't think I won any friends that day. I wasn't trying to provoke or anger her, but the problems associated with repetitive prayer exist whether we are willing to say them out loud or not.

Let me point out again that I'm not talking about any old prayer for the lost; I'm talking about repetitive prayer for the *salvation* of the lost. That point is extremely important to this discussion. I want to be clear that I think we are definitely called to pray consistently for the lost, but the question I'm focusing on is whether or not we should pray for their *salvation* over and over again.

My story about my friend in Sunday school is probably not new to you. All of us have, most likely, heard those stories of how "a relative" prayed for someone's salvation over the years without giving up even though everyone else did. Sometimes it's the other way around, the person telling the story prayed for a lost relative or friend over the years and never gave up. In either case someone doggedly prayed that someone they knew would be saved, and then, *voila*, the moment came and all those prayers were apparently answered at once when the person being prayer for came to faith in Jesus. Many times the teller emphasizes that salvation came after years and years of diligent prayer for the other's soul. What do we say to this sort of thing?

This is one of those discussions that can be a minefield. If you say such repetitive prayer is a waste of time because clearly God had answered "no" numerous times—perhaps for those "years and years" mentioned)—you effectively paint yourself as anti-missionary in some way, or worse yet, as anti-salvation for someone's loved one. After all, what kind of monster wouldn't pray for the salvation of the lost? If you say it is a great thing that someone prayed over and over, doggedly, for salvation and it worked, then you end up tacitly agreeing that dogged, repetitive prayer, with no thought to the actual answer God gives us on a daily basis *does* work.

Before I get into the heart of this discussion, let me say a general word about this topic. Frankly, I don't want it to consume the book; and it probably could. This book is about how we *ought* to pray; it is not a theological treatise on "Prayer for the salvation of the lost." But this topic is always the one "but what about . . . ?" objection I hear concerning repetitive prayer. And since that is the case, I felt it needed some special attention. Please do not become overly obsessed with this one topic, though. Let me play devil's advocate for a moment. Let's suppose that I don't prove my point about repeated prayer for the salvation of the lost. I would still argue my position is still very strong concerning repetitive prayer in general. So, that being said, let us press on.

Repetitive prayer for the salvation of the lost is one of those areas in which we need to do two things: (1) we obviously need the input of scripture; and (2) we need to think through the implications of what we are doing. Scripture is the priority for getting the best information on God's view of praying for the salvation of the lost, but our view of God and the expectations we have, often cloud our understanding of his Word on the issue. For this reason, let me begin with the second task first, thinking about the implications of what we are doing and presuppositions we harbor when we pray for the salvation of the lost. Again, the reason for this is that part of our approach to prayer for the souls of the lost seems to come directly from our pre-suppositions about God and the salvation process rather than from what scripture says.

I like to ask people about whether they pray for the salvation of the lost. (This is just an informal survey of sorts—I casually ask folks at church and work.) I get a lot of "yes" answers. I've actually never gotten a "no" answer without a qualification such as, "but I should" or, "but it's important." In truth, usually the "yes" answers are qualified as well in some way. Here are a few of the qualifications that I often hear when people say they do pray for the salvation of the lost:

- People don't necessarily pray for the lost *every single day*.
- People don't always pray for *all* the lost. (When I further ask why they pray for the ones they do, they usually say they know them in some fashion—co-workers, friends, family.)[96]
- People pray for the lost when their name *comes up* in prayer time. (By this they mean that God brought that person's name to their mind while they were in prayer.)

I usually ask follow up questions as well. When I ask what it is that people pray for when they do pray for the lost, I get a number of similar answers:

- They pray God will make the person receptive to the truth of the Gospel.
- They pray God will help the person see the futility of their life without Jesus and that they will turn to the truth.
- Some pray that they have opportunity to share the gospel with the person, but this answer is not very common.

In all these various answers I see some underlying presuppositions that create cognitive dissonance. That's a five-dollar-phrase meaning we are holding ideas that conflict with one another and that situation creates

---

96. Of particular interest to me was one answer by a theologically informed pastor when I asked him why he prayed for the few lost he did. He said it was because they were family and he saw how miserable they were in their lives. I asked whether he thought he would have prayed for them if they were happy lost people, he said, "probably not"! I truly enjoyed that honesty. I think that often we pray for the lost when we are impressed with just how unhappy they are apart from Christ. Beyond that, I would suspect many of us don't think much about the lost in terms of their eternal salvation or damnation.

contradictions in our heads. Well, it creates contradictions if we continue to think about the issues. Usually, as far as I can tell, people just stop asking questions and thinking about these contradictions at all. If we do continue to think about such things, we often are forced to come to grips with errors we've embraced in our belief system. Let's look at a few of the conflicting ideas that people hold concerning their fundamental beliefs about prayer for the salvation of the lost and the contradictions that they spawn.

One such contradiction relates to the underlying ideas we hold about whether or not prayer is a necessary vehicle of salvation in the first place.

This is a problem that very few of us really think out because it strikes at so many fundamental facets of the whole salvation process. First, the most basic question is, if people are saved by means of the intercessory prayer of others, does that make prayer a requirement for salvation? We can ask this another way: What if no one prays for you—can you still come to faith in Jesus? If prayer for a lost person *is* a necessary element of their salvation, then we are truly in deep trouble when we even partially become lax about praying for the salvation of the lost. For if my prayer is the avenue through which that person is saved, and I don't pray for them, then what will happen? We probably answer: "Someone else will pray for him or her." But how do we know that? What if *no one* prays for the salvation of that person? Are they barred from heaven just because God's people have been faithless in their prayers? I suppose we could argue that God will not let us be faithless like that, but the fact is, we are sure faithless in a lot of other areas. And God is not making us stop being faithless in those areas. Why would he intervene in that one area of prayer for the salvation of the lost alone? Moreover, isn't saying that God will not let us be faithless in that manner really saying God is overriding our own will for his purposes and *making* us pray for the salvation of the lost? That doesn't seem right when we posit such a thing concerning our own belief in Jesus; we don't think God overrides our will and makes us have faith in Jesus. Moreover, we don't really believe God *makes* us carry out Christian good works in any fashion. We believe we do them of our own free, Christian choice. So, in the end, God will not stop us from being faithless in our prayers. He will not make us pray for the salvation of the lost. And because that is the case, theoretically, a person could have no one praying for their salvation. But we don't think for that reason they are barred from salvation.

Let me bring in a similar argument that is sometimes suggested. We might argue that there is a similar problem with saying a person must *hear the gospel* message before they can be saved.[97] But in truth, this is not quite the same situation. In terms of the Gospel message itself, there can be no faith in Jesus if one does not know about Jesus. [98] You cannot have faith in something you don't know exists. We can easily imagine that a person can find out about Jesus, and therefore develop faith in him, without having someone pray for them. On the other hand, it is hard to imagine a person having faith in Jesus if that person has never been introduced to him or the gospel. Even in praying for the salvation of the lost, people pray that the lost will somehow see and understand the message of the Gospel of Jesus. In truth, a person can hear the gospel message without you ever praying for them. Many missionaries I've spoken with have reported how God at times will even draw people to the Gospel of Jesus by means of dreams and visions. But even by those modes, we have the gospel being presented to the unbeliever. Prayer just isn't a required vehicle that is necessary for them to hear the Gospel.

So, for example, one missionary was telling me how people would occasionally walk into her medical center from distant, completely unchurched areas to hear about this *Jesus* they kept dreaming about. These are people no one is praying for, unless we count the abstract prayers of believers who pray for "the lost" with no specific person in mind. Still, what if absolutely no Christian prayed for the lost of the world in any way? Are we saying that no one would then be saved (beyond those faithless, prayer-less Christians who are not doing their jobs)? I don't think most of us would want to accept that. So we are forced to admit that prayer is not a necessary part of someone's salvation process. People can be saved even when no one prays for that salvation because whether

---

97. This could actually be taken down to the foundational question of whether we should pray for *anything* at all since God knows what is going to happen and has ordained it. That's reducing it to non-functionality though. Clearly Jesus *prayed* for things. Clearly He asked things of God. I'm not arguing that we shouldn't ask things of God. I'm just interested in finding out *what exactly* we are asking for and determining whether all the things we request are really profitable for us to be addressing.

98. The Gospel of Jesus is often noted as the means by which we come to eternal life. Look, for example, at John 20:31; Acts 16:31; Rom 3:21–22; 10:8–9; and 1 John 3:23. Acts 4:12 especially notes that there is salvation in no other name. We must have faith in Jesus. The church has understood this from the time of the great commission onward. And in response the Word of truth has gone out into the world that it might be saved through the Word.

we are faithful in prayer or faithless, it is God alone who saves by his own power and decree.

Furthermore, if we say prayer *is* a required element for one to be saved, doesn't this also place us in the driver's seat when it comes to salvation? If my prayer is a required element for a person to be saved, then theoretically I control their salvation to some extent. God forbid I'm an awful Christian and choose not to pray for a particularly evil individual—like Hugo Chavez, Kim Jong Il, or the nasty neighbor down the block. The bottom line is this: Do we want to believe that God will not save someone because we (or someone else) have never prayed for them?

I wonder if anyone was praying for the salvation of the Apostle Paul prior to his experience on the Damascus road. The story of Paul's salvation experience is interesting and may shed some light on this topic. Here is the account:

> [10] Now there was a disciple at Damascus named Ananias; and the Lord said to him in a vision, "Ananias." And he said, "Here I am, Lord." [11] And the Lord *said* to him, "Get up and go to the street called Straight, and inquire at the house of Judas for a man from Tarsus named Saul, for he is praying, [12] and he has seen in a vision a man named Ananias come in and lay his hands on him, so that he might regain his sight." [13] But Ananias answered, "Lord, I have heard from many about this man, how much harm he did to Your saints at Jerusalem; [14] and here he has authority from the chief priests to bind all who call on Your name." [15] But the Lord said to him, "Go, for he is a chosen instrument of Mine, to bear My name before the Gentiles and kings and the sons of Israel; [16] for I will show him how much he must suffer for My name's sake." [17] So Ananias departed and entered the house, and after laying his hands on him said, "Brother Saul, the Lord Jesus, who appeared to you on the road by which you were coming, has sent me so that you may regain your sight and be filled with the Holy Spirit."[99]

When the Lord tells Ananias in a dream that he is to go to Paul and lay hands on him so that he can regain his sight, Ananias has some reservations. Remember at that time, as far as Ananias knew, Paul (Saul) was a zealous anti-Christian rabbi. Instead of jumping to the task, Ananias says he's heard about this Saul and he respectfully informs the Lord that Saul had injured believers previously, and was out to arrest and kill even

---

99. Acts 9:10–17.

more Christians at this very moment! In point of fact then, it looks like Ananias would prefer Saul stay blind and away from the whole Gospel enterprise, doesn't it? It also doesn't sound like Ananias had Paul in his prayers—at least not in terms of salvation. When he is directly told by the Lord Himself to go help Saul out, Ananias even bucks at that directive. If he is unwilling when told directly by his God to go heal Saul, does it make sense to say that he was praying for Saul's salvation? It seems clear that he was *not* excited about helping Saul on the road to becoming a Christian. Yet Saul was drawn directly by the Lord Himself, and with or without Ananias' help, Saul was going to embrace Christ. I am convinced that if Ananias had not given in to God's commands—if he had acted faithlessly—God would have found someone else for the job, or he would have done it himself.

All in all, it doesn't really make sense that prayer would be a required element for a person's salvation. God saves people even when no one is praying for them because he calls them to Himself, regardless of our activities; he calls them by his own sovereign choice. Of course this is not to say prayer *cannot* be a part of someone's salvation process; it is just saying that it doesn't *have to* be a part of the process. So, if prayer for the salvation of the lost does not *have to* be a part of the overall salvation process, then at least we can admit that when a person is lost it is not due to our lack of prayer for his or her salvation. That should be somewhat freeing to our minds, I would think. We can rest in the fact that God will save his elect. And though we may ask for him to save someone, we don't need to resort to nagging him about the issue because we understand that even if we never prayed for the salvation of that lost one, God would not for that reason bar him or her from heaven.

Let me be clear that I'm not suggesting a cavalier attitude about the salvation of the lost by suggesting this. Because prayer for their salvation may not be necessary does not mean that we should not ever pray for their salvation at all or that we should just leave the whole thing to God. It just means that we should not see it as the necessary determiner of whether a person is saved. And, more importantly to this discussion, it should tell us that if we stop praying for someone's salvation we are not "bad" Christians who do not want that person saved. It more likely means that we have tuned in to more important and immediate prayers that could be offered on behalf of someone at any particular moment in their lives.

Another contradiction in our thinking arises when we consider what we expect God to do when we pray for the salvation of the lost.

There are two broad approaches to salvation that must be addressed here. Suppose you come from that sector of Christendom that believes all people (unbeliever and believer) have free will and can choose to believe in or deny the gospel message by their own power. Usually these believers also believe in some sort of grace on God's part extended to all humanity that has raised all of us to this position of freedom from the total depravity we suffered at the fall of man.[100] One of the foundational truths of this system of theology is that mankind now has the ability and right to choose to believe the gospel message. On the other hand, mankind also has the ability and right to reject the gospel message as well. God has gracefully given to us all the *freedom* to believe or disbelieve as we see fit. Hence we, as believers, go out into the world sharing the gospel with everyone, desiring all will believe, and knowing that if they do not, they had a chance to do so and have rejected the truth freely. They were just not convinced for some reason.[101]

Such believers, who adhere to this freewill system, pray for the salvation of the lost. I know this anecdotally because I've asked many such believers. But there is a problem here depending on what they pray for. If they pray that God move in the heart of the lost person, isn't that stacking the deck? Why should God work in that person's heart, essentially giving them the edge in hearing and believing the gospel over anyone else? And if we believe that God *does* work in the heart of unbelievers that way, doesn't that say we really don't think they can choose on their own without some extra help from God? It looks as though we are actually becoming the agent that *takes away* their free will when we call God in to somehow change them enough that they can now understand, appreciate, and believe the gospel. Such a thing just can't happen in a

---

100. This grace is called *prevenient grace*. It is freely given to all people by God in order to restore to them the ability to choose the gospel message when they hear it. It is a measure of redemption in a way. Were it not offered we would all be "dead" in sin and incapable of hearing the gospel of salvation (Eph 2:1–3). A good discussion of prevenient grace can be found in Wiley, *Christian Theology*, vol. 2, 344–57.

101. I must stop here and point out the subtle arrogance I sense in this position. I simply do not see how we can convince ourselves that we are somehow so insightful that we can choose eternal paradise, and yet others are just too spiritually stupid that they would reject it. The fact is, if people really understand the Gospel message, they would choose it. Who would not choose life over death? But that is the very problem; they do not—*cannot*—understand the message of the Gospel on their own.

freewill system. Prayer cannot work that way because it defeats the point of the freewill approach by putting, at the very least, the initial impetus to believe on God rather than on our gracefully elevated free wills. It means God is choosing to work in one person's life over another's. But that is one of the foundational truths of this *freewill* system—God does *not* sovereignly choose one over another for his blessed work. We *all* have the same grace-enabled free will to choose or reject the gospel as we desire.[102]

Furthermore, it doesn't matter what you pray for—that God open their hearts or brains or eyes; that God reveal himself to them; or that God arrange the world in such a way that they would be persuaded. If God does *anything* to help the process, he's violating their free will to choose, or given them an unfair advantage over everyone else. That's not "fair" (to quote such believers).

Suppose on the other hand you come from that sector of Christendom that believes God is completely sovereign and he alone chooses who is *elect* and believes the gospel.[103] These types of believers pray for the salvation of the lost as well. And again, depending on the prayer, it can be a troublesome idea. In this case, such a Christian believes God elects the believer *before the foundation of the world* based solely on God's loving choice.[104] Some even believe God begins the regenera-

---

102. This opens a whole can of worms concerning our real abilities to grasp the gospel in light of our seemingly God–given natural make up as well. I'm assuming for this argument that everyone can, having received some sort of grace from God, choose or reject the gospel. But the truth is many are severely hindered compared to others in that ability. A person with a 50 IQ for instance is not going to grasp the complete gospel as readily as the person with a "normal" IQ. Someone born with a severe mental disability may not be able to grasp the gospel at all. To handle this new set of problems some resort to the idea that God will not condemn anyone who is not "normal" enough to grasp the gospel. Yet God was the one who made them "normal" or "disabled" in the first place. So it looks like, in some respect, he's already stacked the deck in favor of the mentally disabled person—for they get to be saved without even understanding the gospel! And that again goes against the system of free will for all with no interference from God.

103. Just so the reader understands, I am this latter type of believer going to a church that believes the former; a Calvinist among Arminians. My pastor and I are saddened when we discuss it because many in our respective camps can't seem to express the unity of the body across those lines. I see it as a question of presuppositions and broken theology, but not necessarily a determiner of salvation.

104. Eph 1:4. I say this because some suggest that God chooses the elect based on His foreknowledge. He looks into the future and sees the elect person choosing to believe in Christ's sacrifice. Then God (prior to the foundation of the world, but based on

tive process at conception, preparing the person for their acceptance of the gospel. This is the most difficult position to reconcile with prayer because in that case the person is already on the road to salvation and our prayer for their salvation appears redundant. If we believe that the person is chosen by God to be saved or passed over *from the foundation of the world*, what do we expect our prayer will do for the lost person? We would have to believe that our prayer somehow altered God's sovereign choice (prior to the foundation of the world) to overlook that particular lost person. God would then somehow add them into the community of the elect. That sort of defeats the whole idea of God's sovereign election at the decree doesn't it? Do we expect God to go against what he has already determined? It makes God look like an idiot, doesn't it? And if they are *elect*, then our prayers are not altering their end in any real sense anyway.

Maybe we are suggesting God has predestined that person's salvation *and* decreed our prayers to be a part of its process. This just drives us back to the position of asking how my prayer is then required and what happens if I don't pray for that person? Will they still be saved? Or is my prayer required and I have no choice but to offer it? I would feel a bit like a robot in that circumstance.

To be fair, some of these sovereignty-focused believers think there is no regenerative work by God until the *elect person* is effectually called, and after that calling occurs they then accept the Gospel. In this latter case there are still problems however. For example, we do not know who is *elect* and who is non-elect, and we do not know when the effectual calling of God occurs. So, what if a believer spends their whole life praying for their one family member who is *not* elect? What a waste of time that would be. So how could we concretely know if a person was one of the elect or not? I suppose we could listen to God's answer to our prayers—if God saves them we could assume they were of the elect and if he does not we could assume that they are non-elect—at least as far as our prayers are concerned. But such an approach would assume we were listening to God's answers and taking them seriously within the theological system we profess.

---

knowledge of its future) declares that person elect to salvation. In contrast, this second type of believer thinks God elects from all of lost humanity based entirely on His choice. There is nothing we do or possess which influences the choice whatsoever.

Some might argue that this is just the *process* of God's election being worked out. We pray (sometimes without outward effect) and by those prayers we bring to fruition the redemption God had already intended for that lost (but elect) person. But, again, doesn't that just place us back in the position of asking: "What if we didn't pray for their salvation at all?"

Of course the problem here for both types of believer (freewill focused or sovereignty focused) is that it looks like we just do not really need to pray for the salvation of the lost in order for them to be saved. I have suggested this very thing to people now and again. Try that for fun at parties! Suggest to God-fearing, people-loving, faithful Christians that they don't really need to be praying for the salvation of the lost on a repetitive basis. You'll enjoy the scowls you receive as they edge away from you in expectation of the imminent lightning bolt from heaven. But the problem remains whether we like it or not: God cannot intervene in one system and has already elected or passed over in the other. So why are we praying for God to act in either case? The truth is, the salvation of people is in God's hands and we need to learn to trust his judgment.

A final contradiction arises when we think about the actual answer God frequently gives us when we pray for the salvation of the lost: "No."

Unless you are that special person who prays for someone's salvation and it immediately happens, you are in the boat with all the rest of us who have prayed over and over, perhaps for years, for someone's salvation without the result of them actually being saved. (And yes, I've been there in the past as well. That is partially why I have spent so much time thinking about this.) Frankly, I've never met that special type of person—that person who can pray for the salvation of the lost and it immediately happens (i.e., God says "yes.") If anyone reading this book has this ongoing experience I would love to get an email from you. Of course I would be skeptical about your claims, for in my entire life I've never seen such a person, and have never talked to anyone who has. Moreover, I don't see that ability existing even in Jesus. Remember, he even had one of the twelve Apostles turn on him. If anyone could have prayed for someone's salvation and had it happen every single time I would expect Jesus would be that person. But I don't see that recorded anywhere in scripture, and Judas' betrayal is proof positive that Jesus' prayers for the salvation of the lost were not always effective—unless we want to believe that Jesus never prayed for Judas' salvation. Furthermore, when Jesus sends his disciples out, he gives them orders on what to do when people reject their message. Why do that unless you realize that that is going to happen on a consistent basis?[105]

What does it say about God if he does not say "yes" to us when we pray for someone's salvation? Does God *not* want to save that person? This leads to the problem of why we would continue to pray for that person. If God has said "no," what can we posit about why he has done so?

Perhaps we think God has said "no," but he is using those many "no" answers to build *us* up in some way. This answer really just creates other questions and problems. If this is the case, that God is saying no just to work on *us*, then are we saying God actually *denies salvation* to people for a time just to work on us? (And sometimes not just for a time, but for eternity, for some believers pray for others their whole lives and never actually see them accept salvation from God.) If God is doing this, what is it he is trying to accomplish with us? I might hazard the guess that he is developing in us a deep frustration with God. For that is often what people feel when they have been praying repeatedly for the salvation of someone they love and nothing has happened. Perhaps he's teaching us to just ignore what he says and pray for what we think he really wants. I know I'm being sarcastic now, but frankly, the answers I hear from people make little sense. On a more serious note, and in line with this book's position, let me suggest that God is teaching us to accept a "no" answer and to stop asking. Unfortunately, that suggestion doesn't seem to satisfy people.

Perhaps we think God says, "No," but in reality he means, "Not yet." I'm going to address this type of mitigation later in the book, but for now let me point out that that sort of thinking would sure make it hard to know when "no" actually means "no" and when it does not. Can you imagine what it would look like if we implemented that reasoning when raising our own children? I tell my little boy, "No," but really expect him to infer I mean, "Not yet," which in turn should encourage him to badger me with the same request for a few more years—maybe for his whole life. I doubt anyone would think that that is a good approach to utilize in child rearing. If the truth be told, wouldn't implementing a "'no' means 'maybe'" approach just place us in the same old position of having no real idea of what God will answer us with and what he means by the answer we do receive?

105. Luke 10:10–11.

Again, it makes sense to approach this problem from the point of view on prayer that we've developed so far. We should ask, what does it honestly reveal to us that we have to pray for something over and over and over while God keeps saying "No"? Is that *effective* prayer? Is that a prayer that we can say accomplishes much? Are we really listening to God when we keep asking for something that he is not granting? I hate to beat a dead horse, but why not slip in the request for the Chevelle along with the salvation of the lost? Both prayers keep getting a "no" answer, but that should not deter us, right? Perhaps the fact that both requests do get "no" answers actually tells us something. The simplest answer is that we ought to listen to God when he says, "No," and take him at his word. God is not going to give us a Chevelle just because we ask for it a hundred times (or for fifty years) instead of once. If he does not want us to have one, we can ask until we finally lay down in the dust from which we came, and we will not have gotten one. In like fashion, if a person is not to be saved, we can ask for a hundred years and he or she will not be saved. The real question that should be asked is: *Do you trust God to make the right decisions about salvation?*

Okay, enough of these contradictions. Let's get to the foundational question with a look at scripture. I started wondering one day about a most basic question that popped into my head on this subject: Where in the Bible does it actually say we are to repetitively pray for the salvation of the lost? I know it seems like a no-brainer. I can imagine people rolling their eyes at my ignorance, but still the question remained for me. To be frank, I don't see a lot of clear texts that tell us to pray for the salvation of the lost. I have asked many people where they find support for this practice of theirs and have yet to find someone answer back on the spot with a clear verse. In fact, I find much clearer texts admonishing people *not to pray* for others in some instances. Let's turn now to some Bible texts to see if there are some answers for us. I'm going to break these down into different sections of types of scriptures for organizational purposes.

Scriptures that Don't Mention Prayer for the Salvation of the Lost

Let me begin by looking at a few passages that neither support nor deny prayer for the salvation of the lost. Surprisingly, they don't say anything about prayer for the salvation of the lost when you would expect they might.

Moses Going to Egypt (Exodus 3)—Israel spent 430 years in Egypt. You would think that God would instruct them to pray for the salvation of the lost among Israel when they had been in slavery for such a long time. After all, they must have drifted from God a good bit, for Moses even asks God what to do if the people ask what God's name is. They might not even know exactly who Moses represents. Though it could be feasible this question might be a test the Israelites give to Moses. Still, the following story of Israel's time in the desert after their redemption from Egypt pictures them as not really knowing their God very well at all. Additionally, we are told in Exodus 12:38 that a *mixed multitude* went up with Israel when they left Egypt. These others were, in all probability, non-Hebrews who were drawn to follow God along with the chosen people of Israel. They were probably Egyptian and of the other nationalities living within Egypt at the time. It is striking that God does not suggest any prayer for all these people in his directions to Moses. Some might assume that Moses prayed for the work and the salvation of these lost ones. But still, when push comes to shove, scripture simply does not record God advising prayer for the salvation of the lost of Egypt.

Israel and the Promised Land (Joshua 11)—You would think that God would want Israel to pray over those about to die in the Promised Land. After all, God is sending Israel to judge and destroy the lost living in Canaan. It would seem to make sense that he would prefer the people of the land give up and turn to him rather than be destroyed. Yet God tells Israel to destroy all—men, women, children, and livestock. They are told to burn down all the alters and uproot the ways of these nations because they acted abominably and deserved nothing but judgment. In Joshua we are told that "Joshua waged war a long time with all these kings. There was not a city which made peace with the sons of Israel except the Hivites living in Gibeon; they took them all in battle. For *it was of the LORD to harden their hearts* [emphasis added], to meet Israel in battle in order that he might utterly destroy them, that they might receive no mercy, but that he might destroy them, just as the LORD had commanded Moses."[106] There is never a hint of prayer for these cities. Had Joshua prayed that God spare these people—that he save them—it would seem to fly in the face of the fact that God actually *hardened* them to fight so he could dole out the judgment they were due.

106. Josh 11:18–20.

The Lord's Prayer (Matthew 6:9-13; Luke 11:2-4)—Interestingly enough, Jesus doesn't include any mention of praying for the salvation of the lost in the Lord's Prayer. The very fact that Jesus taught his disciples a pattern for prayer that left out any mention of praying for the salvation of the lost seems important to me—especially in light of the fact that he knew he was going to send the disciples out to evangelize the world. It could not possibly be the case that he would leave that out if it was a necessary element in the salvation process and their work as his Apostles.

The Great Commission (Matthew 28:19-20)—The Great Commission is the mission statement of the church: Going therefore, make disciples of all the nations, baptizing them in the name of the Father and the Son and the Holy Spirit, teaching them to keep all that I have commanded you. Here the Greek text is very clear; there is one main directive: *make disciples*. There are three accompanying participles that modify this main directive: *going*—we go to the lost; *baptizing*—we baptize them into the body and Christ; *teaching*—we teach them to follow Jesus. These three things make people into disciples of Jesus. But one would think that when Jesus sent his disciples out into the world that he would have mentioned prayer for the salvation of the people they were trying to reach. Especially if prayer is supposed to be the power that it is for the salvation of the lost. But here again, there is no mention of prayer whatsoever.

The Church as Light to the World (Matthew 5:16)—When Jesus was describing a believer in the Sermon on the Mount (Matthew chapters 5-7), he calls them "lights" of the world. He says nobody lights a light and then hides it away so that it cannot shine and be seen. Consequently, he admonishes the believer to let their light shine before men in such a way that they can see his or her good works and be inspired to glorify God in heaven. Here again, it is interesting that our *works* are the impetus to the unbeliever coming to God. And oddly enough, once again, Jesus leaves out any mention of prayer over those lost ones in the dark. He just says our works will speak about the greatness of God and will draw them in.

Let me run down a rabbit trail here because this last thought raises a serious question. We are told by Jesus to let our lights shine before men so that they can recognize God working and give him glory. Letting our lights "shine before men" is a metaphor for acting out our Christian lives in an open and transparent way so that people can look at us and see that we are followers of Christ. I am afraid to say that there are those of us who seem to think that when they pray their private prayers for the salvation of the lost are letting their light shine—even though the lost never even know they are being prayed for! The very concept of prayer for the salvation of the lost as some means of shining your light before men is ludicrous, for unless we stand in front of them and pray audibly while they hear us, they will see nothing of God in our lives. To be blunt, some use prayer as a replacement for openly *living out* their Christianity before unbelievers. In describing the godly as lights of the world, Jesus is talking about setting our lives out in the open for people to see, as a light is set out and shines on everything that comes near it. Prayer at times seems to be used to dodge this! People think that since they pray for the salvation of the lost they then never need to *say* anything about their Christian worldview, faith, or hope in Jesus.[107] When you think about this, you see that it is nothing more than actively *thwarting* the very thing we are praying for—that the lost might come to Jesus.

Let me make one more point on this topic. Sometimes people will say that they are relying solely on prayer because they have tried previously to share the Gospel with a lost person and been rebuffed. But if they have been rebuffed, what is it prayer is supposed to do? As we have previously noted, prayer is not some sort of magical force that overrides the person's free will and makes them amenable to salvation. I would counter that if you are rebuffed in your presentation of the Gospel, then let your life works shine and be content to move your salvation attention to someone more receptive; God can take care of the first person.

Peter and Simon (Acts 8:20-25)—Acts chapter 8 records an interesting exchange between the Apostle Peter and a former magician but present believer, Simon. At that formative time in the church's history, the Holy Spirit did not necessarily come upon everyone who was baptized in Jesus' name instantaneously. In some instances the Apostles had to lay their hands on people for this to occur in order to reinforce the importance of the Apostles and their message about the true church.

Simon had been going about with the evangelist Philip and the two had ended up in Samaria. Many of the Samaritans had believed in Jesus, but had not as of yet received the Holy Spirit. When the Church

---

107. Peter makes the point of saying we need to always be "ready to make a defense to everyone who asks you to give an account for the hope that is in you, yet with gentleness and reverence" (1 Pet 3:15).

in Jerusalem had heard that God had so blessed the Samaritans, Peter and John were specifically sent to Samaria to lay hands on them and impart the Holy Spirit. In this way the notoriously divisive Samaritans were linked to the founding Church in Jerusalem and the teaching of the Apostles.

As this was going on, Simon had seen the Apostles doing some amazing miracles, even imparting the Holy Spirit by the laying on of hands; and he wanted to have the same abilities. To that end, he offered to purchase the skill from the Apostles. The text then tells of this exchange:

> [20] But Peter said to him, "May your silver perish with you, because you thought you could obtain the gift of God with money! [21] "You have no part or portion in this matter, for your heart is not right before God. [22] "Therefore repent of this wickedness of yours, and pray the Lord that, if possible, the intention of your heart may be forgiven you.[23] "For I see that you are in the gall of bitterness and in the bondage of iniquity." [24] But Simon answered and said, "Pray to the Lord for me yourselves, so that nothing of what you have said may come upon me."[108]

It is interesting that there is no record of Peter actually *praying* for Simon. Peter and John "solemnly testified" about Jesus, but they offered no prayer on Simon's behalf (at least none is recorded). This is another example of where you would expect, at least, to hear Peter pray for Simon, especially since Peter notes that Simon, though he professed belief in Jesus, was actually in the "bondage of iniquity." Still, Peter gave no prayer for the forgiveness of Simon, for his salvation, or for his growth, if he was indeed a Christian.

Let's look at one more example of a place where we might expect prayer for the salvation of the lost but we find none.

Jesus Lamenting the Lost (Matt. 9:35—10:42)—This passage is especially interesting because it begins with a specific directive to pray to God in connection with the lost. The text reads:

> [35] Jesus was going through all the cities and villages, teaching in their synagogues and proclaiming the gospel of the kingdom, and healing every kind of disease and every kind of sickness. [36] Seeing the people, he felt compassion for them, because they

---

108. Acts 8:20–24.

were distressed and dispirited like sheep without a shepherd. ³⁷ Then he said to his disciples, "The harvest is plentiful, but the workers are few. ³⁸ "Therefore beseech the Lord of the harvest to send out workers into his harvest."[109]

Jesus had firsthand experience with the overwhelming job of declaring the kingdom of God to the people. Because he was in the trenches daily, ministering the Word, he saw clearly the need for more workers. In light of this fact, he says to his disciples, "The harvest is plentiful but the workers are few."[110] Now, a number of things could have succeeded that statement. He could have stopped speaking entirely, and we could have understood him to be lamenting an unfortunate fact of ministry: There are often more needs than there are workers to meet them. If the presupposition that we must pray for the salvation of the lost is true, one would expect Jesus to go on to say something like, "Pray for the lost that they hear and respond to the truth of the kingdom." Instead, he directs his listeners to ask God to send out more workers. And that's it. He doesn't add a note to pray over the lost even as an afterthought to asking for more workers to tell them about the kingdom of God.

This little passage, Matthew 9:35–38, acts as a lead in to chapter 10. In Matthew 10 we find the record of Jesus sending out the twelve disciples to do ministry. Notice that Matthew clearly arranged his gospel so that the sending out of the Apostles followed the directive to pray for more workers. Matthew was making a point that some of those workers were the twelve Apostles themselves. What is of interest to us is the directions Jesus gives to them for their work, or more precisely, the lack of one specific directive. He does *not* tell them to pray for the salvation of those they are going to evangelize. So, Jesus initially says the concern of prayer for the lost is that there be enough workers to carry the gospel message, and then, when he sends the disciples out, he tells them to "preach, saying 'the kingdom of Heaven is at hand.'"[111] He also tells them to heal diseases, raise the dead, cleanse the lepers, and cast out demons. He seems to tell them everything *except to pray for the salvation of the lost*. Astounding! How can that be? Yet here it is, in one of the most important pictures of what the disciples did when they were first sent out

109. Matt 9:35–38.
110. Matt 9:37.
111. Matt 10:7.

to share the gospel, Jesus doesn't include any instructions to pray for the salvation of the lost.

So, in summary, in a number of passages (and there are many more like these), where we expect to find prayer for the salvation of the lost, we find no mention of it.[112] Arguing from silence is not the optimum way to support an idea, but this lack of prayer and instructions to pray for the salvation of the lost is intriguing, isn't it?

Let's move on now and look at some rare passages where God tells people specifically *not* to pray for those who are lost or straying from God.

*Scriptures that Tell People **not** to Pray for the Salvation of the Lost*

The book of Jeremiah is one of the sadder books of the Bible. Jeremiah had the unfortunate job of ministering to the sinful tribe of Judah during their demise as a nation. They were ultimately conquered and carried off to bondage in Babylon in 586 BC. Jeremiah was given the unenviable job of telling them about their sin and the need to turn to God. (I say unenviable because we all know how popular a person is when they point out people's sins. Poor Jeremiah was not one of the respected prophets because he had one of the more trying messages to share from the Lord.) It is an unfortunate truth that often even the people of God are beyond prayer in the evil that they do. Judah had apparently reached this point.

Jeremiah chapter 7 opens with the prophet being told to go stand by the Lord's temple and speak to "all you of Judah, who enter by these gates to worship the LORD!"[113] I.e., he is being told to speak to God's children who have abandoned God but still continue on in their stale religious practices. Isn't it interesting that people can continue in the habit of religious practices and yet be far from God spiritually? The prophet was to tell the people that if they amend their ways and trust in the Lord, God would establish them in the land which he promised to Abraham

---

112. Another astounding example is Peter's prayer in Acts 4:24–30. Peter and John had been released from jail after being grilled by the Jewish authorities over their preaching of Jesus and the resurrection from the dead. Peter didn't pray for the salvation of those aligned against them, but rather prayed that God would grant to them the skill and courage to speak the gospel with boldness while God does His part with signs and wonders and what not. Basically, the picture is of Peter and John asking to share the gospel well and that God reveal Himself. There is no mention of expectation that people be moved to be saved.

113. Jer 7:2.

and his posterity. But the problem was that they were trusting in everything *but* God. They were acting wickedly and assuming God would just turn a blind eye and forgive them without any repercussions. God even told them to take a hint from their own history of their dealings with God. They should look at the town of Shiloh where God had previously set his name.[114] Shiloh was now gone, having been destroyed when the Assyrians demolished the northern kingdom of Israel. God's point was that he was not going to keep a worship site safe and prosperous just because he had placed his name there at one time. He was willing to let it be destroyed if it was abused and neglected and misused. He was promising to Judah that the temple in Jerusalem would end up the same way if the people persisted in their sin; his "anger and wrath" would be poured out on this place.[115] At this point, it seems Judah had crossed the line and would, without doubt, need corrective punishment for their sin.

Within this declaration of judgment Jeremiah relays an interesting message from God. He says:

> [13] "And now, because you have done all these things," declares the LORD, "and I spoke to you, rising up early and speaking, but you did not hear, and I called you but you did not answer, [14] therefore, I will do to the house which is called by My name, in which you trust, and to the place which I gave you and your fathers, as I did to Shiloh. [15] "I will cast you out of My sight, as I have cast out all your brothers, all the offspring of Ephraim. [16] "As for you, *do not pray for this people* [emphasis added], and do not lift up cry or prayer for them, and do not intercede with Me; for I do not hear you. [17] "Do you not see what they are doing in the cities of Judah and in the streets of Jerusalem?[116]

Isn't that amazing? God actually tells Jeremiah *not to pray* for straying Judah. Even more startling is the statement: "I do not hear you." Let me be clear about something here. I am not suggesting in any way that God is painted in a bad light in this passage. On the contrary, I'm amazed at how patient God was with his rebellious people and how far he let them wander before he dropped the hammer of correction. What strikes me about this passage is how it shatters so many old "truths" about prayer. Foremost for our discussion is the directive to *not pray* for the evil people

---

114. Jer 7:12.
115. Jer 7:20.
116. Jer 7:13–17.

of Judah. Undoubtedly Jeremiah had done, or desired to do, just that. It is hard to imagine a prophet of God *not praying* for the people he is ministering to. But God specifically tells him, "Do not pray" for them anymore. And to top it off, God says he will not listen to the prayer anyway! That is a very interesting thing as well, isn't it? God says if Jeremiah did pray for Judah, he was not going to listen to it. What would be the point of praying for them in that case? Why spend time praying for something when God is not going to grant your request? Of course we might ask, "How do you tell if he will grant my request?" For Jeremiah the answer was obvious: Listen to God's instructions and stop praying for them.

So how might we tell if God will answer our requests positively? Do we need to be audibly told whether God will grant it or not? That would be quite a drastic alteration of the system God has set up. We don't usually get directly communiqués from God on a daily basis concerning what to put into our prayers. I would again suggest we can tell if he desires to grant our request by the simple fact of whether he grants it or not. If he does not, perhaps we should accept that he is not willing to hear that prayer and move to another more in line with his desires.

I'm not suggesting we pull this passage out of context and use it to teach that we ought to not pray for anyone when they are broken and walking in sin. I'm just noting the fact that at least on some occasions there is a time to *not pray*. It is not so farfetched that we at least ask the question about whether we ought to pray for someone in the body who is straying or for someone outside the body who is lost.

And lest anyone think this is a onetime occurrence, this same directive is given to Jeremiah at least twice more:

- *Jeremiah 14:11-12.* "So the LORD said to me, "*Do not pray for the welfare of this people* [emphasis added]. When they fast, I am not going to listen to their cry; and when they offer burnt offering and grain offering, I am not going to accept them. Rather I am going to make an end of them by the sword, famine, and pestilence."

- *Jeremiah 11:14.* "Therefore *do not pray for this people* [emphasis added], nor lift up a cry or prayer for them; for I will not listen when they call to Me because of their disaster."

Notice that God also says he's not even going to listen to *them* when *they themselves* cry out. In the book of Lamentations (Jeremiah's expression of anguish over the destruction of Judah and Jerusalem) the prophet says of God, "You have covered Yourself with a cloud, So that no prayer can pass through."[117] There are times, apparently, when God will say "no" to the most urgent and insistent requests—such as a call for rescue from destruction. And here we see him making the point quite directly; he will *not* help out when his people call on this occasion because they deserve the discipline coming their way. And one thing we know about God is that he will *not* be partial in his judgment. Judah *would receive punishment* even though she was God's chosen nation.[118]

Now, one last item before we look at some verses that directly tell us to pray for others. Let me point out an interesting passage from 2 Chronicles that depicts prayer and also talks about the prayers of others. King Solomon was tasked with building the temple of the Lord in Jerusalem. It was an eleven year project that finally concluded in 959 BC, and upon completion, Solomon gave a long dedication prayer to inaugurate the new building. Included in this prayer is a request on behalf of the foreigners who live around Israel:

> [32] "Also concerning the foreigner who is not from Your people Israel, when he comes from a far country for Your great name's sake and Your mighty hand and Your outstretched arm, when they come and pray toward this house, [33] then hear from heaven, from Your dwelling place, and do according to all for which the foreigner calls to You, in order that all the peoples of the earth may know Your name, and fear You as *do* Your people Israel, and that they may know that this house which I have built is called by Your name."[119]

Solomon requests that God "hear from heaven" and "do according to all for which the foreigner calls to You." The reasoning for this request is so that "all the peoples of the earth may know Your name, and fear You as do Your people Israel, and that they may know that this house which I have built is called by Your name." In other words, Solomon is

---

117. Lam 3:44.

118. Another example of God telling people not to pray for those who stray is found in Isaiah 1:15, "So when you spread out your hands in prayer, I will hide My eyes from you; Yes, even though you multiply prayers, I will not listen. Your hands are covered with blood." Here we see that the reason is that people are unrighteous, and God is not going to allow them to continue in that vein while still attempting to have a relationship with God.

119. 2 Chr 6:32–33.

not praying that foreigners be saved, but that God answer the foreigner's prayers so that when they see his power revealed, they would believe he alone is Lord of heaven and that he dwells in Israel. You might say that's the same thing, but there is a difference. Solomon seems to take for granted that some foreigners would come to God's Temple to offer prayers, but he does not pray that that would happen. Solomon does not pray that God somehow intervene and draw the foreigner to the Temple and to God. Moreover, nowhere in this prayer does Solomon pray that God open the foreigner's eyes or make his heart receptive to belief in the God of Israel. Solomon is concerned with one thing: That *if* the case arises that a person prays to God at the Temple, then God would listen to that prayer and grant it in order that the answer might provoke people to believe that he exists. This would be similar to our asking Jesus that if someone asks God for help, that God help; or that if someone believes in the Gospel that God act righteously on that faith. The difference here is that we are not asking that God *override* the desires of the person. We are merely asking that God hear their cry, if and when it comes. This is really just asking God to be and do what he, by his very nature, is and does.

Scriptures that Seem to Support Prayer for the Salvation of the Lost

Well, let's move on to the most difficult set of passages—those that seem to tell us to pray for the salvation of the lost. If such scriptures can be found, then the whole idea of not praying repetitively for the salvation of the lost is contradicted and we should resume our practice of such prayers. So let's look at a few of the passages that supposedly imply we ought to repeatedly pray for the salvation of the lost.

The first example I want to look at comes again from Jesus' famous Sermon on the Mount found in Matthew 5–7. Jesus says at one point:

> [43] "You have heard that it was said, 'YOU SHALL LOVE YOUR NEIGHBOR and hate your enemy.' [44] But I say to you, love your enemies and pray for those who persecute you, [45] so that you may be sons of your Father who is in heaven; for he causes his sun to rise on *the* evil and *the* good, and sends rain on *the* righteous and *the* unrighteous."[120]

This statement comes in a large section that is dealing with a question that would have been obvious to any first century Jew listening to Jesus'

---

120. Matt 5:43–45.

words. He had already talked about the *character* of the person of God in Matthew 5:1–12—the famous beatitudes. He noted how blessed people with certain attributes are both now and in the future. He then described the *function* of the person of God in the world: They are like salt and light. They ought to affect the tasteless and dark world around them. After hearing such ideas, the natural question for the first-century Jew was, "Ok, so what about the Law? What about the expression of God's righteousness that had functioned for Israel since Moses' time?" You see, the average Jew had channeled all his or her religious thought and action through the filter of the Mosaic Law. It had expressed the righteousness of God for Israel since Moses brought it down from Mt. Sinai and Israel had adopted it by covenant. Jesus' ideas were great and all, but how do they fit with the Mosaic Law? And, I might add, we must admit that since God is consistent, Jesus' ideas *must* fit with the Law in some way. Here are Jesus' thoughts about the Law and Prophets:

> [17] "Do not think that I came to abolish the Law or the Prophets; *I did not come to abolish but to fulfill* [emphasis added]. [18] For truly I say to you, until heaven and earth pass away, not the smallest letter or stroke shall pass from the Law until all is accomplished. [19] Whoever then annuls one of the least of these commandments, and teaches others *to do* the same, shall be called least in the kingdom of heaven; but whoever keeps and teaches *them*, he shall be called great in the kingdom of heaven. [20] For I say to you that *unless your righteousness surpasses that of the scribes and Pharisees, you will not enter the kingdom of heaven*" [emphasis added].[121]

Jesus makes two important statements in these verses. First, he says he did *not* come to abolish the Law. So the initial fears or doubts of the Jews who have righteously kept the Law for over a thousand years could be laid to rest; the Law has indeed been an acceptable expression of God's righteousness—and Jesus is not discounting it.[122] The second important

---

121. Matt 5:17–20.

122. This is an area where Christians often make an serious mistake. They think somehow the Mosaic Law is bad because it brings death but the Gospel of Faith is good because it brings life. However, Paul says in Romans 10:8 that the two are the exact same thing. Both the Law and the Gospel require faith in God's forgiveness as the avenue of salvation. For this reason it makes perfect sense that Jesus said he had come to fulfill the Law and not abolish it. In dispensational terms, the Law has merely been replaced by grace as the avenue of God's righteous work among men. But both, in their very essence are built on God's overarching grace to mankind and mankind's faithful response of belief.

point Jesus makes is that a person's righteousness must *surpass* that of the Scribes and Pharisees. Many of the latter had adopted a practice of righteousness that resembled what we saw earlier in Israel's history. They went through all the motions, but they did not give their hearts and lives over to God.[123] Jesus is informing the Jews that, yes, the Law is still in force, but their outward observance of it must be better—more honest, authentic, holy–than that of the Pharisees. It is for this reason that Jesus refers to the Pharisees as hypocrites so often.[124]

Once Jesus has laid this foundation, he begins to expound examples of what this might look like in real life. He starts each example with statements like: "You have heard it was said" or, "You have heard that the ancients were told."[125] The people had been given teaching that was supposedly authoritative and representative of God's desires. But in reality, the teachings were just hearsay or inference; they were not actually part of God's instructions to Israel. They had "heard it was said" about a lot of things, but Jesus disagrees with some of the things they have *heard*. Consequently, Jesus goes on in each example he gives to correct what has been taught by supplying his own take on the topic at hand. So, in our portion, we find that the people had heard "You shall love your neighbor and hate your enemy."[126] This statement is not just some little, random teaching produced by a rabbi in the past. It is an altered portion of an important truth found in Leviticus 19, one of the most significant chapters in the Pentateuch.

In Leviticus 19 we find a long section of the Law that deals with how the people of Israel were to treat their "neighbors."[127] In the context of the passage, God is talking about the people of God as a body of believers which has an obligation to care for the other members of the community. The Law lists all sorts of practical measures to accomplish this, such as leaving some food on your land when you harvest for the

---

123. As an example, Isaiah 1 records God's disgust with Israel's continuing outward sacrifices which were disconnected from their inner heart attitude.

124. Cf. Matt 15:7; 22:18; 23:13–15, 23–29; Mark 7:6.

125. Cf. Matt 5:21, 27, 31, 33, 38, 43.

126. Matt 5:43. Interestingly enough, this is written in the future tense, indicative mood; it is not an imperative meaning that it is not in the form of a command morphologically. It is not uncommon to use a future as an imperative however. In this case, it does stand in stark visual difference to Jesus' follow-up commands which are in the imperative mood and are clearly commands.

127. Lev 19:9–18.

needy to gather (19:9–10), not stealing from one another (19:11), and not oppressing others or treating others badly due to their frailties (19:13–14). And at the end of this portion we have the famous statement Jesus called the second greatest commandment: "You shall love your neighbor as yourself; I am the Lord" (19:18). Because God is talking about relations within the body of Israel in the context of Leviticus 19, some of the teachers through the years had assumed that such care for others did not extend outside the body of Israel. As long as you loved your own, you could freely *"hate"* your enemies (i.e., anyone not of Israel or the Covenant Community). Now, it is true that the Law does differentiate between God's Covenant People of Israel and the rest of the Gentiles, but it does not say that Israel should hate their enemies. Differences notwithstanding, Israel should care for those outside the community. For example, Exodus 23:4–5 says:

> [4] "If you meet your enemy's ox or his donkey wandering away, you shall surely return it to him. [5] If you see the donkey of one who hates you lying *helpless* under its load, you shall refrain from leaving it to him, you shall surely release *it* with him."[128]

And also in Deuteronomy 23:7 we find:

> "You shall not detest an Edomite, for he is your brother; you shall not detest an Egyptian, because you were an alien in his land."[129]

In both instances we see that Israel is told to care for people's needs and not detest them even if they are foreigners. They are to treat them with love and respect if only for social reasons. And doesn't this make sense? After all, how would society work if we never aided one another in their

---

128. Exod 23:4–5. Some might suggest that the term translated enemy here is distinct from a true enemy and implies a person one might have a disagreement with (even a violent disagreement at times). So we find King Saul calling David his "enemy," even though they were both of the people of Israel (cf. e.g., 1 Sam 19:17). However, the term is also used of the national enemies of Israel (cf. e.g., Deut 1:42).

129. Deut 23:7. I would point out that earlier in Leviticus 20:23 God had instructed Israel not to follow the ways of the nations they were going to disposes from the Land of Canaan. God says He "abhorred them" because they practiced so many revolting and evil ways. This is a different term than that used in Deuteronomy 23:7. When God says Israel should not "abhor" or "detest" foreigners, he means to say they ought not view these Gentiles as ceremonially unclean just because they are Gentiles. When He says He "abhors" the nations of Canaan, He is talking about disgust over their evil practices. Israel could rightly be disgusted and hate the practices of the nations around them without extending that to hatred and abhorrence of their very beings.

time of need? On this point, some of Israel's teachers had apparently overstepped God's instructions for Israel to love their neighbor. God didn't also intend that they should "hate" their enemies as though the two emotions were opposite and acceptable sides of a single coin. It is this implication by previous teachers that Jesus wants to correct, so he says Israel should not just love their neighbor as themselves, but they should actually "love" their enemies as well.[130] Moreover, they should *pray* for the ones that persecute them.

Now, some may wonder if the term "neighbor" limits the people we should love to a particular group, separate from some other group we would designate our "enemies." We would not be the first to wonder about that, and over in the Gospel of Luke we find that very question arising. So let's look at that idea for a moment before we proceed.

In Luke 10:25–27 we are told a particular lawyer among the Jews wanted to test Jesus concerning ethics and the path to heaven. (Lawyers always seem to have a lot of questions, don't they?) This particular lawyer asks Jesus, "What shall I do to inherit eternal life?" He wants to know what his part is in the road to salvation. How should he act to ensure that he gets to heaven? In response, Jesus does one of my favorite things: He asks the lawyer to think through his own position before Jesus gives his thoughts. As a teacher I find this to be especially useful, and my students will verify that I fill my lectures with questions. My intent is to imitate Jesus and make them think about what it is my students are saying and what implications flow from their thoughts. Counter questions force an inquirer to formulate their own ideas before receiving the answer from someone else. In chewing on their own ideas first, people also sharpen their thinking skills and get better at looking more fully at ideas before they speak. Sometimes, when students do this, they find they already know the answer to what they are asking, or, they realize their own mistakes that formed their question in the first place, and they consequently alter their question for the better. Jesus asks the lawyer two questions in response to his inquiry: "What is written in the Law? How does it read to you?" He's trying to get the lawyer to do two things: (1) remember specifically what the Law actually says about how one ought to act as a child of Israel and (2) analyze how he interprets the Law and explain what he thinks it is saying.

---

130. Matt 5:44.

Interestingly enough, the lawyer answers in a way that echoes Jesus' own teaching on the Law! By this we might assume that he knows the truth pretty well. He zeroes in on the most important thing the Law teaches about how we live and answers Jesus saying, "You shall love the Lord your God with all your heart, and with all your soul, and with all your strength, and with all your mind; and your neighbor as yourself."[131] This is reminiscent of Jesus' own words (on a different occasion) to another lawyer from the party of the Sadducees. Jesus was asked in that instance: "Teacher, what is the great commandment in the Law?" And he answered back:

> "'YOU SHALL LOVE THE LORD YOUR GOD WITH ALL YOUR HEART, AND WITH ALL YOUR SOUL, AND WITH ALL YOUR MIND.' This is the great and foremost commandment. The second is like it, 'YOU SHALL LOVE YOUR NEIGHBOR AS YOURSELF.' On these two commandments depend the whole Law and the Prophets."[132]

Our first lawyer in Luke 10:25–27 is obviously on the right track when he answers Jesus' question about *what* the Law says. Moreover, it must be the case that he intends his quotation from the Law to also encompass his answer to Jesus' second question about what he thinks the Law is saying, for he adds no distinct answer to that question. It would appear that in his mind, his quote tells you clearly what the Law is saying: People ought to love God fully and love their neighbors as they love themselves. That is what the Law says and it is, apparently, self-evident what love of neighbor would look like.

Jesus agrees with this answer saying, "You have answered correctly; Do this, and you will live."[133] So, Jesus is agreeing that one ought to love God with all you are and love others as you love yourself. If the lawyer did that, he would have eternal life. This could be, theoretically, the end of the exchange. But the lawyer, trained to wrangle over each word and phrase, had noted that the Law does not say love "others" as you love yourself, or love "men" as you love yourself. Rather, it says to love your *"neighbor"* as you love yourself—and that seems to him to be an impor-

---

131. Luke 10:27. See also Deut 6:5.
132. Matt 22:37–40.
133. Luke 10:28.

tant distinction in wording. So, for a follow-up question, he asks, "And who is my neighbor?"

We might think our lawyer is merely trying to nail down the facts, as lawyers are wont to do—every thing in its proper place and every place containing its proper thing and all that. But Luke tells us that the lawyer was asking this question not to truly learn but to "justify himself."[134] He was probably thinking of all the people he had *not* loved over the course of his life and was trying to figure out a way to excuse his un-loving behavior toward them. I think if we were in his shoes we might find ourselves doing the same thing. He may also have been one of those who had been teaching that the idea of "neighbor" does not include everyone; a real "neighbor" would only come from the Covenant people of Israel. Who knows, perhaps he even went so far as to distinguish the "good neighbor" Israelites who followed his particular brand of Sadduccean beliefs and the "enemy" Israelites who did not.

But Jesus is not willing to accept any kind of differentiation of people into those I can love and those I can hate; he is calling on Israel to love *all others*—even their *enemies*. In response to the follow-up question about who our neighbor really is, Jesus tells the familiar parable of the Good Samaritan.[135] In this parable a Priest and a Levite both ignore a fellow Jew's distress. In fact, they leave him lying injured on the side of the road after he was robbed and beaten! However, when a Samaritan passes by, he comes to the aid of the Jew and even pays for his medical help. Now remember, the Samaritans were so despised by the Jews that when Jesus met a Samaritan woman by a well one day she even noted the common belief that Jews have no dealings with Samaritans.[136] In Luke 10, Jesus asks the lawyer to judge, "Which of these three do you think proved to be a neighbor to the man who fell into the robber's hands?" And again, the lawyer answers correctly saying, "The one who showed mercy toward him." In other words, the person who really loves their neighbor even crosses social boundaries to care for them. (And don't think it wasn't noticed that the hero in Jesus' parable was a dirty Samaritan! That must have bugged every Pharisee and Sadducee standing about listening to this exchange.) Jesus agrees with the lawyer's evaluation, and tells him to

---

134. Luke 10:29.

135. Luke 10:30–37.

136. John 4:9. In this short story, just in case you didn't get it, the author John tells the reader plainly that Jews have no dealings with Samaritans.

do the same thing the Samaritan did— i.e., cross even social boundaries to care for people, including foreigners you might want to classify as "enemies." Wow! That must have gone over like the proverbial lead balloon, huh?

So, at this point you might be asking why spend this much time talking about Jesus' teaching on loving others. Our topic is praying repeatedly for the salvation of the lost, isnt' it? Well, the reason is this: Throughout this discussion there is no mention of the salvation of that other person. The question asked by the lawyer in Luke 10 was concerning what he should do to gain eternal life for *himself*, not that of the other person. And the Sermon on the Mount passage in Matthew 5 is giving a correction to the false teaching that Israel should love their neighbor but hate their enemy. It has nothing to do with the salvation of the enemy in any way. In both passages Jesus is merely talking about our *view* of others, not how we might help them acquire salvation.

Now, we have yet to note the main portion of the Matthew 5:44 text that is often quoted in support of praying for the salvation of the lost. Jesus corrects the false teaching of loving your neighbor and hating your enemy with the admonition that we ought to love our enemies and—here is the important point—that we ought to *pray* for those who persecute us. Jesus does not say that the disciples are to pray for the *salvation* of those who persecute them. He merely says they are to pray for them. But any number of different types of prayers spring to mind. And this is especially true in light of the fact that Jesus doesn't specifically say that they should pray for the salvation of the one who persecutes you. In fact, if that is what Jesus meant, it would seem important to say it, for what better way of dealing with persecution would there be than the conversion of the one persecuting them?

The very idea of praying for a persecutor is reminiscent of the story of the Apostle Paul's conversion which we looked at earlier. Here was a man who was a great persecutor of the church. As we previously said, Paul was so notorious that Ananias didn't even want to go see him after Jesus directly told him to do so![137] You would think if Jesus taught his disciples to pray for the salvation of those who persecute the church that Ananias would have been on his knees daily praying for Paul's salvation. Yet as we have seen, there is no hint of anyone praying for Paul.

---

137. Acts 9:11–14.

In fact, in Matthew 5:43–48 Jesus actually gives his reason for praying for those who persecute us. He says it is "in order that you may be sons of your father who is in heaven; for he causes his sun to rise on the evil and the good, and sends rain on the righteous and the unrighteous."[138] In other words, the prayer for the persecutor and the love of the enemy is for *our benefit*. It is a way that we become perfect as God is perfect (Matt 5:48). It is not about the salvation of the persecutors; it is about how we handle their persecution, just as Jesus handled the persecution of those who killed him. You don't find Jesus offering up prayers daily for the salvation of all those who were arguing with him, hunting him, spitting on him, and hurling abuse at him. In fact, the closest Jesus ever came to such a prayer is when he declares from the very cross itself, "forgive them father." And that is not a prayer for the salvation of the lost who were murdering him. It is a prayer for God to forgive their foolishness at the murder of the Messiah. The only way we could infer that Jesus meant that statement to acquire forgiveness leading to salvation for all those who were committing the crucifixion is to assume that every person who was involved in his death is now saved—and that seems awfully far-fetched.

All in all, it is better to take Jesus' admonition to pray for those who persecute us as, at most, a call to pray that they see the error of their ways or the good in our lives and leave off the persecution. We might even pray that they be stopped as King David prayed so often in the imprecatory psalms. In either case, it is not a call to pray for the persecutor's salvation.

Let's look at another text related to Matthew's Sermon on the Mount. In Luke 6:17–26 we find either Luke's account of the Sermon on the Mount or an account of another sermon with many of the same topics.[139] In Luke's account it seems that a major theme is found in 6:35–36: "But love your enemies, and do good, and lend, expecting nothing in return; and your reward will be great, and you will be sons of the Most High; for he Himself is kind to ungrateful and evil men. "Be merciful,

---

138. Matt 5:45.

139. It seems a little more plausible that this is a different sermon than that recorded in Matthew 5–7 since Luke prefaces it with the clear statement that Jesus had "come down" from the mountain when he preached this. It's the Sermon Off Of the Mount in this case.

just as your Father is merciful." Again the theme is being like God, not saving the lost enemy.

Actually, the entire Lukan account from 6:27–49 is about how we need to *act* toward others. It is not about how we need to pray for the salvation of those who persecute us—and in so doing stop them from persecuting us. In Luke 6:31 Jesus gives the golden rule: "And just as you want people to treat you, treat them in the same way." In 6:36 he says, "Be merciful, just as your Father is merciful." In 6:38 Jesus notes that, "by your standard of measure it will be measured to you in return." Jesus asks the probing question in 6:46, "Why do you call Me, Lord, Lord, and do not do what I say?" Nowhere in the entire account is there any indication that the salvation of the person who is doing the persecuting is in any way being addressed. The main idea is that we become more like God in our *actions*. Our prayers for those who persecute us should somehow bring us toward perfection, as God is perfect, not just be calls to eliminate the persecution (which the salvation of the persecutor would accomplish).

Let me discuss one final idea in regard to this understanding of the command "pray for those who persecute you." If praying for the salvation of the lost was intended by Jesus when he said pray for those who persecute you, then you would think we would find that being encouraged by the Apostles in their letters. But to the contrary, we find an interesting appeal from Paul in his second letter to the Thessalonians. He writes:

> [1] "Finally, brethren, pray for us that the word of the Lord will spread rapidly and be glorified, just as it did also with you; [2] and that we will be rescued from perverse and evil men; for not all have faith."[140]

Notice that in the process of spreading the gospel, Paul says pray "for us." There are two human participants in the gospel enterprise, the one who preaches and the one who receives the preaching. Paul requests prayer for the preacher, not the receiver. He is asking that his work be made more effective, not that those who hear be saved. Moreover, he even points out that "not all have faith." If there ever was a time to include a word about praying for the salvation of the lost, you would think it would be following this last statement. Maybe something like: "Not all have faith, so pray that they might come to faith" or something similar. But Paul appears to accept the truth that not all have faith, they will persecute the faithful,

---

140. 2 Thess 3:1–2.

and that our prayer should be spent on upholding the faithful in their work rather than on the faithless and their salvation.

In the same vein, let's look at another appeal to prayer that Paul wrote to the Church at Ephesus. He is wrapping up his letter to that church and says:

> [18] "With all prayer and petition pray at all times in the Spirit, and with this in view, be on the alert with all perseverance and petition *for all the saints*, [19] and pray *on my behalf* [emphasis added], that utterance may be given to me in the opening of my mouth, to make known with boldness the mystery of the gospel, [20] for which I am an ambassador in chains; that in proclaiming it I may speak boldly, as I ought to speak."[141]

Note once more that Paul asks for prayer for believers, and that he would be able to preach well, but there is no mention of praying for those who are lost. Paul was in jail when he wrote this, and there was no clear sign that he wouldn't be executed for his crimes of stirring up the nation at this point. These could have been his last written words to the believers at Ephesus, and he doesn't mention praying for the salvation of the lost in any way. Remarkable.

There is one last passage I want to look at because it seems to hold the most promise for a directive to pray for the salvation of the lost; 1 Timothy 2:1–7 reads:

> [1] First of all, then, I urge that entreaties *and* prayers, petitions *and* thanksgivings, be made on behalf of all men, [2] for kings and all who are in authority, so that we may lead a tranquil and quiet life in all godliness and dignity. [3] This is good and acceptable in the sight of God our Savior, [4] who desires all men to be saved and to come to the knowledge of the truth. [5] For there is one God, *and* one mediator also between God and men, *the* man Christ Jesus, [6] who gave Himself as a ransom for all, the testimony *given* at the proper time. [7] For this I was appointed a preacher and an Apostle (I am telling the truth, I am not lying) as a teacher of the Gentiles in faith and truth.[142]

We should begin our examination by noting the fuller context in which this passage occurs. So, up to this point in 1 Timothy Paul has been discussing the need for right doctrine. In 1:3 Paul tells Timothy

141. Eph 6:18–20.
142. 1 Tim 2:1–7.

to "instruct certain men not to teach strange doctrines, nor pay attention to myths and endless genealogies." The problem is that these sorts of concerns "give rise to mere speculation rather than furthering the administration of God which is by faith." In other words, adherence to strange doctrines does not help or advance their stewardship work. On the contrary, true ministerial work is only advanced by means of the proper exercise of faith, not by speculations that sprout from strange doctrines. In contrast to such teaching Paul says that the goal of his (and Timothy's) teaching is "love from a pure heart and a good conscience and a sincere faith."

Paul then highlights in particular the idea of Law, noting that some have turned from their desire for a "sincere faith" and pursued "fruitless discussion."[143] We have probably all met such a person on occasion. They are excited about all sorts of trivial, odd stories that really don't help them be better Christians. They are more interested in the discussing of a matter than their actual growth as believers in a true knowledge of God and sound Christian beliefs.

In this case, these false teachers had been focusing on the Law of Moses in some way. Paul says that they wanted "to be teachers of the Law, even though they do not understand either what they are saying or the matters about which they make confident assertions."[144] It is a concrete case of what James warns about in James chapter 3. It is a very serious matter to take up the mantle of *teacher* in the church, and it is important to understand what you are saying before you spout something off.

Paul then recalls how he himself was saved by grace and not by Law, and in this, he is an example to others who would *believe* in Jesus for eternal life.[145]

Finally, Paul explains why he believes he can tell Timothy to stay in Ephesus and control these false teachers. His command to do so is "in accordance with the prophecies" which had been made about Timothy.[146] In other words, Paul is telling Timothy to do a work that complements what he has been gifted by God to do. Paul also adds that he has given Timothy this command so that Timothy can "fight the good fight, keeping faith and a good conscience." If Timothy had tried to correct these

---

143. 1 Tim 1:6.
144. 1 Tim 1:7.
145. 1 Tim 1:12–17.
146. 1 Tim 1:18.

false teachers in his own power apart from the gifts and abilities given by God, he would have failed, for people are not capable of doing holy work in merely human power. In the same vein, if Paul had commanded someone else to do the work of correction, who was not given the ability by God to correct them, that person would also have failed for the same reason. The bottom line is, Timothy was working within his previously prophesied spiritual gifting, and for this reason he was rightly tasked by Paul to instruct these false teachers not to continue what they were doing. As an example to everyone, Paul finishes this command and chapter 1 of First Timothy by highlighting in 1 Timothy 1:19b–20 the consequences of some who have *not* followed proper belief.[147] It is the last portion of 1 Timothy 1:19 that especially demands our attention in order to understand the context of this discussion. Unfortunately, it is a very difficult portion to translate and it is often misunderstood. Here is 1 Timothy 1:18–20:

> [18] This command I entrust to you, Timothy, *my* son, in accordance with the prophecies previously made concerning you, that by them you fight the good fight,[19] keeping faith and a good conscience, *which some have rejected and suffered shipwreck in regard to their faith* [emphasis added]. [20] Among these are Hymenaeus and Alexander, whom I have handed over to Satan, so that they will be taught not to blaspheme.[148]

Some take this text to be saying that certain people have not kept their personal beliefs—i.e., their faith and a good conscience. Consequently, their faith has "suffered shipwreck." But this interpretation does not make the best sense. It is not really much of an insight to say that someone who rejects their faith and a good conscience has faith problems. This would be like pointing out that when the sky is blue—it is blue. This kind of circular argument is called a *tautology*; it is a needless repetition of an idea. When we see someone reject what they believe, we don't need to be told their faith (i.e., what they believe) is now going to crash. In fact, it would be amazing if someone rejected their faith and then did not suffer shipwreck in regards to their faith—because it's the same thing!

Fortunately, the same difficulties that accompany the wording of the original text in Greek, which make it hard to translate, also allow us

---

147. 1 Tim 1:19–20.
148. 1 Tim 1:18–20.

to posit another translation. Were the text completely clear, with no ambiguity, we would be stuck trying to figure out why Paul included such a repetitive comment about faith. But we do have another choice. We can paraphrase the text like this: "This command I entrust to you, Timothy, my son, in accordance with the prophecies previously made concerning you, that by them you fight the good fight, keeping faith, and a good conscience, which, rejecting faith and a good conscience, also shipwreck the Christian faith." It's a little rough to read in English, but the idea here is that when a person abandons their personal faith, they also bring "shipwreck" or "disaster" to the Christian faith. Now, it is not that they tear the whole Christian faith down in the sense of making Christianity as a system stumble and fall, but in the eyes of others, they make Christianity look silly and worthless. We see this happen all the time in the world around us, especially when a prominent Christian turns their back on their faith—Christianity is ridiculed as weak and silly.

So, in the first chapter of 1 Timothy, Paul is telling Timothy to correct these false teachers, and he is also noting that when people abandon their personal faith they harm the Christian faith's reputation—they bring it to shipwreck—in the eyes of others as well. Although Paul is probably thinking about how Christianity looks to outsiders, I would add that when a person abandons their faith, they also affect others within the body of Christ. Believers watch other believers, and if we reject our faith, they see Christianity in a different light—sometimes a very bad light.

Paul's very last comment in 1 Timothy 1:20 lists two specific people who have done precisely this. Their names were Hymenaeus and Alexander, and they had apparently gone so far in their denial of the faith that Paul says they have "blasphemed."

Now, all this has been a lead-in to establish the context of the passage we are addressing, 1 Timothy 2:1–8. Our question is, does this passage teach us to pray for the salvation of the lost? Paul's main interest is the false teaching that needs correcting in the church, and Paul has tasked Timothy with stopping such activity because it does not lead to sincere faith and it tarnishes the reputation of the Gospel.

To begin with, we make clear that the main topic of 1 Timothy 2:1–8 is not prayer—the topic is *salvation*. Prayer is not even mentioned after 1 Timothy 2:1. The problem in the church was that false teachers were advocating for "true" believers adherence to all or part of the

Mosaic Law and pagan fables.[149] They were limiting who could be saved to a specific group of their own choosing. In contrast to this, Paul says believers should pray for "all men."[150] Paul uses this little phrase again in 2:4 when he says God desires "all men" to be saved. This little phrase creates a few problems for us, which makes it very important.

Fortunately, St. Augustine described and unraveled the problems concisely in a little book called *The Enchiridion*.[151] First, he notes that it is clear that God does *not* "will" all men to be saved in the sense that God will definitely make it so. We can see clearly in scripture that not all people will be saved. Some will reject the truth of the Gospel and end up in hell. In terms of God's will then, Augustine noted that no man is saved unless God "wills" his salvation. That is, no one is saved apart from God's will for it to happen. On the question of God's will then, Augustine concluded that the believer should pray that God *will* our salvation because if God wills it, it will definitely come to pass. His key idea is that salvation is entirely linked to God's will and does not come about without it. This is really just praying the Lord's Prayer—*thy will be done*.

The second point of interest Augustine explains has to do with the definition of the short phrase "all men." Again, God clearly does not will *all* men to be saved—or they would *all* be saved. The alternative to this is to believe that God can "will" anything he wants—such as a person's salvation—but he cannot guarantee that anything will actually happen. Orthodoxy has never adopted this view with good reason—it reduces God to a weakling who has a lot of dreams and no power to get them done. So, when Paul says God desires "all men" to be saved, he must mean something other than *every single* living person. Augustine wisely developed the answer from the other uses of the word "every" found in scripture. In Luke 11:42 we find this statement by Jesus: "But woe to you Pharisees! For you pay tithe of mint and rue and *every garden*

---

149. Note in 1 Timothy 4:3 Paul specifically mentions a few of the ideas that were probably being advanced: forced celibacy, food restrictions, and ascetic practices.

150. 1 Tim 2:1.

151. The full title is "*The Enchiridion on Faith, Hope, and Love*" but it is commonly known as *The Enchiridion*. Augustine makes an interesting comment at the end of his discussion in chapter 103. He says, "God, then, in His great condescension has judged it good to grant to the prayers of the humble the salvation of the exalted." Some might take this to mean he is saying we should pray for the salvation of the lost, but as is noted in the main text, Augustine counseled that we pray that God *will* the salvation of others, not that they be saved.

herb [emphasis added], and yet disregard justice and the love of God; but these are the things you should have done without neglecting the others." Clearly there were herbs that the Pharisees did not tithe, and there were many upon many that they had never even heard of in the great wide world. But Jesus' point was that they tithed many *types of* herbs. It is in this sense of the word "every" that Paul's comment about prayer can be easily understood. God desires *all types* of men to be saved. God is not a God of partiality—as if only the rich, only the poor, only the meek, only the fierce, only the Jew, only the Gentile, etc. are able to be saved. No, God desires that salvation come to every strata of mankind but not necessarily to every individual in every strata.

Now, if there is any stratum of mankind that seemingly will never accept the gospel of faith it is that made up of the rich and powerful. Jesus himself proclaims, "Truly I say to you, it is hard for a rich man to enter the kingdom of heaven."[152] Along the same lines he says, "It is easier for a camel to go through the eye of a needle than for a rich man to enter the kingdom of God."[153] In light of such statements by Jesus, it makes complete sense for Paul to urge Timothy to pray for "all types" of men, but then go on to especially identify the need to pray "for kings and all who are in authority." It would probably be the case that if we were to neglect anyone in prayer, it would be the rich and powerful, wouldn't it? Even if we believed them to be worthy of prayer, we might not feel there is anything they actually need most of the time—after all, they're rich and powerful, they have everything.

Now, you may be saying to yourself that this whole passage still seems to be promoting prayer for the salvation of the lost, and perhaps especially the lost among the rich and powerful. But this is not the case, for at this point we have merely been told that we ought to pray for all types of people, and specifically for kings and all who are in authority. Paul points us to his main interest at the end of verse two. He gives his directive to pray for all types of people, especially for those in authority "so that we may lead a tranquil and quiet life in all godliness and dignity." If his purpose for offering prayer for people was their salvation, you would think he'd have said something like this: "I urge that prayers be made on behalf of all men ... in order that they might be saved," or, "in order that God might open their eyes to the gospel," or something along

---

152. Matt 19:23.
153. Luke 18:25.

those lines. But instead Paul clearly says the object or goal of the prayer is to gain help for the *person praying*, not for the object of the prayer! He urges prayer for all men, "so that *we* may lead a tranquil and quiet life."[154] Clearly, paying attention to grammar, we see that Paul's main purpose is *not* to encourage us to be praying for the benefit of the lost. He says we should offer up this kind of prayer so that *we* might derive the benefit, not they. Paul then comments on the fact that living "a tranquil and quiet" life is good and acceptable to God, "who desires all men to be saved." Again, who desires all *types* of people—even kings and those in authority—to be saved.

Why would it be important that Christians live tranquil and quiet lives? The answer ties in with both the specific problem of the false teachers that existed in Ephesus and the social situation of the church. First, concerning the problem of false teaching, Paul points out later some of the specific problems with teaching false doctrine. 1 Timothy 6:3–5 says:

> ³ If anyone advocates a different doctrine and does not agree with sound words, those of our Lord Jesus Christ, and with the doctrine conforming to godliness, ⁴ he is conceited *and* understands nothing; but he has a morbid interest in controversial questions and disputes about words, out of which arise envy, strife, abusive language, evil suspicions, ⁵ and constant friction between men of depraved mind and deprived of the truth, who suppose that godliness is a means of gain.[155]

Here we see that the fruit of false doctrine is envy, strife, abusive language, evil suspicions, and constant friction between people. All these fruits destroy the serenity and unity that ought to exist in the body of Christ. And when the body is torn up in such a way, it ceases to function as the beacon of salvation in the world, for it resembles the very world to which it witnesses. When the church lives in tranquility and quietness, it resembles the unity, peace, and tranquility of God.

More importantly to our passage, a tranquil life allows for the salvation of all types of people by allowing for the sharing of the gospel. If the church is living tranquilly with kings and rulers, it has an opportunity to share the gospel message by which people come to salvation. Yes, Paul *is* asking that prayers be made for every type of person—we ought not

---

154. 1 Tim 2:2.
155. 1 Tim 6:3–5.

reject praying for someone because of their social status, even kings. But he is not asking that we prayer for their salvation. He's asking that we pray for the situation around us and them—that it be conducive to the sharing of the gospel. A good picture of this same idea comes from the book of Colossians. Near the end of the book Paul writes:

> ² Devote yourselves to prayer, keeping alert in it with *an attitude of thanksgiving;* ³ praying at the same time *for us* [emphasis added] as well, that God will open up to us a door for the word, so that we may speak forth the mystery of Christ, for which I have also been imprisoned; ⁴ that I may make it clear in the way I ought to speak. ⁵ Conduct yourselves with wisdom toward outsiders, making the most of the opportunity. ⁶ Let your speech always be with grace, *as though* seasoned with salt, so that you will know how you should respond to each person.[156]

In this statement Paul does not ask that the Church at Colossae pray for the salvation of the lost but that they pray for Paul and his companions, that they have opportunities to share the gospel. In connection with this, he directs them to act wisely with *outsiders* (i.e., unbelievers), most assuredly because he wants them to have the same sort of opportunity. Strife with someone makes sharing the gospel very difficult, if not impossible, so the more we can minimize social strife, the more we have opportunity to share what we believe.

Here again we see a corrective to an all too common Christian cop out. People pray for the salvation of the lost, but they refuse to share the gospel with them. 1 Timothy 2:1–8 fits the pattern of the rest of the New Testament in encouraging not prayer for the salvation of others, but prayer for the opportunity and circumstances to actually shine the light of the gospel on them through the witness of our lives and speech.

Before I move on, let me discuss a passing statement Paul makes about his fellow Jews in Romans 10:1. I'd been looking through scripture with an eye to portions that might support ongoing, repetitive prayer for the salvation of the lost and I ran upon this statement: "Brethren, my heart's desire and my prayer to God for them is for salvation."

In Romans 9–11 we have a unit of scripture that is dealing with a question of the veracity and trustworthiness of God's word. In Romans 9:1–5 Paul laments the fact that so many of his fellow Jewish brethren were rejecting the Gospel and consequently aligning themselves against

---

156. Col 4:2–6.

Reasons People Don't Enjoy Prayer

God. This is the famous passage where Paul goes so far as to even say he'd be willing to be "accursed" for their sake, that they might be saved (not that such a thing is really possible).

In Romans 9:6 he states the nature of the real problem, "But it is not as though the word of God has failed." This is really the thesis statement that lays the foundation of his discussion in Romans 9–11. But it needs a little unpacking because Paul says it with such brevity. The problem is that God had told Israel that they were his chosen people and heirs of his kingdom (e.g., Deuteronomy 7:6). Moreover, God had based this promise on his own faithfulness and nature. The Jews understood correctly that they were a special people "for Gods own possession," but they had, unfortunately, also come to the conclusion that any Jew was automatically an heir and a member of the chosen people. Additionally, they had come to believe that Gentiles were not, and could not be, included in that group. A Jew could no,t in effect, be lost for any reason, and the assertion that God loved the Gentiles just as much as the Jews was rejected as well.

Paul was arguing, however, that to reject Jesus as the Messiah and Savior was to reject God and was an indicator of damnation rather than salvation. Thus, many Jews were not, in point of fact, part of the people of God. But here is the crux of the problem—how can a Jew be lost if he is saved based on the *unconditional* covenant God made with Abraham? It is the same problem that Jesus faced when he had to tell the Jews that God can raise up "children of Abraham" from rocks.[157] They believed regardless of their actions that they were children of Abraham. He corrected them, in that instance, with the idea that their actions, faith, and repentance are keys to whether they really were or were not Abraham's children.

In Paul's thinking (in Romans 9–11), the problem is a matter of genealogy. He is trying to prove the point that God *did* promise chosen Israel that they would be heirs of his glory, but Israel had to understand that just genetic relationship was not the crucial aspect of the promise. He says bluntly, "For they are not all Israel who are from Israel" (i.e., Jacob).[158] So Paul argues, first of all, that even those from Ishmael's side of Abraham's family are not part of "chosen Israel." During this argument he dwells heavily on the idea that God is sovereign and faithful to his

---

157. Luke 3:8.
158. Rom 9:6.

word. The point being that just because many Jews are apparently being "lost" by rejecting Jesus is no indicator that God has somehow gone back on his word to Israel. The main point Paul is trying to express is that not all Israel were recipients of that promise (even if they thought they should be). Paul makes clear that the key at the present time is how they respond to the gospel of faith in Jesus that Paul was preaching. He even goes so far as to say some Gentiles are in the family of Abraham because they accept faith—even though they are not Jews.

Then, in Romans 10:1, Paul reiterates his concern over his Jewish people by saying, "my heart's desire and prayer to God for them is for salvation." It is obvious that he is linking salvation with their acceptance of the gospel. The problem I see with equating this statement with repeated prayer for salvation lays in its general nature. He could be, theoretically, praying that they listen every time he begins a new sermon to a group of Jews. That would not really be repetitive in the sense we have discussed. It would be more akin to saying I pray for salvation for these sorts of people (Jews in this case) every time I have opportunity to speak to them. That is quite different from saying I constantly pray the same "God save them" prayer over the same people, every day. Paul is also the one who was willing to walk away from some places after they rejected the gospel (such as at Lystra in Acts 14 for example), and it seems more likely his prayer of salvation would walk away with him and move on to the next objects of his ministry. I would also add that the tenor of the statement fits a general description of Paul's overarching attitude about the lost state of many of his fellows. It is meant to convey the fact that he realizes God is in control of their salvation but at the same time he wants to share his own personal desire with the readers.

Now, having surveyed scripture and tried to evaluate our presuppositions, it seems patently clear that we are *not* told in scripture to pray repetitively for the salvation of the lost and that often we do so using somewhat muddled logic. Let me here say again, I'm not advocating that we don't pray for the salvation of the lost at all. Remember, the point of this section is to address the *repetitive* prayers we ask (the nagging of God) that are not effective and are answered with a "no" by God. I'm advocating that when we pray for the lost, we pray for things that God actually answers. Salvation may be one of those prayers we pray, but if and when we receive a "no" answer (i.e., they are not saved) I suggest we move on to prayers to which God will answer "yes."

One more thought before we move on to another approach to prayer that is flawed. We might ask: How did we get into this habit of praying for the salvation of the lost? Why do so many take the practice for granted? Why do we do it repetitively? These are really background questions that take us further into this one topic and it is here that I would like to abandon this topic, for it is a book unto itself. I'm interested in this present work in thinking about how we should pray, not exploring further one particular type of prayer. We have seen there is no reason to treat prayer for the salvation of the lost any differently than any other prayer. Repetitive nagging of God on any subject is fruitless and frustrating and prayer for the salvation of the lost is no different. Such prayer should not be mindlessly repeated in opposition to the answers God clearly gives us.

I will say this however. I believe many of our prayers for the salvation of the lost are motivated by deep love for them. And were we to analyze what we were really requesting from God, we would realize that we are not intending to harp at the same prayer, but to merely express our deep love for the lost person. Perhaps the whole thing could be corrected by just identifying more accurately what we are really doing in our prayers. Very often it is the case that because we do not think about our speech with God prior to blurting it out, we drift into saying things that do not really reflect what we believe. I would venture to guess that there are many out there who agree that praying a repetitive prayer for the salvation of a lost person is fruitless after a time, but they still pray that prayer because they have not stopped to think out what it is they are saying. Were they to stop for a moment, put down their present practice of prayer, and analyze what they really want to say and what is coming out, they would probably readjust their words and express more clearly the fact that they merely want God to know they love the lost person and it hurts to watch them suffer.

Lobbying God with Numbers

After that long section, let me remind the reader of the broader topic we're working on. We're thinking about how our basic approach to prayer is often flawed, and looking at some of the major flaws that exist. So, moving on, another methodology that we sometimes see in prayer is the lobbying of God by groups of people. By this I mean that we seem to think God is like a political entity who, if presented with enough signatures, can be lobbied to change his position to agree with the petitioners. So, we see at the extreme margin, for example, those goofy chain-letter prayers that circulate among our churches that ask us to "pray this prayer ten times and send it on to ten friends," as though the more people we have praying the more likely our request will come to pass. Sometimes we act like our church prayer chains are similar entities, and if we were to get enough people to pray over something God would definitely do what we want.

Part of this view probably stems from a very real concern we have about prayer in general. Either our prayers really matter or they don't, and if they don't—if God is going to do whatever he wants regardless of our prayers—then why pray? At least why pray that something occur? We might pray for other reasons—to talk to God, to sort out our own minds, etc.—but we would probably not want to pray for things to happen one way or the other if we believed God had already laid it all out precisely with no room for our petitions.

If, on the other hand, we accept that our prayers *do* make a difference, that they are somehow important in the flow of God's plan for the ages, then it might also make sense that if a lot of people in the body agree on something, perhaps God will be in line with it too. And if more of the body agrees, then there is a greater likelihood that God will agree as well. The bottom line here is that we want God to agree with what we are praying for. Or more positively stated, we want to agree with and suggest to God in prayer what the best and Godliest course of action is.[159]

Unfortunately, we sometimes fall into the idea that it is just a matter of getting a lot of people on our page, and the deal is done. Furthermore, to support this group-petition idea, some even have pulled out scripture to shore up the argument. One of the most used is Matthew 18:19-20, which says:

> [19] "Again I say to you, that if two of you agree on earth about anything that they may ask, it shall be done for them by My Father who is in heaven. [20] "For where two or three have gathered together in My name, I am there in their midst."[160]

---

159. It doesn't really matter to us that God knows all that will occur. We're interested in whether *we know* what should occur, because we're trying to bring our prayers into focus with God's desires enough that when we pray we are sure that they are "in God's will."

160. Matt 18:19-20.

We take this scripture and apply the old adage, if a little is good, a lot is better. So we think to ourselves how true that must be if *hundreds* agree on something! Jesus says God the father will do whatever just two or three might agree on, but we can do better than those paltry numbers; we can easily get more than that. It's hard to not chuckle at this, but I have honestly heard this suggested. In fact, the "two or three" in agreement statement arises in relation to all sorts of ideas about God. I paraphrased it one day in class as: "God just likes groups and doesn't let them fail."[161] And to that suggestion I got hardy agreement from a good number of students.

Of course this passage says nothing of the sort, for in this specific context Jesus is talking about the functioning of discipline in the church. He means that if two or three leaders in the church agree on some situation concerning church discipline and ask God for something in relation to that, then he will answer them. Jesus is focusing on the idea of two or three here because he's just made clear that problems have to be handled by more than individual leaders—especially when the problem explodes into whether a person is to be treated as an unbeliever (e.g., a tax gatherer) or not.[162] In such a situation one leader cannot make a ruling alone. But when the church in plurality agrees on a ruling, God promises that he will have been in their midst working with them. Of course, this teaching does not negate the other of asking things that are "in God's will." In this case as well, the two or three seemingly need to be agreeing on things that God would also agree to.

So, it is not the sheer number that is being addressed here, it is the leadership of a church, united in dealing with some disciplinary problem. In that decision making process, God says he will be present and will honor their decisions. This is not a blanket statement that God will just give "groups" whatever they want merely because of their numbers.

Another passage that might be of interest to us concerning the group prayer idea comes from the book of Daniel in the Old Testament:

---

161. In this case we were discussing group versus individual interpretation in Ecclesiology class. In support of group interpretation one enterprising student suggested we see a pattern for God in Matthew 18: God likes groups. I suggested that the passage is hardly proof of that assertion, but like so many ideas, in many ways his suggestion "preaches" to people.

162. Matt 18:17.

> ¹⁷ Then Daniel went to his house and informed his friends, Hananiah, Mishael and Azariah, about the matter, ¹⁸ so that they might request compassion from the God of heaven concerning this mystery, so that Daniel and his friends would not be destroyed with the rest of the wise men of Babylon. ¹⁹ Then the mystery was revealed to Daniel in a night vision. Then Daniel blessed the God of heaven; ²⁰ Daniel said, "Let the name of God be blessed forever and ever, For wisdom and power belong to him. ²¹ It is he who changes the times and the epochs; he removes kings and establishes kings; he gives wisdom to wise men And knowledge to men of understanding. ²² It is he who reveals the profound and hidden things; he knows what is in the darkness, And the light dwells with him. ²³ To You, O God of my fathers, I give thanks and praise, For You have given me wisdom and power; Even now You have made known to me what we requested of You, For You have made known to us the king's matter."[163]

This passage in Daniel records events that took place in Babylon, when Israel had been taken into captivity to the "land of Shinar."[164] The king of Babylon, Nebuchadnezzar, had had dreams that disturbed him concerning a large statue that ultimately Daniel interpreted to represent future world powers. The king asked his own servants to explain the dream, but they could not, so in his fury he decreed that all the wise men of Babylon were to be destroyed—among whom was the Israelite Daniel.

When the captain of the king's bodyguard came to round up Daniel for execution with the rest of the Babylonian seers, Daniel asked, "Why is the decree from the King so urgent?"[165] Having learned of the dream, he then offered his services to the king to provide an interpretation, and it is at this point of the story that our text occurs. After Daniel had requested of the king a little time to get the interpretation of the dream, he went to his friends to request that they also might ask God to give Daniel the interpretation. Now, it is clear that Daniel felt it would be helpful to bring his friends into the process of requesting a particular answer from God. But the key here is the timing of the event. Daniel had not apparently asked God one way or the other. The Hebrew text is very clear on the order of events:

---

163. Dan 2:17–23.
164. Dan 1:2.
165. Dan 2:15.

- Daniel requests time from the king in order that "he might declare the interpretation to the king."
- Then, Daniel goes to his friends that they too could pray to God about sparing their lives by revealing "the mystery."
- Finally, the mystery was revealed "to Daniel in a night vision."

Daniel did not ask for the interpretation, receive a "no" answer from God, and subsequently go get his friends to try to persuade God to see reason and change his mind. He clearly felt that since they too were under the death penalty, they should be brought into the situation to pray for an answer; and this occurred *prior to* Daniel ever raising the issue with God.[166]

The reader should take special note of Daniel's prayer of thanksgiving as well, for in it he praises God's sovereignty over world events and the wisdom of men. This is important to our discussion, because it reveals that even in Daniel's prayer request, he understood that God is the one who will either give the answer or will not based on *his* desire, not on Daniel's (or anyone else's). Daniel understood that he and his group of friends were not going to change God's mind if God were not inclined to provide the interpretation of the dream. It would not matter if there were thousands of people praying for the interpretation (which there probably were if you include all the Babylonian wise men who also were in fear of their lives). Daniel and his friends were asking for wisdom from God and they accepted the answer they received in light of the fact that God sovereignly rules the flow of kingdoms and kings in the world.[167]

Although we are discussing the problem of trying to use large groups of people to persuade God to grant our requests, let me take some time here to discuss the positive aspects of coming to decisions with the aid of others. Practically speaking, there is great merit in running our decisions and requests by other Christians in order to see what they think. This

---

166. We see the same sort of thing happen in the Old Testament book of Esther. Esther is tasked with going to see the king of Persia without an appointment. She knew she could receive the death penalty for such an affront. So, prior to going and making her request she asks others to fast along with her (presumably with prayer) that she might be fully prepared and in God's will when she proceeded (Esth 4:15–16). She didn't receive her answer and then gather the assembly to try to change the outcome.

167. Cf. passages such as Job 12:16–25; Prov 8:15; Dan 2:21. There are many passages that speak to God's sovereign rule of the world.

is not merely to get them on our page so we have more ammo to shoot at God in prayer; it is not so that we can say, "Look how many people want this thing, God!" Running our requests by others or asking them to pray with us is a part of the process by which God leads us. Proverbs 27:17 says, "Iron sharpens iron; so one man sharpens another." In terms of maturity, it is often the case that others in the body can point out our failings, sharpen our thinking processes, and give us help in our decision making and growth. In the church body, God has instituted a system whereby the believer has access to other Christians in order to evaluate his or her decisions. This is a good system, if we use it correctly. If we merely call on others to validate our wants in a vain effort to manipulate God, we miss the point of the system, and it fails to function.

A question that underlies the use of the body of Christians as guide to my decision making process is, "How does God lead us?" I believe we often turn to flawed systems of prayer because we do not have a clear idea of how God will actually help us make decisions. Let me relate an incident that occurred at our church not long ago that illustrates the idea.

One day I (and a number of other members) received an email from some people that had attended our church for more than twenty five years. It said they had decided to leave the church because God was leading them into some unknown future, but as far as I could tell, they had not discussed this with anyone in the church. For all intents and purposes, it was a decision made by them, for them, and to the exclusion of any counsel from other believers in the body. I considered them my friends, so I had asked what exactly they saw as God's leading that had brought them to that decision. Unfortunately, I was politely told that they had thought on it for a long time, and that I should not worry—which was a nice way of saying, "Butt out." As you can probably infer, that answer did not really address my question. The problem is, if we cannot identify clearly *how* God leads us, we run the great risk of not following his lead. One way God concretely does lead us is through the input of other godly believers, and when we make big decisions for our lives, without any scriptural or body support for them, we run the risk of doing whatever we want regardless of God's real desires.

An additional and regrettable outcome of this is that frequently we then blame God for our decisions when they go awry saying things like, "God led me to this," or "God told me to trust him," or something like that. This situation reminds me of the story of Potiphar's wife in Genesis 39. She made a bad decision by attempting to seduce Joseph, her husband's house steward. Then, when Joseph rebuffed her advances, she blamed her husband saying, "The Hebrew slave, whom *you* [emphasis added] brought to us, came in to me to make sport of me."[168] Of course in her anger she also added the lie that Joseph was the one who instigated the tryst. But the point is, she made a bad choice on her own; it didn't work out; and she subsequently blamed her husband for the whole debacle. She would probably not have made that bad choice in the first place had she consulted with a few others about the plan.

In truth we often make bad decisions on our own because we've excluded the concrete ways God actually does commonly lead us, such as scriptural instruction and input from other believers. Moreover, we often use prayer as an excuse for not utilizing the many valid methods God uses to guide us, by convincing ourselves that God mystically "miracles" the correct choices directly into our heads, or, as we have been discussing, by thinking we can just gather a group of like minded people together in order to persuade God to honor our decision.

Now, I took time for this last discussion about the benefits of running our ideas past others in the body in order to segue into the next major flaw we sometimes have in our prayer systems: We have not really identified what we expect God to actually *do* when we pray to him.

So, to this point, I've mentioned two large general flaws that can occur in our approach to prayer. First, we sometimes nag God endlessly to get what we want. Second, we sometimes multiply prayer partners to persuade God to change his mind and do what we desire. Now, let me return to an idea that was mentioned in passing earlier, but was not discussed. It's what I call the lottery syndrome.

Lottery Syndrome

In some ways the lottery syndrome is similar to the idea I had mentioned earlier about the need to have some expectations when we talk with God. I had noted that we need to grow in our relationship with God to the point where we can somewhat anticipate how he will *answer* us, and doing so, we can then better formulate our requests of him. Similar

---

168. Gen 39:17.

to this is the idea that we must learn to anticipate how God will *act* toward us.

We know, oftentimes even before we ask, how people will respond to our requests. I know if I ask my friend Joe to help me fix a computer problem I am having that he will not initially refer me to a computer shop. First, he will ask questions about the problem. Second, he will look at the computer himself. Then, as a last resort, he may suggest someone to talk to, or a shop to take it to. I understand how he operates to some extent and therefore I know what to ask and how to ask it. I know one thing that Joe is not going to do: He won't just give me a new computer. He could; he's able to build one and just give it to me. But I know he won't, so I would not say to him, "Hey Joe, I have a computer problem, will you give me a new computer?" I know him well enough to not even ask once, let alone more than once. And if I ask him, "Hey Joe, will you solve my computer problem?" I know, even when he says, "Yes," that his "yes" *answer* does not mean his "yes" *action* will be to give me a computer. He could, but even a "yes, I'll fix your computer problem" answer does not mean he will. Here then is an important point: We interact with people according to what they *will* do, not according to what they *can* do.

I call this flaw in our approach to God the Lottery Syndrome because it seems very similar to the way people play lotteries. Everyone *knows* what real life is like. You work hard, get a pay check, save up money, and budget your expenses. Basically, you just live within your means. I can insert the oft-told joke here: "That is, unless you're the federal government, and in that case you just print money or take it from others." But assuming we're not in that position, then normal life follows this sort of course: Work, earn, save, live, etc. etc. etc. You gloomier readers will want to insert "You die," at the end of the path.

When it comes to the lottery however, things are totally different. In that setting, we buy a one-dollar ticket and have the opportunity to win millions upon millions of dollars—and people do actually win! Lo and behold, people who sometimes have nothing but their lone lottery numbers hit the big one and take home multi-millions of dollars. Cool, huh? But did you ever notice the little warning that is presented to you when you buy the ticket? It says something to the effect of, "Don't use playing the lottery as your form of investing." There is also a little declaration about what your chances really are of winning the ga-zillion dollars: They're miniscule. You have a better chance of being hit by lighting than actually winning the big prize. In truth, you have a *way* better chance of being in a car wreck on the way to the store to buy the ticket than winning that prize.

Now, most people get this concept. They still buy lottery tickets—I'm lobbying my wife to buy one for me even as I write this—but they also order their lives on the premises of real life: Work, get paid, save, etc. They don't buy a million-dollar house because they honestly believe that they will win a million dollars tomorrow at the drawing. Granted, some people do silly things like that, but that's why we call those people "silly," isn't it? Yes, some people really do win the lottery, but even though we know that that is the case, we still don't live our lives as though it will happen to us—because we know the truth. For all practical purposes in making daily decisions about how we live, it won't happen—we won't win. This is a wise truth, and most everyone understands it. Unfortunately, this wise truth does not seem to transfer to our prayer lives and the expectations we have for how God will *act*. We pray as though we are going to win the lottery every day, and we live as though we expect a huge miracle on a daily basis—even though we hardly ever (if ever at all) witness one. No wonder God seems like such a bummer and prayer seems so ... well ... futile. We have a "lottery ticket" mentality in a "workaday" life. We submit our dollar prayer expecting a million dollar answer and when reality hits—no million-dollar miracle—our faith in the power of prayer crashes.

Now, you may be saying to yourself, "Yeah, but lotteries are impersonal roles of the dice whereas God is a personally involved father; lotteries are just numbers coming up randomly—they are not granted requests from an all-knowing, all-loving God." How about I use another familiar analogy: The picture of a child and parent. On occasion a parent will give a special gift of some kind to a child. Out of the blue, a parent may give their child an ice cream cone for instance, just because they love them and want to give them something special. Or, sometimes a parent will give their child something merely because they think the child needs it at that moment in their life. Whatever the reason, children know that now and again, mom or dad will hand over something that is definitely not the norm. Growing up in my family, it was very out-of-the-norm to go out to dinner at a restaurant. When we did, it was a surprise and so we never banked on it happening. And since it truly was a "special" circumstance and not a daily event, we loved it and never expected it. It was special and not mundane.

Now, suppose a child started to build her relationship with her mom solely on the prospect of the "special" thing—say, an ice cream cone. Every time the youngster saw mom she would ask for an ice cream cone. When they sat down to dinner, the first question to mom would be: "Are we having an ice cream cone?" You see the problem, right? Yes, sometimes mom *does* really and truly give the unexpected ice cream cone, but in truth, it is just that—unexpected. It is not something we ought to be asking for on a daily basis. That's what actually makes it "unexpected," isn't it? It *doesn't come* to us on a daily basis. A child ought *not to expect it*. When a child starts to pattern her daily life on the expectation of the unexpected, it becomes a fiasco. She might say to herself, "I'm not eating this breakfast—I'm waiting for the ice cream cone. After all, mom has the money for them." Worse yet, at every turn she may expect the ice cream cone, and incessantly ask for it even when it will surely do her no good. She may even have been told: "No, you're not getting an ice cream cone," but she is undeterred and continues to ask anyway. Or perhaps she is ignored when she asks, which in itself is a "no" answer. In real life, we shouldn't expect the unexpected on a daily basis. We expect the world to move along according to the rhythms God set in motion for it. When we live on a diet of expectation of the unexpected we end up sorely disappointed, frustrated, and confused. I might carry this metaphor a bit further when we think of those parents that *do* constantly hand over the ice cream cone. Look at where that leads—the obesity rate in America is skyrocketing and especially among children. We are not made to subsist on ice cream; it is a treat and not a staple for a reason. To have too much is tremendously bad for you, and I submit that such a state is true of the miraculous as well. It too is not good for us. We need a spiritual diet of work, trust, faith, and growth within the mundane routines of daily life—not a diet of sugary miracles that handle things for us without the need for maturity.

How does something become *unexpected* in the first place? Isn't it because we have some expectations about the nature of something, and when it acts differently, we describe that as unexpected? In fact, we cannot really have the idea of *unexpected* without some sort of idea of the expected. And that is where we have a problem. Many of us seem to know God so poorly, that we somehow have come to expect the unexpected—

as expected. That's a mouthful isn't it? But read that sentence again and think it through. It's important.

Let's go back to my friend Joe. Someone who did not know him at all may, in fact, walk up to him, knowing he is computer whiz, and just ask him for a free computer to replace their broken one. But that ignorance of how Joe typically acts is not really something to be proud of. Joe will consistently say to that person, "No, I'm not going to do that for you." And that person is going to be frustrated if they continue to believe Joe is going to just hand over a computer, when in reality, Joe typically never, ever, just hands over a new computer—even though he is theoretically *capable* of doing so. What Joe *can* do and what Joe *will* do are entirely different things.

The problem then, is expectations. God does guide us. God does give us things. God does help us out with insights. All Christians believe these truths firmly. Yet we must ask, *how* does he *actually* do that? What do we expect him to really, honestly *do*? Does he "miracle" answers, maps, or directions right into our heads? Does he provide visions and dreams as Daniel received? What do we expect him to do? To really get a handle on someone, we need to analyze what sort of answers we expect from them ("yes" or "no") and how we expect them to act. We need to have some expectations for the way they think and what they desire, and we need some expectations about what they typically do. We need to clearly delineate what God *can* do as opposed to what God *will* do. To understand the distinction is to admit that there is a difference between offering realistic, definite, answerable prayers, and merely hurling words at God. It is also to recognize the distinction between a mature believer who speaks intelligently with God and a child who prattles on and to whom no one pays attention because they babble gibberishAllow me to remind the reader of the epigraph of this book: "Do not be hasty in word or impulsive in thought to bring up a matter in the presence of God. For God is in heaven and you are on the earth; therefore let your words be few."[169] We need to think out clearly what we are saying to God, discerning both what he says "yes" to and how he tends to act.

So what are our expectations? How do we think God *will act* with us? How do we think he *will* respond? These are completely different from: How *can* God guide us? How *can* God respond to us? In fact, the difference here is profound for every aspect of our Christian lives. God

169. Eccl 5:2.

can decide one day to make the sky green. Should I then teach people not to rule out the possibility of a green sky occurring? Should I counsel people to pray a "turn the sky green today" pray every now and then because "you never know . . ."? We need to think about this distinction: What God *can* do as opposed to what God *does do*. Let's look at some scriptures and think about this a bit.

In scripture the picture that illustrates how God *can* respond is pretty awesome and miraculous. Let me give some examples of what God *can* do as recorded in scripture. Again, I've grouped them into types of actions that God can accomplish.

God Can Heal the Sick and Broken Miraculously

Genesis 20:1-18. In this story we've seen before, Abimelech had taken Sarah away from Abraham because he thought she was Abraham's sister. In response, God had closed the wombs of all the women in Abimelech's clan to punish him for this indiscretion. When Abimelech found out that Sarah was actually Abraham's wife, he returned her immediately. Abraham then prayed to God that the wombs be healed, and God did so. So we can say positively, God *can* close and open wombs in response to the faithful prayers of the saints.

2 Kings 20:1-6. In this story King Hezekiah of Judah becomes sick to the point of death. Isaiah the prophet tells him that God has said that he needs to "set his house in order, for you shall die and not live." In response, Hezekiah prays to be healed and sure enough, God declares that he would heal him and that he is adding fifteen years to his life. So here we can say that God can stave off death and remove sickness.

Luke 9:1-6. In this narrative, we are told about Jesus' sending out of the twelve Apostles. It says he "gave them authority over all the demons and to heal diseases. And he sent them out to proclaim the kingdom of God and perform healing." And consequently, they did just that; they went out proclaiming the gospel and healing everywhere. Later, following this story, it is said that Jesus as well was "curing those who had need of healing" when they came to him.[170] So here we see that God can heal everyone and anyone with a disease. And it need not be just Jesus doing it, for here we see the disciples also doing the healing.

---

170. Luke 9:11.

Acts 3:1–8. In this story the Apostles Peter and John were going up to the temple after having received the Holy Spirit. They came across a lame man who had been lame in his feet for his entire life, and had therefore been unable to work. He was laid in front of the temple to beg alms from the passers-by as they came and went. As Peter and John came by, he asked them for something as well. Peter said clearly to him that he didn't have any money, but instead he promised to give him what he did have: the power of God. Peter then reached down, grabbed the man and pulled him to his miraculously-healed feet. This healing was so dramatic that it landed Peter and John first in jail, and then in front of the authorities to be questioned about the matter. So we can add to our list that God, through his agents, can make lame limbs whole.

1 Corinthians 12:28. In this passage about unity in the body of Christ, Paul discusses some of the various giftings we find distributed among believers. He says there are "gifts of healings" among the gifts. As a side note, I would point out that he does not discuss gifts in order to lay down a theology of spiritual gifting but does so only to explain how they work to produce unity in the body. His main topic in the entire passage from chapter 12 to chapter 14 is unity in the body and how we ought to be building each other up. However, apparently, God can provide the means for healing as well and has given a gift to do so.

So, my point in mentioning this first set of passages is to state clearly, "yes, God *can* heal," and "yes, he *has* done so in the past as recorded in scripture." I could make the list much longer, but these will suffice. Here, however, is another set of passages to peruse.

God Doesn't Heal the Sick and Broken Miraculously

Genesis 48–49. This is the story of Jacob's final days of life, when he was old, and more importantly, the text tells us he was sick. There is no record of praying for the healing of this sickness. Perhaps the term is intended to just mean weak or frail. Regardless of the distinction, he does not recover—he dies.

2 Samuel 12:1–18. This is a very sad story from King David's life. David had committed adultery with his friend Uriah's wife (Bathsheba). They had conceived a child and we are told that in this case God had struck the child with sickness. David "inquired of God for the child, fasted and went and lay all night on the ground." It did not change things. The child died seven days later.

1 Kings 14:1–13. This is another sad story about a death, but it has a twist that distinguishes it. Jeroboam the son of Nebat was the first king of the northern tribes of Israel when the monarchy divided after the death of King Solomon. He was a terrible king and God severely rebuked him saying, "you also have done more evil than all who were before you ...." Remember before him King David had committed murder and adultery, and King Solomon had married hundreds of foreign wives in opposition to the direct command of God. But Jeroboam had instituted a new religion in Israel to draw his people away from Yahweh, and that was by far a more grievous sin.

During his reign, his child had become sick and Jeroboam had seen the light about Yahweh. This is not to say that he had repented of his sin, but he recognized that the only true healer in the world was the God of Israel. His hand-made cow idols were as worthless as the metal they were made from when it came to real power. So Jeroboam sent his wife to Shiloh to see an authentic prophet of God named Abijah. He thought if she disguised herself the prophet wouldn't recognize her and would tell her what the future held for the sick child.

Well, she went, and as expected Abijah saw right through the disguise, for God had told him what was going to happen. (After all, he was a prophet, right?) Abijah, as expected, delivered a message of condemnation to her about her husband's rule. But what is interesting is what he says about the sick child:

> [12] "Now you, arise, go to your house. When your feet enter the city the child will die. [13] All Israel shall mourn for him and bury him, for he alone of Jeroboam's family will come to the grave, because in him something good was found toward the LORD God of Israel in the house of Jeroboam."[171]

In this instance the child not only dies, but God explicitly says that "something good" was found in him. It was actually a blessing that he died and went to his grave, for the rest of Jeroboam's male family was going to end up food for the animals (dogs and birds). The point being, God did not heal in this instance, even though he describes the death as a blessing given to one who is found "good."

171. 1 Kgs 14:12–13.

2 Kings 13:14. In this verse the great prophet Elisha is described as being "sick with the illness of which he was to die." There is no question of whether he would be healed. He was going to die—and he did.

2 Corinthians 12:7–9. In this interesting passage the Apostle Paul is in the position of having to defend his apostleship to the stubborn and arrogant Church at Corinth. This Church had received a number of letters from Paul and still they seemed to struggle with the problem of boasting and self interest. Paul is relating to them how he was caught up to heaven and given revelations that he was not to speak about. He then says he was also given a "thorn in the flesh" to keep him from "exalting himself." He explains, "Concerning this I entreated the Lord three times that it might depart from me. And he said to me, 'My grace is sufficient for you, for power is perfected in weakness.'"[172] Paul apparently suffered from this malady for the rest of his life.

What is very important about this particular instance is that Paul goes on to say that he is "well content with weaknesses, with insults, with distresses, with persecution, with difficulties, for Christ's sake; for when I am weak, then I am strong."[173] Paul seems to have viewed the difficulties he faced as avenues for the expression of power in some way.

First Timothy 5:23. In this well known verse we find some fatherly advice the Apostle Paul gives to his young pastor-friend Timothy. He says, "No longer drink water exclusively, but use a little wine for the sake of your stomach and your frequent ailments." It seems that Timothy was abstaining from wine for some reason (perhaps a religious reason) and Paul was noting that medicinal use might aid him. Note that Paul says Timothy had "frequent ailments" along with his stomach malady. It is hard to believe that Paul had never prayed over them, but apparently God did not fix the problems.

So, as you can see, the fact that God *can* heal is definitely no guarantee that he *will* heal, and I suggest that if we honestly look at all the people suffering and dying from diseases in the world (including good and faithful Christians) we would have to admit that clearly God does *not heal* on a typical basis or as a matter of daily policy.

---

172. 2 Cor 12:9.
173. 2 Cor 12:10.

Before we go to another set of verses, let's stop for a moment and look at a few reasons why some of the previously mentioned healings may have occurred. They are not just healings for the sake of healings on God's part. These healings served a purpose which was greater than just helping a particular person out. And that appears to be God's mode of operation in healing; his usual approach is not to just heal anyone who asks but to heal for a greater purpose. So let's look at these healings in terms of the broader circumstances in which they occur.

In our Genesis 20 passage about Abimelech and the closed wombs, the healing was in direct response to the correction of Abimelech's sin. It is not as though his women were not bearing because they were too old or infirm. Abimelech did not have to pray on a consistent basis that all the wombs in his kingdom be opened and child-bearing. The closing of the wombs in the first place was caused by God directly intervening in Abimelech's family to bring attention to the problem of Sarah, Abraham's wife. Had Abimelech not taken Sarah, there is no indication that any of the barrenness would have ever happened in the first place. The only reason for the healing was to restore what would have naturally occurred anyway. So God is not reversing any normal activities of life; he is not changing the rules on a lark or because someone asked. He is making a point of protecting his chosen vessel for the seed of Abraham.

Hezekiah's healing recorded in 2 Kings 20 is an especially interesting case on a number of levels, so we should spend some time on it. First, let's begin by trying to get a feel for the tenor of Hezekiah's entire reign before we look at the specific tale of healing. Hezekiah was young when he became king of the southern kingdom of Judah—a mere twenty-five years old we are told.[174] He was a great king and is described in scripture as one who "did right in the sight of the Lord, according to all that his father David had done . . . he trusted in the Lord, the God of Israel; so that after him there was none like him among all the kings of Judah, nor among those who were before him."[175] King David is pretty heady company to be compared to—and in such glowing terms to boot!

---

174. 2 Kgs 18:2. Remember, that the country of Israel had split into two independent kingdoms in 931 BC. The northern kingdom was called Israel and the southern kingdom was called Judah. This division occurred after the death of King Solomon. The story is recorded in 1 Kings 12:1–24 in the Old Testament.

175. 2 Kgs 18:3, 5.

Now, the northern kingdom of Israel had grown more and more evil in the sight of the Lord, and in the fourth year of Hezekiah's reign (in the south; in Judah) Israel in the north was invaded by Assyria. The king reigning in the north at the time was named Hoshea.[176] Of course, the Assyrians were not going to stop invading Palestine at the border of Judah, and ten years later, king Sennacharib of Assyria "came against all the fortified cities of Judah and seized them."[177] From Jerusalem, King Hezekiah could see the writing on the wall and feared his country also would be entirely lost to this marauding gentile. So, he offered to pay tribute to the King of Assyria and he stripped the house of the Lord of all its silver, cut the gold from the doors and doorposts of the temple and handed the whole lot over to Assyria. Moreover, he emptied his own treasuries of silver to add to the gift.

As with most ransom payments to thugs, Hezekiah's appeasement approach didn't work. The King of Assyria proceeded to send ambassadors to Jerusalem to explain how it was going to be overrun and destroyed regardless of the tribute. They even claimed that God *wanted* them to destroy it and approved of their doing so.[178] When the Judean delegates chosen to discuss the matter with Assyria heard this they asked the Assyrians to speak only in Aramaic rather than in Judean. The problem was that the discussion was being carried out by shouting at one another across the wall of the city. Consequently, everyone could hear what was being discussed. The Judean delegates didn't want the people alarmed by the threats. Of course (again) the Assyrians didn't pay any heed, because they wanted to frighten the people of Jerusalem. So, they began to shout directly at them, telling them Hezekiah their king was deceiving them by telling them to trust in either Egypt as an ally or God as a protector.

To sweeten the pot, the Assyrians promised the people of Jerusalem that if they came out they could eat and drink freely of their own produce and water until such time as they were carried off by the army. That didn't sound too good, but they added that the people would be deposited in a "land like your own land, a land of grain and new wine, a land of bread and vineyards, a land of olive trees and honey, that you

---

176. Hoshea's reign can be found in 2 Kings 17 in the Old Testament.
177. 2 Kgs 18:13.
178. 2 Kgs 18:17–25.

may live and not die."[179] Doesn't it seem as though tyrants always promise the same sorts of benefits regardless of what age they inhabit? They promise that if you give up your freedom under their rule you will get it all back and more.

As a final nail in the coffin, the Assyrians asked a very penetrating and perplexing question: "Has any one of the gods of the nations delivered his land from the hand of the king of Assyria?"[180] They were pragmatists and had good, solid, historical reasons for expecting to stomp Jerusalem flat and deport her people. After all, they had done the exact same thing to countless other nations previously. All of those nations had "gods" who could supposedly protect them, but none had actually been able, or desired, to do so. The question was clear, why would the God of the Jews be any different? With good reason we are told "the people were silent and answered him not a word."[181] Of course, King Hezekiah had commanded that they not answer, but one wonders if they could have anyway. It is a sobering question they were posited, and the plain facts of the situation rested like a ton of bricks on their backs. They were faced with a choice between what I like to call "reality" and "real reality." Reality said they were goners. Assyria was going to stomp them flat and take everyone into captivity. Real reality said that God could drive away any army whatsoever. Unfortunately, reality often frightens us more than real reality comforts us and we crumble under our fear.

Now to be sure, Hezekiah was distraught along with the people. He was no idiot. The fact was, in reality, the Assyrians were completely correct. They had razed to the ground every city and country they encountered on their inexorable way to Jerusalem. So, in light of these crushing circumstances, Hezekiah sent to Isaiah the prophet for help. Well, he sent to Isaiah for something—it's hard to tell what exactly. Hezekiah seems to have been totally demoralized, for he dressed himself as if in mourning and went to sit alone in the temple. In truth, he didn't even go to see Isaiah personally; he sent some messengers to relate his message to the prophet:

> [3] They said to him, "Thus says Hezekiah, 'This day is a day of distress, rebuke, and rejection; for children have come to birth and there is no strength to *deliver*. [4] Perhaps the LORD your God will

179. 2 Kgs 18:32.
180. 2 Kgs 18:33.
181. 2 Kgs 18:36.

hear all the words of Rabshakeh, whom his master the king of Assyria has sent to reproach the living God, and will rebuke the words which the LORD your God has heard. Therefore, offer a prayer for the remnant that is left."[182]

Hezekiah sounds totally bummed out doesn't he? With good reason I think. His kingdom is on the verge of total destruction! He seems to have crumbled under this reality and almost lost his trust in God, for he even refers to God as "your God" twice in his words to Isaiah. The Bible tells us the problem he was having, the problem we too face at times—he was *afraid*.[183] Of course he was! Reality can wield a big stick sometimes, and a few *thwaks* by it can break even the most ardent believer if they are not truly tuned in to God. God, however, through Isaiah, tells Hezekiah *not* to be afraid. Real reality breaks in! The blasphemous words of Assyria would be avenged and king Sennacharib would end his campaign in Palestine and return home (where he would die by the sword).[184]

At this point, Rabshakeh (the Assyrian commander and message bearer) had to turn his attention away from Jerusalem for a bit to fight the war in Palestine on another front. Because he was fighting a number of foes in the region, King Sennacharib of Assyria sent another letter to Hezekiah to restate his offer and renew his threats about ultimately tearing Jerusalem apart. At this point, Hezekiah seems to have regrouped, for he then turns to God in prayer. And what a prayer it was! It is worth reading in its entirety:

> [15] Hezekiah prayed before the LORD and said, "O LORD, the God of Israel, who are enthroned *above* the cherubim, You are the God, You alone, of all the kingdoms of the earth. You have made heaven and earth. [16] Incline Your ear, O LORD, and hear; open Your eyes, O LORD, and see; and listen to the words of Sennacherib, which he has sent to reproach the living God. [17] Truly, O LORD, the kings of Assyria have devastated the nations and their lands [18] and have cast their gods into the fire, for they were not gods but the work of men's hands, wood and stone. So they have destroyed them. [19] Now, O LORD our God, I pray, deliver us from his hand that all the kingdoms of the earth may know that You alone, O LORD, are God."[185]

182. 2 Kgs 19:3–4.
183. 2 Kgs 19:6.
184. 2 Kgs 19:21–28.
185. 2 Kgs 19:15–19.

Hezekiah tells it like it is doesn't he? He sees the Assyrian's logic: Every nation has gods and every nation was stomped by Assyria. Yet he also sees the fallacy in that reasoning: *Every nation's gods are but idols.* Hezekiah understands who it is he worships and how his God is not like any of the other gods. Of course *they* would fall, but that says nothing about the power of the true God of Heaven—the God of Judah. So Hezekiah asks that God save Jerusalem, and he does not ask merely because he wants to save his kingdom. He sees God's desire in the situation as well. If God is mocked by the Assyrians and lets his people fall, he too will look weak in the eyes of the nations. Hezekiah asks for deliverance in order that all the nations might see that Israel's God is the true God of Heaven. What a man! What a king! If there was ever a man that God would love and care for, you would think it would be this man. Well, the outcome was as predicted, God did answer his prayer. The "angel of the Lord" went out and struck down the Assyrian army. And, having lost his whole complement of soldiers surrounding Jerusalem, king Sennacharib left Palestine and returned to Assyria and his home in Nineveh, where not long after, he was assassinated by two of his underlings.[186]

Now, let's wend our way back to the main point and Hezekiah's healing. The healing actually occurs at the beginning of this whole episode of the siege of Jerusalem. As we had previously noted, Hezekiah fell ill and Isaiah the prophet told him that he would die soon. This was probably right near the beginning of the problems with Assyria. Hezekiah didn't want to die yet; no one ever really wants to die I suppose. But there were other concerns that probably bothered Hezekiah in along with his personal interests. He was a good king, and as such, he undoubtedly felt a deep responsibility to care for his kingdom and people. Imagine that someone came onto your lawn and said they were going to take away your family and house and possessions. You would not want to die at that moment either. You would want to live and be able to protect your loved ones and defend your home. Were Hezekiah to die during the siege, chances are things would go badly (at least by his reckoning) for both the country and the people. And that would disgrace God and the nation.

So, the purpose of God's statement, through Isaiah, to Hezekiah was to provoke this very train of thought in the king. It is not as though God did not *know* himself that he intended to give Hezekiah fifteen more years of life. Unless we want to believe God really has no future plans

186. 2 Kgs 19:20–37.

or idea about what he intends to do until the moment arises, we must admit he surely knew what was coming and what he intended to do. But just as clearly, Hezekiah did not. He may not have really understood himself as deeply as he could have. Remember that Job had not really appreciated some of his mistaken beliefs until he was drawn into discussion with God either. This proclamation from God that the king would die from his illness seems to have spurred Hezekiah to really evaluate *why* he had served God so faithfully over the years. When push came to shove, he admitted to himself that he truly believed that God *is* faithful and a "rewarder of those who seek him."[187] So he wept and prayed to God. Interestingly, the prayer that is recorded for us in scripture does not include a plea for more life! You would think that that would be the main item to express to God. Instead, the prayer is but one verse: "Remember now, O Lord, I beseech You, how I have walked before You in truth and with a whole heart, and have done what is good in Your sight."[188] His prayer is a command that God look and remember how Hezekiah has conducted his life. That's it. It is asking that God be who he is, in a sense, for surely God does know Hezekiah's life intimately, as he knows all our lives intimately.[189] God had brought Hezekiah to the place of praying with real recognition of the God who had proven himself loving and true over Hezekiah's entire life.

And in the text, God immediately answers; Isaiah has no more than walked toward the gate of the house and God tells him to go back and tell Hezekiah that God has heard his prayer, seen his tears, and would heal the king—Hezekiah would rise and go from his house to the temple in three days time. Hezekiah is incredulous it seems, for he asks for a sign of some kind to really prove that he would leave the house in just three days. He must have been very ill indeed to be that brazen! You would have thought a word from the great prophet Isaiah would be enough, but perhaps Hezekiah was still shaken at how close he had come to death. We may draw from the text that his wish for a sign did not offend God because he granted him the sign he wished to see—a shadow moved the wrong way during the course of the day.

Now, chapter 20, verse 6 is the key verse to notice in this healing. It reads: "And I [God] will add fifteen years to your life, and I will deliver

---

187. Heb 11:6.
188. 2 Kgs 20:3.
189. Cf. 1 Chr 28:9.

you and this city from the hand of the king of Assyria; and I will defend this city *for My own sake and for My servant David's sake* [emphasis added]." Here we are given a piece of information that is important in explaining the healing properly. It tells us that the king's sickness was *during* the siege previously described. If Hezekiah had died during the siege itself, the people would have been thrust into a very difficult situation. On the one hand, their city is under attack; on the other, their godly ruler is seemingly abandoned by God to death at a moment of need. Hezekiah's father, Ahaz, had been a terrible and godless king who had gone so far as to alter worship for his own selfish ends. But still he had died a natural death and was gathered to his people with his city intact.[190] How would God look if a king like Hezekiah, who loved and served him devotedly throughout his reign, was allowed to die at the very moment a king should be in place and ruling with a decisive hand? It would probably seem like God was killing off the good kings and prolonging the days of the evil ones! This healing was vital to the continuity of the country spiritually as well as existentially at that particular point in history. It was no mere healing of one man.

The goal of this closer look at Hezekiah's healing is to point out that it was vital to more than just Hezekiah as a man. His healing is intimately linked to the welfare of the nation of Judah at the time, and the respect its people would give to God. So, yes, God healed Hezekiah; but it was more for God's and the country's benefit than it was for Hezekiah's—even though assuredly Hezekiah was strengthened in his faith through it. But I would also note that it did not prevent Hezekiah from acting very foolishly later in life with the emissaries from Babylon who had come to covertly spy out Judah for attack. The king showed them all the treasures he and Judah possessed as though he believed that since God was on his side he no longer had to use his wits in his position as king. Then God, again through Isaiah, made clear to him the ramifications of what he had done: Babylon was going to come one day and do what Assyria had not.[191] Unfortunately, Hezekiah had deteriorated in his reasoning to the point of just being happy to live strife-free during his own lifetime with no care as to what will befall the nation after he died. And ultimately he did die peacefully, after which his son took over the throne.

---

190. 2 Kgs 16:20.
191. 2 Kgs 20:12–18.

This brings up one last point about this particular healing that no other healing in the Bible explains so forthrightly. There are no "healings" in the Bible in the sense of cures for the curse. We should use a different term, like "reprieve" for example. After all, in every healing that occurs, the object of the healing is really just receiving a reprieve from the ravages of sin for a time. The healing (or reprieve) of Hezekiah is unique in that it tells us outright that his reprieve from death was fifteen years. This point is applicable to the next set of texts we will look at as well which mention resuscitations from death. They aren't "resurrections" of any kind—as though people are given new, immortal bodies. They are just reprieves until the flow of this world finally takes its natural course and kills the object a second time.

I mention this because when we are trying to decipher how God will realistically act, we shouldn't have some vague notion that he is going to stop the laws of nature for us. At best he might suspend them for a time, but we have to face facts my friends: God is going to let you die—unless Jesus comes back and interferes with the flow of reality in the biggest way possible.

Now, we were noting a few reasons why the healings we find in scripture might be special and might be necessary beyond the idea that God is answering a single person's prayer for healing. Next in our list is Luke 9:1-6 and the story of Jesus sending out the Apostles to proclaim the kingdom. In sending them out, he also gives them the ability to heal and cast out demons, and notice particularly what verse six says: "And departing, they began going about among the villages, preaching the gospel, and healing everywhere." These two items, preaching and healing, are inextricably linked. Earlier in the gospel we are told concerning another healing that Jesus performed that the work itself also revealed that Jesus had the power to forgive sins.[192] In the Apostle Peter's first sermon on the day of Pentecost, he says to the crowd that Jesus was "attested" to them "by God with miracles and wonders and signs which God performed through him" in their midst.[193] In the whole book of Acts every time a sign and wonder is mentioned it accompanies the sharing of the word so that people would believe the gospel. Paul also mentions

---

192. Luke 5:17-24.

193. Acts 2:22. Note that Acts was also written by Luke.

signs and wonders accompanying his work of sharing the gospel with the gentiles.[194]

My intent is not to get into a discussion of signs and wonders, per se, but merely to point out that the healings we see in scripture, which must be counted as signs and wonders, surely must have occurred for the advancement of the gospel, not just to heal people because they wanted some healing. Even when Peter's mother in law is healed from a fever, it is so she can wait on Jesus to further his ministry work.[195] This covers the healing in Acts 3 as well, for the healing of the lame man moves seamlessly into Peter and John proclaiming the gospel to the Jews with the healing as a starting point.

Perhaps the vaguest statement on healing in scripture is the one we find in 1 Corinthians 12:28. It tells us that some of the believers in the early church had a "gift of healing." Yet we might wonder, if that was a gift that was supposed to continue in the church, and was to be used on a daily, consistent basis, why Paul could not himself be healed, and why he had to persuade Timothy to drink wine to help his ailments.[196] I think it was probably because neither of them needed a sign proclaiming to them the gospel. They were already saved, and showing the power of God through a miraculous healing in order to inspire faith was not really of any use to them. They already had faith.

Now, we have seen two things: first, God *can* heal, but that the healings seem to come when something more than just fixing an illness is at stake; and second, that God clearly does *not* heal as typically as he is pictured doing in scripture. In point of fact, he even heals very little in scripture if we take into account how many people actually lived during the time of the writing of the Bible. There were millions upon millions in the world who never knew of the God of Israel, let alone received any healing from him.

Let's move on to another form of miracle we know God *can* produce. *God can raise the dead*

1 Kings 17:17–24. This is the famous story of the prophet Elijah and the widow of Zarephath. The widow had wanted a son for a long time, and finally, Elijah had met her and announced to her that she would have

---

194. Rom 15:19.
195. Matt 8:14–15.
196. 2 Cor 12:7–9; 1 Tim 5:23.

one. Unfortunately, later the child grew ill and died— "his sickness was so severe that there was no breath left in him." The widow was angry at Elijah about the loss, suggesting he had come to her just to remind her of her sins and to put the boy to death.[197]

Elijah took the boy and prayed to God over him saying, "O LORD my God, have You also brought calamity to the widow with whom I am staying, by causing her son to die?" Then he stretched himself upon the child three times, and called to the LORD and said, "O LORD my God, I pray You, let this child's life return to him." The LORD heard the voice of Elijah, and the life of the child returned to him and he revived.[198] It seems pretty clear: God definitely *can* raise the dead.

2 Kings 13:21. In this very odd text God raises up a dead man by using the dead bones of Elisha the prophet. The man had died and during the burial his companions saw some marauders at a distance. They panicked and in their haste to get away hurled the man's body into the grave of Elisha. When his body touched the bones of the great prophet, he was revived and lived again.

John 11:1-44. In what is probably the most famous of all resuscitation stories, the story begins with Jesus tarrying long enough to make sure everyone knows that his friend Lazarus is truly dead.[199] Lazarus' sisters, Mary and Martha, are distraught at Jesus' coming because they had hoped he would be there sooner to heal their brother. But amazingly, Jesus overrides even the passage of four days and calls Lazarus to "come forth" from the tomb—which he does, still wrapped for death in burial clothes. This is the most dramatic proof of God's ability to resuscitate the dead, and we can positively say again, God *can* raise the dead.

With the first set of passages I took time to find places recorded where people were sick but were not healed. This time I won't bother to find examples of places where people died and stayed dead. If you wish, you can peruse the thousands of names in the scriptures at your leisure and just append one of the following phrases: "and she died" or "and he died." Unless scripture tells us they were resuscitated, we can

---

197. 1 Kgs 17:18.
198. 1 Kgs 17:20–21.
199. John 11:1–6; 17; 21.

go with Paul's description of mankind in general in Romans: "death spread to all men."[200]

Just as a passing thought, let's run down a different rabbit trail for a moment. The first thing I would point out is how different these two types of miracle (healing vs. resuscitation) seem to be in our own minds and in our prayer lives. People will often pray for healing nowadays, but I've never once heard someone ask in prayer for a resuscitation from the dead. People may wrongly *think* God will heal on a regular basis, but they seem to *know* God *won't* routinely raise the dead. I guess we know we can only go so far before our requests just seem silly. No one will sit around praying for a resuscitation because we just *know* innately that God's not going to do it—even though we know he *can*. I wish people would get that same mentality about *healing*.

To continue, I would also point out that there are a lot of different miraculous actions that we see God perform in the scriptures which never come up in our own daily prayer lives.

How about the story of Elisha when he had his servant make stew for the sons of the prophets? There had been a famine in the land and everyone was pretty hungry. One enterprising man went out and got some wild gourds from a plant he didn't know anything about and threw them into the stew. Unfortunately, they were poisonous! The people all cried out, "There's death in the pot!" thinking they were probably all going to get sick and die. Elisha quickly solved the problem by having them add some meal or flour.[201] It's not an antidote that Elisha provides, but the story is exhibiting the power that Elisha wielded. Now, I don't see people praying that God heal their poisonous meals. Our family had a bad turkey one year at Thanksgiving, and we all got food poisoning. I remember praying grace over that meal, but God still let us all get sick. I know I felt like yelling, "There's death in the pot!" that night. Still, no one got a "yes" from God when we prayed for healing from the "poisonous" turkey.

As we've mentioned previously, Elijah prayed there would be no rain and there wasn't for three and a half years.[202] That would be a good one to imitate if you have a vacation coming up I suppose. Or if you prefer to only use such prayers when you're acting "Christian-y," you could pray for sunny skies when you have a Christian campout at your church.

200. Rom 5:12.
201. 2 Kgs 4:38–41.
202. James 5:17.

But for the most part, people don't usually pray for droughts—even short week-enders—expecting they will really occur. Deep down we know God doesn't do that sort of thing on a regular basis, even though we do sometimes pray that the weather is good. I guess we don't mind having all of our region or the country subservient to our weather needs on specific weekends.

Here is one more from Elisha's life. He wanted to thwart some enemies of the state so he prayed that God strike them with blindness.[203] You would think that would be a good on to always have on hand—striking people with blindness. There are so many people who hate Christianity and want to overtly or covertly hurt Christians and Christian entities. Still, I must say again, you don't see that one being offered over and over during our prayer times. It's in the Bible, so we know God *can* strike the enemies of his people blind, but somehow we just cannot get to the place of imitating that one.

So, I realize I've been a bit facetious at the end here, but my point is that everyone can find examples of both miraculous and non-miraculous answers to prayer in the Bible. And those that pray for miraculous things on a regular basis even seem to innately realize that many of the amazing things God can do (because they are recorded in scripture) he won't actually do for them. And consequently they know well enough not to ask.

But I must emphasize again, we should note well that the fact is, the huge majority of cases are examples of God *not* interposing with a miraculous answer in people's lives. Think about the Bible. How many miraculous happenings are recorded? How many wondrous answers to prayer? One hundred? One thousand? Let's assume 50,000 miraculous and wondrous answers to prayer are recorded in the Bible. (There are nowhere near that many actually recorded with details, but let's assume that gigantic number.) Think now of all the people in the world who were living during the times those miracles occurred. Compared to the mass of people that actually lived during their occurrences, we can see that of that mass, a tiny, very tiny, immensely tiny proportion of people were given a miraculous answer to their prayers. Do you see how infrequently God actually intervened with a healing, or a vision, or something like that? Yes, we could perhaps argue that the others just weren't recorded. But there is no record of such things being *typical* anywhere in the historical

---

203. 2 Kgs 6:17.

life of the church or Israel. There are outbreaks of occasional miraculous answers, but for the most part, daily life is pretty non-miraculous for the believer. I would argue that what makes those records of the miraculous amazing is the very fact that they stand out against a backdrop of utter mundane ordinariness in the lives of believers. We work, we save, we eat, we sleep, we grow old, we get sick, and we die. Everyone is on the road to the grave. And it is not a road populated with towns called "Healingopolis," "FreeMoneytown," or "Resuscitationville."

The scriptures do not paint a picture that encourages us to expect the ice cream cone from God every time we interact with him. To the contrary, the Bible actually paints a rather bleak picture for our present, earthly lives. Jesus tells the disciples that they will be handed over for persecution.[204] He teaches that we, the slaves, ought to expect to suffer just as he, the Master, did.[205] Paul notes the hardships he had suffered for the gospel as opposed to some miracle filled life of Riley.[206] The author of Hebrews exhorts his readers with the statement: "let us also lay aside every encumbrance, and the sin which so easily entangles us, and let us run with endurance the race that is set before us, fixing our eyes on Jesus, the author and perfecter of faith, who for the joy set before him *endured the cross* [emphasis added], despising the shame, and has sat down at the right hand of the throne of God."[207] This is certainly not an exhortation to expect a life of ease and the easy removal of sickness, difficulty, and pain. He is saying life is going to be hard from within because of struggles with sin, and from without because of hatred by the world. Jesus didn't have an out, and neither do we. He endured, and so ought we.

We need to understand that God can do all sorts of things. Yes, you can win the lottery, but that doesn't really matter. What matters is will you win the lottery; what matters is what God does do—what he will do. If we pray with the belief that God will act on a daily basis according to what he *can* do, we will never learn to pray in accordance to what he really *does* do. We will always be praying a lottery prayer that, 99.9 percent of the time, God will definitely say, "no" to. Because like our lotteries, God's miraculous, wondrous answers are very few and far between, and those who receive them are the one-in-a-billion, not the one-in-four.

204. Luke 21:12.
205. Matt 10:24–25.
206. 1 Cor 4:9–13.
207. Heb 12:2.

Moreover, when miraculous events did occur in scripture, it was for very specific purposes that transcended the desire of the one receiving the miraculous answer.

Some might be shaking their head with a sigh at this point. Maybe you're thinking that the idea I'm suggesting here is actually part of the problem, not the solution. Some will argue that we don't see God doing all he can because *we* are restraining him. People like me are the real problem—people who suggest that the bar of prayer should not be raised to expect the miraculous consistently, and in so doing we never allow the possibility of the miraculous occurring. Like the archer, we get what we aim for, and aiming at the mundane gets us just that. Just for the record, I'm not saying that, because I am convinced that God does do the miraculous at times. But I also see in scripture that the miraculous is rare and that there is a deep and important *value* to the mundane and often painful lives we live on a daily basis. This is something that the miracle-hawkers don't seem to get. I'll say it again: There is *real value* in the ordinary life most believers live, and they are not missing out on the *real* Christian life they ought to be experiencing. God, who pervades every aspect of our lives, actually sees great *value* in the daily, trudging existence we endure when we live our lives well and in service to him. Let me add another thought to this: Rather than emphasizing a fully Christian life, the miracle-hawkers out there are actually dismissing the real and faith-filled lives of billions of believers in a blasé and condescending manner. Shame on them! Wonderful Christians all through the ages have suffered and died in honorable, yet "mundane" service to Christ, and they ought not to be dismissed as ignorant, spiritual fools who couldn't access "cool" and "super spiritual" miracles from God.

Even more serious than demeaning the mundane but faithful lives of believers is the problem of what the miracle-hawkers are teaching faithful believers who *want* to walk in the footsteps of their Lord. They hold out the notion that God will act in miraculous ways just because they find a few examples of God acting miraculously in the scriptures, but it escapes their notice that the huge majority of Christendom has gone through life never experiencing such miraculous events. Perhaps they think most Christians are spiritual dolts who couldn't pray up a miracle if their lives depended on it. Hmmm, that's an ironic thought, isn't it?

The miracle-hawkers also seem oblivious to what they are presenting to the world: If God acts according to what he *can* do on a regular basis, then frankly speaking, God can't do much, can he? After all, I alone could name a dozen faithful believers off the top of my head who are in the throes of sickness and death, sorrow and pain, difficulty and fear. Their lives are filled with divorce, death, work layoffs, church difficulties, sin struggles, and other real-world problems, yet they devoutly believe in God with all their hearts. "Weak" faith is not the source of their struggles and the lack of a miraculous solution is not a symptom of their spiritual smallness. The real truth is, God is not sending the miraculous remedy because he chooses not to for the greater good of all involved. Sin and trials are real-life entities and we need to learn how to handle them, and stop telling people to always look for the ice cream cone when God wants us to eat the liver and broccoli. (No offense to you liver and broccoli fans out there; I'm thinking in terms of all the good nutrients in them.) We need mundane tasting spiritual nutrition that energizes the spirit rather than religious sugar that rots our souls.

Taking one more step, the situation that is created when we are constantly telling people they should expect miracles from God is like that which would exist if our ice-cream-cone-wanting child had a number of sadistic siblings. The child may sense in her heart the truth that mom has a regular daily pattern of more common provision—the ice cream cone is truly the "unexpected" gift in a sea of loving, yet mundane care. But her cruel brothers and sisters are telling her, "never mind what we have actually experienced mom doing on a daily basis," ignore reality and pursue fantasy. The girl should just keep hammering away at mom for the ice cream cone; she should at least start every discussion with mom as though she expects some sort of treat outside of mom's daily routine. Moreover, they tell her that if she doesn't get the ice cream cone, and can't get anything else out of the ordinary, there's just something wrong with her because *they* are getting those blessings *all* the time. Of course, they cannot share any of it with her because she doesn't have the proper attitude to receive it—her faith in mom is "weak" or "restrained." Lack of miraculous blessing in her life is really all her own fault come to think of it. Does this scenario even remotely make any sense to you?

I believe many of our brethren teach this "lottery syndrome" approach to prayer in good faith and not because they are cruel. They rightly believe that God *is* great and loving and interested in our lives.

But they also honestly believe that he will answer our prayers according to all he *can* do (i.e., with all the power he can muster). They are deceived and such a belief is a fatal and crushing mistake. They are missing the important truth that our lives here on earth are, in many respects, like a train heading toward a shattered bridge. Every one of us, believers included, and all this creation as well, is headed toward a meltdown (literally for the universe); and God *wants* it to be that way. God could have removed the cross from Jesus' life—but he didn't. He *wanted* it that way. The Apostle Peter says God even "predestined" that trauma for Jesus.[208] Remember, the broken rails we are chugging along are not the *real* reality for us. They are the track we follow now even while we see the golden rails to heaven in our faith. Jesus saw those golden rails as he watched his own earthly tracks plunge off a cliff into death on a cross, and he didn't waste his time asking for the earthly ones to be miraculously repaired.

Look honestly for a moment at Jesus' life, keeping in mind that he is our example.[209] He was described as a "man of sorrows and acquainted with grief" for good reason.[210] His life was not filled with the extraordinary answers to prayer that some expect to occur in our lives. Yes, he healed others, and raised the dead, and allowed others to become prosperous, but he Himself got none of this! We don't like to look at it that way, but it's the plain truth. He even lamented one day that even birds and foxes have homes, whereas he could claim none during his ministry.[211] If we wanted to honestly pray to follow Jesus' model we would pray constantly that God allow anything, painful or otherwise, to enter our lives so that others might prosper.

Let's come back to the main point and ask this: Why do we want to know what God *will do* as opposed to what he *can* do? Well, if we can pin down how God really does typically act, we can start to get a feel for what he desires in terms of actual, recognizable involvement in the world and in our lives. Notice I said "recognizable." We have to be able to see God acting—to recognize his hand—to truly be able to say he has, in fact, acted, don't we? I suggest that we will only see him acting when we understand that he acts all the time in regular, non-miraculous ways. (It's difficult to describe God's intervening in *any* way you know what

---

208. Acts 4:27–28.
209. Cf. 1 Pet 2:21.
210. Isa 58:3.
211. Matt 8:20.

I mean.) We can see him acting all the time when we get on his page and pray for things that he can actually step in and act on. We will never see and recognize him acting any other way, for the truth is, he will not act when all we ask for are ice-cream-cone requests that don't fit his system and desires for our lives.

It does us little good say God *can* do such and such. Frankly, who cares? I know God *can* raise me from the dead if I am hit by a car on the way home. The real question is whether I live in such a way that I give him the opportunity to exhibit that bit of power. It sounds a bit ridiculous when said out loud like this, but that's only because it is a bit ridiculous when we think about it, isn't it? God can do all sorts of things but that is no help to us when we want to know God intimately. Knowing what people *will do* is the only way I can relate to them, and it is the only way to relate to God as well—according to what he really, honestly, typically, wantonly *will* do.

So, to sum this error up, God wants us to resonate with his real goals and desires in life, and not always to be asking for a test of his power. That's what is really happening you know. We want him to miraculously intervene, I believe, because we secretly, maybe unbeknownst even to ourselves, want to see it with our own eyes, not because it will further what God wants for us. We want faith in the visible, not faith in the unseen.

Once we start to resonate with him in real terms our prayer lives become serious, because suddenly we begin to see "yes" answers all over all over our lives. This is because we begin to pray along God's lines and he freely and wantonly will answer "yes" when that is happening. We begin to walk through life as God really wants us to live it, with him at our side aiding us in authentic and realistic ways. We remove the picture of God as the magic unicorn who grants every wish, and replace it with God as a real and active friend walking by our sides.

SUMMARY

One thing I do not want this book to be is merely a list of things that are wrong with our prayer lives. You don't need me to point out all the problems anyway—most likely what you really want are some solutions. And I want to get to that portion as well. But before we move on to the next topic, let me sum up this entire section.

The overarching topic that we are addressing is reasons why people do not enjoy prayer. Under this broad topic I have highlighted a few practices that I think are especially problematic for people and prayer. First, prayer is haphazard. I noted five problems that contribute to this haphazardness: We have no system to follow; we don't know how to pray in the first place; we don't know how God will answer; we don't interpret his answers honestly; and finally, we don't reshape our requests in light of the answers we receive.

Second, I noted that the true goals of prayer often seem to be ignored. Here I listed just three important goals that are key to authentic prayer: Prayer should be effective and accomplish something; it should promote spiritual maturity; and lastly, it should aid endurance in the life before us, not somehow remove all hardships.

Third, I said that often we have been trained to pray in a rather boring fashion. In regular life we often don't want to participate in activities because we find them excruciatingly boring. Our Bible studies are not that way; our church services are not that way. But for some reason we keep teaching prayer in a manner that renders it exceedingly dull—and consequently, we don't want to participate in it.

Finally, I pointed out that there are a few foundational flaws in many of our prayer lives that impede progress and enjoyment in prayer. We sometimes drift into nagging God for the things we want. Sometimes we think that if we can get a lot of people to agree with us, that will persuade God to give us what we desire. Finally, we sometimes us the "lottery" approach where we think God is going to give us the big winnings every time we place a bet—uh, I mean *prayer*.

People aren't praying authentic prayer, for all of these are reasons, and of course, there are undoubtedly many others we could have listed. But the ones we have examined seem particularly important to me. Now, I could just shrug my shoulders and say, "that's the way it is," but of course I wouldn't be writing this book if I thought it *had to be* the way it is—with no solutions. There *are* some solutions and we *are* going to get to them. But, before we do, we need to discuss a few more ideas. First up, in our next section, will address expectations, and ask, "What expectations do we bring to prayer?" We have touched on this in places in the previous discussion, but it's helpful to put them all out in a row and identify them in one place. After that, I want to address how people mitigate the problems I've been describing (and perhaps you've been experiencing). Then, finally, we will end the book with an examination of actual prayers from the Bible, putting our insights together into a more complete and realistic picture of how to pray.

3

What Are Our Real Expectations?

I WAS FLUSH WITH energy and pride as I ran up and down the basketball court in fourth grade. I was on a team that played *real* games with refs and everything! The other team was full of popular kids whereas ours was comprised of individuals from the nameless rabble of fourth grade—yes, I was nameless rabble. The other team even had cheerleaders—five or six of the most popular and pretty girls who attended the popular boys on the other team. We, of course, had none.

Basically, the cheerleaders cheered solely for their boyfriends and ignored the great unwashed rabble on the other teams. Consequently I felt a powerful flush of energy and pride when I heard my name being called out as I stole the ball and began to head up court. One of the cheerleaders (*the cheerleaders! The pretty popular cheerleaders!*) had cupped her hands around her mouth and was screaming at the top of her lungs *directly* at me, "Go Tom! Hey! Tom! Go!" She was ardently trying to get me to hear her. I almost stumbled in my exuberance! She (I'll call her Joan) was cheering for me! She had finally come to realize what a magnificent athlete I was! Or perhaps my personal charm and charisma had finally overwhelmed her at that very moment! She had switched sides *right during the game!* I must admit, I *was* devastatingly handsome in the fourth grade.

As I expertly sped up court with the ball under erratic, semi-control I glanced over at her as she screamed, "Go Tom!" I saw her standing right up at the out of bounds line, her face red with the effort of shouting. She was even wearing a skirt that looked like a cheerleader's outfit, and it flitted about as she squirmed with the effort of screaming *my name*. And then I heard the next line blaring from her lips: "Goooo Toooom! OUT THE DOOR AND OFF THE FLOOR! Go Tom Go!!" In an instant my heart plummeted. Anger rose in my throat. Shame at the foolish ideas of friendship that had arisen in the split second of hearing "Go Tom!"

shouted at me by a pretty, popular, fourth-grade cheerleader. She was not praising me in any way. She was making a point of ridiculing me. My expectations were shattered. And it hurt.

Expectations. We have hinted at this subject briefly by necessity as we have looked at various topics thus far in the book. But let's go back to it now for a little more in-depth discussion.

Have you ever prayed for something and had nothing happen? Have you then asked yourself, "Why aren't my prayers being answered?" Or, conversely, have you ever prayed for something and had an answer immediately? When that has occurred have you asked yourself, "Why did God agree to that?" We don't usually ask this last question do we? It's been my experience that when things go their way people don't usually evaluate why they did. They just assume that's how things should have gone and move on.

We usually wonder about why God responds or does not respond for other reasons. First, when there seem to be no answers at all from God we wonder why our prayers aren't answered. Second, when we consistently receive "no" answers from him we wonder when he will say "yes" to something. Sometimes these situations blend together for us and we equate "no" with no answer. Then, we often will console ourselves, in light of these "no" answers or silences, with the thought that we can't understand God anyway, or that that is just the nature of prayer. As I have said before, sometimes we just go to the ol' standby of throwing up our hands and crying, "Mystery of God!"

No matter how we deal with it, when our expectations are not met, I think we are hurt. Just like when I was led astray by what I thought that cheerleader was doing. I had wrong expectations and they led me into heartache.

In any event, as we have previously said, crying, "Mystery of God!" does not really help us in any real way. And it especially doesn't help us when we are trying to figure out what God will actually do in our lives. If our prayers are always reduced to mystery, it makes prayer similar to a game of roulette. We spin the wheel of prayer and God randomly releases a "ball of answer" either agreeing to or denying that request. Sometimes the ball bounces onto our prayer-bet, and sometimes it doesn't. We don't really know, but we keep on wagering with the hope that God (Lady Luck?) will smile on us and will answer with a "yes." Of course, like so many beliefs that shape our actions we would never characterize our prayer lives that way out loud, but in practical terms, that appears to be the situation.

Such a view, the Mystery-Roulette method of prayer, is not much help. We have as our only option to look at where the ball lands, but we believe that the next time we ask, it will be like another bet on a wheel. God's too mysterious to predict in any way, just like that roulette ball is impossible to predict. I have to ask again, is that what our prayers should be like? Should prayer have this sense of "I have no idea what to expect from God"?

What are our expectations when we pray? Have you ever asked yourself this question honestly? Have you asked it in relation to every type of prayer you offer to God? It can apply to any prayer we offer up, though we amend the question depending on what the prayer consists of. So, for example, "What do I expect God to do with my thanksgiving?" would more likely be phrased as, "How do I expect him to react to my thanksgiving?" Or maybe the question is asked when we have need of comfort: "What will God do to comfort me when I'm hurting?"

I'm thinking here mostly in the context of requests we make of God. Have you ever asked that question of yourself? Do it now. Ask yourself: "What do I expect God to do?" "What do I *really, honestly*, expect God to do?" Better yet, do it when you have a specific prayer request in mind. Ask: "What do I expect God to do (when I want him to *bless* my friends and family)?" "What do I expect him to do (when I am sick and want him to *heal* me)?" "What do I expect God to do (when I need comfort because my life is spinning out of control)?" "What do I expect God to *do*?"

As we have seen, I believe that one of the biggest problems we have in our prayer lives is failing to have any expectations of what God will practically do. It is an old, hackneyed cliché, but it is still true: If you have no target, you will undoubtedly not hit one. We have no expectations of what we would like God to do, or think he will do, so when we pray, we never actually hit on anything. We just float about with no verifiable answers.

Let's begin figuring this out by exploring what we should be praying about. To the question of what we should pray about, people have

What Are Our Real Expectations?

suggested a range of answers. These vary from nothing on the one hand (because God already knows what everyone needs) to absolutely everything on the other (because God is even interested in just hearing our thoughts).[1] Some suggest God only supplies our *needs* while others suggest he meets our *desires* as well.[2] All of these suggestions are accompanied by scripture texts that seem to support whatever is being urged upon us. But let's be honest, a few verses gleaned from scripture are not proof enough to give us a complete picture of what, specifically, we should ask about in prayer.

Jesus did say, "If you ask Me anything in My name, I will do it," but clearly experience has driven home the truth that this is not the case in the coarsest, literal sense of his words.[3] We cannot just tack on "in Jesus' name I pray" and get whatever we might pray for. Some have turned to the model prayer of Jesus recorded in Matthew 6:9–13 as the example of what to pray for:

> [9] "Pray, then, in this way: 'Our Father who is in heaven, Hallowed be Your name. [10] Your kingdom come. Your will be done, On earth as it is in heaven. [11] Give us this day our daily bread. [12] And forgive us our debts, as we also have forgiven our debtors. [13] And do not lead us into temptation, but deliver us from evil. *For Yours is the kingdom and the power and the glory forever. Amen.*'"[4]

Jesus actually prefaces this prayer with the words, "Pray in this way," so it certainly makes sense to incorporate the points he mentions. Yet in all honesty, very few of us would admit to only praying prayers that follow this pattern (let alone actually just repeating this prayer every time we pray). We usually include all sorts of other requests when we pray, and in light of Jesus' encouragement to ask anything in his name, we seem to be justified in doing so.[5]

---

1. Matthew 6:8; John 14:14. Matthew 6:8 says God knows what we need before we even pray for it. Some might infer that there is then no reason to pray at all since God already knows what is needed. However, in the next verses goes on to show them a prayer that includes asking for things (e.g., food, forgiveness, and guidance). So apparently even though God knows our needs, that fact does not preclude us asking for things.

2. Phil 4:19; Ps 37:4.

3. John 14:14.

4. Matt 6:9–14. Cf. Luke 11:2.

5. We are going to spend a good deal of time looking at this model prayer from Matthew 6 later in this book. For now I would merely suggest that we don't pray that prayer through on a regular basis as our daily prayers. We tend to pray more free-style

Let's say that we should bring to God *all* the desires of our hearts in prayer. Is such a view realistic? I would say that it is not, and that our daily experience of prayer proves to us that we ought to curtail our requests in some manner. Let's think about it for a moment. If God really intended us to ask for *anything*, then our experience should bear out one of two occurrences. First, we ought to receive *everything* we ask for. If God wants us to ask *anything* of him, then one would think that he would give us *anything* (i.e., everything we ask for). That would make sense. After all, why tell us to bring all our desires to him if he didn't intend to meet them? But of course reality shows us that we don't receive *everything* we ask for, so we must admit that God must expect us to curtail our requests in some way. He does not really mean that absolutely *anything* we desire we should ask of him.[6]

Now, if we still want to hold to the literal idea that we should bring absolutely anything to God, and yet we also know by experience that we are not receiving absolutely everything we pray for, then we must admit that God intends for us to be told "no" as often as we are told "yes." (Or, by the looks of it, he wants us to be told "no" a *lot more often*.) These are our only two options. If God wants us to ask absolutely anything of him in prayer, then either he will give us anything we ask, or (as reality proves) he wants to say "no" to us a lot. I only say that because I would suggest that many people, praying as they do now, are receiving a lot of "no" answers for all the reasons we've discussed up to this point in the book. I don't believe that many of us interpret "no" as "no," but I do think we are receiving "no." I'll explore this later when we discuss how many of us mitigate the problem of hearing "no" from God.

In any event, I won't beat this horse any longer. I think we would all agree that when we are told to bring *everything* and *anything* to God in prayer, he must expect some sort of limitation on that directive. So the question is, what is the limitation? We are driven back to wondering, will God respond to our prayers? What should we expect God to do when we request things in prayer?

---

prayers. And when we do incorporate it, we don't usually pray it and stop. I will suggest later that we don't pray much of the content of that prayer in any event, even when we do incorporate it into our prayers.

6. The most obvious thing we could point out here is that though we desire sinful things at times, we also realize we cannot and should not bring such requests to God. We assume without even thinking about it that requests of that sort should be excluded.

The Apostle John seems to clarify Jesus' statement for us a bit in his first epistle when he writes, "This is the confidence which we have before him, that, if we ask anything according to his will, he hears us."[7] This is often what people will say when they are limiting the "bring anything" idea—whatever you bring to God should be "in his will." You can hardly argue with John the Apostle, can you? But this is not really of much help in the specific sense. For John seems to be tacitly assuming that we ought to know what actually will be "in God's will." But that's the very question we are trying to answer in different clothes. Whether I ask, "What is in God's will?" or, "What can I expect God to do in response?" I'm basically saying that I need to have some idea of what God wants and how God will act. They are the same thought in different dress. I think in quoting John we are admitting, whether we like it or not, that we *should* know God's will to some extent. We ought to be able to anticipate how he will act in some way. In truth then, 1 John 5:14 states without doubt the underlying belief that we *can* know God's will, we *can* have explicit expectations of how he will act, and we *should* shape our prayers in light of these facts. Our prayers should not be vague and non-specific—crafted haphazardly. They should be to-the-point, with specific expectations that are in accordance with what Jesus would want in any situation. Our prayers should be effective as we described it earlier. But this whole idea seems to presuppose that we know Jesus well enough to anticipate or sense what he might want for us or for others. It presupposes we have some insight into what God wants now and will want in the future in response to the situations around us.

Let me again use a picture to paint this situation for us. As children we probably asked for things from our parents that made them laugh. Perhaps you asked for a pony. They did not berate you when you were seven years old and brought this request to them. But suppose you were forty years old and were still asking for a pony? At that point, everyone would wonder what is wrong with you. By the time you hit forty years old, you should have learned to not even ask for a pony. It has nothing to do with whether your parents love you, but everything to do with maturity, sense, and insight into what they might say and think. In the same way, perhaps our prayers are so often answered with a "no" because we are like 40-year-olds asking for ponies from God. The Apostle Paul says one of his deep desires is that believers grow in their knowledge of

---

7. 1 John 5:14.

Jesus and that they attain full maturity in that knowledge.[8] Paul does not want us to be pony-beggin' 40-year-olds.

Here I would return for a moment to the need for maturity in our lives. Asking things in prayer according to God's will must certainly be linked to our maturity in Christ. When we were new believers, we didn't know God too well, and consequently, we asked for many things indiscriminately. But often times we were answered with a "no." "No I won't make your phone bill magically disappear." "No, I won't make your attitudes miraculously change overnight." "No, I won't force you to go to church when it's boring." "No I won't make you give liberally to others." And on and on it undoubtedly went. But unlike children, many of us haven't grasped the idea that we *can* receive "yes" answers by learning to anticipate what is in accordance with God's personality and desires. We have not learned to shape our expectations of how God will act.

Let's now return to where we began this section: Expectations. I had begun by saying that sometimes we don't have any expectations of how God will act. And I have argued that having no expectations is really not feasible if we want to receive "yes" answers to our requests of God.

Now I want to discuss what I believe is more often the case with believers. It is not that we have no expectations, but that we really *do* have expectations. However, they have been so rarely met in our experience that now we hide them in a deep, dark corner of our psyches thinking no one will know they are there (especially God). We secretly hope that they will be met, but our experience in prayer is that they are seldom (mostly never) realized. We live in constant disappointment. It reminds me of a time as a child when I wanted a specific kind of toy for Christmas. I made that desire known to my parents as all children do—irritatingly, over and over again, incessantly begging and whining. They just didn't believe that I would use the toy as much as I said I would, so they got a cheaper, smaller version. They thought it was the same thing. I remember acting excited and thanking them, and the minute I got outside to play with it feeling that deep sense of dislike for what I actually got. It wasn't the same. It wasn't what I asked for. It would have been better (I thought) to have nothing at all rather than this knock-off. My inner expectation, which I still grasped, had not been met. And I was extremely disappointed and angry. (Let me note for the record that they were right—I didn't use it for more than a short while.)

---

8. Eph 1:17; 4:13.

What Are Our Real Expectations?

I think we end up in the same place in our prayer lives. We secretly have very concrete expectations that we no longer even share with God. They still dwell within us, and as much as we think we have put them down, they still prompt us quietly (or sometimes loudly) for attention. Experience has taught us that God won't give us the answer we desire, so instead of altering our expectations, we drive them underground, where, I suppose, we subconsciously think God can't see them. We tell ourselves on the surface that such expectations are silly, and we actually are right about that. Most of them *are* silly. But we haven't arrived at that conclusion by careful, mature evaluation. We have arrived at it by convention. We are like children that have been told they cannot do something and out of respect (fear?) of their parents they obey. But inside they still seethe with desire to do that thing, and that unmet desire does not just stop. It sits like an unfed lion and waits for an opportunity to assert itself.

I remember seeing in the news a few years back a story about a young man at a zoo. It's a story that recurs on occasion in the news; you just have to change the venue, animals, and participants and there it is. The general plot is this: Zoo visitor thinks the animal is cute and obviously tame; zoo visitor reaches too close to the bars; animal bites, claws, shreds zoo visitor in some way. And the usual summation, offered dryly by a commentator, is: Zoo animals are not tame! They're wild and waiting to exercise their God-given traits. That's what our crouching, hidden, un-reasoned expectations are like. They are not tame. They are wild. We cage them in the dark recesses of our minds thinking we have solved the problem they pose. But in truth, we have not solved anything. Every time we go to prayer, they are there waiting to pounce. They will not stop clawing at us until we really tame or exterminate them. (You should drop my analogy now; I'm not for exterminating lions, tigers or bears—oh my, no!) Consequently, we do not go to prayer very often in any serious way. If we do, it's like walking near the cage. We put our hand out and they suddenly attack and shred us. It's far safer to stay away from the cage entirely. But still, even though avoiding its vicinity, the animal roars and paces and shrieks for attention.

So how do we handle this situation? Again, one answer I'm going to address later is the reinterpretation of God's answers. However, that is a big topic and is, as I have said, for a later section. Let me put forward one very useful tool here and now, however. We put into use what I like to call "Christianese." This is the language of the Christian who does not want to actually speak their honest expectations of God openly. It includes all the terms we find in scripture—things like *bless, fill, love, permit, save, give,* etc. It's really a very useful language. I've seen it used in almost every "Christian" setting, but I'm limiting my discussion of it right now to how we use it to shape our prayers. We think it's a spiritual language. We think it's the language of the mature disciple of Christ. I know this is going to sound cynical, but my estimation is that this language is usually just a thin sheet over empty space. Most of us, though we use it fluently, don't have any idea of what it means and prefer to remain in our ignorance.

It's like those books we read every now and again that are full of big, three- and four-syllable words. We can pronounce them all; we can string the sentences together; we can digest the paragraphs. But at the end of the day, when we are asked what it's all about, we just shrug. We can, perhaps, even repeat some of the words and sentences, but in all honesty, we have no idea what the author is saying. I sometimes talk with people like this in my line of work as a college professor of Bible and theology. I saw it most clearly one day when my wife and I were speaking with another professor from a different school. We all chatted (well, mostly he and I chatted) for about an hour. Later, after we were alone, my wife asked me, "Did you understand anything he said?" I had gotten about forty percent of it; she got about five percent. We both understood all the words, but when they were strung together, they made no sense to us. They didn't convey any actual meaning for us. Even though I could repeat them, and knew their meanings as individual words. In all honesty, I suspect that the professor didn't actually understand what he was saying completely either. He was using a lot of popular Christian buzzwords that all of us who speak Christianese know, but hardly any of us understand in a practical or useful way. Or perhaps my wife and I were not "*nuanced*" enough to grasp the meaning of the words (using the popular lingo now in vogue).

How does this relate to our caged expectations, you may ask? These seem like two different topics on the surface, don't they? But I think there is an intimate relationship. First, we have expectations that we have not thought out, lurking in our heads. They want to be met (or be fed in our animal metaphor). But we also know from experience that they won't be met. God is not going to meet them as they exist. They will stay hungry. So we cage them in the back and try to ignore them. But every time we go to prayer they begin to howl, wanting to be met. So we either must quit praying, because praying makes our hidden expectations howl, or we must somehow pray in such a way as to satisfy them enough that they keep the howling to a low, tolerable murmur. Now, no serious Christian wants to just give up prayer, so that is not really a viable option. We *want* to pray—to converse with God intimately. We want to interact with our heavenly father on a daily basis. Quitting is out of the question for most of us. So we have no other alternative than to adopt a new way to pray.

Here is where Christianese enters. It is a language that is so malleable, so meaningless, that it can meet our need perfectly. It allows us to pray, but never demands we expect anything. It feeds our unwarranted, childish expectations with hope while at the same time it keeps them caged with terms right out of the Bible itself. It embraces dreams of miraculous intervention, but also survives on a diet of constant "no" answers from God. It is the language we can speak to one another, and to God, and not be required to actually have any idea of what we are saying in any meaningful, functional, practical way. It meets the one need of allowing us to talk *at* God, and at the same time suppress what we'd really like to say to him.

Is this too vague? Let's look at this language a bit and think about our expectations. I think in the end, we will have to re-interpret the language on a grand scale and we will definitely have to un-cage the expectations we harbor and slay them.

"BLESS US"

Here is a fine Christianese term: *Bless*. It's so scriptural that I'm sure every single one of you can pull up at least one scripture that uses it. But in prayer, it has completely lost its meaning for many of us. We use it in prayers like, "Lord, bless so and so," "Lord, bless me," "Lord bless my family," or, "Lord, bless this situation." But what do we expect to happen? What do we expect God to *do*? I would suggest that our inner, caged expectations are often along the lines of something like, "Lord, make everything go smoothly for my family," or, "Lord, make me happy all the time," or, "Lord, give me everything I want." Of course we don't parade those expectations outside in polite, Christian society. We don't even admit them to ourselves. As I said, they're kept inside, locked up. Oftentimes we don't even realize we've penned them away.

Most of us know, deep down, that the term "bless" in scripture does not mean give me everything I want. But we have failed to really find out what it does mean. This being the case, we have two tasks to undertake. It probably does not matter what order they come in, but let's put first the task of finding out what "bless" actually means in English. Our second task will be to look at the use of the term in the Old and New Testaments. By doing so we can pin down the meaning of these terms as they are used in a variety of contexts and try to piece together what the concept of "blessing" entails.

So, what about the term "bless" in English? What does it mean? It's an odd question isn't it? The reason we need to ask it, is because sometimes we use terms in everyday speech that are poorly defined in our heads. (This is the whole nature of Christianese.) That can be a problem when we are trying to figure out exactly what we are doing and talking about. Somehow, we have developed a vague notion for a word, but we have not been exactly clear about what it means in specific situations. So when we use it in prayer for example, it is so malformed in our heads that it becomes a fill-in word rather than an actual-meaning word. That is, it functions as a noun or verb, but doesn't function as a real concept for us.

According to Dictionary.com, our term "bless" means:

- To consecrate or sanctify by a religious rite; make or pronounce holy.
- To request of God the bestowal of divine favor on.
- To bestow good of any kind upon.
- To extol as holy; glorify.
- To protect or guard from evil (usually used interjectionally).
- To condemn or curse.
- To make the sign of the cross over or upon.[9]

I'm going to throw out a couple of these right off the bat, if you will allow it. First, I don't think any of us pray, "Lord, bless me," interpreting the term "bless" as "make a sign of the cross." We wouldn't restate our prayer as, "Lord, make the sign of the cross over me." So number seven is scratched. Also, number six is probably out of the question. Again, we would not pray, "Lord, condemn me." So let's dump that one too.

---

9. Dictionary.com, s.v. "Bless."

Of the remaining choices, I think we have used all of these in our prayers, rightly or wrongly. Let's take a look at them.

Notice that the first dictionary definition is an action, not just a statement: "to consecrate or sanctify by a religious rite." We see such a rite in Leviticus 9:22 when Aaron the high priest *blessed* the people of Israel. He was sanctifying them. A rite is a formal or ceremonial *act*. Although to be fair, the second sentence of the first definition does include the idea of speech alone: *pronouncing* something holy. But even that is after a restatement of action: *make* something holy.

I think many of us take the second definition as the one we operate by—"To *request* of God the bestowal of divine favor." This is not just a slight variation of the first definition. It is a completely different meaning. In fact, it is identical to just asking something from God. We could say the term "bless" equals the term "request" according to this second definition. Our prayer would be, "Lord, give me your favor," rather than, "Lord, bless me." The dictionary is not much help here, is it? Do you see another use of Christianese here? I replace "bless me" with "give me Your favor." Pretty cool, huh? And yes, I mean that in a sarcastic way; it's actually not so cool. The problem is, it sounds like we have understood the meaning of "bless," but in truth, we still end up with the problem of undefined expectations. What do we expect God to do in response to the request, "give me Your favor?" What is God's favor? What does it look like? But somehow I feel like I've actually said something different and concrete merely because I've replaced a word or two with some other non-specific word or two.

In fact, now that we have noticed this problem, we can see that all the definitions have this same difficulty don't they?

- "To consecrate or sanctify by a religious rite; make or pronounce holy." And we can ask, "How would I consecrate something?" if I were to pronounce such a blessing today?

- "To request of God the bestowal of divine favor on: Bless this house." And we can ask, "How would God bestow favor?" if I asked him to "bless" me?

- "To bestow good of any kind upon: a nation blessed with peace." And we can ask, "How would God bestow good on me?" if I asked him to do so?

- "To extol as holy; glorify: Bless the name of the Lord." And we can ask: "How would I extol God?" or, "How would I glorify God?" if I wanted to?

- "To protect or guard from evil (usually used interjectionally): Bless you! Bless your innocent little heart!" And we can ask, "How would God guard me from evil?" if I asked him to?

We are consistently stuck with the generic question, "How would God do…*whatever* I think is involved in "blessing"? It's not that the word "bless" itself is the problem. The Bible uses bless a lot. The problem is, what do we understand "bless" to mean when we use it?

Let's look at a few particular instances of the concept in scripture and see how it's used. Perhaps a few examples can shed some light on what we should expect God to do when we ask for "blessing" from him.

Since this book is focusing on what we request of God, I'm going to limit my examples to places where the idea of blessing is used in relation to request in some way. I want those examples that might reflect how we would use it in our prayers. And that typically means we are asking God for blessing on others or ourselves. Or it can mean we are commenting on the blessings God has already given to us. Not all the examples will be specifically prayers then, but they will in some way relate to that idea of how we desire blessing from God.

Let me begin with an interesting example from Psalm 67. I pick it first because it is a clear example of asking for blessing and it just so happens that it gives a purpose for that blessing as well. Since the Psalm is so short, I'll print it here in its entirety:

> [1] "For the choir director; with stringed instruments. A Psalm. A Song. God be gracious to us and bless us, *And* cause his face to shine upon us—Selah. [2] That Your way may be known on the earth, Your salvation among all nations. [3] Let the peoples praise You, O God; Let all the peoples praise You. [4] Let the nations be glad and sing for joy; For You will judge the peoples with uprightness And guide the nations on the earth. Selah. [5] Let the peoples praise You, O God; Let all the peoples praise You. [6] The earth has yielded its produce; God, our God, blesses us. [7] God blesses us, That all the ends of the earth may fear him.[10]

---

10. Ps 67:1–7.

In the first verse, after the introductory remarks, the author calls to God to be gracious to the people, bless them and make his face shine upon them. In verse two we read the most amazing thing. You would expect something along the lines of, "that we may be mighty" or, "that we might be prosperous" or something like that. But instead it says, "that Your way may be known on the earth, Your salvation among all the nations."

The first thing we need to understand about real blessing is that it comes to us *to further the greatness of God*, not just to give us stuff or make us happy. This is the heart of asking for blessing from God in a way that honors him. At least one goal of blessing from God, one expectation that we should have, is that God's way of living and being become more known by everyone. Moreover, we should expect that his salvation (the salvation provided in the blood of Christ) be known among all the nations. How about it? When you offer up that quick, "Lord bless so and so," is that part of what you're thinking? That in granting that blessing, God's ways would be made known more and more in the world? In this instance, God's blessing includes something that relates to *his* desires, not ours.

I think the reasoning is pretty clear on the author's part. He is suggesting that when God blesses his people with concrete things, they respond by praising him among all the nations. Additionally, the blessing that they receive flows, to some extent, to those who dwell around God's people. Verse seven again gives a reason for the blessing God pours on us: that all the peoples may fear him. When we ask God to bless us, part of our reasoning should be that others see and know God. There is no description here of blessing primarily having to do with us getting something, or being comfortable; it is entirely explained in terms of what it does for God in the world. This places quite a responsibility on our heads when God blesses us. It requires us to let people know that all the "blessings" we have are from God, furthering his name and reputation in the world. Do you do that?

There is another line, however, that gives us a glimpse of another expectation we might have of God when we ask for blessings. Verse six says, "The earth has yielded its produce; God, our God, blesses us." The idea presented in this verse is clearly not the main point of the psalm. Remember, the main point is that the blessing poured on the people has effect among the nations, revealing God to them. In verse six the author merely notes his interpretation of the natural cycles of food production.

When the crops grow well, he interprets it as God using that natural function of crop cycles as a means of blessing the people. Here then, is another real expectation for our call for blessing that we can identify in scripture. We might call for God to ensure the natural cycles of life around us. Interestingly enough, I would suggest that often we do the very opposite! We think of blessing, at least internally, as something happening *out of* the ordinary, *out of* the natural cycles of life. But here the author sees the normal flow of good crop cycles as the blessing God is pouring out on the people. This is not a passing thought. Those of us who live in cities (and the majority of Americans do) often lose track of the cycles of nature and the reality of nature.

People often speak idealistically about things like, "getting back to the land" and, "living in rhythm with nature." Usually they are wistfully longing for a "simpler time" when people lived "simply" and in harmony with the world around them.[11] For the most part, the people I hear speaking like that have no idea what reality is like for someone "living in harmony" with the world around them. The truth is, nature is constantly trying to kill you. In reality, food is not guaranteed every year when the crop comes up. We in America can run down to the local market twenty-four hours a day, seven days a week and carbo load on Twinkies and Ho-Hos. Consequently, we get the wrong idea that food is so plentiful and easy to produce that it too can be picked and eaten at any moment. But the reality is that crops fail all over the world. People starve for lack of rain. In much of the world nature is the reality of life and death. When the author of Psalm 67 calls something so mundane (to us) as a crop being a blessing, he's speaking from experience with real nature and difficult farming. He sees God's hand in good crops because bad crops are just as likely, and it truly is a gracious blessing to have abundant food and healthy crops. And it's a blessing that God does not always give.[12] We should include in our calls for blessing the idea of the cycles of the world just working as they should under the steady hand of a gracious God. Wouldn't this put a whole new spin on what we expect from God when we request his blessing? We would, perhaps, stop asking for the miracu-

---

11. I'm highlighting these terms and phrases because they have become buzz words in our society that I am convinced everyone has heard.

12. Note Genesis 12:10 for example where we are informed that "there was a famine in the land." Clearly God does not always give abundant crops. It truly is a *blessing* when he does.

lous and out of the ordinary, and would concentrate on the routine and regular. We would see God more intimately related to the mundane life around us (which then would probably not be so "mundane" after all).

Let's look at another example. An interesting use of the term "bless" is found in another of the psalms: Psalm 65. It too is fairly short, so I have included it in its entirety as well:

> [1] "For the choir director. A Psalm of David. A Song. There will be silence before You, *and* praise in Zion, O God, And to You the vow will be performed. [2] O You who hear prayer, To You all men come. [3] Iniquities prevail against me; As for our transgressions, You forgive them. [4] How blessed is the one whom You choose and bring near *to You* To dwell in Your courts. We will be satisfied with the goodness of Your house, Your holy temple. [5] By awesome *deeds* You answer us in righteousness, O God of our salvation, You who are the trust of all the ends of the earth and of the farthest sea; [6] Who establishes the mountains by his strength, Being girded with might; [7] Who stills the roaring of the seas, The roaring of their waves, And the tumult of the peoples. [8] They who dwell in the ends *of the earth* stand in awe of Your signs; You make the dawn and the sunset shout for joy. [9] You visit the earth and cause it to overflow; You greatly enrich it; The stream of God is full of water; You prepare their grain, for thus You prepare the earth. [10] You water its furrows abundantly, You settle its ridges, You soften it with showers, You bless its growth. [11] You have crowned the year with Your bounty, And Your paths drip *with* fatness. [12] The pastures of the wilderness drip, And the hills gird themselves with rejoicing. [13] The meadows are clothed with flocks And the valleys are covered with grain; They shout for joy, yes, they sing.[13]

Here we find another enlightening use of the concept "bless." In this instance we have two different Hebrew terms for the concept. One implies happiness or blessedness belongs to someone (verse four) and the other refers to God prospering something (in this case the earth, verse ten).

Notice the first instance: "How blessed is the one whom You choose and bring near to You to dwell in Your courts." In this instance, the blessing that the people receive is happiness just to be in the presence of God. How many of us pray, "Lord, bless me," with that expectation? "Lord, choose me and bring me near to you so I can live in your presence." What would that conjure up for expectations in our lives? Certainly it

13. Ps 65:1–13.

envisions something entirely different from what we usually expect when we call for a blessing. And note the comment by David after that line: "We will be satisfied with the goodness of Your house, Your holy temple." For David, there was joy, happiness, and blessing just in being able to go to the temple and worship the Lord, standing in his presence. Do we pray to be blessed with that as our expectation? How could God actually bless us with this blessing when we are asking with the expectations we usually harbor? I cannot recall even once hearing a call to God for blessing that I could have interpreted as a request to merely come into God's presence at church to worship him. Can you?

Of course, David also notes that God answers their prayers with "awesome deeds." Can you say that? Does God answer your prayers consistently with "awesome deeds?" I think David can say that because of the expectations he has. He expects from God what God actually will and does do on a daily basis. God is truly awesome when we see him working as he chooses—regularly—to work.

More often than not, "awesome" means to us something completely out of the ordinary—something miraculous (as we've noted before). But look at David's ideas of "awesome" in this psalm. Just the fact that the mountains are made is God acting "awesomely." The dying out of a storm on the sea, the sunrise and sunset, the flow of fresh water, the growing of crops (again), and that the land is full of animals that are healthy—all are "awesome" to David. For David, blessing is not the miraculous intervention of God with amazing feats of unnatural power. Blessing is the awesome working of God in his sustaining of nature—his power exhibited naturally in the cycles of the world he made for us. It is his abundant supplying of what the earth provides even in its fallen state. David understands how intimately God holds each element in creation together, and he sees the awesome power and blessing of God in the fact that the world even revolves around the sun each day. How petty and sad our modern scientific view is when it thinks by merely describing the orbit of the earth around the sun that it has comprehended the majesty and awesome nature of this planet on which we live. (As a side note, I must admit that the more I learn about science, the more I'm dumbfounded that every scientist in the world is not a firm and joyous believer in the awesome existence and majesty of God.)

How did we get to this place? How is it that we miss God in the daily flow of the world around us? I'm not sure I have an answer to that.

Maybe we've mastered the complex structures of nature well enough at this point to imagine that they are self replicating with no presence of God. Probably we've just taken for granted what previous generations have not come by so easily—food, water, housing, and comfort. In practical terms, we've relegated God out of the ebb and flow of the natural world around us. So we see nothing of blessing in natural process or even the scientific inventiveness that provides so many wonderful things for us.

Let's switch to the New Testament for another example. In Luke 6 is the Lukan version of the Sermon on the Mount. In verses twenty-seven and twenty-eight is the following: "But I say to you who hear, love your enemies, do good to those who hate you, *bless* those who curse you, pray for those who mistreat you."[14] (In the Matthean version, Matthew leaves out the blessing clause.) We find this same instruction to bless others in the Pauline book of Romans in chapter twelve, verse fourteen. The Greek term used in these instances is *eulogeo*, which has a range of meanings:[15]

- "To say something commendatory, speak well of, praise, extol." This is the use found in Luke 6:27–28 and Romans 12:14. It is also intended in 1 Cor 4:12.
- "To ask for bestowal of special favor, especially of calling down God's gracious power, bless." This is a meaning very close to that which we saw in the Old Testament.
- "To bestow a favor, provide with benefits." This use implies acting on behalf of others. We find such a use in Acts 3:26 where it says God raised up his Servant (Jesus) to send him to his people (the Jews) to bless them, turning them from their evil ways.

I wanted to especially note again the active nature of the term "bless." In the first instance, in our example, we see that when we are told by Jesus to bless those who curse us, it means we *say something commendatory*. We could say that the second definition implies the same thing. We might call on God to bless the one cursing us, but certainly that must

---

14. Luke 6:27–28.
15. Bauer, *A Greek-English Lexicon*. This lexicon, often referred to as BDAG, is a standard Greek-English lexicon of the Greek language. It is named for the editors who assembled it—Bauer, Danker, Arndt, and Gingrich.

be in their hearing, so again, we are saying something to them to indicate we are not an enemy (even if they consider us one). The last definition is even more pointed. This idea would imply we actually do more than speak praise to them: We would *provide a benefit* to that person who curses us.

I could go on and on with examples, but the point I wish to make is clear. When we use the term "bless" in our prayers we often use it as Christianese—as a somewhat fuzzy concept with no expectations of either how God would act or even how I would act when mentioning it. But we need to remove its fuzziness and become more concrete in our thinking. We need to ask the question when we call on God for "blessing:" What exactly do I expect him to *do* as a blessing for me? Or if I'm blessing another, what exactly does that require *me* to do?

"COMFORT"

Here is another term we often use both in prayer and conversation. But again, it is regularly stripped of any practical meaning. When we ask God to "comfort" us, what do expect him to do? I believe that much like "bless," "comfort" is frequently used to mean "remove my discomfort" or, "stop my emotional hurt." But here again, I think we've misunderstood what real "comfort" is. Comfort is not necessarily the removal of distress. In fact, comfort more commonly is gaining a right understanding in the midst of distress. It is learning to accept and deal with distress. So when we call on God for comfort, we should be expecting him to provide us some way of dealing with the difficulties that we are facing, not the removal of those difficulties. So how would God do that?

Here are a couple of examples from scripture. The first is from Psalm 119, a great Psalm about the *Torah*, or *"instruction"* from God. *Torah* is the Hebrew name for the first five books of the Bible. We also call them the *Pentateuch* referring to the fact that there are five of them. Psalm 119 is a long, complex psalm that declares the majesty of God's instruction. It is a beautifully crafted alphabetic psalm, meaning in this case, that every eight line stanza begins with a succeeding letter from the Hebrew alphabet. The verses I wish to look at fall in the section that begins each line with the Hebrew letter *Zayin* (119:49–56). This section reads:

> [49] Remember the word to Your servant, In which You have made me hope. [50] This is my comfort in my affliction, That Your word

> has revived me. ⁵¹ The arrogant utterly deride me, *Yet* I do not turn aside from Your law. ⁵² I have remembered Your ordinances from of old, O LORD, And comfort myself. ⁵³ Burning indignation has seized me because of the wicked, Who forsake Your law. ⁵⁴ Your statutes are my songs In the house of my pilgrimage. ⁵⁵ O LORD, I remember Your name in the night, And keep Your law. ⁵⁶ This has become mine, That I observe Your precepts.[16]

The author seems to pack a lot of ideas into these verses. First he notes that he is under affliction, but he has a comfort through it. And that comfort is the reviving nature of the Word of God. And note that he says it *has revived* him. It has *already* done this. I am dismayed at how often I hear of Christians who, when facing difficulties in life, turn from the very things that can provide comfort to them. People become despondent and rather than turning *to* the Word of God, for example, they actually turn *away* from it. I think this must be the influence of evil in the world. What better strategy could Satan have than to convince us that when we are slogging through hard times we would be better off without the input of God's wisdom and hope? In our text we find a very practical answer to our prayers for comfort from God: read his word; meditate on it; trust in it. When we pray for "comfort" from God, we should expect his word to speak to us, and look to it for the comfort it offers.

The author of Psalm 119 also says that even though people deride him, he does not turn aside from the Law of God. He is single minded in the face of opposition. This is a more pointed statement about action than the first about the law reviving him. Here we have a practical way of drawing comfort from God: Keep on walking in his ways. Our author says he has "remembered Your ordinances from of old" and "comforts" himself. How do these relate? In living out our Christian lives (or Jewish lives at the time the Psalm was written) we see practically, on a daily basis the outworking of God's power. From those daily actions which are in accord with God's desires we draw the comfort of knowing that we are in communion with God, knowing that even in trial we are demonstrably walking in righteousness. And righteousness *is* a comfort to us. There is nothing more demoralizing and un-comforting than fretting over sin we are committing. But when we walk righteously with God, we can weather difficulties knowing that we have not brought them on

---

16. Ps 119:49–56.

ourselves. They are there to serve the greater purposes of God, whether that be our maturity, or some other matter.

Finally, take note that the author actually mentions his "indignation" at the fact that the unrighteous have abandoned God's law. It is not as though God's comfort relieves our stress entirley, but it provides a proactive and positive way of living with our stress. It is not a feeling, but a doing that God gives us. And in this case he gives us this comfort through the doing of his commands.

In a New Testament passage we find a very similar thought. First Thessalonians 4:13–18 is an answer Paul sends to the Church at Thessalonica about their loved ones who have died. They had apparently wondered what happens to them—would they still partake of the coming of the Lord? Paul reassures the believers that their loved ones would indeed share in the resurrection and glory of Jesus. And the last line he adds is, "Therefore, *comfort* one another with these words."[17] Again, Paul cites the transmission of God's truths as a source of comfort for believers.

In the second letter to the Thessalonians, Paul encourages them to keep on living their Christian lives well. He says,

> [15] So then, brethren, stand firm and hold to the traditions which you were taught, whether by word *of mouth* or by letter from us. [16] Now may our Lord Jesus Christ Himself and God our Father, who has loved us and given us eternal comfort and good hope by grace, [17] comfort and strengthen your hearts in every good work and word.[18]

Notice verse sixteen: "May our Lord . . . comfort and strengthen your hearts in every good work and word." Again the two main emphases of God's word and our actions are avenues by which God comforts his people. And here the Apostle Paul's blessing is that the readers truly receive that comfort. Certainly the only way for this to practically play out is for them to hear and heed the word of God.

When we pray to God for "comfort" we need to be realistic in our expectations. No Christianese vagaries will do. We need to think in terms of concrete responses from God; how will he comfort us? And we can

---

17. 1 Thess 4:18.
18. 2 Thess 2:15–17.

categorically name two ways: Through his Word already given to us, and through our daily living out of his desires.

Let me mention one more passage that speaks to this idea of comfort from God. It is in the book of 2 Corinthians:

> [3] Blessed *be* the God and Father of our Lord Jesus Christ, the Father of mercies and God of all comfort, [4] who comforts us in all our affliction so that we will be able to comfort those who are in any affliction with the comfort with which we ourselves are comforted by God. [5] For just as the sufferings of Christ are ours in abundance, so also our comfort is abundant through Christ. [6] But if we are afflicted, it is for your comfort and salvation; or if we are comforted, it is for your comfort, which is effective in the patient enduring of the same sufferings which we also suffer; [7] and our hope for you is firmly grounded, knowing that as you are sharers of our sufferings, so also you are *sharers* of our comfort.[19]

Paul says a number of things here about God's comfort of us, but I want to focus on the repercussions of that comfort. He says that God comforts us in all our afflictions, "so that we will be able to comfort those who are in any affliction with the comfort with which we ourselves are comforted by God." Think about that statement. God comforts us with a purpose in mind—that we then might comfort others in their affliction with the same sort of comfort we received from God. This tells us a couple of very important things. First, God will comfort us with the expectation that it ought not to end there. God's comfort is not meant to stop with us (and I would argue the same for all the blessings he pours on us). We are to pass it on. We are to be his hands of comfort in the world around us. When we pray that God comfort us, we should expect something from him that we can *pass on*. This brings us to the second important point. If God comforts us with something that we can pass on, then it must be in a way that *we* can manifest as well. It will not be in some mysterious, spiritual way that we cannot replicate. At least some portion of our comfort from God will be in a material way that we can offer to others in their afflictions. One obvious example would be the Words of God found in scripture. He gives them to us as a comfort; we pass them to others as a comfort.

Sometimes the Word of God is pooh-poohed as hackneyed and out of place when people are under affliction. Relating the promises of God is sometimes viewed as worthless and even antagonistic at times.

---

19. 2 Cor 1:3–7.

Yet in truth, what better way to comfort than to bring the eternal truths of God to people who are suffering? It is not trite to quote real reality to those who are mired in the false and afflicting pain of this world's shell of reality.

Paul says one more thing that flies in the face of what we often expect when we pray for comfort from God. Let me quote him using the Revised Standard Version in this case because I think it captures best the idea he's trying to get across: "If we are afflicted, it is for your comfort and salvation; and if we are comforted, it is for your comfort, *which you experience when you patiently endure the same sufferings that we suffer* [emphasis added]. Our hope for you is unshaken; for we know that as you share in our sufferings, you will also share in our comfort."[20]

Paul is pointing out that comfort flows to us in the process of enduring sufferings or afflictions. God's comfort is not the removal of those difficulties; God's comfort is exhibited in the enduring of affliction. Endurance then, is proof that God is comforting us and we are grasping hold of that comfort. When we fail to endure affliction we are actually exposing the truth that we are declining God's comfort. Paul even goes on to say that sharing in sufferings is an indicator of sharing in comfort from God. Paul sees both as ordained by God—suffering and comfort to endure it. Nowhere does he indicate that the suffering will end. Comfort is not the removal of affliction; it is the ability to endure. And what better example of this do we see than Jesus himself? God met and comforted him through all manner of affliction, even the painful process of crucifixion. God did not remove that affliction, but helped him through it. When we pray for "comfort" from God, let us not embrace Christianese and water down this critical truth.

"PROTECT US"

Here is a Christianese prayer I hear quite often. Though usually it is in rather mundane settings such as, "Lord, protect me as I travel to such and such a place," or something like that. It is undoubtedly prayed with more urgency in other parts of the world than it is here in America. But I believe that it is probably prayed more realistically in those parts as well. When missionaries are faced with having their heads chopped off, for example, they know quite specifically what they are asking for when they

---

20. 2 Cor 1:6–7 RSV.

pray, "Protect me father!" And they know exactly what they expect God to do. Perhaps we need to be in more dire straits to think clearly about our expectations of God and stop using Christianese.

When we pray for protection, what are we asking for? We don't usually mean just safety from dying. We usually mean, "keep us entirely out of harm," though we wouldn't say it that way. I would point out, however, that being out of harm's way, even never falling victim to harm, is not the only indicator of God's protection of our lives. Here we can just scan the many stories of God's faithful people in scripture to see that this is so.

Take the prophets Elijah and Elisha for example. They certainly had to deal with some pretty dangerous tasks and though protected by God, they also fell into harm at times. Of course this might depend on what you mean by "harm." I would think that being hunted by the whole government qualifies as harm. Poor Elijah had to hide in the wilderness and live off of what birds brought him at times. He had to flee for his life constantly. He was "in harm's way" a lot I suspect.

The same is true of the New Testament Apostles. Paul describes the Apostle's call as one train-wreck after another in 1 Corinthians:

> [11] To this present hour we are both hungry and thirsty, and are poorly clothed, and are roughly treated, and are homeless; [12] and we toil, working with our own hands; when we are reviled, we bless; when we are persecuted, we endure; [13] when we are slandered, we try to conciliate; we have become as the scum of the world, the dregs of all things, *even* until now.[21]

Paul also describes his own personal life in 2 Corinthians. In this short passage he is describing his true experience of being an Apostle of God's as opposed to those false teachers who merely claim to be God's Apostles, but are not:

> [23] Are they servants of Christ?—I speak as if insane—I more so; in far more labors, in far more imprisonments, beaten times without number, often in danger of death. [24] Five times I received from the Jews thirty-nine *lashes*. [25] Three times I was beaten with rods, once I was stoned, three times I was shipwrecked, a night and a day I have spent in the deep. [26] *I have been* on frequent journeys, in dangers from rivers, dangers from robbers, dangers from *my* countrymen, dangers from the Gentiles, dangers in the city, dangers in the wilderness, dangers on the sea, dangers among

---

21. 1 Cor 4:11–13.

false brethren; ²⁷ *I have been* in labor and hardship, through many sleepless nights, in hunger and thirst, often without food, in cold and exposure. ²⁸ Apart from *such* external things, there is the daily pressure on me *of* concern for all the churches.²²

I would think that Paul prayed for "protection" from God a few times in all these adventures. And he was protected, but not in the way we often pray for it. The Apostle Peter captures Paul's view of protection in an encouraging word to believers found in his first epistle:

> ³ Blessed be the God and Father of our Lord Jesus Christ, who according to his great mercy has caused us to be born again to a living hope through the resurrection of Jesus Christ from the dead, ⁴ to *obtain* an inheritance *which is* imperishable and undefiled and will not fade away, reserved in heaven for you, ⁵ who are protected by the power of God through faith for a salvation ready to be revealed in the last time.²³

Peter's understanding is that we are indeed protected by God, but it is a protection for our ultimate salvation. It is not necessarily protection from harm here in the world. And even a casual perusal of the saints in the scriptures leaves us with the impression that often God does not "protect" us in the way we pray for it nowadays. We need to have the right expectation of what God will do when he protects us. Protection may involve allowing us to survive, or it may involve allowing us to die knowing we are assured of glorious heaven in the afterlife. Protection by God does not seem to be the necessary prevention of harm coming our way. More often than not, God's emissaries in the world underwent all sorts of harm while living under God's protection of eternal life. How would that truth change the way we pray? I would think that it would at least change our focus from our own safety to a desire to achieve the Lord's ends with the comfort of knowing we are protected from any ultimate harm. Jesus told his followers, "And do not fear those who kill the body but cannot kill the soul; rather fear him who can destroy both soul and body in hell."²⁴ The context was an encouragement to his disciples that they are far more important to God than anything else, so they need not fear those who will persecute them. God will always be with them—even in their afflictions.

22. 2 Cor 11:23–28.

23. 1 Pet 1:3–5.

24. Matt 19:28.

"HEAL US"

We have already talked quite a bit about healing earlier in the book, so I will not add much here. Let me just say again, that part of the problem we have with praying for "healing" is that we have no expectation of what God will actually do. Or, in some cases, we have a caged expectation that he should take our disease entirely away. Yet, as we have noted, that does not seem to actually happen in real life very often, and it does not seem to fit with the whole idea of living under the fallenness of the world.

It does sound very "Christian" to pray for healing. But I don't see people really following up with those prayers much. Have you ever prayed for the healing of a friend's cold? As I wrote this sentence I was struggling with a 3-week cold that was hampering my daily life. I had three or four friends say they were "praying for me." I don't really know what they were praying about because they didn't elaborate. They didn't follow up on it for the most part, though one had asked how I was feeling three or four days after saying she'd pray for me. Maybe she expected me to be better because she asked for me to be healed. Apparently God said "no" to her prayer because I was the same as I was a week before in terms of having a cold. How often have you followed up with someone and found out if the cold left the moment you ask for healing? That's a good experiment to try for a month during flu season. It should sober us to the truth that God doesn't take flu bugs and colds away on a regular basis. And therefore, we ought to expect him to do something else—and perhaps in this case we ought to stop praying for healing altogether.

You may think it's too demanding to expect God to just say "yes" to our prayer of healing and take the cold or flu away instantaneously. But I would counter with, "Why?" If God is going to intervene in the situation with a "yes" to our prayer for healing, then why is it too much to expect that he just do it? I would argue that anything else is really not a "yes" in any real sense anyway. At best it would be God saying, "Yes, I'll heal you when I want to heal you," but that creates other problems. An interesting picture of a similar situation is found in the Gospel of John:

> [46] Therefore he came again to Cana of Galilee where he had made the water wine. And there was a royal official whose son was sick at Capernaum. [47] When he heard that Jesus had come out of Judea into Galilee, he went to him and was imploring *him* to come down and heal his son; for he was at the point of death. [48] So Jesus said to him, "Unless you *people* see signs and wonders,

you *simply* will not believe." ⁴⁹ The royal official said to him, "Sir, come down before my child dies." ⁵⁰ Jesus said to him, "Go; your son lives." The man believed the word that Jesus spoke to him and started off. ⁵¹ As he was now going down, *his* slaves met him, saying that his son was living. ⁵² So he inquired of them the hour when he began to get better. Then they said to him, "Yesterday at the seventh hour the fever left him." ⁵³ So the father knew that *it was* at that hour in which Jesus said to him, "Your son lives"; and he himself believed and his whole household.[25]

I must point out again that John is interested in presenting this vignette as another sign which led the officer to belief in Jesus as God. But he also makes the point that it was at the very hour Jesus said the boy was well that the boy became well. There was apparently no lag time between the order from Jesus and the healing. So why do we expect anything else? We might also ask, what did the official expect when he asked Jesus to come heal his son? I wouldn't think he expected Jesus to come down, look at the boy, and then tell him that it will be a few weeks until his son fully recovers. I would think his expectation was that Jesus would heal the boy then and there, on the spot, without delay. And if Jesus didn't do it, anything he did do would be regarded first as a "no, I'm not going to heal him" answer.

Let me address here an idea that is not directly related to healing but is related to what we expect to happen when we pray. Often when we pray for healing, we are not, in truth, actually praying for healing at all. That sounds like a contradiction, I know, but let's think about it for a moment. I would wager that most people who pray regularly have learned, deep down, that God does not answer their "heal so and so" prayers with a "yes." They have learned by experience that the sickness very rarely, if ever, actually goes away the moment they request it do so. Yet they still pray for "healing" for some reason. We will talk about how they get to the place internally where that is acceptable, but for now let me propose that they are not really praying for healing. They are praying for something else in the guise of healing. They are praying for other reasons and the prayer just comes out as a "heal so and so" prayer.

Most of the time, we feel completely at a loss when others are sick and we cannot fix the problem. I recall one of our friends little one-year-old having seizures for a time. They were so frightened every time one

---

25. John 4:46–53.

occurred, and even after they found out that they were not dangerous, it still bothered them tremendously. It is extremely difficult to be entirely out of control when someone you love is suffering. Even when it's as mundane as a cold, we still want to see those we love released from their pains. But we cannot really do *anything* to help. So we pray. The prayer is expressed as a request of healing, but it is spawned from a sense of love for the other person. We just want to express how we care for them and it hurts us to see our friend suffer, even in the slightest. So even though the prayer is a request for healing, it is really serving the purpose of expressing our anguish over the suffering of the other person. I believe that often we don't really have any expectation of a "real" healing from God. In truth, we aren't actually praying over the other person at all in many respects. We're really expressing our love for them to God. This is a good thing in that respect. But it can be a real detriment when we then think about prayer literally. Because when we start to believe that we really are asking for a healing, then we realize that God keeps saying "no" to us. The Christianese phrase "heal so and so" is a detrimental mask in such a situation, for it makes us think we are saying one thing but it is really hiding what we authentically want to say. And therefore it is hiding reality from us. Or, we are hiding reality from ourselves by using such talk.

We need to be clear about our expectations in order to be clear about what we are saying to God. God knows what we mean, but that is no reason to continue lying to ourselves. God also wants *us* to know what we mean and to know how to say it directly and authentically.

"BE WITH US"

Here I must confess I'm including one of my pet peeves. I've used this one myself many a time. My feeling, after listening to many prayers, and hearing myself pray, is that people ask God to "be with so and so" when they cannot think of anything specific to pray at all. It's become a general catch-phrase which stands for nothing. I doubt we are thinking that God is *not* with the people we are praying over. We are not asking that God suddenly turn his attention to someone, having previously been unaware of them or some such thing.

Now there is a similar phrase that occurs quite often in scripture. That is: "The grace of the Lord be with you." But note, in all of its different forms, it always is a call for the grace, or joy, or peace or something like that to be with a believer. It is not God Himself we call to be with believers; it is his grace, or peace. The difference is immense. We assume God *is* with the person, but we pray that they *experience* the peace, joy, or grace of that relationship. We do not assume that the person needs God's presence or that God has somehow withdrawn Himself from his beloved children. And perhaps we don't really think that when it's said out loud like this, but by not saying what we mean accuratley, one wonders if we ever even think about what we are really saying at all.

What are we really expecting when we ask God to "be with" someone? Isn't it that they experience God's presence on a personal level in some way? And the obvious question is, how would that happen? Again, some of the most basic answers are, by experiencing him in his Word, the Bible; by experiencing him in a robust, productive, and functional prayer life; by experiencing him through the interrelationships of the body of Christ; and on and on. We see an example of this last gone awry when Paul writes in 2 Timothy 4:16 the sad lines, "At my first defense no one supported me, but all deserted me; may it not be counted against them." I wonder if anyone was praying that God "be with" Paul during his imprisonment. Perhaps they should have been praying more fruitfully, "May I have an opportunity to bring God's comfort to Paul as he stands in the courtroom." As a side note, notice the great Apostle's thought on the matter: "may [their desertion] not be counted against them."[26] When we pray for God to "be with" someone, we ought to consider how we can be his representative rather than how God will miraculously conjure up a feeling of being loved when people are abandoned, lonely, or are on their own.

"LIFT UP"

This is the final term from Christianese I want to comment briefly on. Firstly, I want to point out that the term "lift up" is used differently in scripture than it is commonly used in prayer today. We often hear people saying things like, "Lord, we lift up so and so in prayer to you." But that construction, lifting up someone to God in prayer is not present in scripture. We can lift up prayers to God, but not people in prayer. Many times the Bible speaks of people lifting up their hands, souls, or themselves in prayer to God. But this is a metaphor for presenting themselves to God through the avenue of prayer.

---

26. 2 Tim 4:16.

In changing the construction of the phrase to "I lift up so and so" we turn it into a verb of action we are committing on our friend. I suppose we could translate "I lift up so and so" as "I pray for so and so." But at that point, what are we really saying? We're merely telling God what we're doing—we're not actually praying for something for that person. God already knows we are praying for so and so. The more important point is *what* are we praying for so and so? Are we asking for something? Are we praising them to God? Are we merely musing over them? The term "lift up" has become meaningless when we merely utter it alone. And when we connect it with specific prayers, it becomes merely repetitious. Let us pray with specificity for people and not in many worthless words.

Well, although I could multiply examples, I think we've gotten the gist of the problem here. We are praying in Christianese to avoid defining our expectations of God's actions. You might at this point be asking what the real problem here is. So what if people use some undefined terms in their prayers, at least they're praying, right? Well, I would say that this is actually a very serious problem. You see, when we continue to pray with terms that have no real expectations attached, we're actually embracing an unknown god. Our God, Yahweh, Jesus, the Spirit, is intimate and real. He acts overtly and relationally. When we embrace a god who we cannot know due to mystery, we embrace someone who is different from the revealed God of the Bible.

Moreover, when we continue to pray these undefined prayers, we develop an undefined relationship with our God. Assuming we really do believe in the God of the Bible who has entered history for the purpose of saving and interacting with us, we should want to know him for who he really is. Praying in Christianese and harboring unrealistic expectations are actually ways of avoiding getting to know the true God. It is trying to live in his house without ever having to meet up with him. And that is a big problem for us who are heirs to the family treasure of eternal life and rule with the Master of the Universe.

4

Mitigating Our Problems— and Creating More of Them

THE STORM THAT SWEPT through that day was heavy—uncommonly heavy for the northwest. There were even reports of small twisters touching down now and again; and that almost never happens in this area. As Jean sat in the clubhouse of her golf course, she pondered the vehement bellowing both outside the window and next to her.

She had sought refuge from the late afternoon tempest of lightning, thunder, and seemingly gale force winds by scurrying off the greens and fairways and into the safety of the clubhouse diner. But as she sat next to the old codger she began to wonder if she'd chosen the right refuge. For here was a storm every bit as angry as that which buffeted the world outside.

He was old and retired and had played the golf course for years. And he was fed up. Jean had been called in to temporarily replace the superintendant of the course who had needed some personal time— maybe a lot of personal time. And word had gotten out that Jean was the new boss—at least for awhile. In the old man's view, she was the new terrain on which to unleash his storm of frustration.

"He's let this place go to s—t!" "That guy was a complete moron!" On and on his stormy explicative's battered at Jean as he described the former superintendant of the course. Intermixed with the tirade were half veiled threats that Jean had better do a sounder job than the previous buffoon! She sighed after an hour or so and again wondered how she would fair if she just went back out into the squall and took a lightning strike. It might have been a more desirous option than the beating she was taking in this confined luncheonette.

Until a couple of weeks ago Jean had been an *assistant* superintendant at a golf course. She loved that job. She was outdoors; she got to work with her hands; she got to use her head on a daily basis problem solving different issues that came up. But one day things had changed. She was asked to temporarily step in as *superintendant* at this course because the head man who was there needed some time away. She was psyched! She realized it was what she had been working toward for 30 years from the moment she began as a summer gardener on a golf course way back in high school. She relished the chance to step up and run things.

Almost from the get-go she could see a serious problem with the previous superintendant's approach to his job however. He ignored almost everything. The tirade the old man was dumping on her was not all wind. He had a lot of truth behind his disgust. Jean shook her head as she recalled the shocking lack of upkeep she'd seen. Every area of management seemed to show neglect. On the important end, bills had not been paid for a couple months—even minor ones that amounted to mere change were left unpaid for no reason. On the other end of the spectrum, the desk she had inherited was rife with what could only be labeled as filth. Packets of oyster crackers that were years old, stale and crushed, had been stuffed into drawers under piles of unsorted documents to seemingly decompose as if in a land fill. Ketchup packets that were so old they had dried up, still sealed, were laying next to the crackers. The floor didn't look like it had been swept for a year and the desk chair was so neglected that she was sitting on bare metal.

The most glaring problem and the most critical was his refusal to address the fact that his water pumps were failing. When they were lit up, water didn't just flow into pipes to feed the thirsty grass, it also spewed out the bottom of the pumps into their sheds supplying the concrete with wasted irrigation. Those pumps were critical and were they to fail at an inopportune time it would spell death for the golf course in many different ways. Jean had been mostly in charge of irrigation at her previous course, and she knew the importance of a functioning water system. She could just imagine golfers looking out from the first tee and seeing nothing but rolling fairways of brown grass, or upon reaching a green landing their golf balls on dirt rather than mowed bent grass. It would be a nightmare. Golfers don't appreciate colors in the brown spectrum on their greens.

It was not as though the system was just poorly built. The previous superintendant had not even sprung for the sprinkler parts his irrigation system needed to work as it should. The crewman responsible for making sure the sprinklers were working had to stoop to cannibalizing some sprinklers on the course to fix other more important ones! A whole section of the course would go brown and die each year for lack of water. Jean mused over that fact as the old codger blustered on with a list of complaints, not even knowing how trivial they were compared to the water problem.

The previous superintendant had apparently justified the neglect with the belief that he was saving money by not buying parts or spending money maintaining his pumps. The critical key was *saving money*. But it was much like a surgeon would save money by not buying scalpels. Yes, the budget looked good, but it didn't fly so well for a patient who really needed surgery.

Jean had quickly realized the golf course was dangerously close to having its whole irrigation system go down due to neglect. And that would spell disaster. It would not just be the death of the grass. Play would dwindle and revenue would all but cease. All the savings gained by not buying sprinkler and pump parts would not match the loss of income that would occur if there was no water to irrigate for even a few weeks in the hot summer. The previous superintendant had put the whole course at risk trying to mitigate the impact of failing pumps by telling himself he was saving money. But in the end, he was really just creating more, and critical, problems with far-reaching ramifications.

Jean sat shaking her head over the dilemma and the old codger blustered on ignorant of the real storm that might be approaching.

Well, we have finally arrived at the last section dealing with some of the problems we seem to have with prayer. Frankly, this entire discussion on the difficulties of prayer has been hard to write. I'm sure it has been difficult and exhausting to read at times as well. It is just no fun delving into all the problems we find in prayer. But hold firm! After this one last section I will turn to the positive side of prayer and will present some more constructive ideas on how I believe we can make prayer into what it ought to be.

I have called this final section on difficulties: "Mitigating Our Problems—and Creating More of Them." Like my friend's experience at the golf course, sometimes people create more problems by mitigating the ones they have. To mitigate something is defined as:

- To lessen in force or intensity, as wrath, grief, harshness, or pain; moderate.
- To make less severe: to mitigate a punishment.
- To make (a person, one's state of mind, disposition, etc.) milder or more gentle; mollify; appease.[1]

My point in this title, is that people have adopted various practices in their prayer lives to lessen the impact of the many problems that we've discussed in the first half of this book. Like the superintendant at the golf course I mentioned, people try to lessen the impact of failing practices.

Obviously, I don't believe that I've hit on difficulties that no one has seen before. I'm merely parading them out of the cellar and into the broad light of day. If you've read this far, you probably have nodded your head a few times and admitted, "Yep, that's what I do" or, "Yes, that's the problem I see too." I believe we all can see some or all of these problems when we want to look. The most important challenge we face, however, is what we do with them. And I believe the most grievous error we make is to mitigate them—to try to lessen their impact or severity. That is why I've put this section last in this negative account of our prayer lives. It is the biggest problem we face because if we mitigate (lessen the severity of) the problems we are facing in prayer, we have no reason to change. And the effect of those problems does not go away; it merely is camouflaged and hidden from our conscious minds. But whether I tell myself I'm getting wet or that I'm untouched by rain, if I'm walking in a downpour I'm still being soaked. My mind-set about what's happening to me does not change the reality of the situation.

We need to stop denying these problems exist. We need to face them head on. I've been giving some ideas on how to do that so far, and will give a better approach more fully in the last portion of the book. But here we need to be clear about one thing: It is no good pretending these problems don't exist or that we can somehow alleviate them by altering our view of reality. That is merely attempting to mitigate our troubles—and it does not solve them. As the rest of the title for this section says, it creates more problems.

Let me repeat again, emphatically, that people are not idiots. I know, I know, when we drive in rush hour traffic it may seem that they (we?)

---

1. Dictionary.com, s.v. "Mitigate."

are, but in truth, they are not. People know the problems they have with prayer when they take the time to think about it. I'm convinced that when the truth is told, in the quiet of our own heads, we admit that in all practical ways our prayers are often answered with a "no." That's the foundational difficulty with our prayer lives. We seem to get "no" answers a lot. and it bothers us. Furthermore, I think we feel as though we are cornered. The way we've been taught to pray seems to leave us with no other options but to keep praying in ways that experientially, consistently get those "no" answers. So we are between the proverbial rock and a hard place. We keep getting "no" answers that would seem to indicate that we are not praying very intelligently, and yet we have not thought out prayer in a way that allows us to pray and receive "yes" answers. We are stuck. So what do we do? I want to suggest that one of the most popular solutions, mitigating the problems, is the final nail on the coffin. It seals us into a dead prayer life that has no opportunity to ever be revived. And how do we mitigate or lessen the difficulties we are encountering? We redefine the very reality of prayer and the answers we get to make them tolerable.

What I mean is that we redefine our prayers so that we can identify God's answer as a "yes" (or some variant of "wait-yes-sorta") regardless of circumstances. We turn night into day and day into night. We upend the prayer universe so that "no" means "yes." We become people who can reformulate our understanding of prayer to view absolutely anything that happens as a "yes" answer in some mystical way. And this accomplishes two things. First, it locks us into the prayer life we have now. For who would then want to change a system that seems to get so much approval from God? Second, it locks God into the person we make him out to be. We keep getting "yes" answers from God as we have come to know him, so he must *be* what we have come to know. (That sentence even hurts to read, let alone think about doesn't it? But read it again to be sure you get it.)

Let's use an example that is very common—we've seen it before. We pray for healing in a friend. As we've said, there are three possible, real-world outcomes that will occur—miraculous healing, medicinal healing or temporal healing. There is a fourth option if you count the possibility that the illness never goes away, but let's just stick to the three scenarios of healing. First, and least likely I would add, the person is miraculously healed. As we discussed earlier, this is not too likely. Again, ask yourself out of all the healing prayers you've offered, how many times has God instantaneously removed the illness entirely? The second, and more likely, scenario is that over some period of time the medicine the doctors prescribed (or we bought at the store) works and heals the sickness. Finally, if the sickness is something more mundane such as a cold, it may merely run its course and go away over time—which is the typical experience we have with most of our day-to-day illnesses. That's what I call a temporal healing.

I find many who will try to explain these answers to the prayer for healing as a "yes, I will heal them" from God. Basically, when any of them occurs we say to ourselves, "Ah, God healed so and so." We may also add something like, "God healed in his time," by way of further explaining why nothing actually happened at the time we asked for "healing." You have probably heard people say this even when the "healing" takes place years after the prayer was offered. If we think on these conclusions seriously however, we begin to sense problems with such "yes" answers to our prayers. And believe me, if you've ever explained answered prayer in that way to an unbeliever, you would realize how many problems such views harbor!

Let me recount one exchange I had with a friend that seems to me to be the most glaring example of mitigating our problems in relation to colds. I was sick with a cold. It was a bad enough cold that I had missed work for most of a week, and at the end of the week I missed teaching my Adult Ed class at Sunday school as well. The next week was just as bad. However, I decided I could not miss any more classes, so I just went to work and to church with my cold as a companion. The week I returned, I mentioned to my Sunday school class that I appreciated the many prayers people had said for me, but if they were prayers for healing God had answered "no" to them. I was still sick and it had not improved.

One parishioner told me later he disagreed with my assessment. "I think those prayers worked. After all," he said, "you don't know how bad your cold could have been." I've heard that sentiment before, and it never ceases to amaze me. This was just the most clear statement of it. The reasoning seems to be that we have no idea what God is doing now, has done in the past or will do in the future, so I should just interpret any reality in which I exist as an example of God saying "yes" to whatever I requested. In this case people requested I get well, and because I was still sick, I should take that to mean that God said "yes" and healed me from some even more dire disease I could have contracted in the future. (I'm shaking my head even as I repeat that logic.)

Now, I want to say again that I believe such thinking is intended to show a sincere awe and love for our good God. But regardless of that motivation, what do you say to that sort of reasoning? If I had gotten better, that would have been proof that God said "yes" to someone's request for healing. If I had stayed sick, that would have been proof that God said "yes" as well, *with the added bonus* that he kept me from an even more serious illness! I'll say this for such thinking—God can't lose! I wonder what my friend would have said if had I died? Would he have posited, "God answered with a 'yes' by taking Tom home to glory." This kind of talk befuddles believers and makes unbelievers view God and us as simpletons. We offer such ideas in the spirit of expressing our trust that God intends what comes our way, and that it is always good in some literal sense. But when we so blatantly twist logic to the point that anything means God has answered us with a "yes," we do a great disservice to God and his reputation.

Let me illustrate this with a concrete example again just to make sure we are seeing the problem clearly. Suppose I ask my wife to move the car out of the garage so that I can cut up some wood on the table saw. There are only a few possible, true responses. She could say "yes" and then do it. Or, she could just do it, which is a "yes" identified by my request being met. She could say "no" and not do it. Or, she could just not do it, which is a "no" identified by my request being unmet. Now let's apply my friends approach to prayer to my situation with the car. There's not really a problem if my wife says "yes" to me and moves the car, or just moves the car without an identified "yes." Either way my request is met with the identifiable affirmative of moving the car. No problems arise in these situations.

But what if my wife says "no" to me and does not move the car? Or what if she doesn't say "no," but also just doesn't move the car? In both cases, my request is unmet—the car was not moved. Using my friend's approach, I would then reason that although she didn't actually do what I desired, her response was helpful, and good, because she kept me from possibly cutting my finger off in the saw(?). The practical outcome is that I asked for the car to be moved and it was not. How can I possibly say that I have asked for something and that I have received some sort of "yes" answer to that request? In the end my request was unmet and the car was not moved. To posit some completely unknown future as the basis for my interpretation of the answer seems ludicrous. Can we in any fashion apply this sort of reasoning to our usual interactions with people? We must surely say that this makes no sense whatsoever.

Before anyone infers that I'm suggesting that God does not know the unknown future let me say that I'm not. I'm sure God knows the future exactly and sometimes says "no" to us because he knows where a "yes" will go. But so what? That doesn't give us license to take his clear "no" answers to prayers and say that somehow they were "yes" answers. Some of the people in my Sunday school class prayed that I would get well. I didn't. God said "no" to those prayers. I agree wholeheartedly that he definitely said "no" for a good reason. But that doesn't make the "no" any less of a "no." It is just God saying, "No, I'm not going to heal Tom." Even if he then did keep me from some unknown and far worse illness that could have sprung from my cold, his answer was still a "no" to healing my cold. On the contrary, if he did keep me from some other worse illness, that would just be a "yes" to another prayer, such as "Lord, keep Tom from some even more dire sickness that could spring from this cold." But no one said they were praying for that. The unknown future makes no difference to me one way or the other. What matters is that God said "no" to my prayer for the healing of my cold—that is verifiable.

I might ask, why would I want to somehow confuse the matter with this idea that God didn't really give me a full-fledged "no" because he was keeping me from something worse that I couldn't see? I think we do that to somehow lessen the truth that God lets us have colds, and sometimes far worse things. But what use is that sort of thinking? How does it really help me to know how to pray in the future? All it does is soften the fact that God can say anything to me and I, apparently, have no idea what it will be, and why he will say it. Again, all this sort of thinking does is mitigate the problem of not knowing what's going on in our prayer lives. Perhaps it gives us comfort to think this way, but I say it's a small and cold comfort that crumbles under any real scrutiny. I say it is better for us to abandon such ideas rather than to live in such complete, non-functional ignorance. Furthermore I would ask, is that really how we think God wants our relationship with him to work? I think a lot of us have voted our answer with our actions: "No thanks; not interested." We don't want to pray at all under those circumstances. Mitigating the problem of a "no" with such brutal logical gymnastics creates more problems than it's worth. We know that, and consequently, we don't want to pray at all.

Let's go back to the prayer for our sick friend. Here is our main problem: if we asked God to heal our friend and it took months or years and many doctors to do it, should God really get the credit? Is that really a "Yes, I'll heal him" answer? Let's assume we all agree that God *ultimately* should receive the credit in that he is Lord of all and "he does according to his will in the host of heaven and among the inhabitants of earth."[2] Let's also assume God allows healing through doctors at times. We can even put this under some of the blessings God gives to us in the flow of the natural world. We can say that God made all the substances we use to make medicine, and he made our minds with which we find cures with those substances, so in that sense *he* provided the healing through us.

Still, doesn't this seem a bit contrived? Can we honestly give him the *direct credit* for healing if we alter the definition of "healing" to mean anything from supernatural intervention to healing by doctors? Can we give him the direct credit when we further describe "healing" as just getting better over time? How about getting better and tagging on the idea that we *could have been* way worse? If altering our expectations in that manner is the only way we can define a "yes" answer from God, it would seem our prayers end up being nothing but banal, global generalities. Apparently *anything* is a "yes" from God if that is our measure of "yes." I think we must admit that we don't know what the answer will be in any real sense when we produce such explanations. God could do anything and still get the credit for a "yes, I'll heal your friend" answer. It seems a bit like the old joke students use in my Bible classes at Multnomah University. Whenever you don't know the answer to anything just say, "Jesus," because ultimately everything can be traced back to him in some way. They even laugh when the real answer to a question *is* "Jesus" because they understand the opportunity for abuse of this answer.

This is much like the game of identifying six steps of separation. You can always make things trace to other things. That's what it feels like we are doing with this sort of definition of a "yes" answer from God. Miraculous healing? That's a "yes!" Cured through doctoral care? That's a "yes!" Your cold went away after a few weeks? That's a "yes!" And remember, "It could have been worse!" We might as well add, "You died? That's a "yes" too! Of course we don't usually want to add that last one. Being "healed" of our colds by death seems a bit over-the-top for most of us.

---

2. Dan 4:35.

God could have healed my friend in two weeks, or six months. He could have done it with many doctors, or one doctor. He could have let the sickness run its course with no verifiable aid from anyone. Heck, he could have let my friend die. With our "anything goes" policy for interpreting "yes" answers it would make no difference, really, what happened. *Something* changed, and I could theoretically call it God "healing" my friend. At the foundation of this I'm really just saying that what happened, happened—right? It turns out that I don't really have to even bring God into the whole discussion if I'm going to redefine anything that happens as God "healing" my friend.

Maybe an even better approach is to just *assume* God is going to say "yes" to my prayer and watch what actually happens. Then I could categorize whatever did actually occur as a "yes." This would be easier because it cuts out God as the middle man. I can just wander about telling myself that God is saying "yes" (or will say "yes") to all my prayers regardless of what he's really doing and saying. But you know what? All this rationalizing of every outcome as some sort of "yes" from God is not helping, is it? It is really just lessening the problem we run into when God doesn't heal our friends. It is mitigating the harsh truth that God says "no" when we ask for healing. God says "no" when we ask for a lot of important things, doesn't he? "Lord, save my child." "Lord, protect our fellow believers in the Sudan." You see my point. Not accepting God's "no" answers creates all sorts of really difficult problems, the foremost being that I have no real idea what the heck God does or why he does it. And this creates the strange truth that we can wander about in reality having no idea what reality is really like.

Let me beat this horse one more time and ask another question. Let's say I think God healed my friend after he still had to go through six months of medicine and doctor visits. If that is the case, then the natural flow of sickness and recovery is an example of God healing. This is especially true if I redefine healing as "healing in his own time" for the case of the person who just has their cold or flu ease up and finally go away. If that's the case, here is my next question: What is *not* an example of God healing? For all practical purposes, healing and not healing would be, in the end, identical. The only thing that changes apparently is timing. In other words, the outcomes can all be different, but apparently they all can be equated in some way. As we noted previously, at the furthest extreme, to be "healed" in this worldview is the same as to "die" in the real world, for death is then just God's way of ending the disease! Let's face facts; we cannot define a "yes" to healing in this open-ended way. We are better off just dealing with the difficulties of the truth that God does not heal very often—almost never. That is far preferable to creating this monster of irreconcilable actions on God's part.

In the real world the average skeptic would say we're just choosing to interpret normal circumstances in the way we want. And although I believe firmly in what I call the believer's "eyes of faith" by which we can discern the movement of God in seemingly natural events, I must admit, we sometimes take that so far as to skew everything that happens into some marvelous, miraculous working of God. But sometimes, as I've already pointed out, God is just mundane. He did, after all, create the trees and plants with seeds to propagate.[3] The point being that apparently, in some way, he expected the created world to have some natural processes that would continue to just carry on without direct, miraculous, divine intervention. He didn't plan on miraculously making new plants every time one died. He made seeds to take care of that chore. And that in itself seems to auger for the idea that in general God intends natural processes to take care of some things.

Another way we mitigate our problems in prayer and placate ourselves when we receive "no" answers is by saying something that actually seems to agree with the point I'm making. We say things like: "God Always answers all our prayers—but sometimes he answers 'no.'" On the surface this seems to fit exactly with my argument that God actually says "no" to us sometimes. So I would agree with that thought wholeheartedly. In fact, I have been arguing for our honest *acceptance* of God's "no" answers. But when people say, "God answers 'no'" they don't seem to mean it in the way I've been presenting it. I'm saying that when God says "no" we ought to listen and change our prayers and figure out why he said "no" and what might be a better prayer. I'm saying "no" is an answer we should not want to hear from God. It's like when a parent has to say "no" to a request from their child. The parent wants the child to change that request, to learn from the "no" response and align themselves with the parents will so that the next time they can get a "yes" answer to their request. A "no" is *not a good thing,* even if it is useful at times.

But some will doggedly say, "God sometimes answers 'no'" as though it *is* a good thing, or as though they think a "no" is as at least as

---

3. Gen 1:11.

good as a "yes" when it comes to prayer because both are just *answers*. We would never use such logic anywhere else in our lives. We wouldn't use that sort of logic even to order an ice cream sundae. If I ordered it and got a "no" for an answer from the waiter I'd be upset that my desire went unmet. I wouldn't just shrug my shoulders and smile politely. I wouldn't thank him for his response and go on my happy way. I'd want an explanation. I'd want to know why he said "no" and whether I should order something else. "No" is not just as good as "yes." Getting a "no" from God should be something we are unhappy with. It should spur us to ask why he said "no" and what we might ask for instead. In all honesty, I think we use this approach of "no" being as good as a "yes" as an outward admission that we don't really have any clue as to what to pray for. And in truth, any answer *is* a God-send apparently when you are completely at a loss as to what God is like and what he will do. If we think about it, settling happily for either "yes" or "no" reflects the idea that at our core we really don't care what he answers, as long as there is something we can call an answer.

Can you imagine your relationship with your spouse being like that? I don't care what she or he says to me as long as she or he says *something*. I just begin the process of prayer with the belief that God is going to answer me somehow, but I really don't know how, whether it will be with a "yes" or a "no." Again, at that point I wonder if we even care what answer we receive. It would appear that I'm only interested in the *fact* that he answers—not in the *type* of answer. I guess the reasoning is something like this: "I'm not interested in whether the answer is 'yes,' or whether I can even decipher it—after all, God sometimes just answers "no" and there's nothing I can do about it!"

What is the outcome of that sort of reasoning? I think it is exactly what we see many Christians doing in their prayer lives. We slide into hurling the most general, non-specific prayers at God that we can muster, not knowing what the answer will be, but satisfying ourselves with the thought that at least he will say something to us—though perhaps it will be "no." This unfortunately brings to mind the abused spouse who says any interaction is better than none. The ultimate end of this approach is that for some people any answer from God—even resounding silence—is considered a blessing and equal to a "yes." (Of course, this is another one of those things we don't say out loud. It's far too embarrassing to admit to this sort of thinking.) Does this sound like the God Jesus prayed to? One who randomly hands out "yes" answers, "no" answers, and silences in an unfathomable way? Is that the relationship between God and men that Jesus pictured for us? What a train-wreck this thinking has led to.

This view of God's answers is a big reason most believers seem to struggle with prayer, and many ultimately abandon it altogether. We mitigate the "no" answers to our prayers to lessen the fact that they are telling us we have prayed for a wrong thing in God's eyes. We mitigate the "no" answers by generalizing the answers into almost nothing which in turn pushes us to more and more non-descript and non-specific prayers. And when our prayers become so general that we cannot know in any way if they will be answered affirmatively or if they will affect reality in any way, why wouldn't we be discouraged and give up? If we have to go through such interpretive gymnastics to find an answer to prayer, why stick with it? It hurts our heads when we think about it, and the whole process comes off as just plain false. Why pursue an endeavor that's so ill-defined and incomprehensible? How could such a thing be effective at all? Imagine such a situation in a daily relationship: I ask something of my friend or relative, but I have absolutely no idea what they will respond with—"yes," "no," or perhaps just cold silence. Furthermore, even when they answer, half the time I must reinterpret my understanding of words and requests to somehow mesh them with what they actually do in response. Would we not soon throw up our hands in frustration? Of course we would. And we do. We're smart and intentional beings.

Suppose I say to my friend, "Will you water my lawn while I'm out of town for three months?" and she says "yes." Subsequently, she does not do it, but in the third month it happens to rain. Can I fairly say to myself, "Wow, what a great friend, she watered my lawn by waiting until the rains came"? Ludicrous! Preposterous! No wonder skeptics think we are crazy at times. No wonder *we* think we are crazy at times. No wonder we quit praying seriously.

A "no" from God really is a "no." It is not a "yes" cached in a "wait" or something like that. In fact, as we have seen, a "no" is a quite useful answer in the growth process if we receive it honestly. It should be a learning experience that makes us reflect on what we asked for, and figure out how we might make better requests in the future. Instead of doing this, many seem to concoct convoluted explanations of how God really did answer "yes," but in a "marvelous and unfathomable" way. We mitigate the difficulty of receiving a "no."

So, we pray for healing over and over for people and we see no discernable results. Perhaps a friend suffers through years of chemotherapy before finally beating cancer, and healing only comes because advanced medicine finally works. During the entire time we have prayed unceasingly that God "heal our friend!" Our response, when the medicine finally works is to say, "God answered my prayer and healed him in his own time!" (Translation—God did nothing miraculous to intervene and the medicine finally worked.) With this understanding we are encouraged to keep on praying for others in the same way, whether there are any results or not. We never face the reality and admit that God allowed horrible cancer into his life, and the years I spent asking for "healing" in my prayers could have been better spent asking for something my friend really needed—like strength of endurance, patience, a good attitude, inner fortitude, a strong immune system to deal with powerful drugs, and trust in a Good and Loving Savior Who sometimes permits deep suffering to wrack our lives.

So often our prayers lack any recognition of the importance of suffering, inner turmoil, physical pain, and emotional sorrow—they lack recognition of the process of maturity and the need for the sharpening of our spirituality. And we leave our prayers in this state by ignoring "no" answers or by reshaping them into convoluted "yes" answer or "waits." We try vigorously to remove any difficulty from our lives—even difficulty at the thoughts of what God uses to shape us.

Before I move on, let me specifically address this most commonly used mitigating term, "wait." You've probably heard people say that God says, "Yes," "No," or "Wait." Usually it is said in a very sagacious fashion as though they've arrived at a really deep and meaningful thought. I've said it that way myself previously until I began to really think about it. It's helpful to cock your head when you express those deep thoughts because you look even more thoughtful when you say them. I like to squint my eyes too as though my brain is being taxed to its limit. "You know, God says 'wait' sometimes too." As you can tell, I'm a bit jaded on that answer now.

Before I say another word about this, let me say that I actually agree; God does say "wait" on occasion. Let's take King David as a concrete example. David was told that he was to be the King of Israel and was anointed as such in front of his brothers by Samuel the prophet.[4] David

---

4. 1 Sam 16:13.

had, in effect, been told he would be king, but he had not been given the kingship at that point. He had to wait until the proper time. Later, as David was living through the train-wreck life he was given until he could assume the throne, even Jonathan King Saul's son said to him, "Do not be afraid, because the hand of Saul my father shall not find you, and you will be king over Israel and I will be next to you; and Saul my father knows that also."[5] But still, it was awhile before David became king. This is an example of a real "wait" from God.

The question we should ask is, "How did David *know* that God had said 'wait'?" This is the fundamental question about a "wait" answer from God. How do we come to understand that God has said "wait" and not "no"? I propose that a real "wait" answer is accompanied by verifiable assurances that God has said, "Yes, but wait for the right time." If there is no way to verify a "wait" answer, if a "wait" could turn into a "no" just as easily as a "yes," then how would we ever identify a "no"?

David knew he was told to wait by the circumstances and answers God was clearly giving him. David was *anointed* king of Israel. That is a pretty clear sign saying, "Yes, you'll be king." David didn't subsequently pray every day (as far we can tell): "Lord, make me king today" or, "Lord, make me king now." A real "wait" answer does not demand a repetition of the prayer of request. If God says "wait" to us, why should we ask again? Continuing to ask seems to reveal an attitude in us that says we don't want to follow God's timing or that we really don't think he'll follow through. Think of a child again. When you as a parent say "wait," you expect the child to stop asking for whatever they have been requesting. You expect them to trust you to deliver at the right time. When they continue to pester us, it actually makes us angry, doesn't it?

Here is another truth from the human child analogy. We are clear with our children. We tell them to "wait" in such a way that they can't misinterpret it to mean "no." We do so for the very purpose of avoiding the aforementioned problems. Now, God doesn't literally flash the word "wait" to us in the sky, but I believe that when he wants to say "wait" it will not be so cryptic that we have no idea that he has said it. Were he to be cryptic about it, he would be creating problems for us. "Wait" has to be clearly identifiable just as "yes" and "no" do. Otherwise, we will just keep doing what we are doing because we can't really understand a "wait until the right time" as opposed to a "no—that's not going to happen."

5. 1 Sam 23:17.

So why do we use the idea of "wait" as a mitigation maneuver? The "wait" answer is particularly important because it can actually mitigate a "no" into a "yes" that is *on-hold*. When we do this, the bottom line is that a "no" becomes, for all practical purposes, a "yes." It's just a "yes" that is waiting on-hold until the proper time. The really good thing about this sort of "wait" is that it doesn't require anything from us whatsoever. In any measurable way it is identical to God saying to us, "Yeah! Keep up that prayer! I'm just waiting for the right time to say 'yes'!" This is why we like this sort of thinking.

In truth, "wait" ought to build our patience in some way. But often when we hear "wait" from God, we just ignore it. In contrast, if I am told to "wait" by my wife when I ask for a cookie (usually because I want them right out of the hot oven), I have to actually *change my behavior* for it to really be a patience-building moment. If she says, "Wait for it," and I just keep nagging her with the same request, how is that patience-building? How am I "waiting?" At best I'm kept from what I want for awhile. But is that the same as acquiring patience? Is that the same as "waiting"? Is patience just the act of being forced to do without? No, real patience is taking the "wait for it" answer and altering my external behavior entirely. I stop asking for the cookie and actually wait for the time at which my wife decides it is appropriate for me to have it. (Unfortunately my analogy breaks down here. In real life, impatient for cookies, I usually ignore her "wait for it" and pry a steaming-hot one off the pan and burn my mouth wolfing it down. I'm a bad example of patience when it comes to cookies I'm afraid.)

The problem with our interpretation of a "wait" answer from God is that oftentimes we use "wait" to betray our lack of faith in him. We pray for something to happen; it doesn't; and then we tell ourselves he's said "wait" to us. In doing this we justify continuing our same prayer over and over. We say it's just a matter of timing, but in truth we're not really even acknowledging the "wait" answer. We're ignoring it. Just like the cookie example, if we really believed God knew what was best for us, and knew that he was going to give us our request in the future, in his time, we would cease requesting it. We would be patient and trust that it is on its way. But we aren't taught to do that. And often we don't pray that way. We just let the "wait" wash over us, having no discernable impact on how we act, and continue to pray as we always have.

We again can look at a child as an example. When we tell them to wait for something, it's a signal that they don't need to keep asking for that thing. It's most pointedly *not* a signal that they should continue to ask for it. In fact, that's why we say "wait" to them in first place isn't it? So that they will *stop* asking for that thing since it will come at the appointed and proper time. But for many Christians the answer "wait" seems to be interpreted as "wait, but keep on asking for that thing anyway, even though I said 'wait' until the proper time." It doesn't make sense to explain that a "wait" from God is a rationale for continuing repetitive prayer in the same vein, does it?

Let me add one last thought on the whole idea of God answering us with "wait." I'm thinking of the specific prayer of salvation for someone. Oftentimes when we pray for the salvation of someone and it does not happen we console ourselves with the idea that God has said "wait"—and that he means we should just keep offering him that same prayer. I've already argued that I don't think he appreciates such badgering about it, but that is not my point in bringing this up again. I think we have a presupposition that we should be involved in that person's salvation. But here I want to ask, *why* do we assume that? Why do we presuppose that we will be involved in the process of any specific person's salvation? We know from scripture that "some water" and "some plant."[6] That is, the process of salvation is seemingly divided over different workers who serve God's will for the lost. If I pray for the salvation of a lost person and it does not come about, why do I assume that I'm still supposed to be concerned about that lost person's salvation and my part in the process?

Don't get me wrong, of course we are concerned about the salvation of the lost in the general sense. But I mean in relation to any particular person and my personal contact and involvement with them. Couldn't it be the case that God has other people intended for that job (if it is to occur)? If I'm spending time focusing my prayer on someone who is clearly not getting saved, could I be ignoring the person for whom I'm really supposed to be working (praying)? I spend twenty-five years praying for my lost friend, but not a minute for my lost neighbor, who is a passing acquaintance. But what if God placed me in my house, next to my neighbor for the very purpose of praying for him? More to the point, what if he placed me there to not just pray for my neighbor but so that

---

6. 1 Cor 3:5–6.

I will talk to him about salvation in Christ? God still knows who will be saved and who will not. Saying my prayer for their salvation 1,000 times is no more effective than saying it once. Maybe it is the case that when our prayer is answered with a "no" we should take that to mean we should move on to someone else for whom we have been ordained as the conduit of God's message of grace. It's just a thought.

Well, we have looked at many different problems we face in prayer, from its haphazard nature, to our understanding of what it should accomplish, to how we handle the answers God gives us. It has been exhausting to point these problems out. No one wants to admit that important things like prayer can be this broken. I'm sure there are even more problems we experience as we pray in inappropriate ways. But I think I've hit on some of the major flaws and the problems they produce. Now let's leave problems behind, roll up our sleeves, and figure out how to pray in a God-honoring, productive, effective, and encouraging way. Anyone can carp about problems, but the seriously interested will try to find solutions. Let's now pursue some solutions.

5

Models of Prayer in the Bible

I REMEMBER THE HEAT bearing down on me as I stood alone on the hot concrete surface. The sun burned from above and the heat radiated from the concrete below. I didn't care; I exulted in the heat. Next to me was a bucket of tennis balls I had collected through the year—some fairly new, some so old and ratty that the felt was almost completely rubbed away. I had walked the mile or so to the court which was tucked away, out of sight, in a quiet neighborhood so that I could be alone while I practiced.

Each ball was tossed up with all the concentration I could muster. If it went awry, I caught it and tossed it again. Errant tosses led to errant serves. And who wanted to practice an errant toss anyway? My grip on my racquet changed as each serve was hit. Always I was trying to find the perfect position for my hand. My arms swung in different planes as I thwacked the balls over the net—sometimes into the net—gauging where they went, how they flew, how they bounced. I had a goal. I wanted to master three different types of serve: A "kicker" which would hit the ground and bound up high into an opponent; a "slice" which would arc through the air and skid when it hit the ground; and a "bomb" which was flat, hard, and sizzled through the air with as much velocity as I could generate. When I began the summer I could not hit any of them well, if at all.

Now and then I looked down at my book. I think it was by Pancho Gonzalez—one of the world's great tennis players when I was a baby and had never heard of tennis. He was old when I was young. The book was old too. But he was a master at the serve, and his book explained how each one worked. And I followed the instructions to a tee. I wanted to serve like Pancho because people said his name with awe and respect. So I read the book, looked at the pictures, and practiced. And slowly, day by heat-filled day, I began to succeed. Until I had looked to a mentor, I was at a loss as to how to serve. But that small book had provided me with the pattern to master all the serves I desired.

The best place to begin figuring out what prayer should look like and how it should be conducted is in the Holy Scriptures. Now, we all know that there is no place in scripture that lays out a template which tells us explicitly how to pray. But there are many examples of prayer that we can examine and imitate.[1] As I imitated Pancho to learn how to serve, we can imitate the Bible to learn how to pray. So, in this section, we will turn to the Bible and look at a few of the prayers found there. It was common in the history of the church to have newer believers begin by only praying the prayers of the Bible to get the hang of what they were doing. That is good practice that seems to have been neglected in our modern age. But we will take that approach and will submit to Biblical prayers as our instructors.

Before we begin with this however, you might ask, "Why do I think the prayers of the Bible are a model of prayers for me?" We really only want to pattern our prayers on those in the Bible if we believe they are examples that any believer can pray with the same success the original speaker had. In other words, we don't want to imitate *ineffective* prayers.

Let's first think about the make-up of the Bible in general. The Bible can be divided into two broad types of texts:

- Texts that instruct us on how to live our lives.
- Texts that record information for us.

Some have described this division with the terms *proscriptive* and *descriptive*. Some texts are *proscriptive* in that they are intended to show us how to act. Proscriptive texts include commands such as, "Let all bitterness and wrath and anger and clamor and slander be put away from you, along with all malice."[2] But sometimes descriptions of people's actions are intended to be proscriptive as well. For example, in 1 Corinthians 10:6 Paul describes the records of Israel's wanderings as

---

1. Of course the so called "Lord's Prayer" is actually a template of sorts. We will look very closely at it for that reason. But even it is rather sparse in terms of length and obvious content. As we will see, it needs to be filled out in our thinking as we pray it.

2. Eph 4:31.

examples to us to teach us to act differently. We often look at Abraham's obedience to God's command to sacrifice his son Isaac as an example of complete trust in God that we should emulate.[3]

Descriptive texts are texts that describe something, but not necessarily with the intention that we emulate it. Sometimes, even direct commands are not to be understood as commands to us personally, but to the specific historical group to whom they were spoken. So Jesus told the people to do all that the Pharisees commanded, but we don't take that instruction as applicable to our lives today.[4]

Many of the prayers of the Bible are proscriptive in that they are intended to not only record the author's prayer, but to picture for us broadly (or sometimes very specifically) examples of prayers we can also pray. Of course, there are some prayers we don't want to pray because they are not useful, God would not respond well to them, or they just don't apply to us. Some even seem to teach what *not* to do rather than what we should do. We need to keep that truth in mind as we look at prayers. We need to ask ourselves, "Should I pray that prayer?" or, "Should I pray that way?" For example, some have read the imprecatory prayers in the psalms and concluded we should never pray for curses to fall on our enemies.[5]

In this section though, let's look at some key prayers that I think are clearly models for us to emulate. We will start with Jesus, then look at the Apostle Paul and finish with King David. In particular we will focus on the need for maturity which makes effective prayer both possible and enjoyable.

THE LORD'S PRAYER (MATTHEW 6:9-13)

Probably the most recognized prayer of the Bible for the Christian is the so-called *Lord's Prayer* found in the Gospel of Matthew, chapter 6:9-13.[6] This is a somewhat misleading name in that the prayer is not one that records what *Jesus* prayed, but a prayer given *to his disciples* to pray. In Luke

---

3. Not that we want to emulate sacrificing children. But we should emulate the trust that Abraham exhibited in the example that is set before us in Genesis 22.

4. Matt 23:1-3.

5. I am of the opinion that we can pray the imprecatory psalms provided we understand them in the right light and do not use them as a way of just cursing others for our own satisfaction.

6. As I've noted, a variation of the Lord's Prayer is also found in Luke 11:2-4. Jesus probably taught this prayer model any number of times as he went about His work.

11:1 we are told that at least once Jesus gave this prayer as an example for a specific disciple who asked how to pray. In Matthew he is talking to a group of his disciples about various religious acts and how to perform them (including things like fasting, prayer, and alms giving). The prayer is relatively short, and many of us have already memorized it:

> [9] "Pray, then, in this way: 'Our Father who is in heaven, Hallowed be Your name. [10] 'Your kingdom come. Your will be done, On earth as it is in heaven. [11] 'Give us this day our daily bread. [12] 'And forgive us our debts, as we also have forgiven our debtors. [13] 'And do not lead us into temptation, but deliver us from evil. *For Yours is the kingdom and the power and the glory forever. Amen.*"[7]

We can break the Lord's Prayer into seven (or eight) short statements:

1. Our father who is in heaven.
2. Hallowed be your name.
3. Your kingdom come.
4. Your will be done on earth as it is in heaven.
5. Give us this day our daily bread.
6. Forgive us our debts as we also have forgiven our debtors.
7. Lead us not into temptation but deliver us from evil.
8. For yours is the kingdom and power and the glory forever.[8]

Since this is a model prayer given to his disciples specifically by Jesus, it stands to reason that we should look at it closely. I believe it provides us with both a model of how we ought to pray, and a list of what we ought to focus on in our prayers.

---

7. Matt 6:9–13. The final line is in parentheses because it is not included in many Greek manuscripts. Therefore, scholars are unsure as to whether it should be included or not. Because it is found in many manuscripts, most of our modern Bibles include the line.

8. Some of the important early manuscripts don't contain this last line, so it is sometimes left out of our English Bibles or is bracketed as a later addition. Let's assume that it does belong in the text since many of our English Bibles contain it. It certainly is in accord with what Jesus taught.

Our Father Who Is in Heaven

My gut hurt. It was late summer and we had driven the eight hours from Coeur d' Alene, Idaho to Portland, Oregon to find a place to live for the foreseeable future. My wife and I were both unemployed as of the end of the month and I was effectively a seminary student with no job, no house, and no income. We had come to Portland for one week in order to find a place to live when we arrived in a few weeks with all of our worldly possessions. I was nervous and my gut hurt. I'd never been to Portland. The closest sized city I had lived in was Spokane Washington, and it is consistently described as a city that feels like a small town in many ways. Portland wasn't that.

Everything was so different. In Coeur d' Alene we had a 2 bedroom duplex with a basement and full laundry for $275 dollars a month. The first place we drove by in Portland had been advertised for $300 dollars a month, and I thought we had the wrong house when we pulled to the curb. The porch was literally cantered to the left and every window was broken or cracked on the front of the house. The yard looked like a city dump, and the inside was worse. In all honesty, we didn't even want to go in, though we finally did. The street made me a bit afraid for my wife's safety. My brain was calculating and re-calculating our budget for school and living with the new information this trash-heap had supplied. My gut hurt as my eyes were opened to the fiscal realities of Portland.

I recall driving through neighborhoods of nice houses to get to that first rat-hole. Looking at it with my new enlightenment I had realized we could never afford those houses. We could barely afford a good apartment. We weren't those people. Where you live tells something about who you are, or at least where you are in life. We were not well off; we were poor students. Our house was going to have to reflect who we really were. And it was going to be closer to the rat-hole than the mansions.

"*Our Father who is in heaven.*" This first statement of the Lord's Prayer obviously notes who we are talking to—God. Now, we might want to jump directly to the predicate of the line and focus in on the truth that God is *in heaven*. And we will think about that in a moment, but first, let's focus in on the beginning of the sentence. Because of the way the original Greek language is typically constructed, we see more noticeably a profound point Jesus is making prior to the idea that God is in heaven.[9] Literally, the line reads: *father of us, the one in the heavens*. It just seems that the Greek renders a clear truth more obviously than English: *God comes first; he* is the initial emphasis.

In Jesus' mind, a prayer should not begin with the focus on us. This may seem fairly obvious to most of us, but let's add another point: The focus does not begin on other people either. It does not begin on people at all—it begins on God. Most people probably wouldn't need too much convincing that we ought not to pray with ourselves as the focus—which would seem selfish. But we might think that praying for others is paramount and reveals our Christ-like love for them. We might argue that prayer for others is the epitome of good prayer, isn't it? Certainly I would agree that praying over another person is an act of love and is extremely important. James 5:16 tells us to "pray for one another, so that you may be healed." In 1 Thessalonians 5:25 the Apostle Paul asks the believers to "pray for us"—meaning the Apostle and his friends. But still, we must keep in mind, even in the direst of circumstances, God has no equal or better in the created realm. And moreover, we are still praying for others *to God*. This little point, that God is the central focus of our prayers, is actually crucial to the entire shape of what we eventually end up saying in prayer. It might seem to be nit-picky, but here is a case where the English translation accidentally presents a subtle change in the feel of the sentence because of the nature of the language. It's not that the English is wrong—we can trust our English Bibles thoroughly—it's just that translations always introduce subtle distinctions. Therefore I want to make it clear: God is first and foremost on our lips when we pray; not us.

If a friend has cancer, for example, and we are centered on him and his problem, we will often ask things of God based in the declarations of that friend—who often will ask that we pray for healing. And so our prayer is something like, "Lord, heal so and so." Often, our friend passes his prayer request to us and we pray for him without thinking through what he is asking. Consequently, we may begin with our focus

---

9. I'm not implying that the Greek says something the English does not; I'm merely saying here that the Greek's word order makes the point seem even more clear. This is one of those places where the English language is hampered by how it is constructed. In Greek, the words have much more freedom of movement. In English however, word order is far more defined by the syntactical requirements of the language over the desires of the writer.

on *him* rather than God. More importantly, by not beginning with God, we eliminate the opportunity to frame our whole understanding of the situation in terms of God and his desires first. Now, I think we do this, usually, with the best of intentions. We assume our friend is the most knowledgeable about the situation and the best equipped to decide what is needed. We add to this, frequently, the conviction that God always wants to heal people (which, as we have seen, is not true). Or we feel loyalty to our friend and show it by following his lead in prayer without thinking at all about what is really being requested. But quite often we fail to ask whether healing is really what is needed; whether healing is what *God* would want. We pray blindly and hope for the best; and we put our friend's wishes ahead of God.

Just for a moment, let's think again about this example of praying for healing specifically and try to ascertain what it might teach us about prayer in general. If healing *is* the best thing in every circumstance of illness, then the question arises, "Why doesn't God heal the sick among the faithful?"[10] Sometimes we pray for healing and the person never improves, or worse yet he gets sicker or even dies. The answer seems clear: God does not heal the sick every time because healing must *not be the best course of action* in some situations. Otherwise, if our call for God to heal does not result in healing, even though it really *is* the best thing for our friend, then we must admit, God is not willing to give out what our friend needs the most. What sort of God would that be? God even says in Matthew 6:8 that he "knows what you need before you ask him." In Luke 11:11–12 Jesus says of the father: "Now suppose one of you fathers is asked by his son for a fish; he will not give him a snake instead of a fish, will he? Or if he is asked for an egg, he will not give him a scorpion, will he?" Jesus' point is that even earthly fathers know what their children need and will give it to them. It stands to reason that if flawed, earthly fathers act that way, then naturally God, our father, the loving, caring God of the Bible, will do at least the same.

But if healing is what is really needed and God does *not* give it, then he appears capricious and untrustworthy in handling our good, and in

---

10. Let's assume that we are talking about believers alone at this point. We might suggest that God does not ever listen to the prayers of the unrighteous, unless they repent and pray for forgiveness (Cf. Isa 1:15; Jer 11:11; Prov 15:29; 28:9). This makes sense because the unrighteous pray for things that flow directly from their selfish wants, even when the prayers seem altruistic on the surface.

that case is not really of much use in our day-to-day lives. In fact, we might say he is hurtful and not worthy of our worship.

The truth is, we recognize that healing is *not the answer* in every case. Often, later in the course of events, even the sick person recognizes that through the process of pain, helplessness, and fear, he has grown in areas in which he had previously been unchallenged. And we ourselves often admit later, that in the process of dealing with other people's pain, we have grown in maturity. All this is not to say that we don't desire healing for others, but it does suggest that our desire for healing may be in error at times if it culminates in prayer for healing exclusively while ignoring God's desires. And, in terms of reality, the fact is that healing must not be the best course of action because our good and faithful God, who really can be trusted to give us the very best, permits deep pain and sickness at times in our lives. All these difficulties come about when we begin our prayers with the wrong focus. God needs to be highlighted first in order for us to even frame our prayers correctly.

Now, I would suggest that others are only the focus in our prayers secondarily in any event, even when we start our prayers with them on our lips. In reality, our focus is usually on ourselves. Even when we begin our prayers with the intent of putting God at the center of our attention, it is our very nature to center on ourselves, for the world around us must pass though us before it can be experienced. I see this in my marriage all the time. I go with my wife, a trained artist, to the local builders store to pick out a paint color for the new bathroom. I pick up a colored card and say, "I like this red," and my wife invariable will say something like, "You mean that rose?" It turns out my wife's grid of interpretation of colors has a gajillion more colors than mine does. The world that surrounds both of us flows through her view producing the impression of many more colors than in my world. At best I might say the paint chips include "darker" or "lighter" reds, or hues of red. But she actually has names for many more of the colors than I do.

Moreover, my wife is constantly, without conscious thought it seems to me, pairing colors together. One particular red is more toward the blue and therefore inappropriate with some other red. Her experience with colors allows her to define the world in a much more visually detailed way than I can. On the other hand there are those people out there who cannot identify when two colors are discordant even when they are side by side. Furthermore, they might even enjoy the two mismatched colors together even though most people would find them repulsive. In such cases, reality is totally shaped by the person's internal grid of interpretation.

Relating this to prayer again, it is often the case that our own interpretive grid forces some self-determined interpretation of reality and therefore a self-determined shape of our prayers. This innate shaping of reality to our own views works against our ability to truly place God centrally in our prayers. But it is not impossible to do so. In my experience with my wife, I've learned over time to adopt *her* view of colors. I now choose my words more carefully and attempt to define exactly what color I'm looking at. In truth, I've grown in my understanding of color. I'm not sophisticated; I often merely combine colors to explain the hue I'm looking at: Blue/yellow as opposed to red/yellow. But I place her understanding of color over mine to facilitate the interaction. When it comes to prayer we ought to do the same thing.[11] We should look at the world around us from God's perspective (as much as that is possible) and shape our prayers to *his* interests rather than our own. We will discuss this more later when we look at the Apostle Paul's prayer life.

All this has been to say that when Jesus began the Lord's Prayer with *father*, he was making an important point about the initial starting place of our prayers. They focus on *God* first and then move to other subjects. Doing so is not perhaps as easy as we think it is because we inherently tend to view everything in terms of *us* first.

Now we might be tempted to think we have exhausted all we can say about the first word of the Lord's prayer (*father*), and that we are ready to move on to the two descriptors: *our* and *who is in heaven*. But we can't leave the first word without a bit more comment.

Jesus could have begun by saying that we should address God as God: "Our *God* who is in heaven." But he exchanged the more general term "God" with the much more intimate term: "*Father.*" There has been much written about this term, so I do not want to repeat it here. But I would say this however, in terms of our prayers themselves, they ought to be formulated to fit the way that one would address a *father*. Jesus is

---

11. On the other hand, at times I willfully refuse to adopt her more detailed distinctions and stubbornly hold to my *red is red* philosophy. I would liken that to how we often pray with God. We stick to our prays whether they are formatted to God's desires or not.

using the picture of a father to shed some light on the context of our prayer/discussion with God.

It is prudent to note here that Jesus is addressing disciples—people who have a relationship with God. Now, it is true that in some sense we can assert that God is everyone's father. In Luke 3:38 Adam is called the *son of God*. So in a sense humankind has this familial relationship to God best understood in terms of creation in God's image. But there is a special father/child relationship for the believer, and this relationship goes beyond mere creation. It reflects the sympathetic view and love the child and father share. Jesus chastises the Pharisees in John 8:44 saying, "You are of your father the devil, and you want to do the desires of your father. He was a murderer from the beginning, and does not stand in the truth because there is no truth in him. Whenever he speaks a lie, he speaks from his own nature, for he is a liar and the father of lies." Jesus is pointing out the similarity of purpose and desire between the Pharisees and Satan himself. He is not implying that Satan created the Pharisees, much less birthed them.

In this passage the Pharisees had said about themselves, "Abraham is our father" and, "we have one father"—God.[12] In both cases they were trying to point out that they follow in the footsteps of their "father"— whether it be Abraham or God himself. And from their point of view, they believed their opposition and hatred of Jesus was good and right and in line with their father's. In all these instances the idea of father/child is invoked in order to picture the child's special relationship to the father and similarity of thought and action between them.

Some people have had poor earthly fathers, and at times this can get in the way of the metaphor. But we should take the picture of God as *father* for how it was intended, in the context of a loving and caring father/child relationship. Jesus was attempting to picture the intimate, bonded relationship we believers have with God. *Father,* in every best sense of the word is what he is intending to communicate. We might now spend time thinking on what a good (even perfect) father would be like: Loving, compassionate, brave, intelligent, disciplined, forgiving, able to teach, able to discipline, protective—the list of good traits is quite long. This is the context Jesus wanted us to use to shape our address to God. We see him as a *father* to us.

---

12. John 8:39, 41.

Now I make this point because we sometimes forget what a good father is like, and how we should treat him. We read that we can address God as *our father* and degenerate into a smarmy discussion of a loving God who seems more like a giant marshmallow of comfort than a real father. God is a father to us in every sense of that word—even the harder senses.

Although the subject is not prayer, a good picture of the strength of a father is found in Hebrews, chapter 12. Here we read:

> [5] And you have forgotten the exhortation which is addressed to you as sons, "MY SON, DO NOT REGARD LIGHTLY THE DISCIPLINE OF THE LORD, NOR FAINT WHEN YOU ARE REPROVED BY HIM; [6] FOR THOSE WHOM THE LORD LOVES HE DISCIPLINES, AND HE SCOURGES EVERY SON WHOM HE RECEIVES." [7] It is for discipline that you endure; God deals with you as with sons; for what son is there whom his father does not discipline? [8] But if you are without discipline, of which all have become partakers, then you are illegitimate children and not sons. [9] Furthermore, we had earthly fathers to discipline us, and we respected them; shall we not much rather be subject to the Father of spirits, and live?[13]

Here we see a picture of a father with an emphasis on the discipline he must dole out at times. This is no milk-toast father who never demands anything from us and who constantly emotes over our weaknesses. This is a strong father who, in love, realizes that children need to grow, to mature, to be corrected. It is this strong father that is so often lost in our view of prayer.

What would such a father think of a child who continually makes the same mistakes over and over again? Wouldn't such a father step up and rebuke such foolishness?

In terms of prayer, what might we say then? For one thing, we must admit we would not just keep hurling our requests to our earthly fathers without thought. Before long they would surely say to us, "Child, you need to grow up!" We would be foolish or irresponsible to think that our father's want us to continue to act like ignorant children when in fact we are grown adults. In fact, they would probably wonder what's wrong with us. Real fathers expect us to mature into wise adults, and reflect their own maturity. When we do so, they are proud of our ability to act

---

13. Heb 12:5–9.

as adults and be responsible for ourselves. As we noted earlier, asking for a pony at seven years old is cute. Asking for a pony at forty is sad and creepy.

In the end, we should view our prayers as though talking to our perfect father. In that context especially, we should see that prayer cannot be undisciplined, ignorant babbling forever. It must be intentional, reasoned, and maturing speech with our loving mentor and guide. And that should be our starting place in prayer—God our loving *father*.

Ok, let's go on. As I noted earlier, there are two descriptors that accompany the term *father*: "our" and "who is in the heavens." Let's look at each of these for a moment.

First, it is *our* father and not someone else's father that we address. If you think about it, that is a very important distinction. I would often ask things of my father that I would not of someone else's father, even if I knew them well and they cared for me. There is always a special bond between father and child that other relationships cannot copy. In terms of prayer, this is important to remember, for it gives us a freedom in prayer beyond what may be expected of a dispassionate relationship with a deity. We talk to God—*our father*—personally, sharing things that he alone is capable of receiving. I would also add as a reminder that this freedom we have is accompanied by a special respect as well. We can talk openly with our true father, but we also must talk with respect that is grounded in our intimate relationship. Knowing God as we do, as children, requires both freedom of transparency and informed respect. When we lose one or the other, the relationship is hindered.

Additionally, it is *our* father, not *my* father. There is a sense of communal relationship that sits behind our relationship and requests to God. We may ask, "Why does that make any difference?" It is vital in that it shapes our requests from the position of looking for the good of *all of us*—not just myself. Even when we pray over ourselves, we are pointed toward asking for things or sharing ideas from a communal position. For example, we often pray that God remove any troubles we might be having. Yet we forget when we pray that way, that our personal comfort is not always the most important thing for the community at large. An example of this is the Apostle Paul as he sat in jail in Rome. He wrote to the Church at Philippi saying:

> [12] "Now I want you to know, brethren, that my circumstances have turned out for the greater progress of the gospel, [13] so that

my imprisonment in the cause of Christ has become well known throughout the whole praetorian guard and to everyone else, [14] and that most of the brethren, trusting in the Lord because of my imprisonment, have far more courage to speak the word of God without fear."[14]

In this case Paul's unfortunate circumstance of being jailed had actually *encouraged* believers to speak out more boldly for God! It would be far better in most of our eyes to get out of jail at any cost, and we might argue, it certainly would have been better if one of the best evangelists in the history of the church were free from the restrictions of jail. Yet Paul says the *greater* good was accomplished by God *not* releasing him from jail.

I am not suggesting that Paul never prayed to be released from jail. I would think that was one of his first prayers to God at his arrest. Yet I suspect that that particular prayer disappeared rather quickly when he noted the true produce of his arrest and detention. In fact, in many of his prayers from jail, we see that he is not concerned about himself at all so much as for his flocks of believers (whether he had even visited them or not).[15]

The point is, when Jesus says we should begin our prayer with "our" father, he seems to be indicating subtly that our prayers are to be shaped by a communal view of our relationship to God. Our requests to *our* father should, in some way, benefit more than ourselves individually. They should address my personal needs in light of the community—*our* needs. We should ask ourselves when we pray then, "What should I pray for that would best help those around me?" Remember, God is the father of *us all,* so when we pray, "our father," we are focused on that paternal relationship not just in our individual lives, but in the lives of all God's children.

Jesus also describes God as he "who is in the heavens." The plural form here may surprise us today, but it is a reflection of the first century worldview of the Jew that heaven is divided into parts.[16] The idea

---

14. Phil 1:12–14.

15. I say that Paul may have not visited his own flocks at times because he says in Colossians 2:1: "For I want you to know how great a struggle I have on your behalf and for those who are at Laodicea, and for all those who have not personally seen my face." Apparently Paul viewed those believers he had not personally ministered to as equal to those he had.

16. We see Paul referring to the *third heaven* in 2 Corinthians 12:2 for example.

is seen clearly in the Hebrew term for *heaven* which is usually rendered as plural.[17]

More important to our discussion is the idea that God, our father, is *in heaven*. Think back to the story about my wife and I looking for an apartment in Portland. We had noted that where you live says something about who you are. It may not define you totally, but it does say something. God lives *in heaven*. Our prayers ascend to our father who sits in his perfect abode, his *dwelling place* far above the earth.[18] What does this reveal to us? For one, God is above what we experience here on earth. We are told in Psalm 14:2, "The Lord has looked down from heaven upon the sons of men to see if there are any who understand, Who seek after God." God's view from heaven is complete. This father we pray to is not hindered by the uncertainties of this reality that surrounds us here on earth. I may, in my limited sight, pray for release from some trouble that assaults me, but God sees well beyond the trouble itself. He knows where the trouble leads and what situations grow from it, not just in my life, but in those lives around me, and around them, and so on. God brings this idea home forcefully (unfortunately) to Job.

In the Old Testament book of Job, the author had complained that God would not give him an audience to plead his case. Job felt put-upon, even accusing God of bruising him "without cause."[19] In chapter 38 God finally responds to Job by asking him a series of questions that drive home the utter ignorance of humans and the all-knowing, all-powerful character of God:

- "Where were you when I laid the foundation of the earth?" (38:4)
- "Have you ever in your life commanded the morning and caused the dawn to know its place, that it might take hold of the ends of the earth, and the wicked be shaken out of it?" (38:12–13)
- "Where is the way to the dwelling of light?" (38:19)

---

17. The term in Hebrew is *sh'mayim*.
18. Cf. 1 Kgs 8:39; 2 Chr 6:21.
19. Job 9:17.

- "Can you hunt the prey for the Lion, or satisfy the appetite of the young lions, whey they crouch in their dens and lie in wait in their lair?" (38:39–40)
- "Do you give the horse his might?" (39:19)
- "Is it by your understanding that the hawk soars, stretching his wings toward the south?" (39:26)

On and on the questions go, making clear to Job that he is not in any way, shape, or form as informed or powerful as God in heaven. When we pray to our father "who is in heaven," we are tacitly noting the truth that God is beyond this world that spawns our prayers.

This is not to say that God is unfeeling to our situations in the same way we might observe the ant hill and know how it works, but really not have any feeling or inclination toward it. Rather it is to say that God sees and knows intimately *all the ramifications* of what we are asking for in prayer. God "knows what you need before you ask him" because he knows the entire circumstances surrounding your requests.[20]

You may ask, "Why does this matter?" "Why do I care that God is all-seeing as he looks down on the world and hears our prayers?" It provides us with a number of helpful insights. First, we can realize that at times we don't know what to ask, but God still knows what we need. Paul says that at times the Holy Spirit even prays for us because of our ignorance of what we should pray.[21] What an encouragement this is when we face overwhelming trials! Second, God's position in heaven gives *his insight* into a circumstance priority over our own. We ought to come to prayer to the all-knowing, all-powerful father with an attitude of, "You know best, Lord, and I would like to learn what that is." Often we use prayer to persuade God to our view of things—sometimes (as I've pointed out) by brute repetition of the same prayer over and over. But we should understand, God is not the one who needs to be informed and tutored to make better decisions. *We* are the ones whose prayers ought to be conforming to the One who sees all from heaven. God's position in heaven should make us think on the fact that our prayers need to be critiqued at times to fit with what *he* sees.

20. Matt 6:8.

21. Cf. Romans 8:26. "In the same way the Spirit also helps our weakness; for we do not know how to pray as we should, but the Spirit Himself intercedes for us with groanings too deep for words...."

This should be one of our goals in prayer: We should want to get to the place in our prayer lives where we are praying for things with the insight of the all-powerful, all-seeing God. Think how effective such a prayer would be?

Let's us the analogy of a child again. When a little child asks to go across the street, we may at times say "no" because we know the broader situation that a small child does not: Perhaps the street is exceedingly busy and dangerous at that time of day; perhaps it is approached by a tight, blind curve; it may be the case that waiting until we can go along will help the child develop patience; we know that the ice cream he wants from the store across the street is not good for him right before dinner. We, who know more and understand more, are in a position to make better choices of action than the child. The child can watch us and learn, over time, to make those choices as well, and in the process he will, hopefully, give up asking for things that are uninformed and entirely from his childish viewpoint.

Here another question comes to mind: If the child continues to ask to go across the street after being told "no," what does this say of his trust in us? More directly, what does it say about our relationship to God when we continue to ask the same prayers over and over once we have been told "no" by him? Are we asserting that he is wrong to have answered that way? Are we thinking we can nag him long enough to change his mind? We've already addressed this question above; nagging is not a good methodology on which to build prayer.

So, in this first line of the Lord's Prayer we see a number of important concepts. We see that God is to be the focus of our prayers and that focus on him shapes what we say. We see that this is not some impersonal God but one who is a father to us—*all of us* together. This last seems to imply that our prayers are best offered from the standpoint of the community asking rather than personal, individual interest. We also noted that our father is *in heaven* and therefore what he knows and can do far exceeds what we know and can do. Therefore, our prayers should be shaped by the notion that in many cases they will need to be modified according to God's knowledge—they need to mature in content, based on God's input.

Hallowed Be Your Name

Sherri would come to our Bible study without her husband as often as with. I remember the forlorn look that seemed to permanently cloud her eyes. It was a deep dilemma for her. On the one hand her husband was a jerk. On the other, he was the father of her children and she loved him. He was full of promises and heartache in equal measure. He would tell her how special she was to him, and he would rave about her to their friends at church. He would even weep while confessing how she was his better and his love.

Then he'd blow their savings on drugs and whores. Sometimes he'd wheedle money out of fellow congregants with his well-practiced presentation. "I'm trying to get better. I just need a little cash. It's for the kids." Whatever. But often the naturally trusting—those who desperately want a better life for all, would believe, and give. Sherri would believe. She'd give of herself as well. And he would burn it away on sin again. And always after his spasm of sin, Sherri would hear: "Really Sherri, I love you, I need you, you're the most important thing to me, forgive me baby."

But in the end, they split up. How long do you live with the designation "Number One in my life" but the treatment of "I don't give a damn about you!"? How long will a person accept being *told* their special, but being *treated* as though they are not? How long would you live like that?

The next clause, "Hallowed be Your name," is the first of three in the Lord's Prayer that are very similar in sentiment. They are all expressions of what we would like to have come about: May God's name be hallowed, may God's kingdom come, and may God's will be done on earth as in heaven.

So these next three clauses are statements of conviction on our part. In the first clause it is a direct statement about the nature of this father we have in heaven. We declare we would like his name to be *"hallowed."* This sentence needs a little explanation from a technical standpoint. In the Greek language the verb form is called an aorist passive imperative. This tells us a number of things. First, the imperative mood implies that it is a strong wish on the part of the speaker that something takes place.

Sometimes it goes so far as to be the same as a command to others. It is like saying, "I really want this done," or even more forcefully, "Let it be done!" Additionally, the aorist tense tells us that this is undefined action—the speaker was not necessarily thinking of a specific moment in time, but is just referring to some moment and action, whenever it occurs. The aorist tense is also used commonly just to carry Greek texts along. We might call it the usual, standard tense when the author is not committing himself to really defining an action closely. So here we might draw the conclusion that Jesus is thinking generally about the action rather than about a particular occurrence of it. He's not really commenting on a specific occurrence of hallowing God's name, so to speak.[22] So this is a strong wish, even a command of the speaker (the pray-er in this case) that God's name be "hallowed."

This leads us to the next question we may have, "What exactly is 'hallowing' anyway!?" A great many Bible translations use the term "hallowed" but it really is not a very common term that one would use in American English conversation. When you look up the Greek term that is being used, the definition is *to sanctify*. In terms of Israel's history, to *sanctify* something was to set it apart for ritual use. It was marking something off as special and holy to God as opposed to being *common*— meaning it was not ritualistically pure.

Taking this definition with our clause from the Lord's Prayer— Hallowed be your name—we might say the line is a declaration calling us to set God's name apart as pure and righteous and separate from the ordinary things of the world (and from us).

Next, we might also have some problems with the phrase "your name" instead of just saying "may you be hallowed, Father," or something like that. Jesus couldn't possibly be saying that we are merely to hold the words "God" or "Adonai" or "Jesus" in reverence.[23] Jesus is speaking from a Jewish conception that a name is more than incidentally associated with an object. In fact, we can positively say that this idea is typical in

---

22. These ideas can be found in many standard Greek grammars and syntaxes. For example: *The Language of the New Testament* by Eugene Van Ness Goetchius, *A Greek Grammar of the New Testament and Other Early Christian Literature* by F. Blass and A. Debrunner, and *Idioms of the Greek New Testament* by Stanley E. Porter.

23. Notice he doesn't even say what *name* is to be hallowed. God was known by many names in the Old Testament: *El Shaddai* (which we translate *God Almighty*), *Elohim* (which we translate as just *God*), *Yahweh* (which is the divine name, and which we typically translate as *Lord*), *El Elyon* (translated as *Lord Most High*) and others.

societies all over the world. People have names that are meant to reflect something about them. And the name often seems to encompass all the power the person has as well. Sometimes even in America, where names hold less importance, we find people naming their children because of what they mean to them. One couple I know named their boy Kaeo, which is Hawaiian for "victorious one" to signify how their boy would overcome in life. Jesus is using the term "name" in that way. It stands for who God is.[24] He is saying that this is another thing we are to pray for when we come to God: Let God, in all he is, be considered Holy—set apart from all else.

Now this expression is considered so important to Jesus that he includes it as a model statement for his disciples to pray—seemingly whenever they come to prayer. And the question arises, "How can one pray this line *effectively*?" After all, just saying, "Hallowed be Your name" doesn't really accomplish much, does it? Much like Sherri's husband's words in the previous story, talk is cheap. Anyone can *say* someone is important and set apart in their lives, but the real question is how is that accomplished in your daily life?

There are two aspects that stand out in this line of prayer for us. First, we must consider who our God is. This sounds a bit silly to say out loud, but I think it might be a real problem underlying our prayer lives. We sometimes don't remember or consider just exactly *who* God is. Moreover, we are not maturing steadily, so as to discover who he is on a continual basis. The problem here is that stagnation in our maturity functionally hinders our understanding of God's attributes—i.e., the things that are represented by his *name*. When a child thinks of a *car* for example, they may think of the thing that we ride in. Or perhaps some think of the bright color of the car. Others may think of *car* in association with destinations such as grandma's house or nursery school. But as we mature, we realize the idea of *car* represents a lot more than those basic things.

In like fashion, our internal representation of God and his attributes should change as we mature. Our prayer, "Hallowed be your name," should be a reflection of the growing awareness we have of his majesty in every respect. When this is not happening, we lose interest. Think of the adult who still thinks of *car* as merely a means of transportation

---

24. For the interested reader, a very extensive article on the use of *"name"* is found in a book called the *Theological Dictionary of the New Testament*, volume V, pp. 242–81.

as opposed to the mechanic who has continually expanded her understanding of what a *car* is. The mechanic says, "My car is great!" with far more appreciation and awe than I do for example. I hardly think of cars at all, even my own. And when I say, "My car is great," I'm thinking of the few aspects I've ever considered: Color, body contours, it drives when I want to go somewhere. The truth of the matter is that for all practical purposes I rarely ever even say, "My car is great!"

Frankly speaking, I never even think about my car enough to muster up the will to utter that sentence. But what would the mechanic think of me if I said daily, "My car is great!" and never knew any more about it than I did the day I bought it? Why even bother to say such a thing? I'm like the child who appreciates a few things, but over the years never adds anything new to my list. It sounds sort of silly in fact. The mechanic spends time learning about her car, and each time she says, "My car is great!" she is reflecting on new aspects of it, and expressing her joy at having it. She never tires of how great her car is because she's constantly discovering new aspects of its greatness. She is undoubtedly more likely to utter praises of her car than I am. And she may even place herself in circumstances and situations where she has opportunity to praise her car—perhaps at a car club or some such thing. I avoid all possibilities of such a thing happening; it's just a car to me, and I don't want to be bothered too much with it.

This is the same thing that should be happening when we utter, "Hallowed be your name," in our prayers. And if that maturity is not occurring, our prayer becomes hollow. We regurgitate the same old ideas of God we had five, ten, forty years ago, and hardly even consider those ideas let alone set them apart and honor them. It becomes impossible to pray that line after a time with any feeling because we honestly don't have a picture of God worth *"hallowing."* Our God is boring and unchanging, and not in the good sense of *"steady."* He's unchanging in the sense of dead. It reminds me of the before-dinner prayer I was taught to pray when I was a child. I beat it into the ground and it soon lost any meaning to me: "God is great, God is good, let us thank him for our food. Amen." After a time I might as well have just uttered, "Blah blah blah, blah blah blah, blah blah blah blah blah blah blah. Amen." I quit saying grace after awhile because God meant nothing to me. I was not growing in *how* God was great and good in relation to food and the only thing that stuck in my head was the rhythm of the words. When I finally started to mature and consider just how awesome it is that I get food every day, the intricate processes that must occur for me to have it, and how God cares enough to provide it, I began to say grace with some anticipation. I began to say grace even with enthusiasm. I actually like to say grace before eating now. I've thought a great deal about food and God and it spurs me on to prayer over the whole topic. In like fashion I suggest that only with maturity in our understanding of God can we utter, "Hallowed be your name" day after day, year after year, with any sincerity. And Jesus undoubtedly knew that fact. His life is an example of growing daily in the knowledge of God and consequently being able to utter that clause enthusiastically in his prayers.

After considering who God is, the second thing we must consider in this line of prayer is how, practically speaking, we can "hallow" God in our lives in a real way. Remember, we are praying that God's person be considered *set apart* from the daily things we encounter in life. But talk alone is cheap; we need to put word to deed. Such a prayer becomes stale without actually considering some practical expression of this thought. "What does hallowing God look like for me?" is the question we ought to ask. Our prayer can grow cold and stale unless it challenges us to change. Moreover, our expanding maturity is also changing the way we ask it. If I ask God to be set apart in my life—what is going to change? And if we don't expect or want something to change, why make the statement in the first place? I think this is another reason we divest our prayers of that line. We don't really consider what "hallowing" God will look like, so we never see it, and consequently we stop considering it.

It's impossible to express for everyone what "hallowing" God may look like in your life, but an example might spur you to explore this line of thought in your own life. I usually begin with an honest look at myself. I ask myself what activities I participate in that express my awe and respect of God, and conversely what I do that may not fully express that awe.

Let me just pick one that has been on my mind lately. I like to watch movies, and I especially like scary movies and big special-effects sci-fi movies. But lately I've noticed that in more and more of them I'm hearing Jesus' name used as an expletive. I know that some Christians just never watch movies because of this, but I think that approach is really just putting out one fire without dealing with the underlying problem. After all, I may not watch movies, but I find Jesus' name is used as an expletive all around me in the world's daily speech. I even hear Christians occasionally saying "Jesus!" or "Jeez!" when they are shocked, as though it were normal to spout the Lord God's name when we feel amazed about something. If the answer to the problem is to remove the vehicle of sin (movies in this case), I'd surely have to remove more than movies from my life. I'm often offended by what the evening news says about Christianity and Christ as well. I'd have to give up watching news. And the radio often has offensive statements too. Even "Christian" radio sometimes has such bad theology that I could be offended if I wished. The daily paper seems to print things that are offensive to Christianity on a daily basis in my town as well. The fact is, we are always going to have to filter the world around us as it comes into our heads. So I take the good scary movie story, and filter out the offensive portions (sometimes by literally fast-forwarding past them!).

In any event, I always have some expectation of at least a little foul and offensive content whenever I see a movie, listen to radio, read a paper, whatever. It's just a part of living in a fallen world. It does not surprise me to hear characters in movies using that language when the world so consistently does the same on a daily basis. But I don't like it. And although I cannot require the world around me to stop using my God's name in vain when they talk to me, I can control whether I hear that in taped presentations like movies. All of this is to say that for me, one aspect of "hallowing" God is to try to limit my exposure to such profanity. I used to allow more of it, one change I'm making is to be less tolerant. That's a sentence you don't hear proclaimed proudly much these days, but at least in regards to foul language in movies that is my intention: Less tolerance for crudity. At least one aspect of hallowing God for me is the respect of his personal name and the removal of movies that seem to blatantly use course language just to offend. It means I see fewer scary movies, but that is ok. And when I pray along the lines of "Hallowed be Your name" lately, I think about this recent real-life change I expect to make. And that's just a little one. We can easily think of more areas where we can add, subtract, or just alter activities that reflect our respect and awe of God. Another might be the addition of more practical, mature prayer. This process cannot occur without maturity taking place. So we find ourselves in a circle: My maturity spurs prayer to hold God more sacred in my life, which makes me think of ways to achieve that end, maturing me, which leads back to prayer again, and so on, and so on.

Let me finish this portion with a comment on the core nature of God and his name which we hold in awe. God says of Himself in Isaiah 46:9: "Remember the former things long past, For I am God, and there is no other; I am God, and there is no one like Me." When we pray that God's name be held in awe or "hallowed," we must remember that our God is like nothing else anywhere. When we consider him in stale, limited ways, we cannot help but fail in our prayers to hold him in awe. We must constantly be considering God in all the magnificence that accompanies his person. And that is a big and life-long enterprise. But if we can do that, recognizing just how unfathomably different God is from us, we will have a lifetime of rewarding prayer that challenges us to open our eyes to his majesty.

So, in this line of the Lord's Prayer, we have seen that we are calling for God to be considered "holy" or set apart in our lives certainly, but also perhaps by everyone else as well. We are both declaring our intentions to hallow him, and also calling for those around us to do the same. To do this, maturity plays a key role. If we do not have a growing awareness of, and appreciation for God, even to pray this line will grow increasingly difficult. Why, after all, even set something apart as unique and valuable if we don't know anything about it? The truth is, we will probably discontinue even praying that God's person be "hallowed" unless we are actively growing in our appreciation of who that person is.

Now, let's quickly look at another passage that adds import to this idea of regarding God as holy and revering him. The passage discusses how Jesus was given his position as High Priest of God. Here is the text:

> [1] For every high priest taken from among men is appointed on behalf of men in things pertaining to God, in order to offer both gifts and sacrifices for sins; [2] he can deal gently with the ignorant and misguided, since he himself also is beset with weakness; [3] and because of it he is obligated to offer *sacrifices* for sins, as for the people, so also for himself. [4] And no one takes the honor to himself, but *receives it* when he is called by God, even as Aaron was. [5] So also Christ did not glorify Himself so as to become a high priest, but he who said to him, "YOU ARE MY SON, TODAY I HAVE BEGOTTEN YOU"; [6] just as he says also in another *passage*, "YOU ARE A PRIEST FOREVER ACCORDING TO THE ORDER OF MELCHIZEDEK."[25]

---

25. Heb 5:1–6.

The author refers to serving as High Priest as an honor, and "no one takes the honor to himself, but receives it when he is called by God." The point is that Jesus exhibited the right attitude, not just toward God Himself, but toward the service rendered him. Jesus didn't "glorify himself" by *taking* the office, but God glorified him by *bestowing* it. This is described as a clear example of Jesus' reverence for God extending even to his appropriation of service. Jesus waited to take his place until God the father gave it to him.

Hebrews 5:7 then goes on to say, "In the days of his flesh, he offered up both prayers and supplications with loud crying and tears to the One able to save him from death, and he was heard because of his piety." This last phrase is important in this discussion of hallowing God. The word translated as "piety" means, "Reverent awe in the presence of God; awe; fear of God."[26] Our English word "piety" means the same thing—that's why we translate the Greek term with it—but the definition of "piety" in English sometimes includes the idea of acting rightly. For example, Dictionary.com says, "Reverence for God or devout fulfillment of religious obligations."[27] As you can see, the first part of this definition is the part that matches the Greek term, but the second part seems to extend it to actions—"fulfillment of religious obligations."

The Greek term is very rare in the Bible, occurring in the New Testament only in Hebrews 5:7 and 12:28. In both places it is speaking about a person's *attitude* as they approach God. Its interest to us is the fact that we are told specifically that Jesus' prayers were heard because of his piety—because he was in awe and reverence of God the father. It does not explicitly state the other side of that coin in Hebrews 5, but surely we can posit the contrasting idea that Jesus would *not have been heard* had he not been reverent of God. He *was* heard *"because of* his piety." The point is clear: Our attitude about God has a direct influence on whether he listens to our prayers. I suggest the somewhat uncomfortable truth that God will not hear our prayers if we don't show this reverence. And we then should ask, "How does one actually *show* reverence of God?" I would point to Jesus' penetrating question in Luke 6:46 as a guide to the answer, "Why do you call Me 'Lord, Lord', and do not *do* what I say?" The most fundamental expression of hallowing God's name is acting according to what he says. Jesus' piety, his reverence for God, was enacted

---

26. BDAG, s.v. "εὐλαβείας."
27. Dictionary.com, s.v. "Piety."

and revealed in his complete obedience to God's will. Jesus even goes so far as to declare, "My food is to do the will of him who sent Me, and to accomplish his work."[28] For Jesus, his daily sustenance was serving God.

When we pray, "Hallowed be your name," to God, our most clear expression of that line will be found in our daily actions. And when we embrace sin, and thereby show lack of reverence for God, he will not listen to our prayers. Jesus was *heard* because he revered God, and his reverence was the catalyst for *doing* God's will.

One more thing we might note of importance from this little verse in Hebrews as well. It says, "In the days of his flesh, he offered up both prayers and supplications with loud crying and tears *to the One able to save him from death*, and *he was heard* [emphasis added] because of his piety."[29] But we must remember, Jesus died—physically. Isn't that interesting? He didn't want to suffer anymore than any of us do, yet going through the process of the crucifixion was important to his life and purpose. Verse eight goes on to say, "Although he was a Son, he learned obedience from the things which he suffered." The suffering was necessary to train even Jesus, the Messiah God-Man, in the craft of obedience. His reverence for God was expressed through the acceptance and embracing of the suffering given him. It's a lesson we do well to examine. Jesus *was heard* when he prayed to God, who was able to save him. And he was heard in a verifiable way—God saved him from death at the resurrection. But he did not save him from the suffering that the process of death inflicted on him. He saved him from the ultimate consequences of that process—continued death and separation from the Lord. Our prayers to God ought to reflect a deep reverence for him, ought to flow from a life consecrated to his work, and ought to embrace the suffering God allows us.

Your Kingdom Come

That night at Bible study Lori again shouted angrily at her husband, "You won't step up and lead!" In truth, she was partially right; he had given

---

28. John 4:32. What is interesting about this statement from John is the fact that Jesus was probably very hungry when He uttered these words. We are told He had been walking back to Galilee and had stopped in Samaria being "weary" from the travel. He was always intent on making the point that doing what God wanted was paramount in His life—even more important than eating when He was probably quite hungry.

29. Heb 5:7.

up. But it was not all his own failing; she was un-leadable. Whenever he asserted a leadership role in their marriage she would buck against it and create a war.

Lori would resist even the most inconsequential things that her husband wanted to take the lead in. And because of this she got what she really wanted: Total control. But she didn't want it, even as she fought tooth and nail to hang on to it—all the while berating her husband with an ongoing drumbeat of "You're not living up to your role! You're not taking the lead!" Eric would just look down as she railed at him. Or he would glance at me, begging with his eyes, "Is there a way to stop this?" I never found one. As far as I could tell neither did he.

Of course there was the other side of the road as well. He would shake his head and point out that she wouldn't follow either. And in response he would let his responsibilities go until she was forced to act for him. It was a dance that hurt both parties with so much kicking going on. The problem was that both wanted to lead.

Have you ever wanted something that you didn't really want? That's a strange situation isn't it? But it seems to be common as well. People say they want something, but then when the time comes to act on their desires, they balk, they turn, they obfuscate—they cloud the issue as much as they can to escape real action. They act like squid slinking away from something in a cloud of ink. The problem is, we sometimes want things that require a lot from us. And then we realize the wanting is great—the acting is intolerable.

The next statement in the Lord's Prayer, "Your Kingdom Come," is another desire on our part. It is like the previous statement in that it expresses a strong wish or command that something take place. We might rephrase it as, "Let your kingdom Come." Why would Jesus want us to pray that? God surely knows when his kingdom is coming and does not need our direction or encouragement to accomplish it.[30] I would hazard the guess that most of us never pray this line in our prayers.

---

30. The Kingdom he is referring to is probably the Eschatological Messianic Kingdom. Remember, Jesus is talking to Jewish disciples who had an expectation that God would one day come and rule their nation (and the world) personally. Jesus is the King who is to sit on David's throne. That is why so many Jews in general were so excited at Jesus' entry into Jerusalem. Many felt He was the promised *Messiah* who would release them from their persecutions and usher in the rule of God and his eschatological kingdom.

So why should such a sentiment be included in our prayers? What is the point of expressing our desire that God's rule come and be manifest among us? The answer is multifaceted, but let me suggest a few reasons why this is such an important sentiment to pray.

First, we must note again what is being desired: *Your* kingdom—*God's* kingdom. In any kingdom, there is a king who rules, and the king is the sole ruler who trucks no interlopers. In the case of God's kingdom, we have to be clear: The king is *not us*; it is God. This line of the prayer expresses our desire for God's rule to be made manifest right now. But this is hard for us, especially at those times when we prefer to be our own kings and queens. Like the wife in the opening story, we sometimes say we want God to lead, but in truth we do not. After all, to express a desire for God's Kingdom to come is to express the desire for us to step off the throne and bow to the real King. Sometimes that is a desire we really don't desire at all.

How do we get to the place in our lives where we are willing and able to relinquish our self-rule? What process can we follow that will pry us off of the throne of our own lives and bend us to the will of the true King of the Universe? This line of prayer is an outward expression that we want that to happen, but how can it be so?

It is an interesting and somewhat circular problem, compounded by the fact that our human experiences are somewhat different in nature. Think of what children are like as they grow into adulthood. As small children they are ruled almost entirely by their parents. They are fed, put to bed, and taken places all when the parents decide. Everything is controlled. As a child ages, they buck against this control. They want more and more to be the decision makers of their lives. And actually, we as parents expect this to happen as well. Finally, they free themselves from parental control entirely and assume mastery of their own destinies. Consequently, in many respects the world around us seems to paint a picture that is opposite of the line, "Your kingdom come." Rather being established in the rule of another, our life experience is that we ought to be growing into self rule.

But it is a different relationship between us and God for we are his children, and we are always under his wing. There will never come a time when we mature to the point of being independent of him with independent rule of our own lives. As usual, the worldly child-parent relationship cannot exactly represent the human-God relationship. Oddly enough, as we mature as Christians, we tend to grasp this truth more and more clearly. Just the other day for example I was talking with a Bible college professor who was in his mid-sixties. He was noting how the more he teaches scripture, the less he feels he knows! He wasn't saying he was growing more stupid, he was saying that his eyes were opening to the depths of truth to be found in God and his Word and his still growing need to come to his father for help.

To pray the line, "Your kingdom come," demands a good degree of Christian maturity. As we mature as humans, we are expected to take control of our lives more fully until we are completely independent. But in our relationship to God, maturity means not just learning to think and feel independently in a Christ-like manner, but also, oddly enough, it means we learn to rely on God's leading more and more. It is a paradox. We ought to learn how to read God and think as he thinks so that we can come maturely to him in prayer and make decisions on our own that please and honor him. Yet at the same time we become more and more subservient to him, waiting to act on his every desire for us.

How do we reconcile such an odd situation? First, we learn to be independent as mentioned above. We learn to stop asking for foolish things in prayer for example. We learn to think as Jesus thinks, act as Jesus acts. But simultaneously, we learn to recognize our personal inability. There are a great many things in life that, regardless of our maturity, we will never be able to accomplish on our own. Moreover, maturity in Christ is actually the true path to the recognition of how dependant we are. The more we mature, the more it should become obvious how much we need to mature. When we have reached that crossover point where we are mature enough to realize that we are wholly dependent on God, we can pray with earnestness, "Your kingdom come." By that time we will have realized (probably by some trial and error) that we are not king. As mature as we are, we will finally realize that it does not matter how long we rule, we will never have what it takes to be king. We come to the place where we recognize that we are not ignorant children who want daddy to always take care of us, we are mature informed believers who see and accept the truth: We cannot do it alone; we are wholly dependent on God. And in the end, even when we give our all, there are times that our all just will not cut it.

We can only reach this point by *doing* what we ought as Christians. We are called to use our gifts and talents fully. We are called to meet our responsibilities fully. We are called to be God's hands in the world. But as we do these things, we should grow more and more accustomed to identifying what we *cannot* do as much as we recognize what we *can* do. When we don't do all we can, when we are lazy and pray that God do things we ought ourselves to do, we are actually interfering with the process of learning what we cannot do. We give in too early, we flake-out on our responsibilities and try to dump it in God's lap. But he won't do our works for us. He won't make our responsible decisions for us. So we think mistakenly that things aren't happening because God doesn't want them to. But sometimes they are not happening because we won't do them, not because God doesn't want them done.

Let me include a side note on this idea of expecting God to handle what we ourselves should do. An extreme and sad example of this occurred not long ago where I live. A couple, following a twisted theology and believing they were being faithful Christians, withheld medical treatment for their child and opted for prayer instead. They were undoubtedly praying for healing for their ill daughter. And God apparently was saying "No, I'm not going to heal her." Their daughter died of pneumonia which could easily have been cured with antibiotics. Now they are being tried for manslaughter in state court. These parents made a fatal error. The questions are, if God heals that way, why didn't he heal their daughter, and if they were taking the lack of healing as a "no" from God, how does that fit with all sorts of other things they do in life? We can't just assume something should not be done at all when God says he won't do it. Would we use such logic when we need a job? Imagine this scenario: I pray to God for a job and don't immediately get one. Then I don't bother to submit resumes and go out on interviews. Why should I after all? God didn't give me a job so he must not want me to have one. Obviously such reasoning makes no sense. We should know God doesn't do *everything* for us. He does some things for us, and leaves us to handle others on our own.

In the case of these parents he said, "No, I'm not going to miraculously heal your daughter." But all they had to do was get off their lazy prayer-butts and buy a few antibiotics for their desperately ill little girl. There is no moral question here at all. God was probably shaking his head at their ridiculous prayer for healing and wondering why they were abandoning their parental responsibility to spend some of their God given money on a few drugs.

When this sort of topic comes up, I think of the story of the Apostle Peter's arrest recorded in Acts 5:18–21. Peter was cooling his heels in jail for preaching the gospel in Jerusalem, and to remedy the situation, God sent an angel to open the jailhouse doors. When he arrived, the angel said to Peter, "Go your way, stand and speak to the people in the temple the whole message of this Life."[31] Peter did all he could do in the situation. He preached, he walked, he followed, he obeyed. He did not ask God to shoulder *his* responsibility—*his* part of the process of God's kingdom coming. God had to do his part—opening the locked iron bars, but Peter did his—getting out there and preaching. The couple in the previous example needed to do their parts; they needed to get some antibiotics. God didn't need to be directly involved in that transaction. We need to look for how we can be a part of the coming of God's kingdom, and then give our all in doing that part. But keep in mind, in all of our doing, we must also remember clearly from this line of the Lord's Prayer—"Your Kingdom Come"—that *we* are *not* the King; God is.

Your Will Be Done on Earth as It Is in Heaven

Tiffany watched her dad intensely; Jeff just sat in his chair, looking back into his two-year-old daughter's pretty blue eyes. For Tiffany, dad was hard to read, and her two year old hand hovered just above the porcelain knick-knack she had intended to grab. Dad had intervened with a soft, but very clear and direct, "No, no."

Jeff and I just watched her. We could see the wheels turning in her head. Two desires tearing at her from opposite directions: Touch the trinket! Pull your hand back! Her hand quivered just perceptibly as the two options battled in her young brain.

Time hung for a few more moments, and then she huffed loudly and ran off down the hall. "Pull your hand back!" had won this time. But the war was just beginning, and one battle did not determine the outcome of the daily war.

Here is the last of three imperatives that express strong desire on the speaker's part: "Let your will be done on earth as it is in heaven." We could restate this as, "May your will be done on earth as your will is done

---

31. Acts 5:19.

in heaven." And of course we must ask, "What does that mean?" This is a very involved statement for only eleven words.

When we think of heaven, what comes to mind? Perhaps it is the cultural pictures of heaven we typically encounter: Fat, little cherub angels with harps, a big white marble throne, and a white-haired old man with lighting around his head. Some might have a more scripture-inspired picture: God in white robes seated on a throne with flaming wheels of fire, living beings circling all around offering praise to God.[32] Regardless of the details, there is a key idea in our visions of God in heaven: It is *his* home. God is to heaven as we envision ourselves to our own homes: He sits as ruler. We've talked some about God's rule and kingdom earlier, but there is a new element here to the idea of God's rule.

Earlier we were taught to pray the two lines of thought: "Our Father who is in heaven" and "Your Kingdom come." The first reminded us that God is not like us; he is "in heaven" and has a completely different perspective than we do. Additionally, we were told to pray for God's kingdom to come. This led us to the truth that *God* is King—not us. Here in this new line, we again are led to the ideas of God as King and his place in heaven, but we are also focusing on what response is given when God requests (demands, decrees) something.

In this clause of the Lord's Prayer, we are expressing our desire that what God says, be heeded here on earth just as it would be if we were standing in front of him in his own house, seated on his own chair. How can we express such a desire? As with the other expressions of desire we've been taught to pray, I don't hear this one expressed very often in people's prayers. I don't get the feeling that we pray this request too often. Part of the problem is that we may not be sure what it is we are requesting (or demanding) when we say, "Let your will be done on earth as it is in heaven, Lord."

We might begin thinking about this by first asking, "How exactly *is* God's will done in heaven?" If we wish it to be followed in the same way on earth, we should look to see how it is done there first. Although it doesn't explicitly say that God was sitting "in heaven" at the creation of the universe, it seems to make sense that he would be. Genesis One gives us quite a picture of how God's desires are met. We find the repetitive statement, "God said 'Let there be. . . .'" and then something instantaneously exists. It seems as though this first picture of God's word is

32. Cf. Rev 4:4; 20:11; Dan 7:9.

one of complete power. He says, "Let there be light," and there is light. He says, "Let there be an expanse," and there's an expanse. Granted, God causes the response in this case. So maybe this doesn't tell us a great deal about how others receive his desires, but at least we see that God's word itself is powerful, and can even call into existence something that didn't exist. Moreover, his will is executed immediately without questions.

Another picture of the happenings in heaven is given in Job chapter 1. Here we find the "sons of God" (angels) coming to present themselves before God (though we are not told why in the story). Satan also joins the angels on this occasion and God initiates a discussion about Job and how righteous he is. Satan says it's natural for Job to be righteous; God has "made a hedge about him and his house and all that he has, on every side," and has "blessed the work of his hands, and his possessions have increased in the land."[33] Satan argues that were God to withdraw that sustaining protection, Job would turn in a New York-minute and curse God to his face.

Now, Satan clearly had a strong desire to wreak havoc in Job's life, but he couldn't do it, apparently, until given leave by God. Amazingly to many of us, God answered Satan saying, "All that he [Job] has is in your power; only do not put forth your hand on him."[34] It seems as though Satan wanted to crush Job like a bug, but God's will was that Satan only touch Job's possessions and relatives at first. And Satan obeyed. God's will in heaven is law, and even the great dragon of old, the deceiver himself, the defiant one who called himself equal to God, was bound to follow it, though it denied him his overwhelming desire to kill Job outright.[35] So, we also might say that God's will is done in heaven to the letter—even Satan could only carry out what God decreed for him.

When we pray this prayer, "Your will be done on earth as it is in heaven," we ought to be thinking along the lines of immediate and complete response to God's directives. Doing God's will on earth should be immediate and complete; there should be no hesitations and refusals on the one hand or attempts to overstep his desires on the other.

---

33. Job 1:10.

34. Job 1:12.

35. It seems to make sense to assume Satan wanted to kill Job. Otherwise, why would God specifically note that he was not allowed to do such a thing? Satan would probably have not only "let slip the dogs of war" on Job's possessions and household, but would have killed him in summary fashion just for the fun of it.

When we pray, "Your will be done on earth as it is in heaven," we might also ask how that would work in terms of participants. We must face a clear fact at this point: You cannot make other people act the way you want them to. Well, at least not in normal, civil society. The truth is, people will do what they choose to do, and we must rely on things like persuasion and reason to change their activities if they offend us. So, when we pray that God's will be done on earth we are praying solely about ourselves for all practical purposes. The only person I can *guarantee* will do God's will when I hear it is myself. I can hope my wife, my friends, my pastor etc. will do what God wants. But when push comes to shove, I cannot absolutely guarantee they will do God's will, nor can I make them do it if they do not wish to. But for ourselves, we believe that we can direct our paths as believers. We believe we can choose to follow God now that the Holy Spirit is empowering our lives. So when we pray that God's will be done on earth just as it is in heaven, we are really making a statement about our commitment to following God. We're saying, "Lord, I want to do here, on earth, what I would do if were I standing before you in heaven." The only participant I can guarantee will act rightly in this transaction is me.

Let's be clear about another thing too. We should not pray this prayer as though we think God is going to *force* us to act in accordance with his will.

Remember my student Bob—the one who seemed miserable? I had noted that one of the reasons I suspected he was miserable was because he had wrong expectations for the Christian life. One of those wrong expectations was what he should expect from other believers and himself. Bob had a worldview that defined Christianity in one particular way: His Way. When I spoke with him, his attitude seemed to be, "*My* way or the highway," so to speak.

I wasn't alone in that assessment. I had other students actually comment to me on the "attitude" that Bob exuded. He just seemed to ooze the feeling of, "I'm doing Christianity correctly—and you're not!" And people sensed it in what he said to them and how he acted around them. In all honesty, you can't really hide such an attitude when you have it. It always comes out in some way. I'm not even sure Bob would classify such an idea as a failing. It was probably a good thing that he was naturally quiet, because when he did speak, it tended to grate on people.

I believe that one of Bob's problems was this next line of the Lord's Prayer. I think he would have preferred to re-write it as, "Your will be done by everyone as I interpret it should be." But Bob missed an important truth: You can't make other people act as you wish. And it will chew you up inside when you live to do so. You can really only make *yourself* act as you feel people should act.

God's will *will* be done on earth in my life *when I do it*, not when he makes me do it. Now, if you have merely scanned your Bible briefly, you can probably name a few items which fall within "God's will" off the top of your head: Love others, forgive people their failings, bear the weaknesses of other people, denounce evil and sin, etc. Perhaps it is here that we find the real reason behind why we don't hear this line prayed too often. It puts us out there on the hot seat. If we pray that God's will be done on earth as obediently as it is in heaven, then we must start with our own obedience. So that's another one of those standing-alone-in-front-of-the-mirror questions you should ask: "Am I really obedient to what I know God wants me to do?" To tell the truth, it's hard to even write this section because I, along with everyone else, can think of areas where I just flat-out have not desired to do what God wants. We should couple with this line of prayer the additional request that God help our weaknesses and embolden our attempts to follow him because it can be a tough slog at times in this world of temptation to follow God's will. But in the end, make no mistakes, when we pray, "Your will be done," we are really declaring that we, ourselves, need to get with the program and follow. We are not praying that everyone else should get to work—we are praying that we might apply *ourselves* to the work.

Give Us This Day Our Daily Bread

I remember sitting and shaking my head as I watched the television that day. Imelda Marcos was the wife of President Ferdinand Marcos of the Philippines. And she apparently loved shoes. The story was about her collection of *twenty–seven hundred* pairs of shoes! I just had no words to describe what I thought of that at the time. I doubt the shoe store I shopped at had that many pairs of shoes in stock! And my closet never would see that many in my entire lifetime.

Of course, since then I've seen the same story rehashed with different people, items, and quantities. One spoiled rich kid purchases thousands of pairs of shoes. Another rich kid spends one -hundred-thousand dollars for a few purses. The basic theme is the same: I want something, and if it costs more than the yearly salary of most Americans, than too bad. I want it.

Finally in the Lord's Prayer we come to a request that has to do with us and what we might want. Do you see where this occurs? It is well *after* our recognition of God. It is in the second half of the example prayer that we are told to ask for something. Do your prayers resemble that structure? Here is a good overall approach to prayer that we can follow: God first and foremost, then us; praise of God, recognition of God, expression of obedience to God; God, God, God—then us.

Interestingly enough, this is not really phrased as a *request* in the original Greek language. It is in the imperative mood, meaning that it could be construed as a demand or order. In fact that is how we render it in our English Bibles, "Give us!" (I added the exclamation point.) Still, it doesn't seem right that in light of all Jesus teaches about God that he would here tell us to boss God around. So we rightly understand the imperative as a strong request rather than an order. But perhaps the form can still tell us something about the request: It is urgent. It is as though we recognize that our daily bread comes from God and no other. And because that is the case, we urgently want him to know that we would like to continue receiving it. We could paraphrase it as, "Lord, *You* give us our daily bread because we need it!"

Now, what exactly is this first request (or desire) we are to make? "Give us this day our daily bread." What are we asking for here? Initially, I want to point out that we are not asking for extravagances. There are a couple of ways to understand the phrase "daily bread" but in either case we cannot understand it to mean some lavish outpouring of unrestrained giving on God's part.

First, "daily bread" can be understood to mean the bread "necessary for existence." This means necessary for existence on an ongoing basis. Give us, O Lord what we need to keep us fed regularly. We might extend the concept a bit and include the general necessities of life perhaps. Jesus says in Matthew 6:31–32, "Do not worry then, saying, 'What will we eat?' or 'What will we drink?' or 'What will we wear for clothing?' For the Gentiles eagerly seek all these things; for your heavenly Father knows that you need all these things."[36] Jesus seems to imply that food, drink, clothes, (etc.?) are all ongoing necessities for us, and that God understands clearly that we need them. So, we don't have to worry about these things or whether God recognizes this need. Coupling that with this request in the Lord's Prayer, we could say that we should pray our desire to have what we need to exist on an ongoing basis.

The second way to view "daily bread" is more literal. It means our required food for that particular day: "Lord, give me what I need for sustenance today." Clearly with these two interpretations there is no picture of God pouring out lavish answers to extravagant requests for sustenance. Here then is another guideline to more productive prayer. We ought to pray with some sense of modesty. I remember when I was a kid and went on family vacations that sometimes we would stop at a drive-in for lunch. Almost invariably my folks would have to say to my brother or me, "your eyes are too big for your stomach." They were noting that we always seemed to want more than we could actually eat. It seems to me that Jesus is addressing this issue with this line of his example prayer. We are being told to formulate our prayers with eyes appropriate to what we actually need.

This flies in the face of a very popular book that came out in Christian circles a few years back. Its premise was that we ought to pray to God in a way similar to an obscure Calebite mentioned in 1 Chronicles named Jabez:

> [9] Jabez was more honorable than his brothers, and his mother named him Jabez saying, "Because I bore *him* with pain." [10] Now Jabez called on the God of Israel, saying, "Oh that You would bless me indeed and enlarge my border, and that Your hand might be with me, and that You would keep *me* from harm that *it* may not pain me!" And God granted him what he requested.[37]

The important points that the little book highlighted from Jabez' prayer were that Jabez asked to have his *border enlarged* and that God *granted* him what he requested. From the request line, and the fact that God did as he was asked, it was posited that if we just pray like Jabez we can have our borders enlarged too. And most of the time "having our borders

---

36. Just as an aside you should note that these two passages are not in conflict about requesting sustenance from God. One says we should *ask* God for what we need; the other says we should *not worry* about it.

37. 1 Chr 4:9–10.

enlarged" meant getting extravagant blessings from God—sometimes the idea that we get anything we desire. All I can say is, "hmmm." Does that make sense? You would think a lot of smart Jewish Rabbis throughout Israel's history would have figured that one out, wouldn't you? Surely there were a few smart and righteous Jews who would have known that little prayer and prayed it over the years if it worked like that. How about Elijah? You know, the Elijah that was hunted by his own people and sentenced with death. It might have helped if he had known Jabez' prayer. He could have asked for his "border to be enlarged" and all the people hunting him to stop it. Maybe he didn't know about that idea yet. After all, Chronicles was written after his time. Or perhaps Jesus should have prayed the ol' "enlarge my borders" prayer. Maybe that would have softened the crucifixion in some way. How about the Apostles? I bet when Peter was hanging on the cross upside down he wished he could have remembered Jabez' prayer. As you can see, I'm a bit skeptical of this notion.

I think we find in Jabez an example of a prayer that we can pray, but it is one of those prayers that is clearly verifiable or not. Either we get "enlarged borders" or we don't. Once we've prayed it, we should probably move on to something a little more realistic and in line with the more common examples we see in scripture. For the most part, God does not "enlarge our borders" just because we ask it of him. Most often he seems to be quite modest in his blessing to us if we are talking about riches and possessions and what not. God certainly did enlarge the Apostle Peter's borders, but it wasn't materially in any sense of the word.

Historically, I can find many good believers (including Apostles, Prophets, Teachers, and the Lord Christ Himself) who apparently could have availed themselves of the prayer of Jabez. Yet it does not look like God answered them with a "yes" the way that book said it would occur. I suggest that Jesus' line, "give us our daily bread," is more in keeping with the typical way God wants us to pray. We should not think about heaping abundance on ourselves in our requests. We should not be focusing on "enlarging our borders." We should focus on requesting that which is regularly of use to us. Prayer of this nature is truly "in God's will."

We might ask, "Why does that make sense? Why might praying for more than I regularly need become a problem?" I would answer that when we pray for what is useful to us right now (what we regularly need), we are thinking in terms of how we can actually serve God.

We are thinking in terms of how we are going to live today or tomorrow and what will make that productive and useful to God. When we pray for excessive wealth, grand position, or anything beyond what we regularly need, we are probably thinking about something else. We may be thinking about the security such abundance might provide to us. We rationalize that having such security would free us to serve God more easily and fully. But in truth we can serve God fully having much or little. Recall the Apostle Paul saying that he had learned to be content in any circumstances.[38] And if we are building our security in life and subsequent service to God on the presence of wealth or abundance, aren't we really making that *thing* the basis for our lives and our lives' work? Sometimes, granted, we do ask for more than we usually need with the intent of using it for good works. Although it is merely experiential in my life, I have found that these prayers are answered with a "yes" more often than those that request abundance with no plan for using it for good works. I'm not laying down a directive here; I'm merely making an observation about what I've seen in my own prayer life. I usually get a huge abundance of something exactly when I need to give much of it away.

An example of this just occurred not long ago in my life. I am happy with the income my wife and I make. I don't think I should be asking God for more money when he clearly has blessed us already with our "daily bread" and more (in my estimation). But an opportunity came up where a friend could use some money to go on a mission's trip overseas. She was raising support for this project and let us know that any help would be appreciated. I desired to help my friend, but we already support missionaries on a regular basis and I was not sure how to come up with as much as I wanted to give to her. The next day I received a call and was asked to teach an extra course which would provide five times as much as I had intended to give to my friend. I had asked God to give me more than my "daily bread" on this occasion because I wanted a particular amount for this missions work. He responded by giving me that amount plus what I would consider extravagant blessings as well.

Now, by saying all this, I don't want to suggest in any way that God *can't* supply us with an abundance far beyond our regular needs. We can find wealthy and blessed people in scripture who clearly had more than their daily requirements. God at times is more than willing to bless us with more than we regularly need. I think especially in the first world

---

38. Phil 4:11.

nations that he does so on a pretty regular basis actually. I'm merely suggesting that when we come to prayer, we ought to have our focus on what is really needed, not on extravagant excess. I'm reminded of the vignette in Matthew 20:20–28 about the brothers James and John. They had their mom go and ask Jesus if they could sit on his right and left in the coming kingdom. Jesus said they didn't really know what they were asking, and then he began to discuss the proper attitude of the believer. We ought not to be seeking greatness or position, or (I would add) lavish possessions. We ought to view ourselves as servants of all. We should not ask at every opportunity for that which we probably don't understand.

When Jesus' brother James describes himself in the opening line of his Epistle, he does not say, "James, Jesus' brother" or, "James, leader of the Jerusalem Church," or some such thing. He says, "James, a servant (slave) of God and of the Lord Jesus Christ."[39] Apparently that is how he wanted to be viewed—as a servant. This is typically how the Apostles viewed themselves. How does this relate to asking for "daily bread" you may ask? Well, If Jesus, the Apostles, and the great leaders of the church saw themselves as slaves of God, then they also probably requested things of God in accordance with the way a slave might request something from his or her master. A servant or slave would not demand great riches and superfluous abundance. They would request the daily necessities, and be grateful to have them.

Yes, sometimes a slave might request more. Jabez did. Nehemiah did at times. Jesus asked for a lot of bread for all those thousands of people at least a couple of times.[40] Yet the huge majority of cases recorded for us are of people receiving a more modest support from God. And let's just say clearly, if Jesus had wanted us to request more than our "daily bread" than you would think he would have said so in this model prayer. He didn't say that we should pray, "Give us a huge abundance beyond all we can imagine." He didn't say, "You should follow Jabez' example and pray for 'enlarged borders.'" God *can* do that. God has done that in the past with many people. God sometimes does do that now. But Jesus doesn't say we should pray for it. He said we should pray for our "daily bread." We should be somewhat modest in our prayers for support.

Now, I might couple this with one more note about abundance. In terms of money anyway, the Apostle Paul is quite clear about abundance

---

39. Jam 1:1.
40. Matt 14–15.

in 2 Corinthians 9: "And God is able to make all grace abound to you, so that always having all sufficiency in everything, you may have abundance for every good deed."[41] Paul's thought is that we receive abundance from God so that we can use it for every good work. It is not solely for our own benefit that we receive more than what we need for daily life. There seems to be an expectation that when we do receive abundance from God, we have a responsibility to do some good with it. I'm not suggesting that we all live in hovels and walk everywhere because we have given away all that we own. I'm merely suggesting that with some portion of our blessings from God that are beyond the level of "daily bread" we ought to engage in good works. From a survey of the giving found in the Old Testament, it looks as though we ought to at least be giving 10 percent to God's interests. I would suggest that that is a starting point for those of us who have full time jobs and what not. Most importantly to this section of the book, in terms of prayer, we should not be asking for far more than what we have been directed to request—our "daily bread."

Forgive Us Our Debts as We Have Forgiven Our Debtors

It is amazing to me where this next line occurs in the Lord's Prayer. Asking for forgiveness is almost at the end of the prayer! I would wager that many of us *begin* our prayers with these sorts of requests. I had a student say that exact thing to me in class not more than a week ago. We must first ask for forgiveness from God before we do anything else in prayer. But here I think our desire to be right with God is actually missing the mark and guiding us away from him. Let me explain.

There is no question that sin is a problem. It hampers our interpersonal relationships and interferes with our fellowship with God. But we need to put sin in the right perspective. If we don't, it can become just as much a replacement for God as anything else. Now don't misunderstand me. I'm not repeating the obvious truth that we can get so wrapped up in a sin that it becomes our god—we all know that can happen. I would even suggest that every time we sin we actually are placing that thing above God.

No, here I'm talking about how we view our sin, not the practice of it. Sometimes we can become so obsessed with the fact that we've sinned that we begin to make our repentance and sorrow over it the main focus

---

41. 2 Cor 9:8.

of our lives. It is true that we ought to have sorrow over our sins. We ought to repent of them before God. But sometimes, maybe oftentimes, we become so focused on repentance, confession, guilt, and determination to stop sinning, that we forget God. This is where the Lord's Prayer is so amazing and helpful.

Jesus knew that he was talking to disciples with sins in their lives. Yet he did not begin his model prayer with the confession of sin. I believe that that was intentional. Even the confession and request for forgiveness of sin can become a replacement for adoration of God. Sin is already the embodiment of disdain for God in its very nature. But how much more heinous is it that it should make us ignore the priority of God even at the moment we are trying to do away with it? It is as though sin is losing a fight when we desire to confess it to God and repent. But in a last ditch effort sin then uses the very act of contrition as another means of drawing our attention away from praise, honor, and adoration of God. Instead of focusing on God, we focus on the evil of our actions and thoughts, and our need for forgiveness. Have you ever reached the point with a sin that the moment your eyes pop open in the morning the first thing that enters your head is that sin and the need to control it? That is just as harmful to us as continuing in the sin. Both ultimately replace God with some other emphasis in our lives.

Jesus wants us to repent, confess our sins, and ask for forgiveness. But even that is not to take priority over recognition of who God is—his hallowedness, his lordship, his grace and power. That is why the request for forgiveness is so far down on the list. Sin in general is of no value to the Christian. Even worse is when we use confession of sin as another reason to ignore our expressions of love for God our father. We need to always keep in mind that even in our desire to be right with God relationally, we cannot put him in second place in our prayers. It is clear that both removal of sin and pursuit of Godliness are vital to the Christian life—there is no doubt about that. But whenever we have two or more items there is also a sense of hierarchy to follow. Adoration of God always should take precedence over confession of sin—there will always be a chance to seek forgiveness after we recognize the great Forgiver.

A second interesting point about this prayer for forgiveness is the assumption of sin in the person's life. As we've said, Jesus just seems to assume people *will* have sin in their lives that needs confessing and forgiveness. This seems to me to be an important point about our prayer lives. We should not put the concern we have over sin before our relationship with God, but we should also not neglect the fact that we are saints who really do have sins. Sometimes we can drift into the belief that we have no sins. As we noted earlier, when we can't identify any "big" sins in our lives like murder or adultery or stealing, we mistakenly think we have *no* sin whatsoever. But Jesus seems to assume in his model prayer that at least one line of our prayers should be dedicated to the confession of our failings and request for forgiveness of them. Here is what we can do. If you have no blatant, obvious sins, don't stop looking. Start doing a little thinking about your attitudes towards people. Ask God to help you see where you might be abrasive, or hard hearted, or un-feeling (or anything else that might hinder your Christian growth). It's great that so many Christians have done so well with putting aside the gross sins, but we mustn't stop there. We should take captive every thought for Jesus as well.[42] We should try to expose every nook and cranny of our lives and root out every odor of sin. When we have this view, we can be sure we are moving toward maturity in Jesus. When we do this we are walking in daily sanctification.[43]

Notice the communal aspect of forgiveness in this line as well—"forgive us *our* debts." What is happening when we pray this way? I'm surely not responsible for my neighbor's sins, am I? I don't believe that Jesus is telling us that. Rather, Jesus is speaking in terms that reflect the same view of the people of God that the Apostle Paul explained in the book of Ephesians. We are a body; we are interrelated. And because this is the case, we should be concerned when others fail as much as we are concerned when we fail. Praying for the forgiveness of other people's sins reveals our understanding of this interrelatedness.

Now, we may ask, "What might it indicate when we pray solely for our own personal forgiveness and never for that of others?" Well, it may indicate that we feel that we are alone in our sin. We may pray, "Lord forgive *me*," as though we don't really understand that *everyone* has sins.

---

42. 2 Cor 10:5.

43. When I say that we should root out our sins, I'm not saying we should expose our sins to everyone and anyone. Calvin warned about the dangers of letting anyone at all hear of your sins (Calvin, *Institutes,* III.IV.12–14). *I* agree with his assessment that primarily we are called to confess to God—not other people. It can be helpful to confess to other people at times, but just as often (perhaps more often) that can turn into a sordid gossip-fest about sin. Sometimes our sins should be our burden to bear until we can hand it off to our Lord who forgives all.

This can be a very destructive thought and I am sure that Satan enjoys using it against us. He convinces us that we are alone in our sin and it is much like when a big cat isolates a sick member of the wildebeest herd. That one individual feels alone, sees no paths of escape, and panics. It often runs headlong into more trouble. We need to wisely understand that we are a body, a group, a people that are one. We are not alone in our sin and even in our private confession to God we do well to remember that truth. There are others who can sympathize and help in our struggles. Moreover, others need forgiveness just as much as we do. Having this attitude undoubtedly helps with the second half of this directive as well, "forgive us our debts *as we forgive our debtors* [emphasis added]." If we fail to realize that others have sins along with us, we may never feel the need to forgive them.

Praying only for our own forgiveness may also indicate a lack of care and compassion for the plight of others. Perhaps we never take any time to think about the struggles others are having in their Christian walks. What kind of interrelationships would that produce? I would imagine we would be quite impatient with one another; we would always be angry that others are not living up to the Christian lifestyle we expect. We know why in our own lives—we have sin. But what about their lives? Well, we should recognize that they too have sin, and they need God's forgiveness as much as we do. When we remember this in prayer, it helps us to think about others more realistically, love them wherever they are in life, and to pray intelligently over them.

I have not yet discussed in detail the actual word that Jesus uses in this line about forgiveness. In the Lucan version of the Lord's Prayer he uses the term "sins."[44] In the version we are examining from Matthew he uses the term "debts."[45] We usually understand the two terms as synonyms in many ways. But the Matthean term seems to add a distinctive flavor to the idea—that of something *owed*. We are asking God to forgive us what we owe him. Often the term is used in reference to wages. A worker is owed something—a wage—when they work. Paul uses the same word in Romans 4:4, "Now to the one who works, his wage is not credited as a favor, but as *what is due* [emphasis added]." Matthew recorded this version of the prayer to capture the idea that we have something that is due God. Moreover, we are asking God to forgive what we owe him. And what do

44. Luke 11:4.
45. Matt 6:12.

we owe God? We owe God our lives; we owe him all the lost moments we have squandered in sin; we owe him our allegiance.

When we pray, we ought to think of our sins this way, and ask God to forgive us the fact that we have withheld from him what is due. We ask him to forgive the fact that we have a standing debt to our names that we cannot pay. Remember the parable Jesus tells about the servant and the huge debt he owes the king in Matthew 18:23–35? The huge, unpayable debt in that parable is very similar to one particular debt we owe to God. Once we have squandered our time on sin there is no going back to reclaim that time—it is out of our grasp. We have taken possession a debt that we cannot pay back in any way short of time travel itself. At that point the only answer is grace and forgiveness. Matthew wants us to see that asking for forgiveness is recognizing that it is physically and literally impossible to make ourselves right before God by our own strength. He wants us to see that even when we walk in integrity, some debt still lingers which we cannot atone for in any way. It can only be forgiven. When we pray this way we realize the debt in which we eternally live, and it is in this realization that we can embrace real gratitude for God's forgiveness.

The first half of the line, "forgive us our debts," is really an expression of our understanding of our position before God as much as a request for God to do something about sin. The second half of the line, "as we also have forgiven our debtors," is the natural, real-world outcome of our recognition of the implications of the first half. In some respects we *must* forgive the unmet obligations of others—their debts. If someone promises me that they will water my lawn while I'm on vacation and they do not, even if the lawn does not die, it has been subjected to harsh treatment. And that can *never* be redeemed. I think of those poor Jews who were subjected to Nazi atrocities in the concentration camps of World War II. Some of those that lived through it may have been able to forgive the debt incurred by their captors. Yet forgiveness does not cover the actual destruction that their lives endured. Part of the debt owed is the healthy life of the prisoner and the time stolen by captivity. These are debts that cannot ever be repaid even if a contrite concentration camp guard were to attempt it with tears. In the same way, we are asking God to forgive us things that we no longer even have access to. And we likewise pray that we too can forgive others knowing full well that portions of their debt owed to us are never going to be paid for the simple reason that the very time of injury is past. We need to pray with this sort of forgiveness in mind. Portions of all debts cannot be settled. Forgiveness is integral to living because it is indivisible from interactions with others.

Lead Us Not into Temptation But Deliver Us from Evil

What does this next line even mean? How often do you hear this prayer being offered: "Don't lead me into temptation God?" How often do you yourself utter this sentiment? I would suggest that many of us have never really even pondered what this request means. The problem here is that this is such a difficult statement to harmonize with what we already know about God. This line presents an idea that is especially incomprehensible without some interpretive unpacking, for on the surface it seems to imply something about God that is clearly not correct: That God *will* at times lead us into temptation.

So let's begin with an underlying assumption that seems to have been established by the time we pray this thought: God does lead us. This is a basic supposition Jesus makes about our relationship to God. He does, in some way, guide us as we go through life. Now, we humans may struggle to identify his directions for many reasons, but most of us would not argue the initial presupposition that God does guide us. Just as a side note, I would argue that often we cannot decipher how God is leading us because of our own input into the situation not because God is unclear. It seems to me that it would make very little sense for God to want to direct our lives and then be so cryptic about it that we would regularly have no ideas about what he wants us to do. Unfortunately, the topic of how God guides us could be a whole book in and of itself, so we cannot explore it here. However, let it suffice to say that God has given us more than enough clear, undeniable directions in scripture to keep us busy for more than a lifetime.

Assuming God does lead us then, why might it be important to ask that he lead us *not* into temptation? It would seem to me that a loving God would certainly *never* lead me into temptation. If he did, it would give the impression that he wanted me to trip and fall in some way. Or at best, that he wants me to struggle with the possibility of tripping and falling. But I know that God is not like that. Such an interpretation would fly in the face of everything scripture says about our loving father, God.

I think we must begin by pondering what exactly Jesus means by "temptation." I think the meaning of the line hinges on our understanding of that particular word. The Greek term is used in two very different ways in scripture. First, it can mean "an attempt to make one do something wrong."[46] We see a clear example of this in the description of Satan's interaction with Jesus in the desert recorded in Luke 4:13, "When the devil had finished every temptation, he left him until an opportune time." Satan was attempting to trip Jesus up and get him to do wrong. This is not the first definition in the standard Greek dictionaries, but it is the one that most people seem to think of when they hear the English word "temptation." Using this definition, we might restate our line from the Lord's Prayer as, "And do not lead us toward anything that would tempt us into doing wrong." Doesn't that sound like a very strange line of prayer? This is not what Jesus meant when he said this to his disciples. In contrast to this we could note James 1:13, "Let no one say when he is tempted, 'I am being tempted by God;' for God cannot be tempted by evil, and he Himself does not tempt anyone." Here we are given the truth that God does not tempt us, and I would think that we could extend this to the idea that he won't *lead us* to the temptations either.

We might also note 1 Corinthians 10:13 in this discussion: "No temptation has overtaken you but such as is common to man; and God is faithful, who will not allow you to be tempted beyond what you are able, but with the temptation will provide the way of escape also, so that you will be able to endure it." Here we are directly promised that God will not allow us to be tempted beyond what we are able. He does not tempt us Himself, and he controls how much he will let temptation come at us. In fact, he will provide ways of escaping temptation so we can stand up under the pressure. This would also seem to indicate that God will not "lead us" toward temptation. Rather than leading us toward temptation he, in contrast, protects us from it, and provides the ways to escape it when it comes. So, I suggest that "temptation" is not the best translation here in the Lord's Prayer.

The other definition of the term translated as "temptation" is, "an attempt to learn the nature or character of something."[47] When the term is used in this sense it is often translated with the English terms "trial" or "test." So, when we read our English Bibles we can sometimes discern

46. BDAG, s.v. "πειρασμός."
47. Ibid.

how the translators understood the term by noting which translation they used, "temptation," or "trial." Of the many English Bibles, the New Jerusalem Bible and the New Revised Standard Version are two that prefer "trial" or "test" to the term "temptation." I would suggest that either "trial" or "test" does fit better here in the Lord's Prayer. We can translate the line as something like, "Do no lead us toward anything that tests us to determine our character."

I believe this is the proper interpretation for a couple of reasons. First, the tenor of the Lord's Prayer up to this point is one that depicts the believer in close relationship to God. That is, it pictures a mature believer, who has a harmonious and knowledgeable relationship with God. Additionally, the brief presentation of the prayer seems to suggest that Jesus assumes the maturity of one who prays the prayer and their ability to infer its deeper intentions and fuller ideas. Moreover, the fact that the prayer focuses mostly on God first seems to depict a believer who rightly understands who they are and who God is. This trait is most developed in a mature believer. At the very least I think we should say that it is a prayer that a novice could pray, but it comes into fullness when a mature believer utters it.[48]

In light of this fact we might ask what would be wrong with a mature believer facing trials. I've argued previously that trials are of use in developing maturity. But in the context of the Lord's Prayer, a request to be spared the process of testing makes sense. Here the mature believer is asking for something that should be a reflection of his or her maturity. Although trials are a very positive way of producing growth in an undeveloped believer, we must understand that it would be even better if we didn't require such a growth process. It would be better if we were already mature and were not in need of the training. Trials are necessary for the immature areas of our lives that need growth, they are not useful just for the sake of trials. Take particular note here of the fact that *trials* are distinct from *suffering*. Jesus Himself suffered but he did not undergo trials in order to ascertain the quality of his faith and trust in God.[49] We,

---

48. Don't misunderstand me here; I'm not saying that only the mature Christian can pray the Lord's Prayer—it is for the immature believer as well. But I am saying that the mature believer does not need to leave off praying it because of his or her maturity; that they will surpass its use at some point. The prayer is ingenious in that it can be prayed even when one is very advanced in their faith, for it is general enough to impel even the most mature believer to think and meditate on even more advanced ideas.

49. The only time Jesus refers to his suffering as "trials" is in Luke 22:28. Even in that

on the other hand, because of our immaturity have need of testing at times to teach us what we are like, what we believe and as a challenge to produce growth.

When a mature believer prays the Lord's Prayer and says, "Lead us not into temptation," could it be they are praying that they be mature enough not to require that testing of their character? It would then be praying that God not lead them to a test that will be difficult because they are undeveloped and will struggle with it.

So here would be another positive approach for our Christian lives in general. We ought to have as our goal the desire to become mature enough that we can ask God to justly and without reservation spare us from tests of our character. How do you get to that place? First and foremost, don't ask to be spared from all trials that *do* come your way. They are obviously there to teach you something and mature you. Also, when you pray, ask God to spare you such trials, but don't stop there, go on to the end of this line, "but deliver us from the evil one."

This second half of the line is a critical rejoinder to the first request. We prefer to be mature enough to escape further testing and trial, but in sharp contrast, we recognize that it will more likely be the case that we have need of more testing and difficulty. Here is where the power of God is most crucial—when we are in the midst of trials. Here is where God must "deliver" us—must rescue us from danger. And here is the conclusion of the line: "But deliver us from evil."[50] We are to ask God to spare us the necessary trials, hopefully because we are asking out of the mature stance of one who does not need them. In sharp contrast to this, we ask that God instead "deliver" us from evil. The term "evil" is probably better understood as referring to Satan, the "evil one." We are actually asking God to rescue us from the evil one himself. It is the other end of the spectrum. On the one hand we desire to be spared the trials our immaturity needs to grow and on the other we desire protection from the adversity a mature believer incites from Satan and his minions.

There is a cosmic realization in this line of the prayer. We often pray without this recognition of the forces that work around us. On the one hand, we desire to be mature and no longer in need of the constant testing God brings our way to shape us. God allows such testing to come

---

verse, he seems to be using the term as a synonym for "suffering" rather than to mean "test" or "temptation."

50. Matt 6:13.

to us just so that we can grow by means of our passing through it. On the other hand, as mature believers we want to be cognizant of the fact that we are targets for evil. And even as mature believers we still are in need of God's rescue and protection from that which would harm us. This line of the Lord's Prayer is a statement of our recognition of the truth that we are trained by God as children, and we are protected by God as adults. If this line is the original finish of the Lord's Prayer it is a fitting end, for here we see a final statement of the truth that began the prayer: God is the central focus of all aspects of our life. Whether we are children or adults, immature or mature, God is the one who trains and God is the one who oversees. God is the *one*, period.

For Yours Is the Kingdom and the Power and the Glory Forever

Let's address this last line of the Lord's Prayer since it is included in so many of our Bibles. As was already noted, it may not have been in the original manuscript of the Gospel, but it clearly fits what Jesus teaches, so even if it was added later, the church recognized it as authentic. And what does it add? I would suggest it rings true and authentic because it expounds the previous line in a more explicit way. It says as clearly as possible what we saw in more veiled terms a moment before: All power and glory and rule certainly are God's forever.

The line begins in the Greek text with a very common conjunction that could be translated in a number of ways. It regularly means nothing more than "and." Yet sometimes it can point to an explanation of what precedes it. This latter is how it is being used in our text. For this reason many English Bibles begin the line with "for" which we might expand to mean "all that we've just said is true because (for)"—"Yours is the kingdom and the power and the glory forever." This line is meant to vigorously bring home the truth that all belongs to God. It is a final statement that should wrap up the attitude which we bring to our prayers, and which should shape the structure of our prayers. All is Gods. And all that we do and ask should further this truth. So, we should shape our prayers broadly under this directive and with these questions:

- Will what I'm requesting further the rule, dominion, recognition, and glory of God?
- Will my requests short-circuit the revealed plan of God?

- Will my desires be in line with God's explicit statements about how I mature and how I come to love him more?
- Do my requests reveal a heart and mind willing to actually *do* the bidding of God?

Guidance from the Lord's Prayer—Summary

I'm sure there are a number of other questions we could use to guide us, but you see the main point. Prayer, in the image of the Lord's Prayer, should start and end with God's holiness, honor, glory, and dominion. And this truth should overshadow even the most serious requests we bring to him. And if we truly believe in the sovereign position of God, we will not ignore him when he answers. We will take what he says, whether by means of scripture, other believers, internal senses, or any other means, and we will honor it. If scripture tells us that he alone saves, we ought to begin with that truth and not demand he heed us on the matter. We ought not to belabor the point with him. If scripture tells us that God cursed the earth and man for his evil, we ought to take that into account when we request that God ignore that curse and heal us. Over all, we need to truly *listen* when he speaks.

Let's put these ideas into a list we can follow for the overall structure of our prayers:

- Start with your heart, mind, and soul entirely focused on God and in recognition of who he is:
    - Remember his relationship to you. *(Father)*
    - Remember his position in the universe. *(Master and King in heaven)*
    - Remember his holy nature. *(To be hallowed in our lives)*
- Then, consciously place yourself in proper relationship to his desires.
- Understand how your prayers relate to the coming of his rule on earth. *(His kingdom and will)*
- Frame your requests in terms of what is really required in your life, not consistently in terms of what you merely desire. *(Our daily needs or sustaining needs of life)*

- Recognize your sin and the expectation that you forgive others for theirs.
- Recognize the place of struggles in your life for the development of maturity, and don't dwell solely on getting out from under them.
- Have an attitude of joy at the prospect of a learning opportunity.
- Open yourself to God's comfort in the process of struggle. *(This can come from the scriptures, other believers, internal insights from the Holy Spirit)*
- Be prepared to see where you are failing in maturity and need to grow through any struggles in which you are entangled.
- Finish again with an entire focus on God and his rule, power and majesty as it shapes your requests.

In all of these macro-steps we always want to explore the ramifications of what we are praying for. You may not get to all of these steps in every prayer. But I would suggest especially the first and last are more critical than all the others. Focusing entirely on God is the avenue to all the others. We never want to shortchange that aspect if possible. Also, think about the ramifications of what you are asking beyond the mere desire for something. Especially ponder how your requests relate to what God may want for other people and to further his stated purposes found in scripture.

PAUL'S PRAYER FOR THE EPHESIANS (EPHESIANS 1:15-19)

The Lord's Prayer gives us an overarching pattern to our prayers that focuses us on God and his sovereignty. It is a great prayer to use in macro-shaping our prayer lives. It is broad enough to give the general outline of prayer but pointed enough to make us ponder and investigate how we (and God) would realistically carry out what we are praying for. Now let's look at another prayer that gives us great insight into the really important micro-structure of our prayers, Paul's first prayer for the Church at Ephesus in Ephesians 1:15-19.

Let me begin the discussion with a question, and when you answer it, don't ruminate. Just stop on the first thing that comes to mind—like you would with one of those ink-blot tests. Here it is: When you gather with others for prayer, what is the most typical type of request you hear put to God? Was the answer some kind of physical healing? Or perhaps it was for the circumstances of their lives to straighten out? I have made a special note of every prayer offered in my hearing for quite awhile, and it seems to me that these are the predominant types of prayer that we offer for one another. We request that God give others some sort of aid for physical problems or that he fix the circumstances of their lives. As you should have gathered by now in this book, in emphasizing these two types of request, I think we've missed the mark.

If you are honest about your investigation, the prayers we often offer aren't very common in the thoughts of those who are our examples in the New Testament. People in scripture aren't overly focused on obtaining healing for everything through prayer. They are not constantly pictured as praying for the fixing of all their problems. Jesus just doesn't command his disciples to pray those types of prayers. And he himself doesn't offer them either. Neither do Peter, Paul, and the other New Testament authors very often. I think the reason is obvious when we look at how the New Testament authors viewed life in general. The external factors of our lives, whether we are sick or well, whether we are poor or rich, whether we lose a job or get a job—all are secondary to the more important aspects of our Christian lives. They were not looking for escapism through faith. They were soberly accepting of the failings and difficulties of their mundane, daily lives. Physical health, riches, daily work all come and go. Consequently, the prayers for others we find in the New Testament are predominantly not about such external things.[51] The Bible and the people we find in it are not predominantly interested in such passing matters. They are, for the most part, concerned with much more important things. Unfortunately, they are interested in things we seldom hear prayed over in our prayer meetings (if we have prayer meetings) and church services.

The Apostle Paul's first prayer for the Ephesians is a great example of what Paul thinks is most important in our prayers. And the reason it is

---

51. Isn't it interesting that the people of the Bible who have very little practical, scientific health care also don't seem to pray for health issues nearly as much as we do in our medically advanced twenty-first-century lives? This probably has more to do with their understanding of what matters most than their concern over health issues. They, like us, undoubtedly were very concerned about them. Jesus spent a great deal of time healing the ill. But beyond the requests found in the gospels we don't see much emphasis on praying for healings.

so informative is that it is not, strictly speaking, a prayer at all. It is actually Paul's description of what sort of prayers he typically offers for the Ephesians. It is useful to us because it is another template of prayer for us to investigate and use as well. Let's lay the foundation of the passage before we delve into it more closely.

The Background Setting

The first thing we need to recognize about the letter to the Ephesians is that it was written from jail. For Paul, the mission God had set before him was more important than all of the daily circumstances of his life, even whether he was in jail or not. Paul's most clear description of how he viewed the circumstances of life is found in another letter written from jail—Philippians. In 4:11-13, Paul writes:

> [11] Not that I speak from want, for I have learned to be content in whatever circumstances I am. [12] I know how to get along with humble means, and I also know how to live in prosperity; in any and every circumstance I have learned the secret of being filled and going hungry, both of having abundance and suffering need. [13] I can do all things through Him who strengthens me.[52]

Paul is not just speaking with dramatic flair when he mentions going hungry or having needs. He was physically beaten with rods, stoned, ship-wrecked, bit by snakes, attacked verbally, and thrown in prison numerous times.[53] Paul walked the walk that he taught. He definitely lived in a manner worthy of his calling as an Apostle of Christ—which got him in trouble with the authorities on numerous occasions. When he wrote to the Ephesians, he was again in a Roman prison (in the capital city of Rome itself). So, when Paul penned the prayers we find in Ephesians, it was not from the ease of a soft pillow in a warm cottage. It was from a prison cell. That alone gives us quite an insight into his view of prayer.

The next thing we should note at the outset is the circumstances of the Church at Ephesus. They too were under difficulties. They had a lot of the internal problems that plague Christians of all ages. They were struggling with sins such as division of the body, lying, anger, im-

---

52. Phil 4:11–13.

53. For a short summary of Paul's many difficulties you should glance at 2 Corinthians 11:23–28. There Paul is in the midst of a defense of his Apostleship as opposed to the false teachers who were troubling the church at Corinth. It is a frightfully impressive list of hardship and suffering for his Lord's wishes.

patience, stealing, laziness, and drunkenness.[54] They were human, and humans struggle with sin. In addition to these typical, human vices they seem to have been under some attack by false teachers who were trying to bend them to unchristian beliefs and activities. Finally, as if that wasn't enough, they lived under the rule of one of the worst emperors of the Roman Empire, Nero (54–68 AD). It was Nero who first organized a governmental persecution of Christians on a large scale a few years after the prison epistles were written around 61–62 AD.

Now, why do I mention Paul's and the Ephesians' problems at the beginning of this discussion? Why is this important? I do so to make clear that there were many concrete, daily circumstances that could have shaped Paul's prayers. He could have spent a lot of time praying that God fix the Ephesians in many ways. He could also have requested that they pray for his release from jail and that he not undergo such difficult persecutions. But the tenor of Paul's prayers is never centered on such things. Paul is interested in deeper, more important issues. And his explanation of his prayers for the Ephesians reveals this interest. It is an interest we would do well to emulate.

The Over-Arching Theme

Beyond this background setting, we should note the main theme of the letter to the Ephesians. Paul's overall concern for the Church at Ephesus is that they live out their daily lives in accordance with their faith in Christ. He follows a somewhat typical pattern in the book of Ephesians which he uses in many of his letters. First, he lays out some theological ideas, and then he states the practical outworking of those ideas. His theology sections are not like modern theology books, but are written to support the practical points he wants to make later in his discussions. So in Ephesians 1–3 Paul discusses a number of theological ideas:[55]

- How much God has blessed us.
- How we have been saved by grace alone.
- How we have been brought together into the Body of Christ.

---

54. I think we can assume these sorts of things were plaguing them by the admonishments Paul issues later in the letter.

55. Let me make clear that these are not theological treatises by Paul. They form our theology, but they are not in the book to explain theology. They are present to bolster the key directive that he wants the Ephesians to hear (found in 4:1).

- How Paul's ministry of sharing the Gospel came about and functions.

Then, in Ephesians 4:1, Paul gives his main request to the Ephesians: "I . . . entreat you to walk in a manner worthy of the calling with which you have been called." This is Paul's main purpose for the book in general—to encourage the Ephesians to live out their lives in a way that reflects and honors their Christian calling. I like to say it this way: We should act like who we are. The Ephesians were Christians, the called of God—they should act worthy of that title. We should add that we too have been called into Christ's family and we should act like it as well.

The Prayer's Foundation—Knowledge

With this short background in mind, let's now return to the beginning of the book. Paul starts with his usual greeting in Ephesians 1:1–2. Then, in 1:3 he begins a blessing of God saying, "Blessed be the God and Father of our Lord Jesus Christ. . . ." Just as a side note, do you notice how similar this is to the example prayer Jesus gave? Jesus taught us to begin with a total focus on God and who he is. Paul begins his opening lines of this letter with a statement of blessing on God. It is as though Paul is thinking of a prayer here as he begins to write, and it shapes his words. But, in this instance, he doesn't actually finish his blessing of God! He gets side-tracked, which is not unusual for Paul. He likes to run down related rabbit trails a lot, so he sometimes doesn't finish his sentences before he breaks off to discuss something else. And that's what happens here 1:3. He begins with "Blessed be the God and Father of our Lord Jesus Christ" but at the mention of Jesus, he leaves off his blessing of God and refocuses his thought on all that God has done for us through Christ. It is as though just the mention of Jesus' name is enough to start him contemplating all that he's received by the sheer grace of God.

So Paul goes on: ". . . the *God and Father* of our Lord Jesus Christ, *who* has *blessed us* with every spiritual blessing in the heavenly places in Christ . . . [emphasis added]." Paul then proceeds in 1:3–14 to list a long series of blessings that God has poured on us, his children:[56]

---

56. If you ever feel bummed out about how life is going or who you are as a person, read Ephesians 1:3–14 slowly. Take in the ramifications of this short little section of scripture. The truths about who we really are in Christ which are laid out in this passage are mind-boggling.

- 1:3b—He blessed us.
- 1:4—He chose us.
- 1:5—He predestined us.
- 1:6—He poured grace on us.
- 1:7—He redeemed us.
- 1:8—He poured grace on us (again!).
- 1:9—He made his will known to us.
- 1:11a—He gave us an inheritance.
- 1:11b—He predestined us (again!).
- 1:13—He sealed us.
- 1:14—He gave us the Holy Spirit as a pledge of our future inheritance of glory.

These blessings are so overwhelming to Paul that he is driven to prayer. These truths that Paul recites also are clear evidence that Paul understands intimately what God has done for believers (including himself). The listing of them exposes Paul's deep *knowledge* of God and God's love for us. This is important, for it is critical to forming effective and worthy prayers in general. Paul started initially with the intent of stating a blessing of God. That is, he wanted to extol the greatness and majesty of God. But he broke off moments after he began in order to recite the many blessings God has, instead, poured on us. Why is that? How did he get sidetracked? I would say that recognition of the blessings God has given us is the foundation of our blessing (or extolling) of God. Paul began by just skipping to the blessing of God, but seems to have realized that he cannot bless God without acknowledging why God is so marvelous in his sight. And we can only recognize the majesty of God through our knowledge of him.

This is of great instruction to us. When we pray, our prayers can become stale and vacant not because there is nothing to pray about, but because we do not *know* him to whom we pray. We have not meditated on and learned to appreciate deeply what God has truly done for us. Paul doesn't seem to have had that problem. He can barely mention his love of God without also noting what specifically God has done for him that warrants that deep love and reverence. Again, as in the Lord's Prayer, it is

God first. In this case we can add that it is God defined by a full knowledge of who he is, or at least as full a knowledge as we have at any given time. It is not just God first. But the real God, understood by knowing him and his actions well.

Even when we bring praise and honor to God, it is not about our praise and honor—it is about the one being praised and honored. And it is about praising and honoring the true God. I would go so far as to say that we cannot really praise, honor and bless God authentically until we really appreciate and know some aspect of what he has done for us and who he is. It may be that we are brand new believers, and have but one aspect to praise, but that one aspect, understood, bears the honest, authentic fruit of praise. And the more we know, the more we can truly enter into praise, honor, and blessing of God, and, as we've seen from our previous discussion, the more we can pray intelligently to him. This is critical to the growth of our relationship with God. The more we know about God, the better we become at truly offering him our honor (and our requests). Knowledge of God is the focal point of Paul's prayers for the Ephesians.

We now are at the beginning of Paul's explanation of his prayers. He goes on in 1:15 saying:

> [15] For this reason I too, having heard of the faith in the Lord Jesus which *exists* among you and your love for all the saints, [16] do not cease giving thanks for you, while making mention *of you* in my prayers; [17] that the God of our Lord Jesus Christ, the Father of glory, *may give to you a spirit of wisdom and of revelation in the knowledge of Him* [emphasis added]. [18] *I pray that* the eyes of your heart may be enlightened, so that you will *know* [emphasis added] what is the hope of His calling, what are the riches of the glory of His inheritance in the saints, [19] and what is the surpassing greatness of His power toward us who believe.[57]

I have highlighted some key words in this passage in order to bring out the main point for which Paul prays: That God grant them knowledge of himself, and in consequence of that knowledge that they fully understand some crucial components of their salvation. We could slim this explanation of Paul's prayers down to just the bare bones and paraphrase it very broadly this way: "I consistently pray for you all that God might

---

57. Eph 1:15–19.

give you understanding of who he is, so that you will know some critical truths about your salvation."

This is Paul's continual prayer for the believers. And we should note that when he says he prays this way "unceasingly," he does not mean he prays repetitively, in an unthinking way for them. We have already seen that repetitive, unexamined prayer is a waste of time (especially when it is being answered with a "no" on a consistent basis). Rather, this description is of a general outline of the important ideas that come up in many assorted ways in his prayers. And notice the focus: It is not physical or emotional distresses. It is not for Aunt Melba's sore toe or brother Fred's arthritis. It is not for Paul's friend Timothy's ailing stomach. It is not for the easing of persecution Paul himself is presently undergoing. It is not for simplicity of life. Perhaps Paul prayed for those things on occasion, but when it came time for Paul to explain his practice of prayer for the Ephesians, in Holy Scripture which is memorialized for all time, he says he prays that they might grow in their *knowledge* of God and his work in them. He prayed that they might understand more and more what they are and what they have received from God in Christ. He prayed that they might advance to the level of knowledge he himself possessed and which spawned the long recital of all God has done for us, which in turn spawned his own blessing of God. Let me say it one more time: He prayed they would grow, by God's help, in their *knowledge* of God.

When was the last time you heard someone pray for that? When was the last time someone prayed in your church service saying, "Lord, give us wisdom and revelation in the knowledge of you so that we can truly know what our salvation consists of and how you've worked in our lives"? I think we take it for granted that we understand our salvation and God fully (or enough). Consequently we have stopped asking for such knowledge. Someone might argue that of course Paul would pray this for the Church at Ephesus; they were a first century church that may not have understood the gospel very well. But I would counter that they had the best teaching available at any time in history. The Apostles Paul and John both ministered in that church.[58] They among all the churches certainly had the true gospel in all its fullness taught to them. And I must say that I seriously doubt that the average parishioner who sits in our present day churches is a theological sophisticate in comparison to the Church at Ephesus. No offense to my fellow church members in

---

58. Though it is true that John ministered later in the century.

all the churches out there in the world. I just don't think we teach the knowledge of God nearly as systematically as the early church did. The truth is, this is a prayer that is critical to every believer at any time in history—ourselves included. And as such, we should not be neglecting it as we seem to be doing.

We nowadays are no spiritual giants who have no need to ask God for knowledge of our salvation. It is a prayer that focuses on the most important aspect of our practical, day to day lives—knowing God and the hope we have in him. Without knowledge of these, our lives are little more than they were when we were un-saved, at least in terms of practical function. For we cannot be different people, worthy of our calling, if we don't know intimately what our calling is or who it is that called us. A full and true knowledge of God is the foundation to real prayer as well. It shapes what we ask for and how we ask for it. It is far more vital than whether we're sick (even dying), well-fed, well housed, or anything else.

We often waste too much of our time praying over inconsequential things that seem so dire and important, and forget the most important things that occupied the minds and prayers of the Apostles and Christ. How well do you know God and his power working in you? If you knew him deeply, how would that alter your prayer requests? How would it alter your entire life? Does it make a difference in your prayer for healing when you know God and his love as intimately as Paul and Jesus did? I would think it matters quite a bit. I would think knowledge of God would be prayer-altering and life-altering at our very core.

Giving Thanks

There is much more to Paul's explanation than this basic thought, so let's now look specifically at Paul's description of his prayers. He begins by saying he "doesn't cease" doing two things: (1) *giving thanks on behalf* of the Ephesians, and (2) *making mention* of them in his prayers. He is continually praying for them, and part of his prayers consists of giving thanks over them while part consists of requesting something from God for them. The one thing Paul is consistently requesting which he identifies for us in 1:17: That God would give them a spirit of wisdom and revelation in the knowledge of God. Before I discuss this main point let's stop for a moment on the idea of giving thanks over others. I believe it is far more important a topic than the one word found in the text might initially indicate.

Why would it be such a beneficial practice to give thanks over other believers? Why would Paul find it so important that he gives thanks for these people *without ceasing*? There are numerous reasons. First, we might ask, what is it that spurs thanks for another person? Thanks flows from knowledge of that other person. So one reason giving thanks is important is because it demands we know others. It is a practice that spurs us to care about other people's lives. This is another circular relationship among facets of our Christian beliefs. The more we know about people, the more we have to give thanks over them. The more we give thanks over them, the more we sense a desire to know them more fully. Knowledge and thanksgiving build on one another. I cannot really thank God for people authentically without having some idea of what it is that makes them thank-worthy. Usually when we say we are thankful for a person we have some specific thing in mind which spurred our thanks for them. In Paul's case he prefaces this statement saying, "For this reason, having heard of your faith in the Lord Jesus and your love for all the saints...." So here, three elements he knows about the Ephesians seem to be the source of his thanksgiving for them.

First, all the blessings which God poured out on them led Paul to give thanks for the Ephesians. This is a very general insight that we all can adopt about other believers. All have blessings from God. The fact that God had so blessed these people at Ephesus (his children) meant that God valued them. And on this basis, Paul valued them as well. In his recital of these blessings from God, he made eminently clear that they are children of God solely by God's grace. (He will go on later in the book to note that they were entirely "dead" prior to God making them alive in Christ.) They had absolutely no worth in and of themselves that would persuade God to make them alive, let alone bless them as he did. In fact, God *predestined* them to be his sons and daughters and *chose* them to be holy and blameless before the foundation of the world—before they were even born.[59] God's love for these people runs deep, from before all time to the end of time. Paul gives thanks over them because God has made them what they are—his children. Paul realizes they had nothing in and of themselves that brought them to their place as Christians and children of God, and he is spurred by this knowledge to thank God for their very existence because he understands what they would be without

---

59. Eph 1:4–5.

God's intervention.[60] Paul is looking with compassion and knowledge on these people, and his knowledge of what God has done in them is critical to his ability to pray to God in this way.

Thanksgiving over our fellows is vital for so many facets of a mature Christian life. Such thanksgiving for others only comes from a clear understanding of how valuable other believers are to God. Our prayers can falter when we don't take the time to really look at the people around us, recognize how much God values them, and realize what they are as children of God (e.g., co-heirs of the world). And we cannot pray for the deeper, more important aspects of their lives without such understanding either. Instead, we drift into superficial prayers about their daily circumstances as though they are the most important things in their lives. We need to remember Jesus' words when he was tempted by the Devil in the desert. Matthew tells us that Jesus had fasted forty days and nights, and that he was hungry. It might seem to be unnecessary to say that last bit—that he was hungry—but Matthew really wants to point out the struggle Jesus was facing. He was *hungry!* Then the tempter came to him and said, "If you are the Son of God, command these stones to become loaves of bread."[61] Food is important; we get that; people cannot live without it. Yet in a time of gnawing hunger Jesus still kept his eye on the prize and responded, "It is written, 'Man shall not live by bread alone, but by every word that proceeds from the mouth of God.'"[62] There are far more important things than the daily circumstances of life—even when the daily circumstances are very difficult to endure. We need to keep that in mind as we pray for our extremely valuable brethren. They have far deeper needs than their broken arms or cancer strewn bodies.

Thanksgiving for the blessings that God pours on others is also helpful to our own self-evaluation. People can forget how much God cares for them sometimes. Perhaps you have been there in that position. But when we rehearse the blessings that God pours on others, it forces us to think about those same blessings in our own lives. (Or about other ones if you wish.) Paul's list of blessings is not a list of things only for a

---

60. He says this as clearly as he can later in chapter 2, "And you, being dead in your trespasses He made alive with Christ—by grace you have been saved" (Eph 2:5). He says it again a little later, "For by grace you have been saved through faith; and this is not your own doing, it is the gift of God...." (2:8).

61. Matt 4:3.

62. Matt 4:4.

specific few in the Body of Christ. When he thinks of all the blessings that God has poured on believers, he thinks of all the body—himself included. And when we pray our thanks to God for his care and blessing of others, oftentimes we too are drawn into thinking about all that God has done for us. Thanksgiving for others turns out to be beneficial to us in many ways, as well as being honoring of God.

The second reason Paul prays ceaselessly over the Ephesians is because he had "heard of their faith in the Lord Jesus."[63] Here is another aspect of Paul's knowledge of others, and another reason he is thankful to God. He could appreciate other people's faith. Sometimes we can become narrow in our understanding of our Christian faith, defining it in ways that strictly reflect our own expression of it, but no one else's. Paul could see the faith that others possessed. What is interesting about this comment is that Paul will go on to encourage the Ephesians to put away what we usually consider to be pretty blatant sins. Yet Paul, apparently, does not judge solely on the present situation of the believer. He seems to see others in terms of the process of maturity. They had faith worth recognizing, yet they needed to continue along the road of sanctification. This is an important distinction. Paul didn't suffer pagans living among his spiritual children. He was not a milk-toast sugar daddy who just let people wallow in their sin. He expected them to change; he expected growing godliness. But these expectations were tempered with the plain fact that change almost always requires time. So he could see the faith, and yet also acknowledge the sin. This is a useful insight when praying for people: They are not perfect. They may be acting in some pretty sinful ways, but that does not eliminate our giving thanks for the faith they do have. Of course, realizing that that faith is a gift from God helps us to be thankful for it.

Now let me say it again so you don't misunderstand me here. I'm not arguing that believers who participate in open sin should be handed a pass in any way. Paul certainly does not do that. The New Testament writers in general seem to equate real, authentic faith with righteous actions. And righteous actions are not so vaguely defined in scripture that we cannot identify them. Yet always there is the understanding that people are on a *road* to glorification. Freedom from sin is not instantaneous and I must admit that I know personally the battle of besetting sin as many others do. Recognition of this fact allows us to pray with

---

63. Eph 1:15.

real love and thanksgiving over our broken, yet growing, fellow believers. And again, as with recognizing God's value of others, when we are able to see other people's faith, though it be clouded by some sin, we are able to appreciate our own faith more fully. For we know most assuredly that we, ourselves, also sin. That is one truth that every Christian ought to admit to themselves—at least when they are alone and being honest. When we acknowledge that faith can be present along with sin, we can thank God for our lives as well, because we are in the same boat as those we are giving thanks over.

Paul's final reason for giving thanks continually for the Ephesians is that he's heard of their "love for all the saints."[64] Again, Paul is looking with compassion on these people. He knows their sins, but he also sees and acknowledges their obedience to Jesus. In this case he is thankful for the love they show to other believers. We might look at these last two items as a connected pair. Thanksgiving over their faith in Jesus is thanksgiving over their spiritual and mental attributes. Thanksgiving over their love for the saints is thanksgiving for their outward implementation of that faith in Jesus. It is as though Paul is seeing them as whole people with both internal and external dimensions. And this view of them is shaping his prayers over them. This is a good practice to adopt. When we pray, especially when we request things of God, we should consider others in both ways. We should ask, "What is good for them internally and externally?" Sometimes this can clear up why our prayers are answered with "no." We are praying for things that might benefit them externally, how they act, but would hinder them internally, how they think and believe. I believe that if we were to prioritize these two, the internal needs far outweigh the external ones. That, at least, seems to be the example set before us by Christ and the Apostles.[65]

So, Paul makes a note of saying that thanksgiving is an important aspect in his ongoing prayer life for others. He can say and do that because he clearly examines his fellow believers and approaches them with an attitude of love. Failings notwithstanding, Paul seems to see these struggling believers as faithful and loving Christians. And his prayers

---

64. Eph 1:15.

65. For example, Jesus roundly chastises a Pharisee on one occasion saying, "You blind Pharisee, first clean the inside of the cup and of the dish, so that the outside of it may become clean also" (Matt 23:26). His point was that outside actions need to be clean, but inside motivations are more important.

undoubtedly are well thought out in light of who they really are and what they really need. This is a good attitude to hold when we petition God for others.

Now, before we go on, let me point out the fullest sense of this idea of knowledge leading to thanksgiving. If right knowledge of the Ephesians led Paul to giving thanks for them, what do you think right knowledge of God leads to? Ultimately our knowledge of God is critical to our ability to thank him authentically and fully. When we don't fully appreciate some aspect of God, we don't give thanks for it. So if you struggle in your prayer life, one very useful practice is to study the Bible more closely. Take time even over the portions you think you understand. Knowing God intimately and what he has done for you should spur you to prayers of thanksgiving (at the very least). If it does not, I would suggest that you are not really growing in functional knowledge. Notice that adjective—functional. The point is that we can have head-knowledge and not really appreciate what we know. Functional knowledge is knowledge that affects us to the point of moving us to action. Paul had functional knowledge of God, and it spurred him to thanksgiving regularly—and to much more.

Consistency in Prayer

The second thing Paul says about his prayer life is that he is giving this thanksgiving to God "while remembering" the Ephesians in his prayers. Paul is consistent about prayer and remembering others. How often have you said, "I'll pray for you," to someone and subsequently never done so? Unfortunately, I'm afraid that we sometimes use the phrase "I'll pray for you" as a signal to stop the discussion on a matter rather than a statement of real intent on our part. What if we put this scenario into human terms? Suppose I said to my coworker, "I'll talk to the boss for you," and then subsequently never did. What would you say about me? At best I'm unreliable; at worst I'm a liar. Paul's approach to prayer for others seems to be more consistent and reliable. And I would point out that he mentions them unceasingly because they are in unceasing need of help from God. Paul is addressing a real need; he's not just doing spiritual busy work. We might ask ourselves here, "How valuable do I think prayer really is?" I like to use the phrase "we vote with our feet." What I mean by this is that we do what we want. When something asks for our time, we often indicate our decision about it by how we act—no speech is necessary. So we should ask, do we think prayer is valuable enough to actually *do it*—consistently?

Another reason that Paul can unceasingly pray for these Christians stems from the type of prayer he offers. Paul does not offer prayers that constantly request something static or finite in nature. He doesn't make requests that can be answered with a "yes" or "no" and then be forgotten. He does not request *stuff*. Thanksgiving, though not a request, is similar in this respect. It is a malleable entity that changes constantly. Thanksgiving for another's faith in Jesus can look one way on one day and another way on another day. Paul's request is the same sort of thing. He asks that God give the Ephesians "a spirit of wisdom and revelation in the knowledge" of God.

This is an ever changing request because they are ever changing people. Each time wisdom and revelation is requested it is not just a repeat of previous requests for the same thing. It is a request for *new* wisdom and revelation fitting the new person the object has become. It is for this reason that James can say to his readers, "If any of you lacks wisdom, let him ask God, who gives to all men generously and without reproaching, and it will be given to him."[66] The phrase "without reproaching" means that God will give wisdom over and over without any implication that we are asking too much or returning too often to get it. We can ask for knowledge and wisdom over and over because these things are not finite or static. It is ever changing with the circumstances of who we are. And God gives knowledge and wisdom to us willingly on an ongoing basis because we need new aspects of it as we change. He does not, apparently, just give us the big "Box o' Wisdom" for our entire lives all at once. We get what we need for the moment, much like he gave manna to the children of Israel as they needed it—on a daily basis. This is, again, similar to Jesus' instruction to pray "for our *daily* bread."

This malleable nature of our requests is a fundamental and important point. Paul focuses on those things that are less concrete, that are malleable in accordance with the person for whom he prayed. Now, I've already argued that one of the problems we have is that we are way too vague in our requests, so it may look as though I've contradicted myself. Here is the distinction I'm trying to make: We ought to pray more specific prayers, but they ought to be in areas that are malleable. So praying for knowledge could take the form of "Lord, give so and so

---

66. James 1:5.

understanding of his position in Christ" or, "Lord, provide so and so with the information she needs to fully appreciate her sin nature." These can be measured and evaluated as to success or failure. This is not to say that those more mundane, specific prayers should never be put forth. But it is to say that Paul doesn't describe his prayer system predominantly in terms of "things."

Wisdom and Revelation

Why does Paul pray that God give the Ephesians a spirit of wisdom and revelation in the knowledge of him? We can't go right to the answer of this question without first dissecting in more detail what Paul is really saying. Let's begin by making sure we understand the exact request Paul makes. Notice the text does not say that Paul prays that God give the Ephesians knowledge of Himself. It says that he prays that God give them *a spirit* of *wisdom and revelation* in the knowledge of Himself. There is a subtle but important distinction. The fact is, they already *know* God. For one proof of this we can note that Paul refers to them earlier as saints (1:1). Paul will make the broad distinction later in the book between two types of people: Those who are lost (the sons of disobedience; 2:2) and those who are saved (2:4–6). And he notes that all the saved were once among the lost. But the key fact for us is that the readers are *saved* in Paul's mind—they know God. They are not in need of the knowledge of God as are the sons of disobedience who serve the "prince of the power of the air."[67] A more important proof is found in Ephesians 1:18, but you need to look at the English translation you are using to really see it.

Because of the way the Apostle Paul writes, we sometimes have a number of choices about how to translate his thoughts. For example, he will often string together a great number of clauses without period breaks, or he will use somewhat vague descriptive participles.[68] To make his sentences more readable, English Bibles often shorten them to more understandable lengths. Ephesians 1:18 is one of those difficult places. In trying to understand what meaning to give the participle Paul is using and in attempting to make the text readable in English, translations have

---

67. Eph 2:2.

68. In point of fact, early manuscripts had no breaks at all in the lines. Editors came along and put in all the commas, periods, semi-colons, etc. later to make the text readable. So every Bible we look at has some bit of interpretation even at the level of the division of sentences.

varied. The two most plausible possibilities are expressed in the New American Standard Bible and the New English Translation. Here is the NASB's translation:

> [15] For this reason I too, having heard of the faith in the Lord Jesus which *exists* among you and your love for all the saints, [16] do not cease giving thanks for you, while making mention *of you* in my prayers; [17] that the God of our Lord Jesus Christ, the Father of glory, may give to you a spirit of wisdom and of revelation in the knowledge of Him. [18] *I pray that* the eyes of your heart may be enlightened, so that you will know what is the hope of His calling, what are the riches of the glory of His inheritance in the saints, [19] and what is the surpassing greatness of His power toward us who believe.[69]

In this translation, 1:18 begins a new sentence. Notice that in this translation the words "I pray that" (1:18) are in italics, meaning that they are not in the Greek text, but the translators have inferred that they should be present. In this translation, Paul is praying for something in addition to praying for "wisdom and revelation in the knowledge" of God. He is also praying that the "eyes of their heart may be enlightened" so that they could know the hope of God's calling. So Paul is really asking for two things: (1) that God give them a spirit of wisdom and revelation; and (2) that the eyes of their heart be enlightened so they can understand the hope of their calling. But the Ephesians are already saints, already believers, already *enlightened*—they don't need the eyes of their heart enlightened unless we understand that term to mean the same thing as receiving wisdom and revelation. And why would Paul repeat himself in such a way? There is no need to do so. In this case, better is the New English Translation of this one particular phrase:

> [17] I pray that the God of our Lord Jesus Christ, the Father of glory, may give you spiritual wisdom and revelation in your growing knowledge of him, [18]—*since the eyes of your heart have been enlightened* [emphasis added]—so that you may know what is the hope of his calling, what is the wealth of his glorious inheritance in the saints, [19] and what is the incomparable greatness of his power toward us who believe, as displayed in the exercise of his immense strength.[70]

---

69. Eph 1:15-19 (NASB).
70. Eph 1:17-19 (New English Translation).

Obviously these editors have made different decisions about where the breaks in the text go and for this reason we see different punctuation marks. Note also that this is a pretty free translation of the text more akin to a paraphrase. But the important point for our discussion is the key phrase in verse eighteen. Here they have understood it correctly as something that has already taken place in the Ephesians' lives. They have already been enlightened to the truth of the Gospel message. As the writer to the Hebrews puts it, they have "tasted of the heavenly gift and been made partakers of the Holy Spirit."[71]

In fact, it is because of this foundation that Paul can then pray that they receive subsequent wisdom and revelation in the knowledge of God. He is asking for enlightenment that builds on the foundation they already possess. They already have had the eyes of their hearts opened—they know God. But they need to know him more fully and more functionally. Hence, Paul's prayer is not that they know God, but that they receive wisdom and revelation in the knowledge of God. I believe this distinction has been lost to many believers. We don't think to pray for our fellow Christian's growth in the knowledge of God because we don't think of our knowledge of God as a foundation and building. We think of it as a one-shot box of recognition. But knowing God, having had the eyes of our hearts opened to him, is the *foundation* of what is supposed to be a grand structure of intimate knowledge. It is the base to an ever growing building of intimate acquaintance. Knowing God is not a complete action accomplished at re-birth.

Now we must ask two more questions: What is *wisdom*? And what is *revelation*? It is important that we understand these two terms correctly and precisely if we are to understand Paul's request. Let's look at wisdom first. The initial point we must understand is that wisdom is not identical to knowledge. Wisdom is defined as "the capacity to understand and function accordingly."[72] Knowledge is the realization of something. We can know about something and not have wisdom concerning it. Wisdom brings along the idea of functionality. Dictionary.com describes wisdom well: "the ability or result of an ability to think and act utilizing knowledge."[73] This is vital to the theme of Paul's letter to the Ephesians in general. He's going to ask them to live in a manner wor-

---

71. Heb 6:4.
72. BDAG, s.v. "σοφία."
73. Dictionary.com, s.v. "Wisdom."

thy of their calling in Christ, and certainly that means being able to make functional use of—to act utilizing—their knowledge of God. To this end, Paul prays that they be given more and more wisdom—functional understanding—from God. In fact, as we shall see in a moment, he is praying for something they cannot produce in and of themselves. He is requesting something only God can supply—wisdom concerning God.

Before we go on to revelation, let me add one more thought about the prayer for wisdom from God. In a stripped down sense, when we pray for wisdom for people, we are really praying for right action for them. Action that is well thought out and that applies functionally what they know about God. A prayer for wisdom is not just a prayer for knowing something or feeling something. It is ultimately a prayer for the other person to *act* in a useful and practically helpful way. Remember, wisdom is "the capacity to understand and function accordingly." I would note that these are especially verifiable prayers because we can observe the decisions other people make.

If I pray that others receive wisdom when they face some decision, I can then determine whether God has granted my request by seeing if they acted wisely in response to what they are facing. If they do not, then I can assume that for some reason, God has said, "No, I'm not going to give it to them."[74] Now we should again highlight James' statement that God gives wisdom "generously and without reproach" when we ask for it. [75] So when God says "no" to my request that wisdom be given to *another* person, it tells me that they, themselves are not asking for it or that they would reject it if offered. I would think that God will not give us more insight, wisdom, and understanding if we do not bother to use what we have already been given. If we ignore God's insights and guidance, he is not likely to heap even more wisdom and insight upon us—and he will undoubtedly continue to withhold it until we change our attitude. When someone exhibits no wisdom then, after I've prayed that they receive it from God, it lets me in on what might be happening in their lives

---

74. Now, some might be saying to themselves that God did not answer my prayer with a "no" at all. Some might say God gave the wisdom, but the person rejected it. My response is this: I would think that God knows in advance whether or not we will reject the wisdom he offers us. And because he does know, he does not have to go through the motion of giving it just to be rejected. I would say that he does not give it in the first place when he knows we will reject it. So, when I see a person acting foolishly, I assume God has not given the wisdom at all.

75. James 1:5.

and relationship to God. This gives me a better idea of what they might really need me to pray over them about—perhaps they really need to learn trust in God; or perhaps they need to rest in their faith; or maybe they need to learn endurance under hardship; maybe they are at a place in their lives where they cannot ask for wisdom due to pride or fear; perhaps they just need comfort rather than wisdom to tackle more difficulties. All of these are avenues of prayer for me to pursue when wisdom has not been received.

The second item Paul requests for the Ephesians is "revelation." This is the full disclosure of something. Paul desires that they have full knowledge and insight into some aspect of God. We know by sheer experience that we do not receive complete, full disclosure of all that God is upon becoming a Christian. We seem to receive insights about God progressively in our lives as we get to know him better. These insights come in various ways: Sometimes as we read the Bible we suddenly experience a "revelation" of some aspect of God that we had not previously noticed; sometimes when we listen to our pastors preach or our friends talk we hear something that reveals a new aspect of God; sometimes when we meditate or pray on we will have an epiphany about God's nature. You have probably experienced at least one of these occurrences. You suddenly seem to jump to a new level of understanding and insight about God. The point is, we receive this fuller disclosure of God in portions not a data dump of complete knowledge of God. Paul is praying that God give the Ephesians insight and previously unrecognized understanding of himself. And again, as with wisdom, this is something that God alone supplies.

Now, the next thing we need to note is that Paul does not merely pray for wisdom and revelation. The text says literally that he prays for "a *spirit* of wisdom and revelation in knowledge of him." We may wonder what "spirit" he is referring to. Some might suggest that he is praying for a state of mind he would like the Ephesians to possess. With this suggestion we might translate the text this way: May God give you a proper state of mind, full of wisdom and revelation concerning God and his character. But the nature of these two items, wisdom and revelation, discounts this idea. Wisdom and revelation, as we've mentioned, are both given to us by God, they are not manufactured within us, by our own hands. Because this is the case, it is better to understand Paul to be praying that the Ephesians would have wisdom and revelation that is *of the*

Holy Spirit. We might paraphrase our text this way: I don't cease giving thanks for you all, remembering you in my prayers, in order that the God of our Lord Jesus Christ, the Father of glory, might give to you the Holy Spirit's wisdom and revelation in knowledge of God.

These people need *heavenly* insight, not what they can muster in their own spirits, and in like fashion we too need heavenly insight. What a prayer this is for our brethren! What a request for our fellows! *May the Holy Spirit give you His own functional understanding of, and deep insight into, God.* That is a prayer request worth emulating if ever there was one.

Although we have been given a bounty in this portion of the prayer, let's add another layer. Paul says he prays for the Holy Spirit's wisdom and revelation "in knowledge of God." Paul wants the Spirit's guidance and insight in the specific area of our "knowledge of God." The Spirit undoubtedly gives us insights into many areas of our lives, but the most fundamental, the most important, is in our knowledge of God, for with a functional and growing knowledge of God we can continue the sanctification process without hindrance forever.

Let's try to define exactly what we are talking about here when we talk about the Holy Spirit's wisdom and revelation in knowledge of God. First, the Holy Spirit's wisdom in relation to knowledge of God is his godly insight into how to functionally apply what we know about God and his nature. If we do not see how to clearly live out, or functionally apply, what we know about God any knowledge we have of him will be of no use to us practically speaking. In such a situation I am reminded of those inappropriate people we occasionally meet who have knowledge of the world around them but no practical idea of how to use it in a beneficial way. Such people speak at the wrong times, ask for improper things, and are generally inept when making positive choices in their lives. It is as though any knowledge they do have never produces something useful for their daily living.

Second, the Holy Spirit's revelation in the area of knowledge of God is the giving to us of his own godly insight into the nature and personality of God. If we do not have this growing knowledge of who God is and what he is like, we again stagnate like a stunted child who has stopped learning. We may know a few things about God: He "is love," or, "God forgives us." But such limited information about God's nature and person leaves us with an incomplete view of who he really is. In this case we again will act inappropriately in his name not because we cannot apply what little we know about him, but rather because we have very little knowledge of him to act on. So in this example we may completely miss the truth that God is also pure justice or wrathful vengeance. Without the Holy Spirit's revelation into God's nature our actions are based on incomplete foundations.

Obviously, the most sought after position is that of knowing God well, and also being able to apply what we know in a useful way. Without these two attributes, our Christianity is stunted. As you can see, Paul is praying for something pretty important on a regular basis here. How often do we pray a prayer such as this? How often do you pray that God would give your friends the Holy Spirit's wisdom and revelation in the knowledge of God? I would suggest that if we are not praying for such insights from God, we may be stunted ourselves, being incapable of seeing such a prayer's priority.

Better Goals in Prayer

Now, we have not fully exhausted all that we can learn from this short description of Paul's prayer life. There is a last portion that is vital to the whole thing. We have seen that part of functional prayer is having a sense of specificity. We ought not to pray vague, un-measurable prayers. (At least we ought not to do so when we are requesting things of God.) And Paul follows that line of thinking in this discussion, when he asks that they receive the Holy Spirit's insights in the knowledge of God with a specific, threefold purpose: "so that you will know (1) what is the hope of his calling; (2) what are the riches of the glory of his inheritance in the saints; and (3) what is the surpassing greatness of his power toward us who believe in accordance with the operative power of the strength of his might...."[76]

Notice this threefold goal is again based on *knowledge*. Paul wants the readers to *know* these three things. The word in the Greek text for "know" is in a form that implies that they know it consistently and continue to do so. Paul wants them to have an active knowledge of these three things in particular. We can investigate these three goals by asking an opposing question to each one.

---

76. I have provided this more literal sounding translation of Eph 1:18–19 to make more clear what Paul is saying.

Knowing the Hope of Our Calling

So, first, what is the Christian like who does not know the "hope of his calling?" I would suggest the hope we have because we are in Christ is a mainstay to living a Christian life on a daily basis. The Apostle Peter says of our hope, "But even if you should suffer for the sake of righteousness, you are blessed. And do not fear their intimidation, and do not be troubled, but sanctify Christ as Lord in your hearts, *always being ready to make a defense to everyone who asks you to give an account for the hope that is in you* [emphasis added], yet with gentleness and reverence."[77] He is telling Christians that even during suffering we need to be aware of, and willing to share with others, the unique hope we have as believers in Jesus.

What a message this is for us today—we *have* a great hope in Christ. What a request to make of God on another's behalf—that they know this great hope fully. I cannot watch the news without hearing daily of another "crisis" we face in the world. In the last couple of years we've seen a good number of people lose half of their life savings or more. We are told we will be killed indiscriminately by things ranging from terrorists to meteors. We see our government grasping more and more of some people's possessions and wealth and redistributing it to others of their own choosing. Our children face a world arraigned against them with a host of insidious pitfalls from the lure of material wealth to the seduction of sexual pleasure. This world needs hope. In that truth we modern believers are not different than the believers in the first century apparently. Paul's prayer was that the Ephesians *know* the hope they have in Christ and what it means to their daily lives. We have need of such prayers today; in fact, the church has always been in need of such prayers, for this world is a hopeless place.

Paul's prayer for the Ephesians is that they know (and actively appreciate) this hope of their calling more and more. Our hope, put succinctly, is for glory with God. Paul says in discussing his apostolic ministry that he was to expound the mystery of Christ being in the Gentiles as well as the Jews; and he further describes this mystery as *"the hope of glory."*[78] There are many aspects to our hope in Christ—a hope of justification, of sanctification, of resurrection, etc. But the end of all of these is a hope of

---

77. 1 Pet 3:14–15.
78. Col 1:25–27.

glory with God. And it will be a glorious thing when we stand perfected with him in eternity. So what happens to the believer who loses track of this truth? What happens when you don't internalize and really *know* this magnificent hope of being one with God? I would answer that our lives become shallow and a mere shadow of what they ought. We live only with the reality of what we are now—partially redeemed believers under the burden of a broken world.[79] At best this is a shadow of who we are to be in Christ. I think many believers are laboring under this worldview because they have not grown in their knowledge of the hope we have in Christ. How often do we pray for that growth in our fellows? Our hope is not just for a happy life or to get through difficulties. Our hope in Christ is so much more. It is a hope of eternal life in the glory of God himself. Do you *know* that? Do you *really know* it? Do you pray that other believers know it?

Now, before moving on let me be very clear about this hope we possess. It is not a *wish* for something that may or may not occur. We are not hoping in the sense that we really desire a future with God, but have no guarantee that it will actually come about. A "hope" of that kind would hardly be something worth pursuing. Our hope is better understood as a confident *expectation* of our future glory with God. We expect it to happen because it is based in God's promises to us.

Paul's phrasing in Ephesians 1:18 again emphasizes the centrality of God in all aspects of our lives. He says he would like the Ephesians to know what the hope of "*his* calling"—i.e., *God's* calling is. He is trying to get the Ephesians to think about the fact that God himself called them, and this calling is the source and means of the hope in which we live. We can even argue that there is no hope at all apart from that found in his call. Later in the book of Ephesians Paul urges the Christian readers to remember what they used to be when they were apart from Jesus, prior to God's calling them to himself. He says they were "at that time without the Christ, alienated from the commonwealth of Israel, and strangers to the covenants of promise, *having no hope and without God in the world* [emphasis added]."[80] Reality around us is not the only witness we have

---

79. Remember Paul's discussion in 1 Corinthians 15 about being saddled at present with a "natural body." We have not yet received our "heavenly" bodies. We have the first fruit of redemption, the Holy Spirit, but await the transformation of our unredeemed bodies at present.

80. Eph 2:12.

to the hopeless nature of the world. God's word witnesses as well to the hopelessness of the world apart from him. God's call to us and the placing of us under Christ's blood has supplied us with a hope we formerly did not have. We may not, at that time, have appreciated our hopeless state to be sure, but it was there all the same. And Paul urgently wants the Ephesians to know this hope they now have more and more each day. It is a hope founded on God's calling of us. Understanding of this hope must begin with the understanding of the truth that God has called us to him, we did not go searching for him. Again, as in the Lord's Prayer, understanding the hope we have in Christ starts first with understanding that God is foremost in the process. He calls, and we have hope in that call.[81]

Knowing God's Inheritance

The second goal Paul desires for the Ephesians is that they know intimately, more and more, "what are the riches of the glory of his inheritance in the saints."[82] "What exactly is that?" you may ask. Paul wants the readers to know the extent of the excellence of God's inheritance, and to fully see the glory of what God has done in forming fellowship with his people. He wants them to appreciate what sort of bond it is between them and God and to grow in their understanding of this connection.

Again we can ask ourselves what our lives would be like without an appreciation of this relationship. It is no small thing that God has taken an inheritance of believers from among fallen mankind. The Genesis story of the fall of man is clear: Every single person fell from that close relationship to God when Adam and Eve fell. People are lost; and along with being lost, we are "dead" according to Paul.[83] Moreover, we are also enslaved to the "prince of the power of the air," to the "spirit that is now working in the sons of disobedience," and the bottom line is that we are "by nature children of wrath."[84] Of course, Paul is not speaking to

---

81. Probably the most devastating passage we can read on how dead we were prior to God calling us is found in Romans 3:9–18. Paul careens through a series of Old Testament quotes to drive home as deeply as possible the truths that no one is righteous and more unfortunately "there is none who seeks for God." Our hope is entirely wrapped up in God's call, for we didn't even want to seek for God prior to his calling us to him. And consequently, we had no hope, and seemingly didn't even care in many ways.

82. Eph 1:18.

83. Eph 2:1–2.

84. Eph 2:2–3.

Christians here, except to say that we "formerly lived" in this situation. The conclusion of the story for the believer is found in Ephesians 2:4–5:

> But God, being rich in mercy, because of his great love with which he loved us, even when we were dead in our transgressions, made us alive together with Christ....

We have this hope and this new life right now! Do you see how magnificent this is? Small wonder Paul prays that the Ephesians grasp, more and more, the incomprehensible nature of this truth! And yes, I see the irony. But it's true: We need to know what is, in the fullest sense, in many ways, *incomprehensible* to us. But still, we *can* know something of this magnificent blessing and with that knowledge we become more like Christ. For this reason, Paul puts it into the list of important requests he prays for others, and for our part, it is a vital practice to emulate. How often do you hear (or offer) this prayer, "Lord, may we have more and more insight into the marvelous nature of our relationship to you"? Imagine what the Christian world would look like if we reflected in ever more obvious ways a deep and confident understanding of "the riches of the glory of his inheritance in the saints." Imagine what your life would look like.

Knowing God's Power

Paul's final desire in his prayer life is that the Ephesians know, "what is the surpassing greatness of his power toward us who believe in accordance with the operative power of the strength of his might...."[85] Paul is saying that he wants us to recognize and really appreciate the tremendous outworking of God's power on our behalf. Our final question might be, what would our lives be like if we did not appreciate how much God did on our behalf? Have you ever done something that required a good deal of effort for someone and received a lukewarm thank-you for it? They didn't really appreciate how much you put forth on their behalf. And even though they thanked you for it, you could see that they really didn't understand what they had received. If it was something that was life impacting, it seems even more galling, doesn't it? I've seen parents buy their children cars for example. A car is a life changing present to a teenager, for with it you acquire a freedom to go and do things that you didn't have previously. But how disappointing it must be when the child

---

85. I have again provided this translation to capture Paul's thought.

takes the gift and nonchalantly tosses a "thanks" over their shoulders as they speed off. They love having the gift in their life because it truly is life changing, but they don't appreciate the $20,000 dollars of work it took from their parents. Of course this analogy breaks down if we think God is somehow weakened by the outworking of his power. It is not as though God is diminished whenever he puts forth effort on our behalf or gives something to us. But you see the point.

Do we see how much God did? Do we understand how magnificent his out-stretched arm is? What is the extent of his power to us? It is the power of *life* itself. As Paul says in the book of Ephesians we were "dead" in our trespasses. But God "made us alive" in Christ. If you've ever been to a funeral with an open casket you get an idea of what this means. On the physical level, death is a very permanent state. When I was a child I accompanied my parents to a funeral for a dear old friend of our family and the service included an open casket for viewing the body. My folks decided that it was ok for me to walk up and view him with everyone else. I recall feeling shaky as I approached that box, knowing that he was laying there. And when I saw him I knew all through my body that he was thoroughly dead, and it was unnatural and wrong. I didn't know why at the time; I was not even a Christian. But I knew the wrongness of death, and I could see its total grip on his body. He was not leaving that box—ever. It is no wonder Paul wants believers to know intimately the greatness of the power God has extended to us who believe. We are no longer dead (spiritually). We are no longer in a spiritual casket, facing imprisonment in a spiritual box. We are free to live eternally. Amazing! Doesn't that change our entire worldview? It must! And Paul says he prays for such insight consistently in the Ephesians' lives.

So let's summarize what we can learn from Paul's stated system of prayer found in Ephesians 1:15-19:

- First and foremost, we should try to distinguish the vital from the mundane in prayer for others.

- Our understanding of who we and others are in relationship to God is critical *(We need to know God fully)*.

- Really knowing someone is helpful to authentic prayer for them. We should spend more time praying for people we know rather than for those we don't. (Though Paul clearly does pray for people he has not met as well.)[86]

- Thanksgiving over people is important for our focus on God and our personal growth as well as theirs.

- Our maturity into a full expression of Christ is more important than some of our daily needs. *(Prayer for wisdom and revelation in knowledge is more important than getting some "thing.")*

- Remember to shape your prayers for others around things they can actually do and know. Even praying for wisdom is tacitly expecting their ability to *act* in accordance with what they know.

- Focus on the relationship between others and God and what they need to fully appreciate and understand God's working on their behalf. *(E.g., that they might know the hope they have fully, or how much God has done for them.)*

DAVID'S PRAYER OF THANKS (2 SAMUEL 7:18-29)

The Background

Let's move on now to one last example prayer. I've taken this one from the Old Testament—Second Samuel 7:18–29. We need to lay a bit of background before we can understand the prayer, so let's take a moment, and do that first.

King David had occupied the throne over all Israel and Judah not long before this prayer is offered. King David remember, sins notwithstanding, is described in the Bible as a "man after his *[God's]* own heart."[87] He was a man who wanted what God wanted even when in the throes of his imperfections. When he had become king, he desired to bring the Ark of the Covenant back to Jerusalem, the royal city. The ark had been captured when Israel was in battle with the Philistines, and when returned, it was put away for twenty years in the house of a man named Abinadab in a town called Kiriath-jearim (aka Baale-judah). When David became

---

86. In Colossians 2:1 Paul talks about how "great a struggle" he has for "all those who have not personally seen my face." I think Paul was concerned over the whole church, but logistically his prayers were more focused on those he knew because he could pray more intelligent and informed prayers over them.

87. 1 Sam 13:14.

king, he wanted to return the ark to its proper place before the Lord at Jerusalem. Unfortunately, he and his men didn't follow proper protocol for moving the ark. They should have carried it on poles so that it would always be stable when moving over rough terrain; instead they loaded it on a cart. During the trip the ark almost fell off and one of the workmen, Uzzah, reached out and grabbed it to keep it from falling. He undoubtedly thought it was the right thing to do, but being ceremonially unclean, he was not permitted to touch the Holy Ark. God "struck him down for his irreverence."[88] That last word in the description of what happened may also indicate that Uzzah really did not understand the importance of the ark or how it should be treated. In any event, he died on the spot. This frightened king David and the prospect of moving the ark seemed impossible for him then. So, he left the ark at a nearby house belonging to a man named Obed-edom. As before, at the house of Abinadab, God blessed Obed-edom's household due to the presence of the ark.[89]

For three months the ark sat at Obed-edom's house and God blessed him and all he owned the entire time. Seeing this continual blessing on Obed-edom's household, King David was spurred to act and he carefully and reverently brought the ark up in the manner it was supposed to be moved. He even added sacrifices to God along the way to really prove how serious his reverence was. The whole city rejoiced and the ark was placed in a tent especially prepared for it by David. Although this seemed good, it was not the solution that David ultimately wanted however. Later, after he had moved into his house and had quelled the resistance of the neighboring states, it bothered David that he had so much good in his life, but the ark of God still sat in a tent rather than a proper temple. David laments in 2 Samuel 7:2, "See now, I dwell in a house of cedar, but the ark of God dwells within tent curtains." We can see his point; the article over which God appears to the priests ought to be in more prestigious surroundings one would think. It is God who uses it, after all. A good believer, like King David, certainly would understand the majesty of God and not want to give the appearance of having better digs than God does.[90] So David's plan was to build a proper temple; God was to have a house of his own.

---

88. 2 Sam 6:7.

89. 2 Sam 6:1–12; 1 Chr 15:13–15.

90. It is not that David thought God actually lived in the tabernacle, but God certainly did appear there when He came to talk to the priests.

David initially got the go-ahead for this plan from the prophet Nathan. He had asked Nathan what he thought about the plan and Nathan, undoubtedly reasoning as the rest of us would, agreed that it was a good idea. He even gave God's endorsement for it saying "Go, do all that is in your mind, for the Lord is with you."[91] However, later that night God spoke to Nathan telling him to reject David's plan for a temple.[92]

God did not have Nathan nonchalantly go and tell David the plan's off however. Instead he had Nathan discuss it in terms of a bigger picture which concerns the future. Let me make one observation about that before we go on.

I don't want to spend much time on this, but it is worth noting that here we have another example of the fact that men (David and Nathan) do not always know the bigger picture. And we ought to accept God's "no" answers when they come because *he does* understand it fully. Notice also that in response to this news that he was not to build the temple, David did not just keep haggling with God about building a smaller temple. Nor did he whine to be given a chance to prove he could build a nice temple. He didn't pout because he was barred from building one, nor did he go out and try to manipulate the circumstances of his life so that he could get the opportunity to build one later. The one thing he did do is recorded in 1 Chronicles 22:1–5—he prepared the raw materials for the work Solomon would be doing later. The text says, "He made

---

91. 1 Chr 17:2.

92. This is an interesting side story concerning Nathan the prophet. He seems to express God's will on the topic from his own reasoning. That is, he doesn't have a direct word from the Lord initially with which to respond to David's plan. So, he answers from his own thinking on the topic, knowing what he does about David, God and the situation. You would think that if Nathan had broken the rules here, he would have been roundly disciplined by God for this breach. But we don't find any chastising of Nathan in the text. God doesn't seem to be angry with Nathan for his initial answer. It was common for prophets to be counselors as well as foretellers and Nathan apparently had acted out of sincere logic and what he thought God would really want. In truth, God seems to let us all do that a good deal of the time. We think and act in accordance with what we believe God would want in any given situation. Ultimately, Nathan was right, for God did have a temple constructed. Perhaps that is why Nathan was not chastised. His intention was good, and his advice normally would have been fine. He just didn't know that God was going to bypass his chosen King and let David's son build the temple instead. So, in this case, God had to directly intervene with an overt "word" to Nathan that night telling him that the plan for David to build a temple was to be rejected. And as a good prophet, Nathan goes right back and tells the king this news. No one in the story seems upset at the change of plans whatsoever, so apparently this process was acceptable.

ample preparations before his death." We are also told in 1 Chronicles 28:11–12 that David even had the plan God had given him drawn up so that his son Solomon would have something to start with. All in all, he facilitated what God had told him he wanted: Solomon was to build the temple, not David. So David submitted to serving that plan.[93]

Having this background of events, we can now look at what God said to David through Nathan the prophet. The whole text is instructive, so I've included it here. I've also divided it into four broad areas and noted those with headings in italics. After each section I will insert some comments.

> [3] Nathan said to the king, "Go, do all that is in your mind, for the LORD is with you." [4] But in the same night the word of the LORD came to Nathan, saying,

(God's Questions)

> [5] "Go and say to My servant David, 'Thus says the LORD, "Are you the one who should build Me a house to dwell in? [6] "For I have not dwelt in a house since the day I brought up the sons of Israel from Egypt, even to this day; but I have been moving about in a tent, even in a tabernacle. [7] "Wherever I have gone with all the sons of Israel, did I speak a word with one of the tribes of Israel, which I commanded to shepherd My people Israel, saying, 'Why have you not built Me a house of cedar?'"[94]

In this first section we find what are sometimes called rhetorical questions. God asks David, "Are you the one who should build Me a house to dwell in?" and, "Wherever I have gone with all the sons of Israel, did I speak a word with one of the tribes of Israel, which I commanded to shepherd My people Israel, saying, 'Why have you not built Me a house of cedar?" I don't think they are really meant to be rhetorical however if we mean that they are for style and emphasis alone and do not expect a reply. I believe when they were being asked of David by Nathan, that Nathan paused and waited for David to think through them and truly answer them. They were legitimate questions that needed answers.

---

93. In David's old age he charged his son Solomon with building the temple. He noted for him that he had collected a vast quantity of supplies to help the work, and he even ordered the leaders of the people to help the work (1 Chr 22:14–19).

94 2 Sam 7:5–7.

Was David really the best choice to build God a house in which to dwell? David's life had been pretty blood-soaked up to this point, and God knew he was headed for even more moral difficulties in the future. Seeing just what he could see of his life so far, David probably could have arrived at the truth that he was not the best man for the job. His heart was right, but his life had (and would have again) some pretty big trenches in it. We're actually told in 1 Chronicles 22:7–8 that God had bluntly told David why he was not being allowed to build the temple, "You have shed much blood and have waged great wars; you shall not build a house to My name, because you have shed so much blood on the earth before Me."[95] All in all, truth be told, David really wasn't the right man for the job.

I want you to notice something else here about this truth. When we look at David, it is not as though he wasn't *capable* of building the temple. He had the money, the resources, the will, the manpower, and even the support of his advisors. He was even given the plan for the temple by God and had amassed a huge amount of the material! There is no reason that he couldn't have physically built the temple for God. The truth was that God didn't *want* him to. It is often the case that we are more than capable of rendering all sorts of varied services to God, but that is not the point. What matters is doing what God actually *wants* us to do. When we don't listen to God's "no" answers we oftentimes will not actually feel the brunt of difficulty. The reason for this is that we are *able,* with all our resources, to do many works in our lives. But the question is not about *can* we do some work, but *should* we do some work. Would God *want* us to do it is the real question. So we ought not to use ease or ability of service as the only determiner of whether we should do something or not.

David could have gone on and built the temple regardless of God's desires because he had all the resources to easily do so. And unless God had inflicted some catastrophe on him to stop the work, as king, he would probably not have been inconvenienced much at all. But that's not the point. The point is that he would have diverted all that effort to something that God *didn't want.* When we don't listen to "no" we divert what we have to things we ought not to pursue. And in consequence, we divert resources from things we should be doing.

---

95. See also 1 Chr 28:1–10 where David talks about the temple and God's directions to him.

Between the two questions is a clear statement of the facts as well: God had always had his worship articles placed in a tent when he was with Israel. Never had he enjoyed the setting of a temple in the history of the nation up to that point in time. It is my belief that Nathan probably stopped after this line as well and let it sink in. Whatever prompted David to build a temple for the Lord, it wasn't a logical assessment of Israel's past interaction with God. There is no historical indication at all that God ever was in need of a temple or ever even wanted one. He functioned perfectly from a tent, and in all truth he didn't even need that. It was only provided so that Israel would have a worship center. But that's an aside. The point is, history wasn't informing this decision on David's part. We might take a note of that. There are plenty of things God directly told Israel to do. Perhaps it is a much better approach to pattern our desires on those clear things rather than planning for things God has never indicated he would want. After all, God can easily suggest things to us if we haven't come up with them. And frankly speaking, I don't think most of us have fully carried out what we already have from God anyway. We don't need another project to tackle. David was described by God as a "man of war" and he undoubtedly needed to correct some habits he developed in that profession.[96] His plate was full with being king as well. He didn't need to extend himself to building a house for God.

So, am I saying that we ought not to suggest new plans to God? No, not at all. I'm saying however, that the best things to suggest to God are those that at most are expressions of what he's already made clear he wants from us. If there is some plan that is way beyond us in every way and seems unnoticed by God thus far in our lives, it may be best to leave that alone until God calls us to it. Yet here we must be open-eyed to God's speech. Again, a circular relationship exists. I pray and talk to God within his interest circle for me, yet by getting to know how he talks with me, I am open to hearing him suggest what might turn out to be wildly different plans for my life. And just as a reminder, he will speak to us through the scriptures, through prayer itself, through friends, the church, strangers, and all sorts of ways. And one last thing we should be aware of, he will speak to us with plans that others' will see as well. God doesn't seem to call lone-rangers too often.

The other question God asks David is, "Wherever I have gone with all the sons of Israel, did I speak a word with one of the tribes of Israel,

---

96. 1 Chr 28:3.

which I commanded to shepherd My people Israel, saying, 'Why have you not built Me a house of cedar'?"[97] This is really the direct, pointed question that voices what the previous statement said. But it's asking David to again think through it. Has he got a concrete example of God ever hinting at the idea that he wanted a temple? David should get the hint clearly: God has never asked for, nor needed a temple. So the idea to build one came wholly from David's head. There was never any actual prompting for it from God. Not even in the daily circumstances of Israel's travels.

This is instructive on a number of levels for our prayers in particular but also for our general Christian lives. We often will attribute our actions and desires to "God's will." It is definitely a good thing to want to walk in God's will, but if we applied the same criteria to our actions and desires as David was being given, I wonder how many of them would be acceptable? I see students all the time at college who profess, "God called me to this school." But I also see those who have made that statement and subsequently dropped out a year later. What does that mean? Did God call them to start a four year program and not finish it? What good would one year of a four year college program be to a person? Maybe God wanted them to see how crummy they are at college? Maybe God was filling time before something better came up? These aren't very satisfying answers. In terms of our discussion we might ask, has God ever in the past called people to start a work and then called them to just drop it, unfinished? That doesn't seem like God's style. In the book of Ezra we see the Israelite's chastened by the prophets Haggai and Zechariah to get back to work on the second temple when the Jews had dropped it out of fear.[98] I think the best I could realistically say about my student dropouts is that they jumped into school without really thinking about what it demands and what it costs. Or perhaps they are just lazy and don't like the difficulties they encounter. Or perhaps they just flit from focus to focus as their hearts desire, declaring along the way that it is "God's will" to do whatever is the latest thing of interest. I wonder how many of us do that as well. God's questions to David seem to indicate that history should inform us somewhat as to what we do and desire; the history of our lives in particular and the history of God's interaction with people in general.

97. 2 Sam 7:7; 1 Chr 17:6.
98. Ezra 5:1–2. Cf. Hag 1:1–11.

(David's Past)

In this next section of God's discussion with David, he focuses on their personal interaction.

> ⁸"Now therefore, thus you *[Nathan]* shall say to My servant David, 'Thus says the LORD of hosts, "I took you from the pasture, from following the sheep, to be ruler over My people Israel. ⁹ I have been with you wherever you have gone and have cut off all your enemies from before you; and I will make you a great name, like the names of the great men who are on the earth."'"[99]

Why would God tell this to David? It must be related to the previous section, but it seems a bit disjointed. First, God makes clear that he never took an interest in a temple for Himself. However, that does not mean that God is silent. In contrast, he has been very direct and involved with David personally in the past. David had no plans for kingship when he was sitting out in the elements tending sheep. At best he was planning his life from the socio-economic position in which he found himself: he was the youngest in the family, and would inherit very little. All in all, his experience was rather limited: He was trained to tend sheep. Realistically planning out his future from that base, his prospects were modest to say the least. But when God needs someone or something, he goes and gets them or it. God reminds David that he didn't come up with the idea of being king on his own, God did; "I took you from the pasture, from following the sheep, to be ruler over My people Israel." It's sort of funny that God even phrases it in a way that sounds as if the sheep were guiding David at that point in his life! He was "following" the sheep rather than "shepherding," "tending," or "guiding" them. God sometimes says some pretty funny things to us if we really listen, and I imagine David smiled when he heard that line and thought back upon his shepherding work. He undoubtedly would have previously described it as he, himself in charge, leading the sheep—not following them.

David came up with the idea to build the temple without any historical indicators that would spawn such an idea. Why didn't he come up with the same thing for being king? The answer is clear. He was being more honest in his views. He was only king because God intervened in his life and made it happen. David needed to get back to his roots on this, and here is a lesson for us as well: Do not try to manufacture things

---

99. 2 Sam 7:8–9.

to do when there is no precedent to do them in your personal history or the history of God's people.

God goes on to say that he has always been watching out for David in his past and would do so in his future as well. This is in sharp contrast to the mere *desire* David has of caring for God by providing him with a temple. David's got to get his facts straight; it is God who really does all the providing.[100] I wonder if God is not saying that it would be enough if we would just do what we are given to do. Rather than desiring more to do for God, even desiring more *great* things to do for God, wouldn't it be nice in God's eyes if we just did what he actually allows to come to us? Rather than praying for the salvation of a million unbelievers you don't know, maybe it would be pleasing to God for you to personally share the gospel with one you actually do know and have some relationship with.

Like David, I think believers of all ages want "projects." We want "organizations" and "institutes" and "benefits" and all sorts of things to do for God. But so many of those things are just the stacking of bureaucracy on top of real actions. And so often those things are tools for *not doing* what we can just *do* on our own if we so desired. Sometimes it seems as though we want a new project to pursue so that we can avoid the real actions that we can perform. David was all excited to build a temple for God. He felt so moved by his love for God and so thankful for all that he had that he wanted to express it by undertaking a big project on God's behalf. Where was that love and thankfulness when he was standing on his balcony ogling his friend's wife and plotting out how he could bed her? Where was it when he had his friend murdered (along with who knows how many others) to hide his actions? We all have sin in our lives, just as David did, so don't get me wrong here—I'm not saying there won't be times of failure. But my point is that we sometimes want great "projects" to show our love for God, when all he really would desire is that we *do* what we already know to do. And that we do it rightly. That can be difficult enough for us.

David had desired to give to God this great temple. God points out that his dreams are nothing compared to the reality which God brought about in his life. God is actually the one who gives great things to us.

---

100. David seems to have gotten this point later in life. When he begins to collect materials for Solomon to use, his prayer makes clear that he understands that all he gives to God's work comes from God in the first place as well. He really is bankrupt on his own (1Chr 29:10–20).

We do well to remember that when we are requesting some project from him or trying to implement one on our own.

(Israel's Prospects)

In this next little section God speaks about the nation he has given David to rule.

> [10] "I will also appoint a place for My people Israel and will plant them, that they may live in their own place and not be disturbed again, nor will the wicked afflict them any more as formerly, [11a] even from the day that I commanded judges to be over My people Israel; and I will give you rest from all your enemies."[101]

In this portion of the text God is pointing out that it is not just David that is under his wing. The whole nation of Israel is God's and receives care from him as a father loves his child. God's great plan is for the future glory and rest of his people in general as well as for David personally. David wants to build a place for God to rest, a temple, but in truth God has plans for giving him and Israel a place of rest. God is driving home the point that he has plans that are set to come true and that he himself will carry out. David is just dreaming at this point of a desire he has to build a temple. And it's a desire not even founded on a realistic view of God's actions in the past. God's words here seem to be making David's desire to build a temple seem rather like a puny offering, don't they? I don't think God is mocking David though; he's just making crystal clear the real situation before him.

(David's Future)

Finally, God speaks to David about his family and their future:

> [11b] The LORD also declares to you that the LORD will make a house for you. [12] "When your days are complete and you lie down with your fathers, I will raise up your descendant after you, who will come forth from you, and I will establish his kingdom. [13] He shall build a house for My name, and I will establish the throne of his kingdom forever. [14] I will be a father to him and he will be a son to Me; when he commits iniquity, I will correct him with the rod of men and the strokes of the sons of men, [15] but My lovingkindness shall not depart from him, as I took it away from Saul, whom I removed from before you. [16] Your house and your

---

101. 2 Sam 7:10–11a.

kingdom shall endure before Me forever; your throne shall be established forever."[17] In accordance with all these words and all this vision, so Nathan spoke to David.[102]

This final section is almost comical in the terminology that God uses. David wanted to build a "house" for God to dwell in, but here in 7:11 God turns the tables and says that he will "make a house" for David. If it were Jesus standing next to David and telling him these things I can imagine a wry smile on his face as he utters these words. Perhaps he would even pat David on the arm with a grin as the irony of the situation oozes around them. David wants to build a house for God. Funny isn't it? David, who would still be following sheep around in a field somewhere had not God reached out and elevated him to the rule of all Israel. David, who is up to his neck in bloodshed. David, who has so misunderstood history that he didn't even notice that God never asked for a temple.

In this last section God says David has it all wrong. God would build a house for *him!* He would not build one for God. Moreover, God would guide that house into an eternal kingship. More than just some temporal temple, the house built by God would endure forever before him. And David's line would be the central pillar in its construction. What does this tell us? One thing is that God's plans certainly are better than ours. David thought that to build a temple for God was all that and a bag o' chips. God's plan is all that and a whole lot more.

This last section brings to my mind the benediction in the book of Ephesians that extols the greatness of God:

> [20] Now to Him who is able to do far more abundantly beyond all that we ask or think, according to the power that works within us, [21] to Him *be* the glory in the church and in Christ Jesus to all generations forever and ever. Amen.[103]

God is able and willing to do far more than we ask or even think. That last word is amazing isn't it? God is able to do more than we can even think of. This seems to be the situation with David. God had consistently done far more than David could think of in his life. But a key here is that God didn't expect David to come up with the wild, abundant, amazing plans of what he should do. God can do that; God is the one who does the amazing. I propose that it is enough if we would just settle

---

102. 2 Sam 7:11b–17.
103. Eph 3:20–21.

for doing what we ought. That would be a good start. And it would probably be enough to keep us quite busy.

Well, this is one of the great promises of the Bible from God to anyone. David had a plan to bless God by building him a temple and instead of being allowed to do so, God turns and declares blessing on Israel, David, and his house instead. It was an amazing turn of events for David and probably an eye opening one as well. He was forced to really think about how God has acted in the past and what his own life was like. And it is on this foundation that he offers his wonderful prayer to God. Let's get into the actual prayer of David now.

David's Prayer

For David, prayer begins with a physical action.[104] Nathan had apparently given God's word to David at David's house, or perhaps at his office—if he had one. David took in the message from God and went to God's tent to "sit before the Lord."[105] In the original Hebrew it is written in a way that seems to emphasize the going of the king to God: "And he went, the king, David, and he sat before the Lord." In truth, that's actually a pretty typical way of describing such an action in Hebrew. But to our western minds it seems to stand out, doesn't it? David was overwhelmed. He needed to put aside the regal position of king and go sit before the true King of kings. It doesn't say how long he sat. My personal belief is that he sat for quite awhile pondering what to say and how to say it. He didn't just blurt out a string of words. I believe this because of where he begins his prayer to God.

David doesn't begin his prayer with thanksgiving or praise, which we would expect under the circumstances. Think if God had just made these magnificent promises to you and your family. Wouldn't "Thank You Lord!" be the default exclamation on your lips? Yet instead David zeroes in on the facts that God had brought up in his words. He focuses on who he is in the world and how he got to where he is. And he frames his thought with a question, "Who am I, O Lord God, and what is my house, that You have brought me this far?" This is a great question! It really is rhetorical, for David has already been told exactly who he is and what

---

104. David's prayer to God is also recorded in the book of 1 Chronicles 17:16–27. There are a few small alterations in the text, as though the author or 1 Chronicles wanted to emphasize particular things that the author of 2 Samuel didn't.

105. 2 Sam 7:18.

his house means to God. But David is saying it for his own benefit. He's trying to express his incredulity at the whole situation. In fact, 7:18–19 really are just David restating what God has already brought to his attention: David and his house were nothing in and of themselves, and God didn't care about that fact at all. So much did it not matter that God even stated what he was going to do in the "distant future" with David's family. It was set in stone. The text even says "And this is the custom of man, O Lord God."[106] The word "custom" is the word "torah" which is used for God's rule or instruction. David is saying that God's plan is the rule of how men live. And specifically God's plan for the house of David and its kingship is the rule of mankind's future. In the opening of David's prayer he expresses to God his new and complete understanding of the relationship between himself and God, and he emphasizes his appreciation of the fact that he really doesn't have anything to offer God from his own resources (i.e., those that he earned on his own).

Verse twenty starts with a question as well, "Again what more can David say to You?" Can you envision David's total bewilderment as he thinks through the implications of the situation? God knows not just the past and present, but the future as well. And he has determined the blessing on David's house already; it is a rule for mankind that will guide all things to come. David's question is totally understandable—what more would *you* say to God if you had been told these things? The last part of verse twenty is almost laughable and I imagine David saying it with a shrug of his shoulders as though he is resigned to the improbability of the whole situation, "For You know Your servant, O Lord God!" David knows himself; God actually knows him so much better, and yet God blesses him. I doubt many of us would want to bless ourselves if we honestly were to assess all of our failings. Most of us would never even want to attempt to do that assessment! If we did, we would probably consign ourselves to punishment rather than blessing. God knows you even better, and yet, just as he chose David, he says he "chose you" before the foundation of the world to be his own.[107] Such things are amazing, aren't they?

David states next what I believe is a vital truth, "For the sake of Your word, and according to Your own heart, You have done all this

---

106. 2 Sam 7:19.
107. Eph 1:3–4.

greatness to let Your servant know."[108] Now, to really appreciate and understand what he's saying, we need to look at the grammar a bit more closely and we need to make some assumptions about the text and about David's topic. Here is a literal rendering of the text, "For the sake of Your word, and according to Your own heart, You did all this greatness; to make known to your servant." The break at the word "greatness" is indicated in the Hebrew text specifically with a little mark called an *atnah*. It is there to divide the verse into two logical units of thought. So we could view the last clause, "to make known to your servant," as a distinct idea. The question then arises, "Make *what* known to Your servant?" The New American Standard Bible translates this clause with, "to let Your servant know." That's fine too, but we still need to ask, let your servant know *what*?

Before we answer that question, let's rephrase the line so we understand exactly what David is saying. He is commenting on all the great things God has done—calling David from the field, putting him into the role of king, blessing his life and his family, and promising a future name for him. All these things, David says, God did for the sake of his word and in accordance with his will or heart. That is, God's great blessings on David were in agreement with what God had committed to in the past and what he wants in the world for the future. They fit perfectly into God's plans. So we could paraphrase the line this way, "You, Lord, did all these great things to make your servant know. And all these great things fit perfectly with what you have said and with what you think."

So, again, our question now is, "God did all these great things to make David know *what*?" In context, it seems as though God's focus has been narrower than the broad flow of history. David, and we, can always do without information about the distant future or even a completely accurate interpretation of the past and present. We can get along just living day to day. But critical to living each day of our lives properly is the understanding of how much God loves us and what our relationship to him is. God has driven home that truth in his words to David, and David is expressing that he gets it. He understands how God has acted to show *his love* for him; "God did all these great things to make David know how much God loves him regardless of his personal attractiveness." Not only this, God has done it in accordance with his own word and counsel.

---

108. 2 Sam 7:21.

God has acted as he saw fit to act and it was for blessing on David, who, frankly speaking, had nothing to offer in return.

David builds on this truth saying, "For this reason You are great, O Lord God; for there is none like You, and there is no God besides You, according to all that we have heard with our ears."[109] David finally arrives in his prayer at the place Jesus where says we should start ours: Praise and honor of God. But in David's defense, he was not snubbing praise and honor of God when he began his prayer. He was just offering it in the dress of complete bewilderment at the situation. I still think Jesus' approach is the best, but David's is understandable in light of the circumstances. And now, after rehashing the truths about God's blessing he finally says outright what can be the only response: God is GREAT! God is UNIQUE! Nothing compares to our GOD! Nothing.

Actually, I think in this situation, David needed to go through the first few portions of his prayer to get to that place. He was reasoning out why God was so great and then expressing it. If you need to, this is a good practice for us to adopt as well. Sit before God. Think about what he's told you. Recognize your place before him and in his scheme of things. Then offer informed and thankful praises. These are far more acceptable to God than ignorant, rote "thanks God" offerings to get our praise out of the way because we haven't taken the time to even think of something specific that God has done (or been) to deserve our praises.[110]

David goes on to express how great Israel is, but the entire portion is centered on God and his work and how he produces her greatness. Here I've highlighted the text a bit to bring this out:

> [23] "And what one nation on the earth is like *Your* people Israel, whom *God* went to redeem for *Himself* as a people and to make a name for *Himself*, and to do a great thing for *You* and awesome things for *Your* land, before *Your* people whom *You* have redeemed for *Yourself* from Egypt, *from* nations and their gods?

---

109. 2 Sam 7:22. This is so true when we think of the gods of the peoples around Israel. They are cruel and selfish gods who give their care only when there is something in it for them. The God of Israel is the unique God who sacrifices himself for his people and serves them for their benefit.

110. Let me be clear here. I'm not saying we withhold our praises until God proves himself. I'm saying we are often too dense and ignorant of His loving care to offer authentic praises. That is a failing in us, not God. But when we do take time to think about God's actions, care, and being, praise springs from us because we understand how much God truly deserves our praise.

> [^24] For You have established for *Yourself Your* people Israel as *Your* own people forever, and *You*, O LORD, have become their God" [emphasis added].[111]

You really can't miss the point here, can you? David has swung full circle from "I want to build God a temple," to "You, God, have pretty much done *everything* for me and the whole nation!" It's an important change in tone for David, and it shapes his prayer of request to follow.

David's request is really just that, *one* request. But he repeats it four times with different facets of interest. Just in case you were concerned, this is not an example of someone just praying the same prayer over and over. He is distinguishing different aspects of his request and what they mean, this might be another example for us. Sometimes certain things just stick in our heads. When we pray for them repetitively, with the same prayer over and over, I've already noted that we run into problems. But when we tear these things down and pray over specific elements of them and explore those parts individually, we can sometimes come to terms with our requests in a more full and satisfying way. And we can pray them to God in a more acceptable way as well. That's what David does here. Here is the remaining text of his prayer:

> [^25] "Now therefore, O LORD God, the word that You have spoken concerning Your servant and his house, confirm *it* forever, and do as You have spoken, [^26] that Your name may be magnified forever, by saying, 'The LORD of hosts is God over Israel'; and may the house of Your servant David be established before You. [^27] For You, O LORD of hosts, the God of Israel, have made a revelation to Your servant, saying, 'I will build you a house'; therefore Your servant has found courage to pray this prayer to You. [^28] Now, O Lord GOD, You are God, and Your words are truth, and You have promised this good thing to Your servant. [^29] Now therefore, may it please You to bless the house of Your servant, that it may continue forever before You. For You, O Lord GOD, have spoken; and with Your blessing may the house of Your servant be blessed forever."[112]

His request can be paraphrased as, "Lord, do what you said you'd do." We find this request in four places:

- "The word that You have spoken ... confirm it forever."

---

111. 2 Sam 7:23–24.
112. 2 Sam 7:25–29.

- "Do as You have spoken."
- "May the house of your servant ... be established."
- "Bless the house of your servant."[113]

Each of these is a subtle alteration of the main idea of God doing just what he said he would do. It is interesting that David started with the request, "Lord, I would like to build a house for you," but now he ends with the more authentic request, "Lord, do what you have already said." He has understood that God's plans for him far out-shadow his own plans for himself (and his own plans for God). The highest request he could think of in the end was that God just *be* who he is, and *act* as he says he will.

This actually makes complete sense if we honestly believe what the scriptures tell us about God. If God knows us perfectly and does everything for our redemptive good, and nothing is out of his purview, and all is the best for us as it would be for any child of a loving and powerful heavenly father, then of course his will is the highest and best desire we can have. Our prayers should elevate us to the greatness that is in God, they should not lesson his intentions and actions for us because we are incapable of envisioning more than that for which we ask. Why would God want to give us less than the best? David had finally gotten to that understanding. God's blessings and desires *really are the best* for his life—so he settles himself on just praying for what God desires.

You might ask, "Why pray at all then?" Why should I ask for what God already declares for me? That seems redundant. Well, for one thing the process of knowing what God declares is ongoing. This prayer of David seems to be the most pure in that it is based on a complete understanding of God's intentions for David's rule. But not all portions of our lives are so clearly marked out. We need at times to work up to this point of understanding. That is probably why Paul does pray so often for wisdom and knowledge. He knows that we are not fully informed about God and our lives. Our goal is to be at the place David had reached on this one topic in the whole of our lives. We ought to be in complete

---

113. Notice that David uses what I have previously called a bit of "Christianese" when he says "bless the house of your servant." But he is not really using Christianese as I have defined it above, for he qualifies exactly what his concept of "blessing" is: it is the continuance of his house. He is actually envisioning a specific thing that is encapsulated in the broad description of a "blessing" from God.

accord with what God has said and desires for us and the world. We shouldn't have a need to suggest more to him.

Another good example for us at this juncture is Jesus himself. He said on more than one occasion that he and God the father were in complete harmony about what was to be done, how to do it, and what the outcomes would be.[114] But just because Jesus was in complete harmony with God didn't mean that he stopped praying, or that he viewed his prayer as redundant. Knowing what exactly God wants, and praying for it is not a bad thing. I suggest it is a reflection of that unity for which Jesus asked when he said he wanted us to be one with father even as he was one with the father.[115] I don't think Jesus was presenting new options to God all the time (such as David offering to build a temple). That's not because Jesus was ungrateful to the father, or uncaring about the honor due to God. It was because he was in perfect unity with the father, and that meant following his lead at all times.

Jesus says plainly in John 10:30, "I and the Father are one." We must believe that his prayers reflected that truth as well. So what does that mean for his prayer life? I would think it means at minimum that he was not constantly suggesting things to God that God would not go along with. But if God went along with everything Jesus prayed for, then in point of fact, Jesus was just praying for what God already wanted. Jesus was merely saying it audibly in prayer (because he was human as well). The point is, he was not bringing up anything that God didn't already want. That's our goal—to pray in such a way that we mesh perfectly with what God already wants. And the reason is because this benefits *us*. Since God knows what is the very best thing for us, praying for what he wants and knows is asking for the very best thing for us as well.

I've heard Christians dismiss this idea because we would just be praying for what God already is going to do or what he already wants. I would counter that that is exactly where we want to arrive because it would reveal that we are in complete harmony with our perfect God, and also that we want what is best for our lives as well. It would indicate that we really were "one" with the Godhead even as the Godhead is "one" among themselves. I seriously doubt that one member of the Godhead would bring a thought to the others that they didn't already

---

114. Cf. e.g., John 4:34; 5:19; 8:28; 10:37–38.
115. John 17:11.

resonate with. That should be our goal as well. To pray prayers God can resonate with.

An interesting picture of this is seen in the raising of Lazarus found in John 11:38–44. Jesus says a prayer before he calls Lazarus forth from the tomb, but it is not just a prayer such as, "God help me raise this guy." Here's what he says:

> Then Jesus raised His eyes, and said, "Father, I thank You that You have heard Me. [42] I knew that You always hear Me; but because of the people standing around I said it, so that they may believe that You sent Me."[116]

This isn't really even a request, is it? Jesus just says "thanks" to God for his continual support. And he then adds that he only said it out loud so that those around him would see that he and the father were on the exact same page, and that the father had indeed sent Jesus as his Messiah. This incredible miracle is not presented to us as an outworking of the second person of the trinity. It is presented as a man, Jesus, who is in complete harmony with the father and therefore hardly needs to even ask something of him. In fact, the asking (if he did ask) is not even recorded for us. More important to John the author is the fact that Jesus was so in tune with the father that he could say, "You always hear Me." Rather than being viewed as redundant and boring prayer, that should be a *goal* of our prayers. That we can say God always hears our prayers because they are so aligned with what he wants in the first place.

Let's get back to David's request to God. He was fundamentally doing the exact same thing Jesus did at the raising of Lazarus. He called to God to do what he said he would do. He says, "The word that You have spoken . . . *confirm* it forever," "*do* as You have spoken," "may the house of Your servant . . . be *established*," "*bless* the house of Your servant." These last two are merely restatements of what God had already said he was going to do, so they don't really qualify as requests for something different at all.

If we are going to say that prayer that just centers around what God already wants is redundant and of no use, than I suggest David's wasting his time. But in fact, David's prayer is the height of perfection in terms of a mature believer in God. He realizes that there is no better thing to ask than that which God has already declared for him.

---

116. John 11:41–42.

Now you might be thinking, "Yeah, but David had his promises for future blessing explicitly stated to him. We don't." But I would say that's just not true. Look at God's promises to David. They are rather general promises. There are no detailed accounts of how this all will come about. Isn't that exactly the same situation in which we find ourselves as well? God gives us a lot of general promises about our future as his children:

- We will inherit the earth (Matt 5:5).
- We shall be made like Jesus (1 John 3:2).
- We will share in the resurrection (Rom 6:5).
- We will stand as rulers of heavenly beings (1 Cor 6:3).

These are just a few, but as you scan through scripture sometime, make a note of all the future blessings promised to you. Additionally, take a moment and think about all the direct commands God has already given you concerning the conduct of your life. I have just this moment randomly flopped my Bible open and my eyes alit on this passage from 1 Peter:

> [13] Therefore, prepare your minds for action, keep sober *in spirit*, fix your hope completely on the grace to be brought to you at the revelation of Jesus Christ. [14] As obedient children, do not be conformed to the former lusts *which were yours* in your ignorance, [15] but like the Holy One who called you, be holy yourselves also in all *your* behavior; [16] because it is written, "YOU SHALL BE HOLY, FOR I AM HOLY."[117]

My point is that there are enough directives for our conduct and actions in scripture that we hardly need to suggest to God more things to do. The first in this little passage is "gird your minds for action." That alone seems like a life consuming project in many ways. It would seem to easily entail concrete activities for our lives such as, reading your Bible, meditating, praying, interacting with other believers, studying—all with the goal of "girding" our minds. The term "girding" is often used to refer to a person binding up their robes to prepare them to walk or do some work. Peter is picturing us preparing our heads for serious Christian activity. Depending on how seriously and deeply you wish to take this, that one command could become a consuming endeavor. And I've not really

---

117. 1 Pet 1:13–16.

even investigated what specific actions the whole context of the passage might entail.

All this is to say, our prayers need not be filled with requests for more projects from God when we have so many obvious tasks right in front of us. David had no evidence from past interaction with God to support his initial desire to build a temple. He had enough to work on already. In like fashion, we don't need to constantly be praying for more action from God. We need to get in line with what God has already declared for us. And if something that seems outside the ordinary is required, we need to trust that God will bring that to our attention in a verifiable way. Just as David had his shepherd's world rocked by being told he would be king one day. God can easily break into our lives with the amazing at any time. He probably would appreciate us pursuing the ordinary a little more diligently.

6

Suggestions for Prayer Summary

One of the most difficult decisions for a writer to make is determining the moment to stop writing. Most authors would probably want their books to be ten times longer than they are because they can see how much more might be said about any topic they're discussing. I am no different. I know that you have not had all your questions answered or all your objections satisfied. If you have found yourself agreeing with me, you probably have not had enough investigation either. No one is completely satisfied at the end of a book, but we are at the end nevertheless.

The first thing I want to remind you of is that God *does* say "no." And it's not that hard to hear if we just admit that it happens and expect it to happen in the same way we expect anyone would say, "no." It is easily seen in all the prayer requests we make that seem to be ignored. Do you pray to be healed and aren't? That's a "no." Do you pray a friend will accept Jesus and they don't? That's a "no." Do you desire a new job and don't get it? That's a "no." Do you pray that God would give you a bigger house and never have the money? That's a "no." "No" is "no" and it's not that hard to recognize. Even children grasp this concept at a very early age.

More important for us is to think about all the opportunities for growth that arise when God answers "no." You pray your friend will be saved, and God says "no." So now what? Well, now you can open your mind to other prayers for your friend and yourself. "Lord, give me opportunity to share the gospel clearly." "Lord, may I see quickly and accurately where my friend needs some help from me." "Lord, help me learn to trust you to do what needs doing in my friend's life." And on and on. Use "no" as a means of growth.

Let me finish on the positive side by summarizing a few of the most important suggestions I've presented for improved and authentic prayer.

1. Start with God as your focus. I cannot emphasize this enough. Your needs are important. Your friend's needs are important. The world's needs are important. But no needs are as important as God himself. In this book I have not really investigated the philosophic reasons why this is true—that's a book in itself. But it is true. And the sooner we come to terms with this truth, the sooner our prayer lives will begin to be truly effective.

2. Listen to God's answers honestly. This is probably the most important thing we can do. It is only by recognizing honestly whether God has said "no" or "yes" that we can learn to adjust our prayers and align them with his will. Honesty is a difficult quality to develop, and you must be willing to face up to the fact that things may not be as you want them to be. Honesty is the ability to accept the "no" answers from God and recognize you were off the mark. It is tough to hear a "no" especially when you feel it's a rebuke. But remember, "No" is not a rebuke of you; it is a rebuke of the idea you presented. You are dearly and infinitely loved by your father in heaven, and his "no" can be translated as, "I love you, but you need to rethink this request a little more and ask something else."

3. Be concrete in your prayers. This entails a number of points we made about prayer. We should have a system to our prayers that is measurable and definable both at the macro-level and the micro-level. We should think of functional, concrete applications of what we are praying for, and thereby we can measure whether we are hearing "yes" from God or "no." Without concrete prayer requests, we are never forced to really identify what we are talking about. And we also are never forced to evaluate whether God has said "yes" or "no" to us. There is nothing like being specific in your prayers to show you whether your prayer life is really in tune with God's desires. If your specific requests are being met concretely then you can be assured you are on God's page. If not, then it's time to reassess your program.

4. Aim for maturity. Every prayer request we make should be considered in light of the question, "Will I be more mature if I receive this?" If your requests are really just your attempts to alleviate problems in your life without helping you grow in maturity, they are probably not worth much. Remember, God is like a good father. Good fathers don't bail their children out of every mess in which they have mired themselves. They sometimes let them struggle through life, gaining wisdom as they go.

5. *Think of the effects.* Always keep in mind that your life is wrapped up in the Body of Christ (that is, your fellow believers) and in Christ himself. Your requests should reflect what is important to both of them.

6. *God is first.* Again, like the Lord's Prayer, God is our focus at the start and at the end. What he wants in accordance with his perfect, wise, loving will is the paramount guide to our requests.

"Go in peace; and may the God of Israel grant your petition that you have asked of Him."[1]

---

1. 1 Sam 1:17.

Bibliography

Aland, Barbara, Kurt Aland, Johannes Karavidopoulos, Carlo M. Martini, and Bruce M. Metzger, eds. *The Greek New Testament (GNT)*. Fourth revised ed. Stuttgart: Deutsche Bibelgesellschaft, 1993. BibleWorks, v.8.

Aland, Kurt, Barbara Aland, Johannes Karavidopoulos, Carlo M. Martini, and Bruce M. Metzger, eds. *Novum Testamentum Graece (BNT)*. 27th ed. Stuttgart: Deutsche Bibelgesellschaft, 2001. BibleWorks. v.8.

Augustine of Hippo. *The Enchiridion on Faith, Hope, and Love.* Ed. by Henry Pauolucci. Washington: Regnery Gateway, 1961.

Bauer, Walter. *A Greek-English Lexicon of the New Testament and Other Early Christian Literature.* Edited by Frederick W. Danker. 3rd ed. Chicago: University of Chicago Press, 2000. BibleWorks. v.8.

Blass, F. and A. Debrunner. *A Greek Grammar of the New Testament and Other Early Christian Literature.* Translated and revised by Robert W. funk. Chicago: University of Chicago Press, 1961.

———. *A Greek Grammar of the New Testament and Other Early Christian Literature.* Translated by Robert W. Funk. Chicago: University of Chicago Press, 1961. BibleWorks, v.8.

Bless. Dictionary.com. *Dictionary.com Unabridged.* Random House, Inc. http://dictionary.reference.com/browse/bless (accessed: October 02, 2010).

Calvin, John. *Institutes of the Christian Religion—Volume I.* Translated by Ford Lewis Battles. Edited by John T. McNeill. The Library of Christian Classics. Vol. XX. Philadelphia: Westminster Press, 1960.

Crump, David. *Knocking on Heaven's Door: A New Testament Theology of Petitionary Prayer.* Grand Rapids: Baker Academic, 2006.

Discipline. Dictionary.com. *Dictionary.com Unabridged.* Random House, Inc. http://dictionary.reference.com/browse/Discipline (accessed: October 02, 2010).

Foster, Richard J. *Celebration of Discipline.* San Francisco: HarperSanFrancisco, 1988.

Goetchius, Eugene Van Ness. *The Language of the New Testament.* New York: Charles Scribner's Sons, 1965.

Hughes, R. Kent. *Disciplines of a Godly Man.* Wheaton, IL: Crossway Books, 1991.

Lockyer, Herbert. *All the Prayers of the Bible.* Grand Rapids: Zondervan, 1959.

Mitigate. Dictionary.com. *Dictionary.com Unabridged.* Random House, Inc. http://dictionary.reference.com/browse/Mitigate (accessed: October 02, 2010).

Piety. Dictionary.com. *Dictionary.com Unabridged.* Random House, Inc. http://dictionary.reference.com/browse/Piety (accessed: October 02, 2010).

Porter, Stanley E. *Idioms of the Greek New Testament.* 2nd ed. Sheffield Academic Press, 1995.

Sloppy. Dictionary.com. *Dictionary.com Unabridged.* Random House, Inc. http://dictionary.reference.com/browse/sloppy (accessed: October 02, 2010).

The NET Bible, New English Translation Bible (NET). n.p.: Biblical Studies Press, LLC, 1996. BibleWorks, v.8.

The New American Standard Bible (NAU). La Habra, CA: The Lockman Foundation, 1995. BibleWorks, v.8.

Kittel, Gerhard, Gerhard Friedrich, and Geoffrey W. Bromiley. *Theological Dictionary of the New Testament (Abridged)*. Grand Rapids: Eerdmanns, 1985. BibleWorks, v.8.

Wansbrough, Henry, ed. *New Jerusalem Bible (NJB)*. New York: Doubleday, 1985. BibleWorks, v.8.

Whitney, Donald S. *Spiritual Disciplines For The Christian Life*. Colorado Springs: Navpress, 1991.

Wiley, H. Orton. *Christian Theology*. Vol.2. Kansas City: Beacon Hill, 1952.

Willard, Dallas. *Hearing God: Developing a Conversational Relationship With God*. Downers Grove: InterVarsity Press, 1999.

———. *The Spirit of the Disciplines: Understanding How God Changes Lives*. San Francisco: HarperSanFrancisco, 1990.

Wisdom. Dictionary.com. *Collins English Dictionary—Complete & Unabridged 10th Edition*. HarperCollins Publishers. http://dictionary.reference.com/browse/wisdom (accessed: October 02, 2010).

www.ingramcontent.com/pod-product-compliance
Lightning Source LLC
Chambersburg PA
CBHW050617300426
44112CB00012B/1546